PROBLEMS OF MEN

JOHN DEWEY

DISCARDED
PROBLEMS OF MEN

PHILOSOPHICAL LIBRARY
NEW YORK

Printed in the United States of America

PREFATORY NOTE

THE INTRODUCTION WHICH IMMEDIATELY FOLLOWS THIS NOTE was written expressly for this volume and has not been published elsewhere. The other essays in this book are reprinted from periodicals in which they originally appeared. Most of them have appeared, as is shown by the dates attached in the Table of Contents, fairly recently. One of them was written, however, half a century ago and has not been previously reprinted. Naturally, there has been some modification of my position in respect to various philosophical matters as the years have passed. The articles of recent date most nearly represent, of course, my present views. Considering the time which has elapsed, the older essay seemed worth reprinting as an anticipation of the direction in which I have moved during the intervening fifty years.

A few of the essays that are included are so technical that on their face they are not about *The Problems of Men*. But a place has been given them because they present aspects of that work of self-criticism, of purging, which, as I said in the Introduction, philosophy needs to execute if it is to perform under present conditions the role that properly belongs to it.

J. D.

Introduction

INTRODUCTION

The Problems of Men and the Present State of Philosophy

A REPORT WAS RECENTLY ISSUED BY A COMMITTEE OF AN ORGAN-
ization whose members are concerned with teaching and writing philosophy, *The American Philosophical Association*. It was
invited to "undertake an examination of the present state of
philosophy and the role philosophy might play in the postwar
world." The invitation came from and was financed by a non-
professional body, The Rockefeller Foundation. This fact is an
indication that the theme is considered to be of public, not
merely professional, concern. This intimation is borne out by a
statement regarding the task entrusted to the Committee. It
was asked to inquire into "the function of philosophy . . . in
the development of a free and reflective life in the community."
It was also asked to discuss "the function of philosophy in
liberal education." The title of the book is *Philosophy in American Education*.

This title suggests that the Committee confined itself to the
narrower of the two tasks confided to it. With a few exceptions
the body of the book bears out this impression. After asking
"What are we trying to do? Where do we think we are going?",
the Introduction to the Report goes on to say, "There is not in
our contemporary situation an authoritatively accepted body of
doctrine called 'philosophy' for which duly accredited spokesmen can pretend to speak. There are philosophies and philosophers, and they *differ philosophically on just the issues with
which we are called upon to deal*." The Committee deserves
every credit for the frankness of this admission. But as far as
concerns interest outside the circle of philosophers, the words
I have italicized are, I believe, more revealing about the present

3

state and role of philosophy than anything else said in the whole volume.

This is a strong statement. The reason for making it is that the internal divisions which kept the Committee from dealing with the more important of the two tasks entrusted to it is the reflection in intellectual form of confusions and conflicts by which the public community is divided. Before reproaching philosophers for failure to agree, we should recall that in the present state of the world agreement among them would be proof positive that philosophy is so technical as to be wholly out of touch with the problems and issues of actual life.

I propose, then, to discuss the present state of philosophy in its human bearings. Within the circle of professional philosophers and in the teaching of philosophy in institutions of learning, differences in the conclusions that constitute systems and isms have their place. But for the public, they are of slight importance compared with the question of what philosophers are trying to do and might do if they tried. The interest of the public centers in such questions as: What is the distinctive purpose and business of philosophy anyway? How is it related to those concerns and issues which today stand out as the problems of men?

I

Discussion may well begin with the fact that there *does* exist at the present time one philosophy which holds that it possesses "an authoritatively accepted body of doctrine," having "duly accredited spokesmen" to declare its contents. The fact that representatives of this type of philosophy do not figure in the Report is itself indicative of a profound cleavage in present life. For that philosophy is that of an institution that claims divine origin and continued divine support and direction. Its doctrines are held to be authoritative because of their source in supernatural revelation. The philosophies represented in the Report formulate a standpoint according to which philosophical doctrines should be formulated on grounds that are independent of supernatural revelation, and not requiring any special institution as their organ. The supernatural and theological philosophy took shape in the medieval period. The philosophies represented in the Report took shape in ways away from, largely in protest against, the attitudes and interests which controlled the formulation of the older philosophy.

Roughly speaking this division within philosophy represents a cleavage in life between older and newer factors in present life, between the supernatural and what by contrast may be called the secular. It is an expression of conditions which led Matthew Arnold more than a generation ago to speak of contemporary man as

> wandering between two worlds, one dead,
> The other powerless to be born.

Nevertheless, an account of the present state of philosophy must note that, as far as concerns the *aim and office* of philosophy, there is one basic agreement between the philosophy of the theological type and at least some philosophies of the secular type. Rejection of the supernatural origin and foundation makes of course a vast difference. But the philosophical tenets that are presented in the Report cling largely, although not exclusively, to the view that the primary aim of philosophy is knowledge of Being or "Reality" which is more comprehensive, fundamental, and ultimate than the knowledge which can be provided by the organs and methods at the disposal of the "special" sciences. For, according to this view, the sciences, with the possible exception of mathematics, deal with things that are temporal, changing, contingent, while philosophy aims at knowledge of that which is eternal and inherently necessary, so primary and so final that it alone can give sure support to the claims to truths put forth by the lesser forms of knowing.

It is the fact of a profound cleavage that is here important, not the question of which is right and which is wrong. The cleavage in life that has been brought about by "modern" departures from and revolt against older practices and tenets is so widespread that nothing is left untouched. In politics, it is manifested in the movements which in practically every country have resulted in separation of church and state. Developments in industry and commerce have substituted mobility for the relatively static conditions of rule by custom which once prevailed. They have also introduced interests and enjoyments that compete with those made supreme in the period of medieval ecclesiastic control. With respect to natural and historical knowledge the rise of new methods of inquiry has profoundly shaken the astronomy, physics, biology, anthropology, and the historical learning with which the theological philosophy had identified itself. The cleavage that has resulted between theology and positive science, between the mundane and the heavenly, between temporal interests and those called eternal has created the special divisions which in the form of "dualisms" have determined the chief problems of philosophies that are "modern" in the historical sense.

Nevertheless, the most striking fact about these modern philosophies is the extent in which they exhibit the influence of the postmedieval movements in politics, industry, and science, but without having surrendered the old, the classic, view that the chief business of philosophy is search for a kind of Reality that is more fundamental and more ultimate than are or than can be the facts disclosed by the sciences. The outcome has been the controversies as to the organ of knowing that constitute the philosophical isms of the last few centuries. Because of the view that the aim and business of philosophy is with Reality supposed to be behind and beyond the subject-matter of the various authentic knowings that form the sciences, the "possibility of knowledge," conditions of knowing set up before knowing can take place, became the chief "problem" of philosophy. The more actual knowings flourished, the more philosophies, mutually contradictory among themselves, occupied themselves with furnishing "Foundations for Knowledge," instead of employing what is known to direct it in discovering and performing its own tasks. The work that once gave its name to philosophy, Search for Wisdom, has progressively receded into the background. For wisdom differs from knowledge in being the application of what is known to intelligent conduct of the affairs of human life. The straits of philosophy are due to the fact that the more this available knowledge has increased, the more it has occupied itself with a task that is no longer humanly pertinent.

For practical problems that are so deeply human as to be the moral issues of the present time have increased their range and their intensity. They cover practically every aspect of contemporary life, domestic, industrial, political. But during the very period in which this has occurred, philosophy, for the most part, has relegated them to a place that is subordinate and accessory to an alleged problem of knowledge. At the same time actual knowing and the applications of science in life by inventions and technological arts have been going on at such a rate that the alleged problem of its foundations and possibility of knowledge are of but remote professional concern. The net result of neglect with issues that are urgent and of preoccupation with issues that are remote from active human concern explains the popular discredit into which philosophy has progressively fallen. This disrepute is in turn a decided factor in determining its role in the world.

For what can philosophies do which, in spite of change of conditions in science and in human affairs of basic import, go on occupying themselves with the problem of the *conditions* of knowledge in neglect of the vital problem of its *consequences,* actual and potential? Inquiry that should devote itself to systematic investigation of the consequences of science; of why they are what they are at present; of the causes of that limitation in which scientific method affects the conditions of life only through the medium of institutions to which scientific inquiry is *not* applied; to what the consequences of science *might* be were they so applied; such inquiry might hope to have some role, to play some part in development of attitudes in the community that are liberal, well tested, and grounded in fact.

II

Under present conditions scientific methods take effect in determining the concrete economic conditions under which the mass of men live. But they are not employed to determine freely and systematically the moral, the humane, ends served by engrossing practical conditions, the actual state of ends and values. Hence the more important things are left to decision by custom, prejudice, class interests, and traditions embodied in institutions, whose results are mostly fixed by the superior power in possession of those who manage them. Under these conditions, a recent movement in philosophy demands especial notice. It retains the notion that philosophy's concern is with superior reality, taking its cue in search for it, mainly from mathematics and quasi-mathematical symbolisms, but completely repudiating that aspect of philosophy that has gone by the name of search for wisdom. It converts the practical neglect by modern philosophies of political and moral subjects into systematic theoretical denial of the possibility of intelligent concern with them. It holds that the practical affairs of men which are of highest and deepest significance are matters of values and valuations, and that *therefore* they are by their very nature incapable of intellectual adjudication; of either justification or condemnation on rational grounds. The movement retains in the most emphatic form possible the ancient Greek conception according to which "theory" is intrinsically superior to any and every form of practical concern—the latter consisting of things that change and fluctuate in contrast with the eternity of Being. But the movement in question goes, so to speak, the classic doctrine one better. The latter held that practical affairs were the material of inferior sorts of knowledge. The present movement holds that moral affairs, concerned as they are with "intrinsic" values, or "ends-in-themselves," are wholly outside the reach of any sort of knowledge whatever.

A distinguished member of this school of contemporary thought has recently written that "the actions of men, in innumerable important respects, have depended upon their theories as to the world and human life, as to what is good and evil." But he has also written that what men hold about "what is good and evil" is wholly a matter of sheer likes and dislikes. They, in turn, are so completely private and personal—in the terminology of philosophy so "subjective"—as to be incapable of judgment having "objective" grounds. Likes and dislikes are immune to modification by knowledge since they dwell in inaccessible privacy. Values that are "extrinsic" or "instrumental" may be rationally estimated. For they are only means; are not ends in any genuine sense. As means their efficacy may be determined by methods that will stand scientific inspection. But the "ends" they serve (ends which are truly ends) are just matters of what groups, classes, sects, races, or whatever, happen irrationally to like or dislike.

The actual or concrete condition of men all over the world with respect to their opportunities and their relative disadvantages of position, their happiness and their misery, their kind and degree of participation "in good and evil in innumerable respects" is now decided by things which, on this view, are mere means. In addition they are said to be totally arbitrary and irresponsible with respect to the ends they finally produce although these ends are all that mankind prizes! What is the probable destiny of man on earth if regulation of the concrete conditions under which men live continues to increase at its present rate, while the consequences produced by them are necessarily left at the mercy of likes and dislikes that are, in turn, at the mercy of irrational habits, institutions, and a class and sectarian distribution of power between the stronger and the weaker? However technical the "theoretical" view of this school about ultimate reality may be, the truth or falsity of this part of their doctrine is assuredly of public concern.

Were this philosophy to be generally accepted the movement for a "moratorium on science" would be greatly strengthened. For it is from science that are derived the values which are "means" and only means, according to this brand of philosophy. According to it, there is no difference capable of intelligent use and test between use of energy due to splitting of the atom for destruction of mankind and its use in peaceful industry to make life more secure and more abundant. This fact does not prove the doctrine to be false. But it certainly gives ground for serious consideration of the grounds upon which it rests. The problem of values and valuations has been coming to the front of late in any case. The challenge here issued should make it the central issue for some time to come.

Meantime, such popular vogue as may accrue to this doctrine will operate, almost automatically, to promote supernatural theological philosophy. For the latter also holds that ultimate ends are beyond the reach of human discovery and judgment. But it also holds that revelation from on high has provided the all-sufficient remedy. In a time as troubled as the present, a philosophy which denies the existence of any natural and human means of determining judgments as to what is good and evil will work to the benefit of those who hold that they have in their possession superhuman and supernatural means for infallible ascertainment of ultimate ends, especially as they also claim to possess the practical agencies for ensuring the attainment of final good by men who accept the truths they declare.

III

Another phase of the present state of philosophy demands notice. It repudiates that which the last named movement affirms and it affirms that which the latter denies. It breaks completely with that part of the philosophical tradition which holds that concern with superior reality determines the work to be done by philosophical inquiry. It affirms that the purpose and business of philosophy is wholly with that part of the historic tradition called search for wisdom—namely, search for the ends and values that give direction to our collective human activities. It holds that not grasp of eternal and universal Reality but use of the methods and conclusions of our best knowledge, that called scientific, provides the means for conducting this search. It holds that limitations which now exist in this use are to be removed by means of extension of the ways of tested knowing that define science from physical and physiological matters to social and distinctly human affairs. The movement is called, in its various aspects, by the names of pragmatism, experimentalism, instrumentalism. Not these names are important but the ideas that are held regarding the distinctive aim and business of philosophic inquiry and of how it should be accomplished.

The accusation brought against it of childlike trust in science omits the fact that it holds that science itself is still in its babyhood. It holds that the scientific method of inquiry has not begun to reach maturity. It holds that it will achieve manhood only when its use is extended to cover all aspects of all matters of human concern. It holds that many of the remediable evils of the present time are due to the unbalanced, one-sided application of the methods of inquiry and test that constitute everything that has a right to the name "science." It holds that the chief present task of philosophy is with issues and problems that are due to this state of things, including the projection of liberal hypotheses as to ways in which the required social change may be brought about.

This view of the aim and office of philosophy involves a decided shift in the meaning of such words as comprehensiveness and ultimacy in their application to the work of philosophy. They lose the significance that was given to them when philosophy was supposed to be an effort to achieve knowledge of "reality" superior to that with which the special sciences are concerned. There are issues in the conduct of human affairs in their production of good and evil which, at a given time and place, are so central, so strategic in position, that their urgency deserves, with respect to practice, the names ultimate and comprehensive. These issues demand the most systematic reflective attention that can be given. It is relatively unimportant whether this attention be called philosophy or by some other name. It is of immense human importance that it be given, and that it be given by means of the best tested resources that inquiry has at command.

Reference to place and time in what has just been said should make it clear that this view of the office of philosophy has no commerce with the notion that the problems of philosophy are "eternal." On the contrary, it holds that such a view is obstructive, tending to be of use chiefly in defense of the practice of continually rehashing issues which were timely in their own social condition but that are no longer urgent, save from the standpoint of historical scholarship. The latter is as important in philosophy as in any other humane field. But when it is permitted to monopolize philosophical activities it chokes out their life. Eternity that is permitted to become a refuge from the time in which human life goes on may provide a certain kind of consolation. But emotion and comfort should not be identified with understanding and insight, nor with the direction the latter may supply.

This movement is charged with promotion of "relativism" in a sense in which the latter is identified with lack of standards, and consequently with tendency to promote chaos. It is true that the movement in question holds since the problems and issues of philosophy are not eternal they should link up with urgencies that impose themselves at times and in places. The "state of philosophy" if it is to be its present state must have to do with issues that are themselves actively present. The word "relativity" is used as a scarecrow to frighten away philosophers from critical assault upon "absolutisms." Every class interest in all history has defended itself from examination by putting forth claim to absoluteness. Social fanaticisms, whether of the right or the left, take refuge in the fortress of principles too absolute to be subject to doubt and inquiry. The absolute is the isolated; the isolated is that which cannot be judged on the ground of connections that can be investigated. The kind of "Relativity" characteristic of the movement in question is that which marks all scientific inquiry. For the latter also finds its only workable "standards" are provided by the actual connections of things; connections which, when they are generalized, are given the name of space-time.

Dependence upon space-time connections now marks all the victories won by scientific inquiry. It is silly to suppose they terminate in mere particulars. On the contrary, they constantly move toward the general, provided only the generalizations have to do with wider and wider connections, so as not to swim in wordy vacuity. And so it is with a philosophy that employs the methods and conclusions of authentic inquiry as instruments for examination of values that now operate in regulating human habits, institutions, and efforts. No span of connections in space-time is too wide or too long, provided they are relevant to judgment of issues that are urgently here-and-now. Not "relativity" but absolutism isolates and confines. The reason, at bottom, that absolutism levels its guns against relativity in a caricature is that search for the connection of events is the sure way of destroying the privileged position of exemption from inquiry which every form of absolutism secures wherever it obtains.

IV

The foregoing remarks need illustration. What special problems and issues does this philosophical movement substitute for those which it takes to be now so irrelevant as to obstruct philosophy from performing the role it might exercise in the present world? Were I to reply that, at the very least, philosophy should clean its own house, I might seem to be retreating from human issues and problems back into the more technical concerns of professional philosophy. This would be the case if the things in philosophical doctrines that need to be got rid of were not also obstructive and deflecting in the human situation. Here is one outstanding illustration. Separation of mind and matter, the elevation of what was called ideal and spiritual to the very summit of Being and the degradation of everything called material and worldly to the lowest position, developed in philosophy as a reflection of economic and political division of classes. Slaves and artisans (who had no more political freedom than did outright slaves) were occupied with the "material," and hence with mere means to the good life in which they had no share. Citizens who were free stood totally above the need of any share in these activities, which were only menial. Division between high knowledge which was rational and theoretical and practical knowledge which was low, servile, and a matter of mere routine, and the split between the ideal and the material followed as matter of course.

We have moved away from downright slavery and from feudal serfdom. But the conditions of present life still perpetuate a division between activities which are relatively base and menial and those which are free and ideal. Some educators suppose they are rendering a service by insisting upon an inherent difference between studies they call liberal and others they call mechanical and utilitarian. Economic theories of great influence have developed out of and are used to justify the isolation of economic, commercial, and financial affairs from the political and moral. Philosophy relevant to present conditions has a hard task to perform in purging itself of doctrines which seem to justify this separation and which certainly obstruct the formation of measures and policies by means of which science and technology (the application of science) would perform a more humane and liberal office than they now do.

This example of the kind of issue and problem with which present philosophy might well occupy itself suggests another problem so closely allied as to be, in fact, the same problem in another guise. The distinction, current in present-day opinion, inside and outside of professional philosophy, between values that are intrinsic and extrinsic, final and instrumental, is an intellectual formulation of the separations set up between means and ends. This form of philosophic "dualism" is a further projection of pre-scientific, pre-technological, pre-democratic conditions into present philosophy in a way so obstructive as to demand total obliteration. Here again, philosophers have a difficult and exacting work to do if they are to take an active part in enabling the resources potentially at our disposal in present science and technology to exercise a genuinely liberating office in human affairs.

It follows that the whole notion of ends-in-themselves as distinct from ends that are called mere means represents a perpetuation of earlier conditions that is now definitely obstructive. In its theoretical aspect it is a striking case of adherence to an absolute after *science* has everywhere substituted connectivities. The hold still exerted by the notion is shown when philosophies that regard themselves as peculiarly modern and emancipated—like the type previously described—retain in full flower the notion that there are actually in existence such things as ends which are not also means. Give up the notion and there vanish all the grounds that are offered for holding that moral ends are not, in theory, capable of the same kind of "objective" factual determination as are technological ends. Democratic abolition of fixed difference between "higher" and "lower" still has to make its way in philosophy.

Reference to this matter of values serves to introduce another example of the work to be done by a philosophy that desires a role in the present world. One reason that is given for eliminating values as values from any contact with grounded judgment is their alleged *subjective* nature. No student of philosophy needs to be told how largely the dualism of subjective and objective has figured in modern philosophy. At one time, in the earliest days of modern science, this dogma was of some practical use. Science had many foes with which to contend. It adopted the device of setting up the "internal" authority of a knowing mind and ego over against the "external" authority of custom and established institutions. Maintaining the separation when the actual advance of science has shown that man is a part of the world, not something set over against it, is one of the chief obstacles now standing in the way of intelligent discussion of all social matters. Wholehearted acceptance in philosophy of the fact that no grounds now exist for fixed division of events into subjective and objective is prerequisite if philosophy is to have a role in promoting inquiry in social matters.

The things just discussed are examples of matters in which philosophy has now to do a hard and, for many of us, a disagreeable job. This is the work of getting rid, by means of thinking as exact and critical as possible, of perpetuations of those outworn attitudes which prevent those engaged in philosophic reflection from seizing the opportunities now open. This is the critical or, if one please, the negative, aspect of the task to be undertaken in the present state of philosophy. But it is not merely negative. It is one side of the positive and constructive work philosophy can, and therefore should, do. Philosophy cannot of itself resolve the conflicts and dissolve the confusions of the present world.

Only the associated members of the world can do this work in cooperative action—a work of which institution of conditions of peace is sufficiently striking example. But intellectual instruments are needed to project leading ideas or plans of action. The intellectual instrumentalities for doing this work need sterilizing and sharpening. That work is closely allied with setting better instruments, as fast as they take shape, at work. Active use in dealing with the present problems of men is the only way they can be kept from rusting. Trial and test in and by work done is the means by which they can be kept out of the dark spots in which infection originates. The fact that such plans, measures, policies as can be projected will be but hypotheses is but another instance of alignment of philosophy with the attitude and spirit of the inquiries which have won the victories of scientific inquiry in other fields.

Only a few centuries ago physical science was in a state that today is only of historical interest—so far away is it in method and subject matter from what we now call "science." Obstacles to creation and use of new methods were not once just theoretical. Old beliefs and old ways of knowing were so connected with traditional habits and institutions that to attack one was taken to be an attack on the other. Nevertheless, a few men had the courage to engage in systematic adverse criticism not only of accepted conclusions but of the standpoint and methods that had obtained for centuries. In addition, they projected new hypotheses to direct the conduct of physical inquiry from that time on. Some of these hypotheses were so broad in scope that today they would rate as "philosophical" rather than as "scientific." Nevertheless, in the end they, as well as the work of purging, played a definite role in leading inquiry into the paths along which dependable tested results have been secured.

Today social subjects, as far as concerns effective treatment in inquiry, are in much the same state as physical subjects three hundred years ago. The need is that there be now the kind of systematic and comprehensive criticism of current methods and habits and the same projection of generous hypotheses as, only a few hundred years ago, set going the revolution in physical knowledge. The opportunity is as great as the need. The obstacles to undertaking the work in social questions are greater than they ever were in dealing, say, with the heavenly bodies. The initial step is to promote general recognition that knowing, including most emphatically scientific knowledge, is not outside social activity, but is itself a form of social behavior, as much so as agriculture or transportation. For it is something that human beings do, as they plow the earth and sail ships. On the critical, or "purging" side, systematic rejection of all doctrines that associate knowing with "mind" and an alleged individual ego, as something separate and self-enclosed, is required. On the positive side, this initial step demands systematic observation of the natural, the biological and societal, conditions by means of which knowing actually goes on.

This work is preparatory. On the whole, it is a case of philosophy cleaning its own house, together with doing a certain amount of refurnishing. The important work is to make evident the social conditions—economic, political, moral, and religious—which have restricted scientific inquiry so largely, first to physical and then to physiological matters; conditions that have kept inquiry penned in so that large fields of utmost human concern are treated as if they were sacrosanct, not to be contaminated by contact with concrete investigations. A deeply entrenched and fortified habit of treating economic affairs, industry, trade and business, as mere means having no intrinsic connection with "ultimate" ends which are moral, illustrates the penning-in theory and perpetuates it in practice.

The result is that what pass for moral ideals in the most important forms of social practices are so "ideal" as to be utopian. They are treated as matters of personal exhortation supplemented with use and threats of use of force in reward and punishment. Separation of the "materialistic" and the "ideal" deprives the latter of leverage and impetus, and prevents the things to which the former name is applied from rendering the humane service of which they are capable. The example of what physiological science and its applications have already accomplished in public health, limited as it is, is an instance of the kind of thing the method and results of competent inquiry might bring about in all aspects of human well being. The pragmatic philosophy, so called, has made a start in helping to break down in the field of education that separation of the "utilitarian" and the "liberal" which restricts alike the former and the latter. The belief that "vocational" education cannot be humane is an illustration that would be humorous were it not so disastrous in effect.

Political theory and practice provide another example. Liberalism once did a work of emancipation. But it was so influenced by a heritage of absolutistic claims that it invented the myth of "The Individual" set over in dualistic separation against that which is called "The Social." It obscured the fact that these words are names for traits and capacities of human beings in the concrete. It transformed that which they actually name into entities by themselves. It thereby obscured, indeed prevented, recognition of the fact that actual realization of these traits and capacities depends upon the specific conditions under which human beings are born and in which they grow up. The words *individuality* and *society* under this influence became names for something ready-made and inherent—not differing in substance from that belief in occult essences which the new movement in physical knowledge had to assault and eliminate before it could do its work.

V

In what precedes I have mentioned, by way of illustration, some of the tasks that lie open to systematic generalized inquiry. Any inquiry, whatever name be given it, which undertakes this kind of inquiry, critical and constructive, will not have to worry about its role in the world. In closing, I shall say a few words about the atmosphere and climate in which the work will have to be carried on. A passage taken from a writing of a distinguished American thinker, written well over a generation ago, will point a contrast. Josiah Royce wrote: "You philosophize when you reflect critically upon what you are doing in your world. And what you are doing is, of course, in the first place living. And living involves passions, faiths, doubts, and courage. The critical inquiry into what these mean and imply is philosophy."

Provided that customs, arrangements, institutions, to which passions, such things as doubts, faiths, and courage, are attached, are brought into this view of the office of philosophy, it is not far different from what I have been saying. But then another note is struck. The passage continued: "We feel ourselves in a world of law and significance. Yet why we feel this homelike sense of the reality and worth of the world is a matter of criticism. Such a criticism of life, made elaborate and thoroughgoing, is philosophy." In this further passage it is assumed, as a matter of course, that the world in which man lives is of such significance and worth that we cannot escape the sense of its homelikeness. The work assigned to philosophy is thereby limited to the office of finding, by systematic and thorough reflection, justification for a fact which philosophy is entitled to take for granted.

Times have altered since these words were written. They probably express an assumption and aim common to most classic systems of the past. But a peculiar hopefulness existing during the period when the words were penned made this assumption of worth, significance and unitary order especially easy. We now live in a situation when the world seems alien rather than home-like; in a period in which the tendency of scientific knowledge modifies the earlier faith in "overruling laws." And in most practical matters there is no more widespread sense than that of insecurity. The type of philosophy which now tries to show that, all "appearances" to the contrary, the world in which we live is "really," fundamentally, one of fixed order, significance and worth takes on the air of theological apologetics.

Philosophy still has a work to do. It may gain a role for itself for turning to consideration of why it is that man is now so alienated from man. It may turn to the projection of large generous hypotheses which, if used as plans of action, will give intelligent direction to men in search for ways to make the world more one of worth and significance, more homelike, in fact. There is no phase of life, educational, economic, political, religious, in which inquiry may not aid in bringing to birth that world which Matthew Arnold rightly said was as yet unborn. Present-day philosophy cannot desire a better work than to engage in the act of midwifery that was assigned to it by Socrates twenty-five hundred years ago.

January, 1946.

PART I

Democracy and Education

I

THE DEMOCRATIC FAITH AND EDUCATION

NOT EVEN THE MOST FAR-SEEING OF MEN COULD HAVE PREDICTED, no longer ago than fifty years, the course events have taken. The expectations that were entertained by men of generous outlook are in fact chiefly notable in that the actual course of events has moved, and with violence, in the opposite direction. The ardent and hopeful social idealist of the last century or so has been proved so wrong that a reaction to the opposite extreme has taken place. A recent writer has even proposed a confraternity of pessimists who should live together in some sort of social oasis. It is a fairly easy matter to list the articles of that old faith which, from the standpoint of today, have been tragically frustrated.

The first article on the list had to do with the prospects of the abolition of war. It was held that the revolution which was taking place in commerce and communication would break down the barriers which had kept the peoples of the earth alien and hostile and would create a state of interdependence which in time would insure lasting peace. Only an extreme pessimist ventured to suggest that interdependence might multiply points of friction and conflict.

Another item of that creed was the belief that a general development of enlightenment and rationality was bound to follow the increase in knowledge and the diffusion which would result from the revolution in science that was taking place. Since it had long been held that rationality and freedom were intimately allied, it was held that the movement toward democratic institutions and popular government which had produced

23

in succession the British, American, and French Revolutions was bound to spread until freedom and equality were the foundations of political government in every country of the globe.

A time of general ignorance and popular unenlightenment and a time of despotic and oppressive governmental rule were taken to be practically synonymous. Hence the third article of faith. There was a general belief among social philosophers that governmental activities were necessarily more or less oppressive; that governmental action tended to be an artificial interference with the operation of natural laws. Consequently the spread of enlightenment and democratic institutions would produce a gradual but assured withering away of the powers of the political state. Freedom was supposed to be so deeply rooted in the very nature of men that, given the spread of rational enlightenment, it would take care of itself with only a minimum of political action confined to insuring external police order.

The other article of faith to be mentioned was the general belief that the vast, the almost incalculable, increase in productivity resulting from the industrial revolution was bound to raise the general standard of living to a point where extreme poverty would be practically eliminated. It was believed that the opportunity to lead a decent, self-respecting, because self-sufficient, economic life would be assured to everyone who was physically and morally normal.

The course of events culminating in the present situation suffices to show without any elaborate argument how grievously these generous expectations have been disappointed. Instead of universal peace, there occurred two wars worldwide in extent and destructive beyond anything known in all history. Instead of uniform and steady growth of democratic freedom and equality, we have seen the rise of powerful totalitarian states with thoroughgoing suppression of liberty of belief and expression, outdoing the most despotic states of previous history. We have an actual growth in importance and range of governmental action in legislation and administration as necessary means of rendering freedom on the part of the many an assured actual fact. Instead of promotion of economic security and movement toward the elimination of poverty, we now have a great increase in the extent and the intensity of industrial crises with great increase of inability of workers to find employment. Social instability has reached a point that may portend revolution if it goes on unchecked.

Externally it looks as if the pessimists had the best of the case. But before we reach a conclusion on that point, we have to inquire concerning the solidity of the premise upon which the idealistic optimists rested their case. This principle was that the more desirable goals in view were to be accomplished by a complex of forces to which in their entirety the name "Nature" was given. In practical effect, acceptance of this principle was equivalent to adoption of a policy of drift as far as human intelligence and effort were concerned. No conclusion is warranted until we have inquired how far failure and frustration are consequences of putting our trust in a policy of drift; a policy of letting "George" in the shape of Nature and Natural Law do the work which only human intelligence and effort could possibly accomplish. No conclusion can be reached until we have considered an alternative: What is likely to happen if we recognize that the responsibility for creating a state of peace internationally, and of freedom and economic security internally, has to be carried by deliberate cooperative human effort? Technically speaking the policy known as *laissez-faire* is one of limited application. But its limited and technical significance is one instance of a manifestation of widespread trust in the ability of impersonal forces, popularly called Nature, to do a work that has to be done by human insight, foresight, and purposeful planning.

Not all the men of the earlier period were of the idealistic type. The idealistic philosophy was a positive factor in permitting those who prided themselves upon being realistic to turn events so as to produce consequences dictated by their own private and class advantage. The failure of cooperative and collective intelligence and effort to intervene was an invitation to immediate short-term intervention by those who had an eye to their own profit. The consequences were wholesale destruction and waste of natural resources, increase of social instability, and mortgaging of the future to a transitory and brief present of so-called prosperity. If "idealists" were misguided in what they failed to do, "realists" were wrong in what they did. If the former erred in supposing that the drift (called by them progress or evolution) was inevitably toward the better, the latter were more actively harmful because their insistence upon trusting to natural laws was definitely in the interest of personal and class profit.

The omitted premise in the case of both groups is the fact that neither science nor technology is an impersonal cosmic force. They operate only in the medium of human desire, foresight, aim, and effort. Science and technology are transactions in which man and nature work together and in which the human factor is that directly open to modification and direction. That man takes part along with physical conditions in invention and use of the devices, implements, and machinery of industry and commerce, no one would think of denying.

But in practice, if not in so many words, it has been denied that man has any responsibility for the consequences that result from what he invents and employs. This denial is implicit in our widespread refusal to engage in large-scale collective planning. Not a day passes, even in the present crisis, when the whole idea of such planning is not ridiculed as an emanation from the brain of starry-eyed professors or of others equally inept in practical affairs. And all of this in the face of the fact that there is not a successful industrial organization that does not owe its success to persistent planning within a limited field—with an eye to profit—to say nothing of the terribly high price we have paid in the way of insecurity and war for putting our trust in drift.

Refusal to accept responsibility for looking ahead and for planning in matters national and international is based upon refusal to employ in social affairs, in the field of human relations, the methods of observation, interpretation, and test that are matters of course in dealing with physical things, and to which we owe the conquest of physical nature. The net result is a state of imbalance, of profoundly disturbed equilibrium between our physical knowledge and our social-moral knowledge. This lack of harmony is a powerful factor in producing the present crisis with all its tragic features. For physical knowledge and physical technology have far outstripped social or humane knowledge and human engineering. Our failure to use in matters of direct human concern the scientific methods which have revolutionized physical knowledge has permitted the latter to dominate the social scene.

The change in the physical aspect of the world has gone on so rapidly that there is probably no ground for surprise in the fact that our psychological and moral knowledge has not kept pace. But there is cause for astonishment in the fact that, after the catastrophe of war, insecurity, and the threat to democratic institutions have shown the need for moral and intellectual attitudes and habits which will correspond with the changed state of the world, there should be a definite campaign to make the scientific attitude the scapegoat for present evils, while a return to the beliefs and practices of a prescientific and pretechnological age is urged as the road to our salvation.

The organized attack made from time to time against science and against technology as inherently materialistic and as usurping the place properly held by abstract moral precepts—abstract because divorcing ends from the means by which they must be realized—defines the issue we now have to face. Shall we go backwards or shall we go ahead to discover and put into practice the means by which science and technology shall be made fundamental in the promotion of human welfare? The failure to use scientific methods in creating understanding of human relationships and interests and in planning measures and policies that correspond in human affairs to the technologies in physical use is easily explained in historical terms. The new science began with things at the furthest remove from human affairs, namely with the stars of the heavens. From astronomy the new methods went on to win their victories in physics and chemistry. Still later science was applied in physiological and biological subject-matter. At every stage, the advance met determined resistance from the representatives of established institutions who felt their prestige was bound up with maintenance of old beliefs and found their class control of others being threatened. In consequence, many workers in science found that the easiest way in which to procure an opportunity to carry on their inquiries was to adopt an attitude of extreme specialization. The effect was equivalent to the position that their methods and conclusions were not and could not be "dangerous," since they had no point of contact with man's serious moral concerns. This position in turn served to perpetuate and confirm the older separation of man as man from the rest of nature and to intensify the split between the "material" and the moral and "ideal."

Thus it has come about that when scientific inquiry began to move from its virtually complete victories in astronomy and physics and its partial victory in the field of living things over into the field of human affairs and concerns, the interests and institutions which offered resistance to its earlier advance are gathering themselves together for a final attack upon that aspect of science which in truth constitutes its supreme and culminating significance. On the principle that offense is the best defense, respect for science and loyalty to its outlook are attacked as the chief source of all our present social ills. One may read, for example, in current literature such a condescending concession as marks the following passage: "Of course, the scientific attitude, though often leading to such a catastrophe, is not to be condemned," the immediate context showing that the particular "catastrophe" in mind consists of "errors leading to war . . . derived from an incorrect theory of truth." Since these errors are produced by belief in the applicability of scientific method to human as well as physical facts, the remedy, according to this writer, is to abandon "the erroneous application of the methods and results of natural science to the problems of human life."

In three respects the passage is typical of such organized campaigns in active operation. There is first the assertion that such catastrophes as that of the recent war are the result of devotion to scientific method and conclusions. The denunciation of "natural" science as applied to human affairs carries, in the second place, the implication that man is outside of and above nature, and the consequent necessity of returning to the medieval prescientific doctrine of a supernatural foundation and outlook in all social and moral subjects. Then thirdly there is the assumption, directly contrary to fact, that the scientific method has at the present time been seriously and systematically applied to the problems of human life.

I dignify the passage quoted by this reference to it because it serves quite as well as a multitude of other passages from reactionaries to convey a sense of the present issues. It is true that the *results* of natural science have had a large share, for evil as well as for good, in bringing the world to its present pass. But it is equally true that "natural" science has been identified with *physical* science in a sense in which the physical is set over against the human. It is true that the interests and institutions which are now attacking science are just the forces which in behalf of a supernatural center of gravity are those that strive to maintain this tragic split in human affairs. Now the issue, as is becoming clearer every day, is whether we shall go backward or whether we shall go forward toward recognition in theory and practice of the indissoluble unity of the humanistic and the naturalistic.

What has all this to do with education? The answer to this question may be gathered from the fact that those who are engaged in assault upon science center their attacks upon the increased attention given by our schools to science and to its application in vocational training. In a world which is largely what it is today because of science and technology they propose that education should turn its back upon even the degree of recognition science and technology have received. They propose we turn our face to the medievalism in which so-called "liberal" arts were identified with literary arts: a course natural to adopt in an age innocent of knowledge of nature, an age in which the literary arts were the readiest means of rising above barbarism through acquaintance with the achievements of Greek-Roman culture. Their proposal is so remote from the facts of the present world, it involves such a bland ignoring of actualities, that there is a temptation to dismiss it as idle vaporing. But it would be a tragic mistake to take the reactionary assaults so lightly. For they are an expression of just the forces that keep science penned up in a compartment labelled "materialistic and anti-human." They strengthen all the habits and institutions which render that which is morally "ideal" impotent in action and which leave the "material" to operate without humane direction.

Let me return for the moment to my initial statement that the basic error of social idealists was the assumption that something called "natural law" could be trusted, with only incidental cooperation by human beings, to bring about the desired ends. The lesson to be learned is that human attitudes and efforts are the strategic center for promotion of the generous aims of peace among nations; promotion of economic security; the use of political means in order to advance freedom and equality; and the worldwide cause of democratic institutions. Anyone who starts from this premise is bound to see that it carries with it the basic importance of education in creating the habits and the outlook that are able and eager to secure the ends of peace, democracy, and economic stability.

When this is seen, it will also be seen how little has actually been done in our schools to render science and technology active agencies in creating the attitudes and dispositions and in securing the kinds of knowledge that are capable of coping with the problems of men and women today. Externally a great modification has taken place in subjects taught and in methods of teaching them. But when the changes are critically examined it is found that they consist largely in emergency concessions and accommodation to the urgent conditions and issues of the contemporary world. The standards and the controlling methods in education are still mainly those of a prescientific and pretechnological age.

This statement will seem to many persons to be exaggerated. But consider the purposes which as a rule still govern instruction in just those subjects that are taken to be decisively "modern," namely science and vocational preparation. Science is taught upon the whole as a body of ready-made information and technical skills. It is not taught as furnishing in its method the pattern for all effective intelligent conduct. It is taught upon the whole not with respect to the way in which it actually enters into human life, and hence as a supremely humanistic subject, but as if it had to do with a world which is "external" to human concerns. It is not presented in connection with the ways in which it actually enters into every aspect and phase of present human life. And it is hardly necessary to add that still less is it taught in connection with what scientific knowledge of human affairs might do in overcoming sheer drift. Scientific method and conclusions will not have gained a fundamentally important place in education until they are seen and treated as supreme agencies in giving direction to collective and cooperative human behavior.

The same sort of thing is to be said about the kind of use now made in education of practical and vocational subjects so called. The reactionary critics are busy urging that the latter subjects be taught to the masses—who are said to be incapable of rising to the plane of the "intellectual" but who do the useful work which somebody has to do, and who may be taught by vocational education to do it more effectively. This view is of course an open and avowed attempt to return to that dualistic separation of ideas and action, of the "intellectual" and the "practical," of the liberal and servile arts, that marked the feudal age. And this reactionary move in perpetuation of the split from which the world is suffering is offered as a cure, a panacea, not as the social and moral quackery it actually is. As is the case with science, the thing supremely needful is to go forward. And the forward movement in the case of technology as in the case of science is to do away with the chasm which ancient and medieval educational practice and theory set up between the liberal and the vocational, not to treat the void, the hole, constituted by this chasm, as if it were a foundation for the creation of free society.

There is nothing whatever inherent in the occupations that are socially necessary and useful to divide them into those which are "learned" professions and those which are menial, servile, and illiberal. As far as such a separation exists in fact it is an inheritance from the earlier class structure of human relations. It is a denial of democracy. At the very time when an important, perhaps *the* important, problem in education is to fill education having an occupational direction with a genuinely liberal content, we have, believe it or not, a movement, such as is sponsored for example by President Hutchins, to cut vocational training off from any contact with what is liberating by relegating it to special schools devoted to inculcation of technical skills. Inspiring vocational education with a liberal spirit and filling it with a liberal content is not a utopian dream. It is a demonstrated possibility in schools here and there in which subjects usually labelled "practically useful" are taught charged with scientific understanding and with a sense of the social-moral applications they potentially possess.

If little is said in the foregoing remarks specifically upon the topic of democratic faith, it is because their bearing upon a democratic outlook largely appears upon their very face. Conditions in this country when the democratic philosophy of life and democratic institutions were taking shape were such as to encourage a belief that the latter were so natural to man, so appropriate to his very being, that if they were once established they would tend to maintain themselves. I cannot rehearse here the list of events that have given this naive faith a shock. They are contained in every deliberate attack upon democracy and in every expression of cynicism about its past failures and pessimism about its future—attacks and expressions which have to be taken seriously if they are looked at as signs of trying to establish democracy as an end in separation from the concrete means upon which the end depends.

Democracy is not an easy road to take and follow. On the contrary, it is, as far as its realization is concerned in the complex conditions of the contemporary world, a supremely difficult one. Upon the whole we are entitled to take courage from the fact that it has worked as well as it has done. But to this courage we must add, if our courage is to be intelligent rather than blind, the fact that successful maintenance of democracy demands the utmost in use of the best available methods to procure a social knowledge that is reasonably commensurate with our physical knowledge, and the invention and use of forms of social engineering reasonably commensurate with our technological abilities in physical affairs.

This then is the task indicated. It is, if we employ large terms, to humanize science. This task in the concrete cannot be accomplished save as the fruit of science, which is named technology, is also humanized. And the task can be executed in the concrete only as it is broken up into vital applications of intelligence in a multitude of fields to a vast diversity of problems so that science and technology may be rendered servants of the democratic hope and faith. The cause is capable of inspiring loyalty in thought and deed. But there has to be joined to aspiration and effort the formation of free, wide-ranging, trained attitudes of observation and understanding such as incorporate within themselves, as a matter so habitual as to be unconscious, the vital principles of scientific method. In this achievement science, education, and the democratic cause meet as one. May we be equal to the occasion. For it is our human problem. If a solution is found it will be through the medium of human desire, human understanding, and human endeavor.

2

DEMOCRACY AND EDUCATION IN THE WORLD OF TODAY

IT IS OBVIOUS THAT THE RELATION BETWEEN DEMOCRACY AND education is a reciprocal one, a mutual one, and vitally so. Democracy is itself an educational principle, an educational measure and policy. There is nothing novel in saying that even an election campaign has a greater value in educating the citizens of the country who take any part in it than it has in its immediate external results. Our campaigns are certainly not always as educational as they might be, but by and large they certainly do serve the purpose of making the citizens of the country aware of what is going on in society, what the problems are and the various measures and policies that are proposed to deal with the issues of the day.

Mussolini remarked that democracy was passé, done with, because people are tired of liberty. There is a certain truth in that remark, not about the democracy being done with, at least we hope not, but in the fact that human beings do get tired of liberty, of political liberty and of the responsibilities, the duties, the burden that the acceptance of political liberty involves. There is an educational principle and policy in a deeper sense than that which I have just mentioned in that it proposes in effect, if not in words, to every member of society just that question: do you want to be a free human being standing on your own feet, accepting the responsibilities, the duties that go with that position as an effective member of society?

The meaning of democracy, especially of political democ-

34

racy which, of course, is far from covering the whole scope of democracy, as over against every aristocratic form of social control and political authority, was expressed by Abraham Lincoln when he said that no man was good enough or wise enough to govern others without their consent; that is, without some expression on their part of their own needs, their own desires and their own conception of how social affairs should go on and social problems be handled.

A woman told me once that she asked a very well-known American statesman what he would do for the people of this country if he were God. He said, "Well, that is quite a question. I should look people over and decide what it was that they needed and then try and give it to them."

She said, "Well, you know, I expected that to be the answer that you would give. There are people that would *ask* other people what they wanted before they tried to give it to them."

That asking other people what they would like, what they need, what their ideas are, is an essential part of the democratic idea. We are so familiar with it as a matter of democratic political practice that perhaps we don't always think about it even when we exercise the privilege of giving an answer. That practice is an educational matter because it puts upon us as individual members of a democracy the responsibility of considering what it is that we as individuals want, what our needs and troubles are.

Dr. Felix Adler expressed very much the same idea. I am not quoting his words, but this was what he said, that "no matter how ignorant any person is there is one thing that he knows better than anybody else and that is where the shoes pinch on his own feet"; and because it is the individual that knows his own troubles, even if he is not literate or sophisticated in other respects, the idea of democracy as opposed to any conception of aristocracy is that every individual must be consulted in such a way, actively not passively, that he himself becomes a part of the process of authority, of the process of social control; that his needs and wants have a chance to be registered in a way where they count in determining social policy. Along with that goes, of course, the other feature which is necessary for the realization of democracy—mutual conference and mutual consultation and arriving ultimately at social control by pooling, by putting together all of these individual expressions of ideas and wants.

The ballot box and majority rule are external and very largely mechanical symbols and expressions of this. They are expedients, the best devices that at a certain time have been found, but beneath them there are the two ideas: first, the opportunity, the right and the duty of every individual to form some conviction and to express some conviction regarding his own place in the social order, and the relations of that social order to his own welfare; second, the fact that each individual counts as one and one only on an equality with others, so that the final social will comes about as the cooperative expression of the ideas of many people. And I think it is perhaps only recently that we are realizing that that idea is the essence of all sound education.

Even in the classroom we are beginning to learn that learning which develops intelligence and character does not come about when only the textbook and the teacher have a say; that every individual becomes educated only as he has an opportunity to contribute something from his own experience, no matter how meager or slender that background of experience may be at a given time; and finally that enlightenment comes from the give and take, from the exchange of experiences and ideas.

The realization of that principle in the schoolroom, it seems to me, is an expression of the significance of democracy as the educational process without which individuals cannot come into the full possession of themselves nor make a contribution, if they have it in them to make, to the social well-being of others.

I said that democracy and education bear a reciprocal relation, for it is not merely that democracy is itself an educational principle, but that democracy cannot endure, much less develop, without education in that narrower sense in which we ordinarily think of it, the education that is given in the family, and especially as we think of it in the school. The school is the essential distributing agency for whatever values and purposes any social group cherishes. It is not the only means, but it is the first means, the primary means and the most deliberate means by which the values that any social group cherishes, the purposes that it wishes to realize, are distributed and brought home to the thought, the observation, judgment and choice of the individual.

What would a powerful dynamo in a big power-house amount to if there were no line of distribution leading into shops and factories to give power, leading into the home to give light? No matter what fine ideals or fine resources, the products of past experience, past human culture, exist somewhere at the center, they become significant only as they are carried out, or are distributed. That is true of any society, not simply of a democratic society; but what is true of a democratic society is, of course, that its special values and its special purposes and aims must receive such distribution that they become part of the mind and the will of the members of society. So that the school in a democracy is contributing, if it is true to itself as an educational agency, to the democratic idea of making knowledge and understanding, in short the power of action, a part of the intrinsic intelligence and character of the individual.

I think we have one thing to learn from the anti-democratic states of Europe, and that is that we should take as seriously the preparation of the members of our society for the duties and responsibilities of democracy, as they take seriously the formation of the thoughts and minds and characters of their population for their aims and ideals.

This does not mean that we should imitate their universal propaganda, that we should prostitute the schools, the radio and the press to the inculcation of one single point of view and the suppression of everything else; it means that we should take seriously, energetically and vigorously the use of democratic schools and democratic methods in the schools; that we should educate the young and the youth of the country in freedom for participation in a free society. It may be that with the advantage of great distance from these troubled scenes in Europe we may have learned something from the terrible tragedies that have occurred there, so as to take the idea of democracy more seriously, asking ourselves what it means, and taking steps to make our schools more completely the agents for preparation of free individuals for intelligent participation in a free society.

I don't need to tell these readers that our free public school system was founded, promoted, just about 100 years ago, because of the realization of men like Horace Mann and Henry Barnard that citizens need to participate in what they called a republican form of government; that they need enlightenment which could come about only through a system of free education.

If you have read the writings of men of those times, you know how few schools existed, how poor they were, how short their terms were, how poorly most of the teachers were prepared, and, judging from what Horace Mann said, how general was the indifference of the average well-to-do citizen to the education of anybody except his own children.

You may recall the terrible indictment that he drew of the well-to-do classes because of their indifference to the education of the masses, and the vigor with which he pointed out that they were pursuing a dangerous course; that, no matter how much they educated their own children, if they left the masses ignorant they would be corrupted and that they themselves and their children would be the sufferers in the end. As he said, "We did not mean to exchange a single tyrant across the sea for a hydra-headed tyrant here at home"; yet that is what we will get unless we educate our citizens.

I refer to him particularly because to such a very large

extent the ideas, the ideals which Horace Mann and the others held have been so largely realized. I think even Horace Mann could hardly have anticipated a finer, more magnificent school plan, school building and school equipment than we have in some parts of our country. On the side of the mechanical and the external, the things that these educational statesmen 100 years ago strove for have been to a considerable extent realized. I should have to qualify that. We know how poor many of the rural schools are, especially in backward states of the country, how poorly they are equipped, how short their school years are; but, in a certain sense, taking what has been done at the best, the immediate ideals of Horace Mann and the others have been realized. Yet the problem we have today of the relation of education and democracy is as acute and as serious a problem as the problem of providing school buildings, school equipment, school teachers and school monies was a hundred years ago.

If, as we all know, democracy is in a more or less precarious position throughout the world, and has even in our own country enemies of growing strength, we cannot take it for granted as something that is sure to endure. If this is the actual case, one reason for it is that we have been so complacent about the idea of democracy that we have more or less unconsciously assumed that the work of establishing a democracy was completed by the founding fathers or when the Civil War abolished slavery. We tend to think of it as something that has been established and that it remains for us simply to enjoy.

We have had, without formulating it, a conception of democracy as something static, as something that is like an inheritance that can be bequeathed, a kind of lump sum that we could live off and upon. The crisis that we have undergone will turn out, I think, to be worthwhile if we have learned through it that every generation has to accomplish democracy over again for itself; that its very nature, its essence, is something that cannot be handed on from one person or one generation to another, but has to be worked out in terms of needs, problems and conditions of the social life of which, as the years go by, we are a part, a social life that is changing with extreme rapidity from year to year.

I find myself resentful and really feeling sad when, in relation to present social, economic and political problems, people point simply backward as if somewhere in the past there were a model for what we should do today. I hope I yield to none in appreciation of the great American tradition, for tradition is something that is capable of being transmitted as an emotion and as an idea from generation to generation. We have a great and precious heritage from the past, but to be realized, to be translated from an idea and an emotion, this tradition has to be embodied by active effort in the social relations which we as human beings bear to each other under present conditions. It is because the conditions of life change, that the problem of maintaining a democracy becomes new, and the burden that is put upon the school, upon the educational system is not that of stating merely the ideas of the men who made this country, their hopes and their intentions, but of teaching what a democratic society means under existing conditions.

The other day I read a statement to the effect that more than half of the working people in shops and factories in this country today are working in industries that didn't even exist forty years ago. It would seem to mean that, as far as the working population is concerned, half of the old industries have gone into obsolescence and been replaced by new ones. The man who made that statement, a working scientist, pointed out that every worker in every industry today is doing what he is doing, either directly or indirectly, because of the progress that has been made in the last half century in the physical sciences. In other words, in the material world, in the world of production, of material commodities and material entities, the progress of knowledge, of science, has revolutionized activity (revolutionized is not too strong a word) in the last fifty years.

How can we under these circumstances think that we can live from an inheritance, noble and fine as it is, that was formed in earlier days—one might as well say pre-scientific and pre-industrial days—except as we deliberately translate that tradition and that inheritance into the terms of the realities of present society which means simply our relations to one another?

Horace Mann and other educators 100 years ago worked when the United States was essentially agricultural. The things with which we are most familiar that enter into the formation of a material part of our life didn't exist. Railways were just beginning, but all the other great inventions that we take for granted were hidden in the darkness of future time. Even then in those earlier days, Thomas Jefferson predicted evils that might come to man with the too-rapid development of manufacturing industries, because, as he saw it, the backbone of any democratic society was the farmer who owned and cultivated his own land. He saw the farmer as a man who could control his own economic destiny, a man who, therefore, could stand on his own feet and be really a free citizen of a free country. What he feared was what might happen when men lost the security of economic independence and became dependent upon others.

Even Alexander Hamilton, who belonged to the other school of thought, when speaking of judges, maintained that those who controlled a man's subsistence controlled his will. If that is true of judges on the bench it is certainly true to a considerable extent of all people; and now we have economic conditions, because of the rapid change in industry and in finance, where there are thousands and millions of people who have the minimum of control over the conditions of their own subsistence. That is a problem, of course, that will need public and private consideration, but it is a deeper problem than that; it is a problem of the future of democracy, of how political democracy can be made secure if there is economic insecurity and economic dependence of great sections of the population if not upon the direct will of others, at least upon the conditions under which the employing sections of society operate.

I mention this simply as one of the respects in which the relation of education and democracy assumes a very different form than it did in the time when these men supposed that "If we can only have schools enough, only have school buildings and good school equipment and prepared teachers, the necessary enlightenment to take care of republican institutions will follow almost as a matter of course."

The educational problem today is deeper, it is more acute, it is infinitely more difficult because it has to face all of the problems of the modern world. Recently we have witnessed activities of an armed coalition of democratic nations, formed to oppose and resist the advance of Fascist, totalitarian, authoritarian states. I am not going to discuss that issue, but I do want to ask a few questions. What do we mean when we assume that we, in common with certain other nations, are really democratic, that we have already so accomplished the ends and purposes of democracy that all we have to do is to stand up and resist the encroachments of non-democratic states?

We are unfortunately familiar with the recent racial intolerance of Germany and Italy. Are we entirely free from that racial intolerance, so that we can pride ourselves upon having achieved a complete democracy? Our treatment of the Negroes, anti-Semitism, the growing (at least I fear it is growing) serious opposition to the alien immigrant within our gates, is, I think, a sufficient answer to that question. Here, in relation to education, we have a problem. What are our schools doing to cultivate not merely passive toleration that will put up with people of different racial birth or different colored skin, but what are our schools doing positively and aggressively and constructively to cultivate understanding and goodwill which are essential to democratic society?

We object, and object very properly, to the constant stream of false propaganda that is put forth in the states for the suppression of all free inquiry and freedom, but again how do we stand in those respects? I know we have in many schools a wonderful school pledge where the children six years old and up probably arise and pledge allegiance to a flag and to what that stands for—one indivisible nation, justice and liberty. How far are we permitting a symbol to become a substitute for the reality? How far are our citizens, legislators and educators salving their conscience with the idea that genuine patriotism is being instilled in these children because they recite the words of that pledge? Do they know what allegiance and loyalty mean? What do they mean by an indivisible nation when we have a nation that is still more or less torn by factional strife and class division? Is that an indivisible nation, and is the reciting of a verbal pledge any educational guarantee of the existence of an indivisible nation?

And so I might go on about liberty and justice. What are we doing to translate those great ideas of liberty and justice out of a formal ceremonial ritual into the realities of the understanding, the insight and the genuine loyalty of the boys and girls in our schools?

We say we object, and rightly so, to this exaggerated, one-sided nationalism inculcated under the name of devotion to country, but until our schools have themselves become clear upon what public spirit and good citizenship mean in all the relations of life, youth cannot meet the great responsibilities that rest upon them.

We had reasons to deplore, also, and deplore rightly, the dependence of these authoritarian states in Europe upon the use of force. What are we doing to cultivate the idea of the supremacy of the method of intelligence, of understanding, the method of goodwill and of mutual sympathy over and above force? I know that in many respects our public schools have and deserve a good reputation for what they have done in breaking down class division, creating a feeling of greater humanity and of membership in a single family, but I do not believe that we have as yet done what can be done and what needs to be done in breaking down even the ordinary snobbishness and prejudices that divide people from each other, and that our schools have done what they can and should do in this respect.

And when it comes to this matter of force as a method of settling social issues, we have unfortunately only to look at our own scene, both domestic and international. In the present state of the world apparently a great and increasing number of people feel that the only way we can make ourselves secure is by increasing our army and navy and making our factories ready to manufacture munitions. In other words, somehow we too have a belief that force, physical and brute force, after all is the best final reliance.

With our fortunate position in the world I think that if we used our resources, including our financial resources, to build up among ourselves a genuine, true and effective democratic society, we would find that we have a surer, a more enduring and a more powerful defense of democratic institutions both within ourselves and with relation to the rest of the world than the surrender to the belief in force, violence and war can ever give. I know that our schools are doing a great deal to inculcate ideas of peace, but I sometimes wonder how far this goes beyond a certain sentimental attachment to a realization of what peace would actually mean in the world in the way of cooperation, goodwill and mutual understanding.

I have endeavored to call your attention first to the inherent, the vital and organic relation that there is between democracy and education from both sides, from the side of education, the schools, and from the side of the very meaning of democracy. I have simply tried to give a certain number of more or less random illustrations of what the problems of the schools are today with reference to preparing the youth of the country for active, intelligent participation in the building and the rebuilding and the eternal rebuilding—because, as I have said, it never can be done once for all—of a genuinely democratic society. And I wish to close (as I began) with saying, that after all the cause of democracy is the moral cause of the dignity and the worth of the individual. Through mutual respect, mutual toleration, give and take, the pooling of experiences, it is ultimately the only method by which human beings can succeed in carrying on this experiment in which we are all engaged, whether we want to be or not, the greatest experiment of humanity—that of living together in ways in which the life of each of us is at once profitable in the deepest sense of the word, profitable to himself and helpful in the building up of the individuality of others.

3

THE CHALLENGE OF DEMOCRACY
TO EDUCATION

ANYONE WHO HAS READ ANYTHING OF HORACE MANN KNOWS THAT he is a sort of patron saint of progressive education not only because of his ideas (very advanced for his day) about the way children should be treated, not only because he advocated a personal and humane atmosphere in the school in the relation of children and teachers, but because, above all, he was the prophet of the idea of the absolute necessity of free public education for the existence and preservation of a democratic way of life; or, as he said in the phraseology of his time, "republican institutions of self-government."

In an eloquent speech which he made after he had held his office some years, he insisted that while he believed thoroughly in the capacity of men and women for self-government, yet he also knew that it was *only* a capacity, not a complete inborn gift, and that public education for all was the only means by which the capacity should be made a reality.

"Education," he said, "is our only political safety; outside of this ark is the deluge." And again, he said: "The common school is the greatest discovery ever made by man. Other social organizations are curative and remedial. This is preventive and an antidote."

So far as the institution for which he labored is concerned— namely, a public school system supported by public taxation and open to all children, training schools for teachers, and so on —the dream of Horace Mann, although not completely realized, has in the passage of a hundred years been realized to a sur-

46

prising degree. But the problem for the solution of which Horace Mann labored is still with us. We have now in a very large measure the institution which he strove to bring into being. But we still have with us, and perhaps in an even more urgent and difficult way, the problem of how this institution is to be made to serve the needs of democratic society, of the democratic way of life. We certainly cannot rest on our accomplishments with respect to the school as the means of political democratic security.

Horace Mann asked in one of his public addresses whether the children in our schools are being educated in reference to themselves and their private interests only, or with regard to the great social duties and prerogatives that await them in adult life. We may well ask the same question today.

To my mind, the greatest mistake that we can make about democracy is to conceive of it as something fixed, fixed in idea and fixed in its outward manifestation.

The very idea of democracy, the meaning of democracy, must be continually explored afresh; it has to be constantly discovered, and rediscovered, remade and reorganized; while the political and economic and social institutions in which it is embodied have to be remade and reorganized to meet the changes that are going on in the development of new needs on the part of human beings and new resources for satisfying these needs.

No form of life does or can stand still; it either goes forward or it goes backward, and the end of the backward road is death. Democracy as a form of life cannot stand still. It, too, if it is to live, must go forward to meet the changes that are here and that are coming. If it does not go forward, if it tries to stand still, it is already starting on the backward road that leads to extinction.

In the fact that democracy in order to live must change and move, we have, I think, the challenge that democracy offers to education. One hundred years ago in the simpler conditions of life, when the social group was the neighborhood or the small community, before most of the inventions that have transformed modern society had come into existence—or, at least, before they had made any great impress on modes of living—it was not altogether unreasonable to advance the idea that individuals are born with a kind of democratic aspiration; and that, given this innate disposition and tendency, schooling would enable them to meet the duties and responsibilities of life in a democratic society. In the comprehensive conditions of today, such an idea is fallacious. Only as the coming generation learns in the schools to understand the social forces that are at work, the directions and the cross-directions in which they are moving, the consequences that they are reproducing, the consequences that they might produce if they were understood and managed with intelligence—only as the schools provide this understanding, have we any assurance that they are meeting the challenge which is put to them by democracy.

Are our schools accomplishing these things? In what measure are they failing to accomplish them? For unless they are accomplishing them, the ark is not an ark of safety in a deluge. It is being carried by the deluge of outside forces, varying, shifting, turning aimlessly with every current in the tides of modern life. Just as democracy in order to live must move and move forward, so schools in a democracy cannot stand still, cannot be satisfied and complacent with what has been accomplished, but must be willing to undertake whatever reorganization of studies, of methods of teaching, of administration, including that larger organization which concerns the relation of pupils and teachers to each other, and to the life of the community. Failing in this, the schools cannot give democracy the intelligent direction of its forces which it needs to continue in existence.

Only as the schools provide an understanding of the movement and direction of social forces and an understanding of social needs and of the resources that may be used to satisfy them, will they meet the challenge of democracy. I use the word "understanding" rather than knowledge because, unfortunately, knowledge to so many people means "information." Information is knowledge about things, and there is no guarantee in any amount of "knowledge about things" that understanding—the spring of intelligent action—will follow from it. Knowledge about things is static. There is no guarantee in any amount of information, even if skillfully conveyed, that an intelligent attitude of mind will be formed. Indeed, whatever attitude it may form is very largely left as a matter of chance, and mostly of the conditions, circumstances, contacts, intercourses and pressures that are brought to bear on the individual outside the school.

I do not mean that we can have understanding without knowledge, without information; but I do mean that there is no guarantee, as I have just said, that the acquisition and accumulation of knowledge will create the attitudes that generate intelligent action.

I remember that years ago when I was in China I was told that the first elections held there were very honest. Before the next elections, Bryce's *American Commonwealth* was translated into Chinese. China got information about how bosses and machines, Tammany Hall and other institutions of the kind worked. This knowledge developed an attitude in some politicians, but not one that was intelligent or socially helpful.

The distinction between knowledge, information, and understanding is not a complicated or philosophical matter. An individual may know all about the structure of an automobile, may be able to name all the parts of the machine and tell what they are there for. But he does not understand the machine unless he knows how it works and how to work it; and, if it doesn't work right, what to do in order to *make* it work right. You can carry that simple illustration through any field that you please.

Understanding has to be in terms of how things work and how to do things. Understanding, by its very nature, is related to action; just as information, by its very nature, is isolated from action or connected with it only here and there by accident.

We have heard a great deal in recent years about the isolation of the school from life and about methods of overcoming or reducing that isolation. The point that I am emphasizing is that the isolation of the school is the isolation of knowledge from action. For social life, whatever else it is, is always a composite of activities that are going on and that are producing consequences.

I would ask, then, how far are studies, methods, and administration of our schools connecting knowledge, information, and skills with the way things are done socially and how they may be done. For only in this connection of knowledge and social action can education generate the understanding of present social forces, movements, problems, and needs that is necessary for the continued existence of democracy.

Consider, for example, two of the more modern tendencies in education which seem to support the idea that the isolation of knowledge from social action is breaking down. The first of these is the increasingly important place held by the social studies in the American school.

It certainly seems as if the social studies have a more intimate relation with social life than a great many of the other subjects that are taught in the school, and that accordingly their increasing introduction into the curriculum, the increasing emphasis upon them ought to be a means by which the school system meets the challenge of democracy.

But the crucial question is the extent to which the material of the social studies, whether economics or politics or history or sociology, whatever it may be, is taught simply as information about present society or is taught in connection with things that are done, that need to be done, and how to do them. If the first tendency prevails, I can readily imagine that the introduction of more and more social studies into the curriculum will simply put one more load onto a curriculum that is already overburdened, and that the supposed end for which they were introduced—the development of a more intelligent citizenship in all the ranges of citizenship (the complex ranges that now exist, including political but including also much more)—will be missed.

I may illustrate the point by reference to that subject which is supposed to train particularly for political citizenship—the study of civics. There is, I think, considerable danger that this phase of social study will get submerged in a great flood of miscellaneous social study. When the subject was first introduced, I think there was a good deal of evidence of faith in the truly miraculous and magical power of information. If the students would only learn their federal and state Constitutions, the names and duties of all the officers and all the rest of the anatomy of the government, they would be prepared to be good citizens. And many of them—many of us, I fear—having learned these facts went out into adult life and became the easy prey of skillful politicians and political machines; the victims of political misrepresentation, say, on the part of the newspapers we happen to read.

There was a modicum of knowledge or information acquired in the school, but it wasn't connected; and I fear isn't today much connected with how government is actually run, with how parties are formed and managed, what machines are, what gives machines and political bosses their power. In fact, it might be dangerous in some cities if pupils in the schools were given not merely a formal and anatomical knowledge about the structure of the government but also acquired an understanding of how the government of their own community is run through giving special favors and through dealings with industrial powers. But without so rudimentary a preparation for intelligent voting or for intelligent legislation, how could we say that we were preparing for any kind of democratic self-government?

In a lecture entitled "The Retreat From Reason," Lancelot Hogben says: "As soon as you ask yourself what would have to be done to increase, diminish, or maintain at some fixed level the population of a community, you discover that you need to know a host of different things which would not occur to you if you set to yourself the more general question, How do populations grow?"

The question of population is certainly an important question of social welfare. But the principle involved may be applied to the entire field of politics. If the classes in our schools asked, "What would have to be done to give us genuine democratic government in our states, local communities, and nation?" I think it is certainly true that a great many things had to be looked into and a great deal more knowledge obtained than is acquired as long as we simply take our democratic government as a fact and don't ask either how it is actively run or how it might be run.

Science as an area of the curriculum, although not so recent a development as the social studies, is also fairly recent. The natural sciences had to struggle to find any toe-hold in the school system. They had to find a place there against the very great resistance offered by the old classical, mathematical, and literary curriculum.

Certainly in modern life the natural sciences have a much closer connection with actual life and actual human relations than a great many of the studies that have come down from earlier times. It is not too much to say that science, through its applications in invention and technologies, is the greatest force in modern society for producing social changes and shaping human relations. It is no exaggeration to say that it has revolutionized the conditions on which human beings have associated for the last one hundred and fifty years, and that with the transition from the machine age to the power age, still greater social changes are in store because of science.

Again, in this matter of the isolation of school material from life versus that connection with it which would give the kind of understanding of social forces that alone will prepare students to take an intelligent part in the maintenance and growing development of democracy, I ask: "How far is science taught in relation to its social consequences, actual and possible, if the resources which science puts at human disposal were utilized for general democratic social welfare?" I know that very great improvements are being made, but I am afraid that science is still taught very largely as a separate and isolated subject and that there are still those, including many scientists themselves, who would think that that wonderful thing "pure" science would be contaminated if it were brought into connection with social practice. And yet without this connection, students are certainly getting very little intelligent understanding of the forces that are now making human society and that might remake it.

I don't know that I am particularly enthusiastic about the question of choosing between communism and fascism. I am afraid that too much attention to that subject will give people the impression that sooner or later we have got to make such a choice. As far as I can see, the hope of maintaining democracy lies in using the enormous resources that science has put in our hands to inaugurate not merely an age of material plenty and material security, but also of cultural equality of opportunity—the opportunity of every individual to develop to his full capacity.

Unless our schools take science in its relation to the understanding of those forces which are now shaping society, and, still more, how the resources of the organized intelligence that is science might be used in organized social action, the outlook for democracy is insecure. The resources of organized intelligence are working in present society, but working under political and economic conditions that are not favorable to the maintenance of democracy. If for a single generation psychology and physical science were related systematically and organically to understanding not merely how society *is* going, but how it *might* be intelligently directed, then I should have no fear about the future of democracy.

I may be thought to have omitted the fact that, after all, the schools spend a good deal of time not only with acquisition of knowledge but also with acquisition of skills. In a competitive and acquisitive society, I don't know that we need to be surprised that so much emphasis is placed upon acquisition either of information or of skills in the schools. It may be said, however, that the movement in the direction of vocational education of some form or other (including professional) is the most marked feature of education in, let us say, the last forty years, and that it, more than any other one thing, gives such unity of direction as exists.

This emphasis upon education for vocations or professions, like the increasing emphasis on the social studies and sciences, may also seem to be a contradiction of the idea that our schools are isolated from contemporary life.

But the question is: With what phases and aspects of social life has the whole vocational movement been most closely connected? Today it is most obviously intended to be an aid in preparing young people to get jobs and so earn a livelihood. It may prepare them quite effectively on the technical side and yet leave graduates with very little understanding of the place of those industries or professions in the social life of the present, and of what these vocations and professions may do to keep democracy a living, growing thing.

It seems to me to be a somewhat sad commentary on our educational system that there have to be separate schools that are called "labor schools" to prepare leaders in the struggle of labor in modern society, and that these few separate schools have a very great struggle to keep going. Wouldn't it seem as if in a really democratic system of education, in a really democratic society, that the history of labor, the significance of labor, the possibilities of labor, would be an important, integral part of the whole education scheme? Or, turning to another aspect of the matter, how shall we account for the fact that, with some notable exceptions, the medical profession is heartily opposed to the socialization of medicine and to making public health a common public asset? How are we to explain the fact that to such a large extent the lawyers who have had a professional and supposedly a competent professional education seem to be the advocates of the most reactionary political and social issues of the community at any given time?

These questions are at least worth asking, even if we can't find the answer. They seem to indicate that to a very considerable extent the movement in the direction of industrial, vocational, technical, and professional education has not come to grips either with the understanding of what the social forces and needs of the present are or of how things might be done to insure an ever-growing democratic life.

Hogben, in the lecture already referred to, says: "The training of the statesman and the man of letters gives him no prevision of the technical forces that are shaping the society in which he lives . . . The education of the scientist and the technician leaves him indifferent to the social consequences of his own action." Those are strong statements. They indicate that there is a very great split in our educational system. The people who are active in the direction of public affairs lack prevision because they have no understanding of the scientific technological forces that are actually shaping society. The education of the average scientist and the average technician, on the other hand, is such that he is left indifferent to the social consequences of his own activities. Hence, it is nobody's business to take stock of the resources of knowledge now available for social betterment.

The question I am raising is whether it isn't the educator's business to see that the education given by schools be such that those who go out from them can take stock of the knowledge that is available for social betterment.

Part of the discredit of representative government in Europe today has come because of the feeling that politicians are able to talk glibly and write elegantly and argue forcibly; but that when it comes to the crises and necessities of action, they are not competent. It might be worthwhile to sacrifice a little of the purity of pure knowledge, to contaminate it here and there with relation to action, if we could save our country from a reaction against politics and politicians who can talk and argue, but who do not know how to act competently with reference to the social problems that have to be dealt with.

Education must have a tendency, if it is education, to form

attitudes. The tendency to form attitudes which will express themselves in intelligent social action is something very different from indoctrination, just as taking intelligent aim is very different from firing BB shot in the air at random with the kind of vague, pious hope that somehow or other a bird may fly into some of the shot.

There is an intermediary between aimless education and the education of inculcation and indoctrination. The alternative is the kind of education that connects the materials and methods by which knowledge is acquired with a sense of how things are done and of how they might be done; not by impregnating the individual with some final philosophy, whether it comes from Karl Marx or from Mussolini or Hitler or anybody else, but by enabling him to so understand existing conditions that an attitude of intelligent action will follow from social understanding.

I don't know just what democracy means in detail in the whole range of concrete relations of human life—political, economic, cultural, domestic—at the present time. I make this humiliating confession the more readily because I suspect that nobody else knows what it means in full concrete detail. But I am sure, however, that this problem is the one that most demands the serious attention of educators at the present time.

What does democracy really mean? What would be its consequences in the complex life of the present? If we can answer those questions, then our next question will be: What direction shall we give to the work of the school so that the richness and fullness of the democratic way of life in all its scope may be promoted? The coöperative study of these questions is to my mind the present outstanding task of progressive education.

4

DEMOCRACY AND EDUCATIONAL ADMINISTRATION

I

My experience in educational administration is limited. I should not venture to address a body of those widely experienced and continuously engaged in school administration about the details of the management of schools. But the topic suggested to me has to do with the relation of school administration to democratic ideals and methods and to the general subject of the relation of education and democracy, to which I have given considerable thought over many years. The topic suggested concerns a special phase of this general subject. I shall begin, then, with some remarks on the broad theme of democratic aims and methods. Much of what I shall say on this subject is necessarily old and familiar. But it seems necessary to rehearse some old ideas in order to have a criterion for dealing with the special subject.

In the first place, democracy is much broader than a special political form, a method of conducting government, of making laws and carrying on governmental administration by means of popular suffrage and elected officers. It is that, of course. But it is something broader and deeper than that. The political and governmental phase of democracy is a means, the best means so far found, for realizing ends that lie in the wide domain of human relationships and the development of human personality. It is, as we often say, though perhaps without appreciating all that is involved in the saying, a way of life, social and individual. The keynote of democracy as a way of life may be expressed, it seems to me, as the necessity for the participation of every mature human being in formation of the values that regulate the living of men together: which is necessary from the standpoint of both the general social welfare and the full development of human beings as individuals.

Universal suffrage, recurring elections, responsibility of those who are in political power to the voters, and the other factors of democratic government are means that have been found expedient for realizing democracy as the truly human way of living. They are not a final end and a final value. They are to be judged on the basis of their contribution to end. It is a form of idolatry to erect means into the end which they serve. Democratic political forms are simply the best means that human wit has devised up to a special time in history. But they rest back upon the idea that no man or limited set of men is wise enough or good enough to rule others without their consent; the positive meaning of this statement is that all those who are affected by social institutions must have a share in producing and managing them. The two facts that each one is influenced in what he does and enjoys and in what he becomes by the institutions under which he lives, and that therefore he shall have, in a democracy, a voice in shaping them, are the passive and active sides of the same fact.

The development of political democracy came about through substitution of the method of mutual consultation and voluntary agreement for the method of subordination of the many to the few enforced from above. Social arrangements which involve fixed subordination are maintained by coercion. The coercion need not be physical. There have existed, for short periods, benevolent despotisms. But coercion of some sort there has been; perhaps economic, certainly psychological and moral. The very fact of exclusion from participation is a subtle form of suppression. It gives individuals no opportunity to reflect and decide upon what is good for them. Others who are supposed to be wiser and who in any case have more power decide the question for them and also decide the methods and means by which subjects may arrive at the enjoyment of what is good for them. This form of coercion and suppression is more subtle and more effective than is overt intimidation and restraint. When it is habitual and embodied in social institutions, it seems the normal and natural state of affairs. The mass usually become unaware that they have a claim to a development of their own powers. Their experience is so restricted that they are not conscious of restriction. It is part of the democratic conception that they as individuals are not the only sufferers, but that the whole social body is deprived of the potential resources that should be at its service. The individuals of the submerged mass may not be very wise. But there is one thing they are wiser about than anybody else can be, and that is where the shoe pinches, the troubles they suffer from.

The foundation of democracy is faith in the capacities of human nature; faith in human intelligence and in the power of pooled and cooperative experience. It is not belief that these things are complete but that, if given a show, they will grow and be able to generate progressively the knowledge and wisdom needed to guide collective action. Every autocratic and authoritarian scheme of social action rests on a belief that the needed intelligence is confined to a superior few, who because of inherent natural gifts are endowed with the ability and the right to control the conduct of others; laying down principles and rules and directing the ways in which they are carried out. It would be foolish to deny that much can be said for this point of view. It is that which controlled human relations in social groups for much the greater part of human history. The democratic faith has emerged very, very recently in the history of mankind. Even where democracies now exist, men's minds and feelings are still permeated with ideas about leadership imposed from above, ideas that developed in the long early history of mankind. After democratic political institutions were nominally established, beliefs and ways of looking at life and of acting that originated when men and women were externally controlled and subjected to arbitrary power, persisted in the family, the church, business, and the school; and experience shows that as long as they persist there, political democracy is not secure.

Belief in equality is an element of the democratic credo. It is not, however, belief in equality of natural endowments. Those who proclaimed the idea of equality did not suppose they were enunciating a psychological doctrine, but a legal and political one. All individuals are entitled to equality of treatment by law and in its administration. Each one is affected equally in quality if not in quantity by the institutions under which he lives and has an equal right to express his judgment, although the weight of his judgment may not be equal in amount when it enters into the pooled result to that of others. In short, each one is equally an individual and entitled to equal opportunity of development of his own capacities, be they large or small in range. Moreover, each has needs of his own, as significant to him as those of others are to them. The very fact of natural and psychological inequality is all the more reason for establishment by law of equality of opportunity, since otherwise the former becomes a means of oppression of the less gifted.

While what we call intelligence be distributed in unequal amounts, it is the democratic faith that it is sufficiently general so that each individual has something to contribute, whose value can be assessed only as it enters into the final pooled intelligence constituted by the contributions of all. Every authoritarian scheme, on the contrary, assumes that its value may be assessed by some *prior* principle, if not of family and birth or race and color or possession of material wealth, then by the position and rank a person occupies in the existing social scheme. The democratic faith in equality is the faith that each individual shall have the chance and opportunity to contribute whatever he is capable of contributing and that the value of his contribution be decided by its place and function in the organized total of similar contributions, not on the basis of prior status of any kind whatever.

I have emphasized in what precedes the importance of the effective release of intelligence in connection with personal experience in the democratic way of living. I have done so purposely because democracy is so often and so naturally associated in our minds with freedom of *action*, forgetting the importance of freed intelligence which is necessary to direct and to warrant freedom of action. Unless freedom of individual action has intelligence and informed conviction back of it, its manifestation is almost sure to result in confusion and disorder. The democratic idea of freedom is not the right of each individual to *do* as he pleases, even if it be qualified by adding "provided he does not interfere with the same freedom on the part of others." While the idea is not always, not often enough, expressed in words, the basic freedom is that of freedom of *mind* and of whatever degree of freedom of action and experience is necessary to produce freedom of intelligence. The modes of freedom guaranteed in the Bill of Rights are all of this nature: Freedom of belief and conscience, of expression of opinion, of assembly for discussion and conference, of the press as an organ of communication. They are guaranteed because without them individuals are not free to develop and society is deprived of what they might contribute.

What, it may be asked, have these things to do with school administration? There is some kind of government, of control, wherever affairs that concern a number of persons who act together are engaged in. It is a superficial view that holds government is located in Washington and Albany. There is government in the family, in business, in the church, in every social group. There are regulations, due to custom if not to enactment, that settle how individuals in a group act in connection with one another.

It is a disputed question of theory and practice just how far a democratic political government should go in control of the conditions of action within special groups. At the present time, for example, there are those who think the federal and state governments leave too much freedom of independent action to industrial and financial groups, and there are others who think the government is going altogether too far at the present time. I do not need to discuss this phase of the problem, much less to try to settle it. But it must be pointed out that if the methods of regulation and administration in vogue in the conduct of secondary social groups are non-democratic, whether directly or indirectly, or both, there is bound to be an unfavorable reaction back into the habits of feeling, thought and action of citizenship in the broadest sense of that word. The way in which any organized social interest is controlled necessarily plays an important part in forming the dispositions and tastes, the attitudes, interests, purposes and desires, of those engaged in carrying on the activities of the group. For illustration, I do not need to do more than point to the moral, emotional and intellectual effect upon both employers and laborers of the existing industrial system. Just what the effects specifically are is a matter about which we know very little. But I suppose that everyone who reflects upon the subject admits that it is impossible that the ways in which activities are carried on for the greater part of the waking hours of the day, and the way in which the shares of individuals are involved in the management of affairs in such a matter as gaining a livelihood and attaining material and social security, can only be a highly important factor in shaping personal dispositions; in short, forming character and intelligence.

In the broad and final sense all institutions are educational in the sense that they operate to form the attitudes, dispositions, abilities and disabilities that constitute a concrete personality. The principle applies with special force to the school. For it is the main business of the family and the school to influence directly the formation and growth of attitudes and dispositions, emotional, intellectual and moral. Whether this educative process is carried on in a predominantly democratic or non-democratic way becomes, therefore, a question of transcendent importance not only for education itself but for its final effect upon all the interests and activities of a society that is committed to the democratic way of life. Hence, if the general tenor of what I have said about the democratic ideal and method is anywhere near the truth, it must be said that the democratic principle requires that every teacher should have some regular and organic way in which he can, directly or through representatives democratically chosen, participate in the formation of the controlling aims, methods and materials of the school of which he is a part. Something over thirty years ago, I wrote: "If there is a single public-school system in the United States where there is official and constitutional provision made for submitting questions of methods of discipline and teaching, and the questions of the curriculum, text-books, etc., to the discussion and decision of those actually engaged in the work of teaching, that fact has escaped my notice." I could not make that statement today. There has been in some places a great advance in the democratic direction. As I noted in my earlier article there were always in actual fact school systems where the practice was much better than the theory of external control from above: for even if there were no authorized regular way in which the intelligence and experience of the teaching corps was consulted and utilized, administrative officers accomplished that end in informal ways. We may hope this extension of democratic methods has not only endured but has expanded. Nevertheless, the issue of authoritarian versus democratic methods in administration remains with us and demands serious recognition.

It is my impression that even up to the present democratic methods of dealing with pupils have made more progress than have similar methods of dealing with members of the teaching staff of the classroom. At all events, there has been an organized and vital movement in the first matter while that in the second is still in its early stage. All schools that pride themselves upon being up-to-date utilize methods of instruction that draw upon and utilize the life-experience of students and strive to individualize treatment of pupils. Whatever reasons hold for adopting this course with respect to the young certainly more strongly hold for teachers, since the latter are more mature and have more experience. Hence the question is in place: What are the ways by which can be secured more organic participation of teachers in the formation of the educational policies of the school?

Since, as I have already said, it is the problem I wish to present rather than to lay down the express ways in which it is to be solved, I might stop at this point. But there are certain corollaries which clarify the meaning of the issue. Absence of participation tends to produce lack of interest and concern on the part of those shut out. The result is a corresponding lack of effective responsibility. Automatically and unconsciously, if not consciously, the feeling develops, "This is none of our affair; it is the business of those at the top; let that particular set of Georges do what needs to be done." The countries in which autocratic government prevails are just those in which there is least public spirit and the greatest indifference to matters of general as distinct from personal concern. Can we expect a different kind of psychology to actuate teachers? Where there is little power, there is correspondingly little sense of positive responsibility. It is enough to do what one is told to do sufficiently well to escape flagrant unfavorable notice. About larger matters, a spirit of passivity is engendered. In some cases, indifference passes into evasion of duties when not directly under the eye of a supervisor; in other cases, a carping, rebellious spirit is engendered. A sort of game is instituted between teacher and supervisor like that which went on in the old-fashioned schools between teacher and pupil. Other teachers pass on, perhaps unconsciously, what they feel to be arbitrary treatment received by them to their pupils.

The argument that teachers are not prepared to assume the responsibility of participation deserves attention, with its accompanying belief that natural selection has operated to put those best prepared to carry the load in the positions of authority. Whatever the truth in this contention, it still is also true that incapacity to assume the responsibilities involved in having a voice in shaping policies is bred and increased by conditions in which that responsibility is denied. I suppose there has never been an autocrat, big or little, who did not justify his conduct on the ground of the unfitness of his subjects to take part in government. I would not compare administrators to political autocrats. On the whole, what exists in the schools is more a matter of habit and custom than it is of any deliberate autocracy. But, as was said earlier, habitual exclusion has the effect of reducing a sense of responsibility for what is done and its consequences. What the argument for democracy implies is that the best way to produce initiative and constructive power is to exercise it. Power, as well as interest, comes by use and practice. Moreover, the argument from incapacity proves too much. If it is so great as to be a permanent bar, then teachers cannot be expected to have the intelligence and skill that are necessary to execute the directions given them. The delicate and difficult task of developing character and good judgment in the young needs every stimulus and inspiration possible. It is impossible that the work should not be better done when teachers have that understanding of what they are doing that comes from having shared in forming its guiding ideas.

Classroom teachers are those who are in continuous direct contact with those taught. The position of administrators is at best indirect by comparison. If there is any work in the world that requires the conservation of what is good in experience so that it may become an integral part of further experience, it is that of teaching. I often wonder how much waste there is in the traditional system. There is some loss even at the best of the potential capital acquired by successful teachers. It does not get freely transmitted to other teachers who might profit by it. Is not the waste very considerably increased when teachers are not called upon to communicate their successful methods and results in a form in which it could have organic effect upon general school policies? Add to this waste that results when teachers are called upon to give effect in the classroom to courses of study they do not understand the reasons for, and the total loss mounts up so that it is a fair estimate that the absence of democratic methods is the greatest single cause of educational waste.

The present subject is one of peculiar importance at the present time. The fundamental beliefs and practices of democracy are now challenged as they never have been before. In some nations they are more than challenged. They are ruthlessly and systematically destroyed. Everywhere there are waves of criticism and doubt as to whether democracy can meet pressing problems of order and security. The causes for the destruction of political democracy in countries where it was nominally established are complex. But of one thing I think we may be sure. Wherever it has fallen it was too exclusively political in nature. It had not become part of the bone and blood of the people in daily conduct of its life. Democratic forms were limited to Parliament, elections and combats between parties. What is happening proves conclusively, I think, that unless democratic habits of thought and action are part of the fiber of a people, political democracy is insecure. It cannot stand in isolation. It must be buttressed by the presence of democratic methods in all social relationships. The relations that exist in educational institutions are second only in importance in this respect to those which exist in industry and business, perhaps not even to them.

I recur then to the idea that the particular question discussed is one phase of a wide and deep problem. I can think of nothing so important in this country at present as a rethinking of the whole problem of democracy and its implications. Neither the rethinking nor the action it should produce can be brought into being in a day or year. The democratic idea itself demands that the thinking and activity proceed cooperatively. My utmost hope will be fulfilled if anything I have said plays any part, however small, in promoting cooperative inquiry and experimentation in this field of democratic administration of our schools.

II

The general question of educational administration makes appropriate a consideration of the problems of public school administration in this country and of the ways of meeting them. It is not necessary to insist upon the fact that the problems are complex and difficult. They present at least three phases, each of which in turn is composed of obscure and conflicting factors.

There is, first, what may be called the intellectual-professional problem. Superintendents, principals, supervisors, etc., are engaged in the direction of an *educational* enterprise. It may seem superfluous to italicize the word "educational." But I do so in order to suggest what is meant by the intellectual phase of the responsibility and function of the administrator. He—or she—not only participates in the development of minds and character, but participates in a way that imposes special intellectual responsibilities. Indeed, the sense of responsibility for distinctively intellectual leadership may take a form that defeats its own purpose. It may take the form of laying out, in a good deal of detail, the whole scheme of the curriculum and promulgating methods to be followed. Even when the idea is not carried to this extent, there are too few cases in which the teaching corps takes an active and cooperative share in developing the plan of education.

In the second place, administrators are particularly charged with problems arising from personal relations. Anyone who has faced the task of helping to maintain harmonious and effective personal relations in family life can imagine the difficulties that emerge in connection with a large teaching staff made up of persons of different temperaments, who have had different training, and are possessed of different outlooks on life. But the problems that arise in connection with these personal relationships are only a part of those which an administrator has to face. He has to maintain cooperative relations with members of a school board; to deal with taxpayers and politicians; to meet parents of varied views and ideals. Moreover, the problems of personal adjustment that offer themselves are often conflicting, because of the opposed demands of different groups. A superintendent is an intermediary between the teaching staff and the members of the public. He is compelled to face two ways, and is fortunate if he can escape the tendency towards a divided personality. At least, there are some administrators who are "diplomatic" and even subservient in one relation and arbitrary and authoritative in the other.

In the third place, the administrator by the nature of his calling has a large amount of detail and routine to which he must attend. There is always the danger that he will become so immersed in this phase of his work that the other two phases of his activity are submerged. Especially in large systems is the danger acute. Large systems work almost automatically toward isolation of the administrator. Business and other details are so pressing that connection with the intellectual and moral problems of education is had only at arms' length. Impersonal matters take the place of personal relations, and are always mechanical. The tendency in this direction is increased because the powerful influence of business standards and methods in the community affects the members of an educational system, and then teachers are regarded after the model of employees in a factory.

The reason I have mentioned these rather obvious things is because they indicate, to my mind, that an administrator can deal effectively with these various problems only as he is able to unify them all in some comprehensive idea and plan. If he parcels them out and tries to deal with them separately he is lost. Especially is it important that his conception of the directly educational phase of his work be unified with his conception of the social relations of administration, both inside and outside the school.

The different aspects of the administrator's work tend in fact to cut across each other in such ways as to nullify their proper effect. The only way for the administrator to avoid this dispersion is to have a definite idea of the place and function of the school in the ongoing processes of society, local and national. Only from a definite point of view, firmly and courageously adhered to in practice, can the needed integration be attained.

The first step in this integration is a clear and intelligent decision upon a basic issue. Is it the social function of the school to perpetuate existing conditions or to take part in their transformation? One decision will make the administrator a timeserver. He will make it his business to conform to the pressures exercised by school boards, by politicians allied with heavy taxpayers, and by parents. If he decides for the other alternative, many of his tasks will be harder, but in that way alone can he serve the cause of education. For this cause is one of development, focussing indeed in the growth of students, but to be conceived even in this connection as a part of the larger development of society.

In the second place, in the degree to which the administrator achieves the integration of the educational phase of his work with the human and social relations into which he necessarily enters, he will treat the school itself as a cooperative community. His leadership will be that of intellectual stimulation and direction, through give-and-take with others, not that of an aloof official imposing, authoritatively, educational ends and methods. He will be on the lookout for ways to give others intellectual and moral responsibilities, not just for ways of setting their tasks for them.

In the third place, the administrator will conceive adult education to be a necessary part of his job, not in the sense of providing adult classes and lectures—helpful as these may be— but in the sense that only as the public is brought to understand the needs and possibilities of the creative education of the young, can such education be vitally effective. He will realize that public education is essentially education *of* the public: directly, through teachers and students in the school; indirectly, through communicating to others his own ideals and standards, inspiring others with the enthusiasm of himself and his staff for the function of intelligence and character in the transformation of society.

5

THE TEACHER AND HIS WORLD

I

SHOULD TEACHERS BE AHEAD OF OR BEHIND THEIR TIMES? PERHAPS someone with a logical turn of mind will object to the question. He will point out that there is another alternative—teachers might keep even with their times, neither ahead nor behind. One might ask whether this middle course is not the wisest course for teachers to steer. The idea seems plausible. But it suffers from a fatal defect. As I pointed out elsewhere, our time is not consistent with itself. It is a medley of opposed tendencies. It is enough to point out two or three familiar matters. One hears on every hand of the economy of scarcity and the economy of abundance. We are living in times in which both are present and they are fighting each other. Unless there were abundance, the banks would not be congested with money; factories would not be idle; cotton would not be plowed under; cattle would not be destroyed. But unless there were scarcity, millions would not be idle; twenty millions or more would not be living on charity, public and private; schools would not be closed, the size of classes increased, valuable social services eliminated. We are also living in times when private and public aims and policies are at strife with each other. What I mean by "private" may be indicated by reference to Mr. Hoover's rugged individualism. What I mean by "public" may be indicated by the fact that Mr. Hoover himself, while President, organized the Reconstruction Finance Corporation and other agencies of public action in an effort to stem the tide of depression. He and those who agreed with him in his emphasis upon private initiative and management in business assumed that it is the business of Government to help restore national prosperity. These contradictions in an individual are typical of the state of the times. Let me give one more illustration that comes close to the occupation of teachers. Our country is committed to the policy of public education. In pursuit of this policy we have increased five or six fold the number of students in high schools and colleges during hardly more than a generation. On the other hand, the young people whom we have trained in these institutions now find themselves to a very large degree without the opportunity to use their training. They cannot find jobs. Does this state of affairs look like consistency or evenness in the times in which teachers live?

The sum of the matter is that the times are out of joint, and that teachers cannot escape, even if they would, some responsibility for a share in putting them right. They may regard it, like Hamlet, as a cursed spite, or as an opportunity. But they cannot avoid the responsibility. Drifting is merely a cowardly mode of choice. I am not trying here to tell teachers with which of the antagonistic tendencies of our own time they should align themselves—although I have my own convictions on that subject. I am trying only to point out that the conflict is here, and that as matter of fact they are strengthening one set of forces or the other. The question is whether they are doing so blindly, evasively, or intelligently and courageously. If a teacher is conservative and wishes to throw in his lot with forces that seem to me reactionary and that will in the end, from my point of view, increase present chaos, at all events let him do it intelligently, after a study of the situation and a conscious choice made on the basis of intelligent study. The same thing holds for the liberal and radical.

It is desirable, if I understand the situation, to promote among teachers, and among parents and others who are responsible for the conduct of education, just this intelligent understanding of the social forces and movements of our own times, and the role that educational institutions have to play. This cannot be accomplished save as teachers are aware of a social goal. I suppose some teachers are impatient at the amount of space given to general discussion. Teachers are unfortunately somewhat given to wanting to be told what to do, something specific. But is it not true that understanding of forces at work, of their direction and the goal to which they point, is the first prerequisite of intelligent decision and action? What will it profit a man to do this, that, and the other specific thing, if he has no clear idea of why he is doing them, no clear idea of the way they bear upon actual conditions and of the end to be reached? The most specific thing that educators can first do is something general. The first need is to become aware of the kind of world in which we live; to survey its forces; to see the opposition in forces that are contending for mastery; to make up one's mind which of these forces come from a past that the world in its potential powers has outlived and which are indicative of a better and happier future. The teacher who has made up his mind on these points will have little difficulty in discovering for himself what specific things are needed in order to put into execution the decisions that he has arrived at. Justice Holmes once said that theory was the most practical thing in the world. This statement is preeminently true of social theory of which educational theory is a part.

II

At first view it may seem absurd to say that teachers are not adequately organized. In large places, especially, many teachers probably feel that, if anything, they are over-organized. There are associations by grades, associations by subjects, and general organizations, city, state, and national. If there is inadequacy, it is not in number and variety. But organizations exist for a purpose, not as ends in themselves. If adequate organization is lacking, it is on the side of aims and functioning for these aims.

Some existing associations serve to bring teachers together, to get them acquainted with one another, and to cultivate a professional spirit. Indeed, all associations serve this end to some extent. The purpose is good and no one will say it nay. Other associations exist for stimulation and direction of their members in the subject-matter of the studies they teach and to improve by exchange of ideas their methods of instruction. No one questions this value in so far as such organizations accomplish it, and are reasonably free from perfunctory and conventional oratory and from exploitation by those seeking publicity and prominence. At critical times, teachers' organizations have operated successfully to bring pressure on law-making bodies for protection of salaries and tenure of position. The campaign for equal pay for equal work on the part of women teachers in some states is a notable instance. In a few cases, teachers' organizations have exposed unequal, scandalous methods of tax assessment and collection, and their work has effected reforms by which the public school system has received increased revenue.

Yet organizations for these purposes do not cover the entire ground. I should be the last to question the value of associations for professional improvement, for raising the economic status of teachers with respect to wages and security of tenure, and for protection from politicians who would use the schools to procure jobs for their friends. But such ends as these do not exhaust the function of organization by teachers. They hardly touch the place of the teacher in relation to society. Organizations of teachers to secure their own immediate economic ends have proved indispensable. But their campaigns when carried on in isolation from other groups of workers, whether civil-service employees or workers in shops, factories, and offices, have a tendency to produce a reaction that is unfavorable to the cause of education. Anyone who has read the letters published in newspapers during the late depression regarding the efforts of organized teachers to prevent salary cuts knows how true this is. Of course there were some who defended the teachers' claims. There were more who attacked the teachers for seeking special favors at the expense of other workers and of the taxpayer.

I do not mention this fact for the purpose of endorsing these attacks. I call attention to it because it indicates the isolation of teachers as a body. Speaking generally, that is for the country as a whole, teachers are not adequately organized for protection of their economic status. This statement is particularly true of rural districts and small towns. But where teachers organize for economic protection, they suffer from the imputation of selfishness as long as they stand aloof from other organizations of workers—and this quite apart from the efficacy of their efforts as isolated organizations.

I refer to the economic phase of teachers' organization not as a thing by itself but as an illustration of the general point of the relation of teachers to society and to social organization. Upon the whole, teachers have preferred to regard themselves as a special class. They have made, in effect if not purposely, a division between themselves as intellectual laborers and others who labor with their hands. At times, indeed, one hears deliberate defense of this position. I propose to discuss what is involved in this position, not only with respect to other workers, but in relation to the social function of the teaching profession and to the conditions under which teachers can genuinely perform their educative function.

First, the isolation of teachers, created and perpetuated by setting up a division between intellectual workers and other workers, has reflected itself in the administrative and instructional set-up of the schools. It has been a strong force in maintaining academic and literary overemphasis. Teachers usually come from that part of the community which is more favored economically; there is danger of aloofness in this very fact. The mass of the pupils in the public-school system comes from the less favored class. One cause for the persistence of a system of education that was originated to serve a small class is found in the fact that educators as a body have not been in close contact with the needs of the greater part of the population. Vocational and industrial education has had a great growth. But even here, the tendency has been to separate vocational or industrial from "cultural" education, when the obvious need is to organize a system which serves both ends by means of the same curriculum and methods. The fact that the great depression has lopped off the studies and courses that are connected most closely with the needs of the young in contemporary life, and has created a reaction toward the old type of education with the three R's as its staple goods, has roots in the isolation of the teaching profession.

Teachers can learn something about the defects and requirements of existing types of organization by the study of economic and sociological literature and by reading such newspapers and periodicals as state the facts honestly. But the understanding thus gained is cold and at arms' length compared with the understanding and sympathy that would spring from direct and vital contact with the troubles and aspirations of the mass of the population, the productive workers. The economic literacy of teachers and administrators would be immensely furthered by an alliance with the great masses of workers.

Secondly, an open alliance of teachers with workers would greatly strengthen the educational as well as the economic position of the teaching body. It is a historic fact that the movement for free public education had one of its most influential sources in the demands of the workers of the country who were engaged in pursuits regarded as non-intellectual. When a school system has been in difficulties, it has always drawn its strongest support from this source. The reason is obvious. The well-to-do class can afford to pay for private schooling; some of its influential members are interested in public schools only when their tax bills come in. The mass of the workers must depend upon the public schools or nothing. The latter fact is sufficiently in evidence in the present crisis in the organized drives of heavy tax-payers for cutting off educational services, reducing salaries, increasing the size of classes, and so on. Considering the disposition of so many teachers to keep themselves aloof from the struggle of manual labor to hold its own, the loyalty of the latter to the schools is touching, if not surprising.

III

I am not especially fond of the phrase academic freedom as far as the adjective *academic* is concerned. It suggests something that is rather remote and technical. Indeed, it is common to use the word as a term of disparagement. But the reality for which the phrase stands has an importance far beyond any particular expression used to convey it. Freedom of *education* is the thing at issue—I was about to say at stake. And since education is not a function that goes on in the void, but is carried on by human beings, the freedom of education means, in the concrete, the freedom of students and teachers: the freedom of the school as an agent of education.

The inclusion of students in the idea of freedom of education is even more important than the inclusion of teachers; at least it would be if it were possible to separate the two. Freedom of teachers is a necessary condition of freedom for students to learn.

I referred elsewhere to "free schools" as the aim to which the American people are historically committed with a devotion that probably exceeds that given to any other aim in our common life. The full significance of free schools is, however, far from realization in the public mind and in the workings of our educational system. Freedom from payment of fees, support by public taxation, is a necessary condition for schools that are to be free of access to all. This aspect of free schools has been extended to free textbooks, free libraries, and, in some public schools, to free dental and medical service and free lunches for those who cannot pay. But in final resort, these manifestations of freedom are tributary to freedom of education as the social enterprise in which education forms character and intelligence. There are plenty of restrictions put upon moral and intellectual freedom of education within the school system itself. It is bound, often hidebound, by hampering traditions that originated under conditions alien to the present. These traditions affect subject-matter, methods of instruction, discipline, the organization and administration of the schools. These limitations of free education, serious and weighty enough in all conscience, have been the objects of attack by educational reformers at all times. But there is another limitation added to these onerous ones that is especially dangerous at the present time. It is the attempt to close the minds, mouths, and ears of students and teachers alike to all that is not consonant with the practices and beliefs of the privileged class that represents the economic and political status quo.

The question of teachers' oaths is so familiar that I refer to it only by way of illustration. Since our Constitution provides for its own change, though by awkward and cumbrous methods, and since it expressly reserves to the people (as well as to state governments) all rights not conferred upon the Federal Government, and since this reservation of rights to the people includes the right of revolution when conditions become intolerable—as both Jefferson and Lincoln have pointed out—a teacher need have no conscientious scruples in taking an oath of loyalty to the Constitution. But the selection of teachers as the class of persons who must take the oath is socially serious because it is one phase of the general movement calculated to prevent freedom of education in all matters that relate to economic and political conditions and policies.

I have more than once pointed out that liberty is a social matter and not just a claim of the private individual. I have argued that freedom is a matter of the distribution of effective power; that, finally, the struggle for liberty is important because of its consequences in effecting more just, equable, and human relations of men, women, and children to one another. In no phase of social endeavor is the realization of the social content of freedom more important than in the struggle for academic freedom. Everyone who has read the pleas made in the early struggle for universal and free schools in this country knows the emphasis that was put upon education as a necessary condition for creation of the kind of citizenship indispensable to the success of democracy. Today freedom of teaching and learning on the part of instructors and students is imperatively necessary for that kind of intelligent citizenship that is genuinely free to take part in the social reconstructions without which democracy will die. The question is now whether democracy is a possible form of society when affairs are as complex and economic power is as concentrated as today. Since freedom of mind and freedom of expression are the root of all freedom, to deny freedom in education is a crime against democracy. Because academic freedom is so essentially a social issue, since it is intimately bound up with what the future citizenship of the country is going to do in shaping our political and economic destiny, it is not surprising that those who either give only lip-service or who openly strive to restrict it, should also strive to present it to the public as a matter that concerns teachers only as individuals, and to represent those *active* in supporting its cause as more or less unbalanced individuals who want more liberty to assert their personal views. There is nothing paradoxical in saying that it is just because of the social significance of liberty of education that it is presented as something that affects only individual teachers.

It cannot be denied that there is a large number of young people who find themselves deprived of opportunity, who find their legitimate desires and aspirations so blocked that they become converts to the idea that social change cannot be effected by democratic methods, but only by violent force. The idea sedulously cultivated in certain circles that this attitude is the result of teachers' imposition to subversive ideas under the camouflage of academic freedom is laughable to all those who know the facts about our schools. This attitude is the product of the restrictive and oppressive effect of the present industrial system, aided by a school system which discounts the value of social intelligence. The feeling that social change of any basic character can be brought about only by violent force is the product of lack of faith in intelligence as a method, and this loss of faith is in large measure the product of a schooling that, because of its comparatively unfree condition, has not enabled youth to face intelligently the realities of our social life, political and economic.

There are ultimately but three forces that control society— habit, coercive and violent force, and action directed by intelligence. In fairly normal times, habit and custom are by far the strongest force. A social crisis means that this force has in large measure ceased to operate. The other forces, therefore, come more conspicuously into play. Reactionaries who strive to prevent any change of the old order are possessed of the power that enables them to use brute force in its less overt forms: by coercion, by intimidation, and by various forms of indirect pressure. From lack of understanding of social affairs, a lack of understanding owing to faulty education, as well as to deliberate refusal to learn, reactionaries unintelligently resist change. Those who have suffered from the old order then react by appeal to direct use of force as the only means at their command. Because of the intellectual suppressions experienced in the course of their own education they have little knowledge of means of effecting social changes by any method other than force.

In short, the social significance of academic freedom lies in the fact that without freedom of inquiry and freedom on the part of teachers and students to explore the forces at work in society and the means by which they may be directed, the habits of intelligent action that are necessary to the orderly development of society cannot be created. Training for good citizenship is one thing when conditions are simple and fairly stable. It is quite another thing when conditions are confused, complicated, and unsettled, when class divisions and struggles are imminent. Every force that operates to limit the freedom of education is a premium put upon ultimate recourse to violence to effect needed change. Every force that tends to liberate educational processes is a premium placed upon intelligent and orderly methods of directing to a more just, equitable, and humane end the social changes that are going on anyway.

IV

Indoctrination involves a basic issue which, it seems to me, has not been made wholly clear. Upon this point I wish to say a few words concerning the function of the public press. The point at issue is that of method. Let it be admitted that the school *must* have some social orientation. Let it be admitted that this necessity "is implicit in the nature of education. . . . in the personality of the teacher, in the life of the school, in the relation of pupils to pupils and pupils to teachers, in the administrative organization and arrangements, in the very architecture of the school building"—as well as in the subject-matter taught. And when I say "admitted," I do not mean admitted for the sake of argument, but admitted as the fact of the situation, and a fact that cannot be escaped.

Let it be admitted also, and for the same reason, that broadly speaking the teaching profession is now faced with choice between two social orientations. Of these two orientations, one looks to the past, the other to the future. And this is but a part of the story. That which looks to the past, looks also by the necessities of the situation to the interests of a small class having a highly privileged position maintained at the expense of the masses. That which looks to the future is in line with the scientific, technological, and industrial forces of the present, and, what is more, it is in the interest of the freedom, security, and cultural development of the masses. Everything that is said about the reality of the contest between these opposed interests and groups, I believe to be also true. In one way or another, teachers as a body and individually do and must make a choice between these opposed social orientations and all they practically imply.

But the more these things are admitted, the more urgent

becomes the question of method. And method is much more than a matter of method in classroom instruction. It includes all the items already mentioned: architecture and equipment of buildings; the composition and control of and by school boards; the relations of administrators to classroom teachers; the prevailing modes of "discipline" and drill and use of memory, of texts and subject-matter. The tendency of these things by and large is toward undemocratic social consequences, and the almost automatic maintenance of the privileges of a small class.

When we face the problem of method in relation to a new social orientation, the place of intelligence looms as the central issue. I cannot agree with those who think that making intelligence central in education signifies a neutral, aloof, and "purely intellectual," not to say mechanical, attitude toward social conflict. How do those of us who believe that the advance of science and technology is creating a new pattern of social life, and is producing a new type of social conflict between the privileged and underprivileged, come to that belief? Did we arrive at it by a process of inculcation or by what we regard as an intelligent study of historical and existing forces and conditions? If the latter, and if the method of intelligence has worked in our own case, how can we assume that the method will not work with our students, and that it will not with them generate ardor and practical energy? The realization that the school has and must have some social orientation raises but does not settle the question of the method by which a new social orientation shall be brought about. Till the latter issue is faced, the whole subject of indoctrination remains ambiguous.

I said that this question is connected with the educational force of the press. It is not surprising in an economic order based on business enterprise for profit that the press should itself be a business enterprise conducted for profit, and hence carry on a vast and steady indoctrination in behalf of the order of which the press is a part. There is rather more cause for surprise that under these circumstances, there is as much intelligent report-

ing of actual conditions as exists. The subject of the relation of
the press to genuine public education, which is the education
of the public, and of what professional educators can do about
it, is too vast for discussion in a page. I content myself with two
somewhat incidental yet important remarks. The first is that
teachers, out of professional self-respect, must not take mis-
representations and efforts at intimidation lying-down. It is a
healthy sign that such attacks on education have in the past
called out vigorous and courageous counter-attacks. Their connection with the method of intelligence is evident. If teachers
do not stand fighting in the front rank for freedom of intelligence, the cause of the latter is well-nigh hopeless, and we are
in for that period of intimidation, oppression, and suppression
that goes, and goes rightly, by the name of Fascism.

My other remark is to the effect that one great business of
the schools at present is to develop immunity aganst the propaganda influence of press and radio. Julian Huxley in his book
on *Scientific Research and Social Needs* (a book which every
teacher should read) says that, "one aim of education should
be to teach people to discount the unconscious prejudices that
their social environments impress upon them." The press and
the radio are two of the most powerful means of inculcating
mass prejudice. War propaganda and the situation in Hitlerized
Germany have proved that unless the schools create a popular
intelligence that is critically discriminating, there is no limit to
the prejudices and inflamed emotion that will result. An intelligent understanding of social forces given by schools is our chief
protection. Intelligent understanding of conditions and forces
cannot fail, in my judgment, to support a new general social
orientation. There are difficulties enough in the way of the
schools obtaining the power to promote this understanding.
Concentration on this task is directly in line with the professed
function of public education, and it alone will give the educators concerned with a new social orientation a herculean task
to perform.

6

THE PROBLEM OF THE LIBERAL
ARTS COLLEGE

NOTHING IS MORE STRIKING IN RECENT DISCUSSIONS OF LIBERAL education than the widespread and seemingly spontaneous use of *liberating* as a synonym for *liberal*. For it marks a break with the traditional idea that a certain group of studies is liberal because of something inhering in them—belonging to them by virtue of an indwelling essence or nature—as opium was once said to put persons to sleep because of its dormitive nature. This latter view of the liberal arts has the merit, for some writers and educators, of rendering it unnecessary to inquire closely into what the subjects actually accomplish for those who study them. If a particular group of studies is "liberal" in and of itself, such an inquiry is irrelevant. Failure to exercise a liberating educative effect in given cases is not the fault of the studies but of external conditions, such, perhaps, as the inherent incapacity of some students to rise to a truly "intellectual" level. To define liberal as that which liberates is to bring the problem of liberal education and of the liberal arts college within the domain of an inquiry in which the issue is settled by search for what is actually accomplished. The test and justification of claims put forth is found in observable consequences, not in an *a priori* dogma.

The concrete significance of the foregoing generalities in locating the present problem of the liberal arts college is found in outstanding historic considerations. The theory that certain subjects are liberal because of something forever fixed in their own nature was formulated prior to the rise of scientific method.

It was consonant with the philosophical theory which was once held about every form of knowledge. For according to that doctrine if anything is knowable it is because of its inherent nature, form or essence, so that knowledge consists of an intuitive grasp by pure "intellect" of this nature. This doctrine is completely repudiated in the practices which constitute the scientific revolution.

In the second place, the traditional doctrine was embodied in educational institutions in a period that was pre-technological as well as pre-scientific. The liberal arts were sharply contrasted with the useful arts. This contrast had its basis in social and cultural conditions. The useful or industrial arts were acquired by means of sheer apprenticeship in fixed routines in which insight into principles played a negligible part. The industrial revolution which marks the last few centuries is the result of the scientific revolution. Only the most backward "useful" arts are now matters of empirical routine. They are now technological, a fact which signifies that they are founded in scientific understanding of underlying principles.

In the third place, and most important of all, social organization has also undergone a revolution. The distinction between "liberal" and "useful" arts is a product of the time when those engaged in industrial production were mechanics and artisans who occupied a servile social status. The meaning attached to the traditional doctrine of liberal arts cannot be understood except in connection with the social fact of division between free men and slaves and serfs, and the fact that only the former received an "intellectual" education, which under the given conditions necessarily meant literary and linguistic training. At the time in which a scientific revolution was radically changing the nature and method of knowledge, understanding and learning, and in which the industrial revolution was breaking down once for all the wall between the hand and the head, the political revolution of the rise of democracy was giving a socially free status to those who had been serfs. It thereby destroyed the very foundation of the traditional separation between the arts suitable for a "gentleman" and the arts suited to those engaged in production of useful services and commodities: that is to say, the separation between "liberal" and "useful" arts.

It is not possible to grasp and state the present dilemma of the liberal arts college, and of the function it should undertake in our society, except as they are placed and seen in this context of irreversible historic movements. Nothing can be sillier than attributing the problems of the contemporary liberal college in this country to the activities of a number of misguided educationalists, instead of to the impact of social forces which have continually gained in force. If there is anything equally silly, it is the assertion (by those who would resolve these problems by a return to an outworn identification of "liberal" with the linguistic, the literary and metaphysical) that their opponents are complacently satisfied with the present situation. For, in fact, the latter anticipated the former by many years in pointing out the confusions, conflicts, and uncertainties that mark present collegiate education.

When the situation is viewed in historic perspective (a kind of view quite foreign to the victims and adherents of an exclusively literary and metaphysical training) it is seen that scientific studies made their way into the college, against the resistance of entrenched orthodoxy, because of their growing importance in the conduct of social affairs, not because of intrinsic love of scientific knowledge—much less because of widespread devotion to scientific method. When Latin lost its monopoly as the universal language of communication among the learned, living languages were added to the curriculum. Not only were the degrees of S.B. and Ph.B. added to the old A.B. (or else the latter extended to cover the new studies), but the curriculum became congested and its aim wavering and unsure.

The new modes of social pressure did not stop at this point. A large number of new callings and occupations came into existence. They competed vigorously with the three traditional "learned" professions, and the effect of this competition found its way into the colleges. At the same time, two of the learned professions, medicine and law, were undergoing great changes. New discoveries in chemistry and physiology so changed medicine as to render it virtually impossible to crowd preparation into the time previously allotted. Studies which in effect, if not in name, were pre-medical found their way into the college. The great changes that were going on in industry and commerce together with their social effects affected the practice of law. The consequences for college education were less overt than in the case of medicine, but they are genuinely present.

The net result of the alterations produced by the social changes here briefly noted has been to render the name "liberal arts college" reminiscent rather than descriptive when it is applied to many of our collegiate institutions. Under these circumstances it is hardly surprising that representatives of the older literary and metaphysical point of view who have been on the defensive have now taken the offensive. Consistently with their view that certain subjects are inherently liberal, they are proclaiming that other subjects, notably those that are scientific and technological, are inherently illiberal, materialistic, and utilitarianly servile, unless they are kept in strict subjection. Social revolutions rarely if ever go completely backward in spite of reactions that occur. I do not believe that there is great likelihood that the American undergraduate college will, in any large number of cases, return to the literary and metaphysical course of study of the traditional liberal arts institutions. I seem to notice that those who are verbally active in this direction are not discouraging receipt of funds to add still more new scientific and semi-vocational courses to an already swollen curriculum.

The danger, to my mind, lies elsewhere. It is possible to freeze existing illiberal tendencies and to intensify existing undesirable splits and divisions. At a time when technical education is encroaching in many cases upon intelligent acquaintance with and use of the great humanistic products of the past, we find that reading and study of "classics" are being isolated and placed in sharp opposition to everything else. *The problem of securing to the liberal arts college its due function in demo-*

cratic society is that of seeing to it that the technical subjects which are now socially necessary acquire a humane direction. There is nothing in them which is "inherently" exclusive; but they cannot be liberating if they are cut off from their humane sources and inspiration. On the other hand, books which are cut off from vital relations with the needs and issues of contemporary life themselves become ultra-technical.

The outstanding need is interfusion of knowledge of man and nature, of vocational preparation with a deep sense of the social foundations and social consequences of industry and industrial callings in contemporary society. On the face of this need we have urged upon us a policy of their systematic separation. I lately received from a man distinguished in public life, not a professional educator, a letter in which he writes: "Millions of our soldiers are coming back reactionaries of a kind through their lack of cultural education to appraise their surroundings and the events that are taking place." I would add that there are at home many other millions who are confused and bewildered, at the mercy of drift and of designing "leaders," because of their lack of an education that enables them to appraise their surroundings and the course of events. The present function of the liberal arts college, in my belief, is to use the resources put at our disposal alike by humane literature, by science, by subjects that have a vocational bearing, so as to secure ability to appraise the needs and issues of the world in which we live. Such an education would be liberating not in spite of the fact that it departs widely from the seven liberal arts of the medieval period, but just because it would do for the contemporary world what those arts tried to do for the world in which they took form.

7

THE NEED FOR ORIENTATION

FOR ONE WHOSE LIFE HAS BEEN GIVEN IN ONE FORM OR ANOTHER to education, it is no gratification to say things that may be construed as an attack on our educational system. But we are living in a time when discriminating criticism is a necessary condition both for progress and for cashing in on the many good things that are already in the schools. And it is not teachers that are primarily criticized but the system under which they work. I am glad to believe there were never so many teachers in this country as there are now who are trained for their work and who are eager to improve themselves professionally. But the setup of the system distracts and confuses their minds as well as their work. It is to these things I shall refer.

The system is a system only by courtesy. In fact, it is more like a patchwork, and a patchwork whose pieces do not form a pattern. It is a patchwork of the old and the new; of unreconstructed survivals from the past and of things introduced because of new conditions. This statement applies equally to the things taught, the ways they are taught, the social control of the educational system, and its administration. In consequence, the new studies that have been introduced have split up the curriculum into unrelated parts and created congestion. There are too many studies and too many courses of study, and the result is confusion.

Return to the strict and narrow curriculum of the past is urged by some as a remedy. But there is no use in discussing its desirability, because it is impracticable. The forces of the

modern world are here, and they are going to continue to act
upon the schools. The demands of an industrialized and technological society cannot be ignored. The old education, even
in this country, was a continuation or an imitation of an education designed for a small and select class. The number in high
schools and colleges has increased sixfold and more in about
a generation. This irruption is something unprecedented in the
history of any nation. Its members proceed from those who do
not have the background, traditions, or needs of the class to
which the old system catered. New studies and courses are
brought in as a response to their needs. But they are brought in
piecemeal, without a unified aim. And the old studies persist,
with little modification, side by side with the new ones. Only
those pupils who have a strong natural bent come out with any
clear idea either of their own capacities or of the world in
which they are to live. The schools are a drift rather than a
system.

The methods of discipline and instruction in such schools
as are adequately supported have been revolutionized in a
generation or so, and mostly for the better—though the rural
schools in a large part of the country are still in a condition that
should be a public scandal. There is much more recognition of
the make-up of individuals and much more adaptation to individual needs than there used to be. But in our large cities, with
their inhuman aggregations of students and their overstuffed
classes, the change has affected the general spirit of the teaching much more than its actual impact upon students. Methods
are still largely mechanical—even more so oftentimes than in
many of the old, small rural schools. The worst thing is that,
even in the schools where pupils are not treated as intellectual
robots, their individual traits are stimulated more or less at haphazard, rather than directed.

It is certainly not the fault of teachers that so many of the
recent graduates of the school now find themselves at a tragic
standstill, without an occupation and without prospect of one.
It is not the fault of teachers that so many young men and

women still in high schools and colleges find themselves in a state of painful and bewildering insecurity about the future. But it is the fault of the system that so many of these young persons have no intellectual legs of their own to stand upon, no sense of perspective by which to take their bearings, no insight into the causes of the economic and social breakdown, and no way of orienting themselves. It is bad enough to be without a job. The evil is increased when these young people find themselves with no clue to the situation in which they are to live and are at a loss intellectually and morally, as well as vocationally and industrially.

I do not mean that the schools should have prepared the young to understand the problems that baffle mature and experienced persons. But I do mean that education, if it is really education, should send them forth with some unified sense of the kind of world in which they live, the directions in which it is moving, and the part they have to play in it. The schools should have given them some sort of intellectual and moral key to their contemporary world. But the hodgepodge of studies pursued for so-called cultural, vocational, and disciplinary aims (that conflict moreover with one another) and by methods that in part appeal to individual powers and that in part mechanize their minds and activities are poor preparations for facing the scene that now confronts the young. In other countries, the combination of economic insecurity with lack of insight into the forces and movements of society have made the young the readiest and most enthusiastic adherents of Fascism. We shall be fortunate if the same sort of thing does not take place here.

What I have said is general in character. But anyone who knows much about our schools can make it concrete, considering how much of the time and energy of pupils is still spent in mere accumulation of information and the acquisition of mechanical forms of skill. Moreover the information that is first memorized and then poorly remembered is selected upon no particular principle; much of it simply on the ground that it was taught in the past. There is little attempt to overhaul the whole structure with a view to selection and organization that would send out students with a sense of the bearing of what they learn upon the present world.

As for methods, the prime need of every person at present is capacity to think; the power to see problems, to relate facts to them, to use and enjoy ideas. If a young man or woman comes from school with this power, all other things may be in time added to him. He will find himself intellectually and morally. But, in the mass of things that have to be "learned," the ability of individuals to think is submerged. In consequence, too large a part of our citizens has left our schools without power of critical discrimination, at the mercy of special propaganda, and drifting from one plan and scheme to another according to the loudest clamor of the moment. Many who have escaped this tendency have found that they had to start their own education afresh. In this connection, I may say that our present system is highly defective in opportunities for directed continuation of education. It is no disparagement of present efforts in "adult education" to say that the *continued* education of those who have left school should long ago have been made a paramount interest of public education.

There is little genuine relation between the existing social control of the school system and its educative work. In fact, the connection that exists is detrimental to the truly educative work of the schools. School boards at present, taking the country as a whole, are representative of a special class or group in the community, not of community interests. They regard themselves after the analogy of private employers of labor and the teaching staff as their hired men and women.

This situation is reflected in the administrative organization of the schools. On the one hand, there is little real cooperation between administrative officers and classroom teachers. The former make out courses of study, prepare syllabuses for instruction, and lay down methods of instruction. The latter take orders, and, in the degree in which they do so, their professional initiative is blunted, and their own work rendered routine and mechanical. On the other hand, the administrators are dependent for their jobs upon undue conformity to the desires of the economic class that is dominant in school boards as the agents of social control.

It should now be clear why I am not engaged in wholesale indictment of teachers. The defects of the school are reflections within the school of the disorder and confusion of our society. It mirrors social planlessness and drift. But the mirror is not passive. It serves to perpetuate the social and economic conditions out of which it arises. I do not mean that teachers and administrators are impotent in this situation. There is no present event more significant than the assertion on the part of courageous and intelligent educators of the responsibility of the schools for a definite share in the evolution of a reconstructed social order. This assertion is as necessary for society as for educational advance. But it is met by a campaign of newspaper vilification, notably on the part of the Hearst press. It is met also by repressive legislation. The responsibility of those engaged in these movements for production of still-greater social chaos is enormous. At the time when intelligence in social matters, in their widest meaning, political and economic, is imperative, there are persons striving to reduce even the amount of social intelligence that now exists. "After me, the deluge," as long as my immediate power remains, is as truly their principle of action as it was that of any Bourbon king.

8

AUTHORITY AND RESISTANCE TO SOCIAL CHANGE

THE LAST FOUR CENTURIES HAVE DISPLAYED AN EVER-INCREASING revolt against authority, first in the forms in which it was manifested and then against the principle itself. None of its important forms has been immune from assault. The assault was first directed against dominant institutions of church and state. But the control exercised by church and state in combination had entered into all phases and aspects of life, in belief and conduct alike. Hence attack upon ecclesiastic and political institutions spread to science and art, to standards and ideals of economic and domestic life. For the practical movement of assault, like every other such movement, had to defend itself on intellectual grounds. The best intellectual defense was attack, and so defense grew into systematic justification, and a social philosophy developed that was critical of the very idea of any authoritative control.

The theoretical system spawned watchwords, rally-cries, slogans for popular consumption. One of the latter, by constant iteration, has assumed the status of a comprehensive social and political idea. To many persons it seems to be itself the summary of a profound social philosophy. According to the formula, the one great intellectual problem is the demarcation of two separate spheres, one of authority and one of freedom; the other half of the formula is to maintain this theoretical demarcation as a sharp division in practice. The formula has a corollary. The inherent tendency of the "sphere" of authority is to extend itself unduly, to encroach on the "sphere" of freedom, thus enstating oppression, tyranny and, in the language of to-day, regimentation. Hence the right of way must belong to the idea and actuality of individual freedom; authority is its enemy, and every manifestation of social authority and control is there-fore to be zealously watched and almost always to be vigorously opposed. However, since the sphere of liberty has its bound-aries, when "liberty" begins to degenerate into "license" the operation of authority is properly to be called upon to restore the balance.

The formula, like most slogans that attain popularity, owes its vogue and influence to the fact that it seems to afford a solution of an outstanding problem, while in fact it evades the problem; and, by postponing effort at genuine solution, gives temporary support, sometimes to one of the contending forces, sometimes to the other, and always at the expense of both. For even when it is accepted in its own terms at face value, it leaves the fundamental issue of the rightful extent of the two alleged spheres undecided, their rightful metes and bounds a matter of constant dispute.

The genuine problem is the *relation* between authority and freedom. And this problem is masked, and its solution begged, when the idea is introduced that the fields in which they respec-tively operate are separate. In effect, authority stands for sta-bility of social organization by means of which direction and support are given to individuals; while individual freedom stands for the forces by which change is intentionally brought about. The issue that requires constant attention is the intimate and organic union of the two things: of authority and freedom, of stability and change. The idea of attaining a solution by separation instead of by union misleads and thwarts endeavor whenever it is acted upon. The widespread adoption of this false and misleading idea is a strong contributing factor to the present state of world confusion.

The genuine import of the formula which divides and apportions the total field of human life and action between free-dom and authority is to be found, not in its theoretical statement, but in its relation to the historic events of the last few centuries. As a purely theoretical formula, it claims an inherent validity and universal application which I, for one, find absurd. But when the formula is taken to be the record of a historic period, the case is otherwise. The formula then achieves the significance of a symbol of the distinctive crisis of western civilization in recent centuries; it becomes representative of a great historic struggle. In its dual character, the formula celebrates, with one hand, the decay of the institutions which once exercised sway over men's minds and conduct; and, with the other hand, it signalizes the rise of the new social and intellectual forces. The old traditions and established social organizations resisted the new forces in human life and society as dangerous; even as mortal rivals who came to dispute for the power and privileges they had hitherto exclusively enjoyed. The formula, instead of supplying a means of coping with solving this historic struggle, offers as a solution what is none other than a theoretical transcript of the nature of the conflict itself. As a guide to understanding and action, the formula is, as I said, absurd. But as a symbol of historic events it is deeply revealing.

Unfortunately, when the struggle first got under way, the newer forces tended to accept the established institutions at their own evaluation, namely, as necessary expressions of the very principle of authority. Finding the existing institutions oppressive, the new movement reacted against authority as such, and began to conceive of authority as inherently external to individuality, and inherently hostile to freedom and to the social changes that the overt expression and use of freedom would bring to pass. In consequence, while the new movement should have the credit for breaking down a system that had grown rigid and unresponsive, and for releasing capacities of individuals that had been dormant—its virtual denial of the organic importance of *any* embodiment of authority and social control has intellectually fostered the confusion that as a matter of practical fact in any case attends a time of transition. More particularly, as I shall show later, the new movement failed to acknowledge as authoritative the very power to which it owed its own vitality, namely, that of organized intelligence. Such are the propositions I desire to advance.

For, in the first place, I think a survey of history shows that while the individualistic philosophy was wrong in setting authority and freedom, stability and change in opposition to one another, it was justified in finding the organized institutional embodiments of authority so external to the new wants and purposes that were stirring, as to be in fact oppressive. The persons and classes who exercised the power that comes from the possession of authority *were* hostile to the variable and fresh qualities, the qualities of initiative, invention and enterprise in which change roots. The power possessed was the more oppressive and obstructive because it was not just physical but had that hold upon the imagination, emotions and will which properly belongs to the principle of authority. Underneath, it was not a conflict between social organization and individuals, between authority and freedom, but between conservative factors in the very make-up of individuals—factors that had the strength that is derived from the inertia of customs and traditions engrained by long endurance—and the liberating, the variable and innovating factors in the constitution of individuals. It was a struggle for authoritative power between the old and the new; between forces concerned with conservation of values that the past had produced and the forces that made for new beliefs and new modes of human association. It was also a struggle between groups and classes of individuals—between those who were enjoying the advantages that spring from possession of power to which authoritative right accrues, and individuals who found themselves excluded from the powers and enjoyments to which they felt themselves entitled. The necessity of adjusting the old and the new, of harmonizing the stability that comes from conserving the established with the variability that springs from the emergence of new needs and efforts of individuals—this necessity is inherent in, or a part of, the very texture of life. In the last few centuries the necessity of effecting this adjustment has manifested itself on an unparalleled scale in the arena of human culture. The philosophy which transforms this historic and relative struggle into an inherent and fixed conflict between the principle of authority and the principle of freedom tends, when accepted and acted upon, to present authority as purely restrictive power and to leave the exercise of freedom without direction. To a considerable extent these untoward conditions depict our contemporary estate.

Let me explain briefly what is meant by calling the struggle one between forces that belong to individuals and that, in the interest of individuals as such, need to be adjusted to one another. It is folly psychologically and historically to identify the structure of the individual simply with the elements of human nature that make for variation and that mark one person off from another. The force of habit that leads individuals to cling to that which has been established is as genuine, and in the main, an even stronger part of the constitution of individuals. When tradition and social custom are incorporated in the working constitution of an individual, they have authority as a matter of course over his beliefs and his activities. The forces that exert and exercise this authority are so much and so deep a part of individuals that there is no thought or feeling of their being external and oppressive. They cannot be regarded as hostile to individuals as long as they are built into the habitual beliefs and purposes of the individual. They support him and give him direction. They naturally compel his allegiance and arouse his devotion. Attack upon the authoritative institutions in which custom and tradition are embodied is, therefore, naturally resented by the individual; it is deeply resented as an attack upon what is deepest and truest in himself.

For by far the greater number of millennia man has lived on the earth, man has been, for the most part, content with things as they, from time to time, are. This is true even of social organizations that seem to us arbitrary exhibitions of despotic force. For ages untold, the human disposition has been to attribute divine origin and sanction to whatever claimed for itself the authority of long tradition and custom. Individuals instead of seeking change were more generally afraid of it. If we were justified in putting authority and freedom, stability and change in opposition to one another, we should be compelled to conclude that for the greater period of human history individuals have preferred authority and stability.

This state of affairs has been reflected in theory. Until a very recent time, the accepted doctrine was that authority existed by nature; or else, by that which was beyond nature—the supernatural. In either case, it was held to exist in virtue of the inherent constitution of the universe and of individual man as part of the universe. In philosophy the conception that social authority exists by nature was formulated by Aristotle. In subsequent periods, the underlying idea was restated by the Stoics, in that quasi-idealistic, quasi-materialistic form that has always been—and still is—the means by which ideas obtain their strongest hold on the popular mind. The Christian philosophers of the Middle Ages reinstated the doctrine of Aristotle—but with a significant revision. Ultimate authority, they said, must be sought in the supernatural Author of Nature and in the Redeemer of man, for in them alone does it reside. This authority had its earthly representative, interpreter and agent in the divinely instituted and constituted church.

Even when the rise of secular dynastic states challenged the supremacy of the church, the basic idea was not even questioned, let alone challenged. The secular state only claimed that it also existed by divine right or authority and that its authority was therefore supreme in all the affairs of this life, as distinct from those of the soul in the life to come. Even when popular governments began to flourish, they continued the old idea in a weakened form: the voice of God was now the voice of the people.

The new science endeavored to smooth its thorny path by asserting that it was engaged in thinking the thoughts of God after Him. The rise of new economic forces in turn threatened the supreme authority of existing political institutions. But the new economic forces also claimed the right to supreme authority on the ground that they were pure and literal expressions of natural law—in contradistinction to political laws and institutions which, in so far as they did not conform to the play of economic forces, were artificial and man-made. Economic forces, through their representatives, interpreters and agents—the official economists and industrialists—claimed the divine prerogative to reign supreme over all human terrestrial affairs. The economist and industrialist and financier were the new pretenders to the old divine right of kings.

The conclusion that emerges from this brief historical survey—a conclusion that would be confirmed by any intensive study of the field—is that the identification of the individual with the forces that make freely for variation and change, to the exclusion of those forces in his structure that are habitual and conservative, is something new and recent. Speaking in general terms, the identification is an expression of special and specific historic events. These events may be condensed and summarized. New methods and conclusions in natural science and their technological application in new modes of industrial production and commercial exchange of goods and services found themselves checked and limited by the institutional agencies of church and state which were the possessors of actual social power and the claimants for exclusive and rightful authority in all the variegated fields of human endeavor. In this conflict, the new forces defended and justified themselves by restricting the very idea of authority to the ecclesiastical and political powers that were hostile to their own free expression and by asserting that they and they alone represented and furthered the interests of the individual and his freedom. The formula mentioned at the outset of this address, the formula of two separate and independent spheres of authority and freedom, in which primacy in case of doubt belongs to the individual and to freedom—this formula is the net product of the historic conflict.

The final result was a social and political philosophy which questioned the validity of authority in *any* form that was not the product of, and that was not sanctioned by, the conscious wants, efforts and satisfactions of individuals in their private capacity —a philosophy which took the form of *laissez-faire* in economics, and individualism in all other social and political affairs. This philosophy claimed for itself the comprehensive title of liberalism.

Two general conclusions, it seems to me, clearly emerge. First, the older forms of organized power that had exercised authority were revealed as external and oppressive with respect to the new forces that operated through the medium of individuals, and as hostile, in consequence, to all important social change. Second, the new philosophy so tended to decry the very principle of authority as to deprive individuals of the direction and support that are universally indispensable both for the organic freedom of individuals and for social stability.

The result is the present scene of confusion, conflict and uncertainty. While decrying the principle of authority, and asserting the necessity of limiting the exercise of authority to the minimum needed for maintenance of police order, the new philosophy in fact erected the wants and endeavors of private individuals seeking personal gain to the place of supreme authority in social life. In consequence, the new philosophy, in the very act of asserting that it stood completely and loyally for the principle of individual freedom, was really engaged in justifying the activities of a new form of concentrated power— the economic, which new form, to state the matter moderately, has consistently and persistently denied effective freedom to the economically underpowered and underprivileged. While originating as a social force that produced widespread social change in opposition to, indeed, despite of, the powers that had authority when it began to emerge, economic power has now become, in its turn, an organized social institution that resists all further social change that is not in accord with itself, that does not further and support its own interests as at present existing.

It is for such reasons as these that I affirm that the real issue is not that of demarcating separate "spheres" for authority and for freedom, for stability and for change, but of effecting an interpenetration of the two. We need an authority that, unlike the older forms in which it operated, is capable of directing and utilizing change, and we need a kind of individual freedom unlike that which the unconstrained economic liberty of individuals has produced and justified; we need, that is, a kind of individual freedom that is general and shared and that has the backing and guidance of socially organized intelligent control.

The evidence of past history is that our problem has not been solved. We have had organized social authority that limited the expression of the variable factors in individuals from which orderly and intentional change proceeds. We have had a time of relatively unconstrained and unchecked individualism; and of resultant change going on rapidly on a wide scale. The suppressive and stagnating effect of institutional authority of a political type has been weakened. But security, cooperative, ordered and orderly change are conspicuous by their absence.

It is completely possible, in my opinion, to recognize the need and important social consequences of the individualistic movement and yet also see that in its past mode of operation it has already run its socially justified and justifiable course. It is possible to acknowledge not merely the valuable historic services it has rendered, but also that its emphasis, practical and theoretic, upon the variable tendencies of human beings—those that mark off one person from another and that are expressed in initiative, invention and energetic enterprise—are values that should be permanently embodied in any future social order. It is possible, I say, to acknowledge all these admirable traits and products and yet also hold that the movement as it has operated up to the present has suffered from a great defect, owing to its absolutistic opposition to the principle of authority.

It requires little if any argument to prove that the institutional forms in which authority has been embodied in the past are hostile to change. It suffices, perhaps, to recall that those who have labored to change the forms authoritative power had taken were denounced as heretics, as elements subversive of social order. And, I need hardly add, those who are engaged in similar labor today are similarly denounced. The point that does require emphatic attention is that in spite of possession of power and in spite of persecution of heretics and radicals, no institution has in fact had the power to succeed in preventing great changes from taking place. All that institutions have ever succeeded in doing by their resistance to change has been to dam up social forces until they finally and inevitably manifested themselves in eruptions of great, usually violent and catastrophic, change.

Nor is argument necessary to prove that the individualistic movement has been allied with a period of immense and rapid changes, many of which, taken one by one, have brought positive benefit to society. The facts speak so loudly for themselves, argument is unnecessary. The intimate connection between the new individualism and social change is seen in the watchwords of the movement: Initiative, Invention, Enterprise. For all these words stand for the variable elements in the constitution of individuals; they point to the loci of departure from what has been; they are the signs which denote the sources of innovation. It is just because they are these signs that they can be so effectively used as watchwords, as signals that arouse the individual to effort and action. Indeed, the connection with change is so intimate that the movement produced that glorification of change as sure and necessary progress, which marked the heyday of its influence. But I venture the statement that just as the past manifestation of the principle of authority failed precisely where its claim was most vehement, namely, in the prevention, or at least in the guidance, of change, so the individualistic movement, taken historically and in the large, has failed to secure freedom for individuals on any commensurate scale— and in any assured way—even for its temporary possessors. The individualistic movement has tended to identify the exercise of freedom with absence of any organized control and, in this way, it has in fact identified freedom with mere *de facto* possession of economic power. Instead of bringing freedom to those who lacked material possessions, it has imposed upon them further subjection to the owners of the agencies of material production and distribution.

The scene which the world exhibits to the observer at the present time is so obviously one of general instability, insecurity and increasing conflict—both between nations and within them —that I cannot conceive that any one will deny the *desirability* of effecting and enstating some organic union of freedom and authority. Enormous doubt may well exist, however, as to the possibility of establishing any social system in which the union is practically embodied. This question, it will be justly urged, is *the* issue that emerges even if the substantial validity of the points so far made is admitted. In fact, it may even be justly urged that this question confronts us as the controlling and decisive question, just because or to the degree that validity of the argument thus far is granted.

The weight of the evidence of the past is assuredly strongly against the realization of any such possibility. As far as the idea of organized authority is concerned, the pathos of the collective life of mankind on this planet is its exhibition of the dire human need for some authority; while its ever-mounting tragedy is due to the fact that the need has been repeatedly betrayed by the very institutions that claimed to satisfy it. That all is not well, on the other hand, with the principle of individualistic freedom in the form in which it has been influential up to now, is shown by more than one fact in the present scene of discord and insecurity. Above all is this manifested by the recrudescence of the principle of authority in its most extreme and primitive form—the rise of dictatorships.

As if in substantiation of the old idea that nature abhors a vacuum, it might be contended that economic competitive individualism, free from social control, had created a moral and social vacuum which recourse to dictatorships is filling. In many countries, the demand for collective and organized guidance and support has become so urgent that the very idea of individual freedom has gone into discard and become an idea not to be praised but to be despised. The régime of economic individualistic liberty is attacked by dictatorships from both the right and the left. In countries in which there are no open and acknowledged dictatorships, the conceptions of liberty and individualism seem to be losing their magic force; and security, discipline, order and solidarity are, by social transfer, acquiring magic power in their stead. The actual concrete conditions that produce resort to dictatorships vary from country to country. But the phenomenon is so widespread it demands a generalized explanation. The most obvious one is the virtual bankruptcy and moribund state of a régime of individual initiative and enterprise conducted for private gain and subject to no control by recognized, collective authority.

Neither the past nor the present afford, then, any ground for expecting that the adjustment of authority and freedom, stability and change, will be achieved by following old paths. The idea that any solution at all can ever be attained may seem to some romantic and utopian. But the most fantastically unrealistic of all notions is the widely prevalent belief that we can attain enduring stable authority by employing or by re-exhuming the institutional means tried in the past; equally fantastic is the belief that the assured freedom of individuals can be secured by pitting individuals against one another in a pitiless struggle for material possessions and economic power. The issue, in my judgment, can be narrowed down to this question: Are there resources that have not as yet been tried out in the large field of human relations, resources that are available and that carry with them the potential promise of successful application?

In raising this question I am aware that it is almost inevitable that what I have said about the human necessity for some kind of collective authority to give individuals direction in their relations with one another and to give them the support that comes from a sense of solidarity, will appear to be a plea for a return to some kind of social control brought about through, and perpetuated by, external institutional means. If my question is so taken, then the criticism I have made of the alliance that has taken place between the principle of individual freedom and private initiative and enterprise in economic matters will necessarily also seem to be merely an argument for social control by means of a collective planned economy—put forward, of course, with some change in vocabulary. However, the argument in fact cuts in both directions. It indicates that while movements in the direction of collective, planned economy may cure evils from which we are now suffering, it will in the end go the way of all past attempts at organization of authoritative power unless some hitherto untried means are utilized on a large and systematic scale for bringing into life the desired organic coordination. Otherwise we shall finally find ourselves repeating on a different plane the old struggle between social organization and individual freedom, with the oscillation from one principle to the other that has so characteristically marked the past.

The resource that has not yet been tried on any large scale in the broad field of human, social relationships is the utilization of organized intelligence, the manifold benefits and values of which we have substantial evidence in the narrower field of science.

Within a limited area, the collective intelligence which is exemplified in the growth and application of scientific method has already become authoritative. It is authoritative in the field of beliefs regarding the structure of nature and relevant to our understanding of physical events. To a considerable extent, the same statement holds true of beliefs about historical personages and historical events—especially with those that are sufficiently remote from the present time. When we turn to the practical side, we see that the same method is supreme in controlling and guiding our active dealings with material things and physical energies. To a large and significant extent, the

Baconian prophecy that knowledge is power of control has been realized in this particular, somewhat narrowly circumscribed, area. To be sure, it cannot be said that intelligence, operating by the methods that constitute science, has as yet completely won undisputed right and authority to control beliefs even in the restricted physical field. But organized intelligence has made an advance that is truly surprising when we consider the short time in which it has functioned and the powerful foes against which it had to make its way: the foes of inertia, of old, long-established traditions and habits—inertia, traditions and habits all of them entrenched in forms of institutional life that are effulgent with the prestige of time, that are enveloped in the glamor of imaginative appeal and that are crowned, severally and collectively, with an emotional halo made of values that men most prize.

The record of the struggle that goes by the name of "conflict between science and religion" or, if you please, "conflict between theology and science" was essentially a conflict of claims to exercise social authority. It was not just a conflict between two sets of theoretical beliefs, but between two alignments of social forces—one which was old and had institutional power that it did not hesitate to use and one which was new and striving and craving for recognition against gigantic odds.

What is pertinent, what is deeply significant to the theme of the *relation* between collective authority and freedom, is that the progress of intelligence—as exemplified in this summary story of scientific advance—exhibits their organic, effective union. Science has made its way by releasing, not by suppressing, the elements of variation, of invention and innovation, of novel creation in individuals. It is as true of the history of modern science as it is of the history of painting or music that its advances have been initiated by individuals who freed themselves from the bonds of tradition and custom whenever they found the latter hampering their own powers of reflection, observation and construction.

In spite of science's dependence for its development upon

the free initiative, invention and enterprise of individual inquirers, the authority of science issues from and is based upon
collective activity, cooperatively organized. Even when, temporarily, the ideas put forth by individuals have sharply di-
verged from received beliefs, the method used in science has
been a public and open method which succeeded and could
succeed only as it tended to produce agreement, unity of belief
among all who labored in the same field. Every scientific
inquirer, even when he deviates most widely from current ideas,
depends upon methods and conclusions that are a common
possession and not of private ownership, even though all the
methods and conclusions may at some time have been initially
the product of private invention. The contribution the scientific
inquirer makes is collectvely tested and developed. In the measure that it is cooperatively confirmed, it becomes a part of the
common fund of the intellectual commonwealth.

One can most easily recognize the difference between the
aim and operation of the free individual in the sphere of science
and in that of current individualistic economic enterprise, by
stretching the fancy to the point of imagining a scientific inquirer adopting the standards of the business entrepreneur.
Imagine the scientific man who should say that his conclusion
was scientific and, in so saying, maintain that it was also the
product of his private wants and efforts goading him on to seek
his private advantage. The mere suggestion of such an absurd-
ity vividly discloses the gap that divides the manifestations of
individual freedom in these two areas of human activity. The
suggestion brings into bold relief the kind of individual freedom that is both supported by collective, organic authority and
that in turn changes and is encouraged to change and develop,
by its own operations, the authority upon which it depends.

The thesis that the operation of cooperative intelligence as
displayed in science is a working model of the union of freedom
and authority does not slight the fact that the method has operated up to the present in a limited and relatively technical area.
On the contrary, it emphasizes that fact. If the method of intelli-

gence had been employed in any large field in the comprehensive and basic area of the relations of human beings to one another in social life and institutions, there would be no present need for our argument. The contrast between the restricted scope of its use and the possible range of its application to human relations—political, economic and moral—is outstanding enough to be depressing. It is this very contrast that serves to define the great problem that lies before us.

No consideration of the problem is adequate that does not take into account one fact about the development of the modern individualistic movement in industry and business. There is a suppressed premise in all the claims and reasonings of the individualistic school. All the beneficial changes that have been produced are attributed to the free play of individuals seeking primarily their own profit as isolated individuals. But in fact, the entire modern industrial development is the fruit of the technological applications of science. By and large, the economic changes of recent centuries have been parasitic upon the advances made in natural science. There is not a single process involved in the production and distribution of goods that is not dependent upon the utilization of results which are the consequences of the method of collective, organic intelligence working in mathematics, physics and chemistry. To speak baldly, it is a plain falsehood that the advances which the defenders of the existing régime point to as justification for its continuance are due to mere individualistic initiative and enterprise. Individualistic initiative and enterprise have sequestrated and appropriated the fruits of collective cooperative intelligence. Without the aid and support of organized intelligence they would have been impotent—perhaps even in those activities they have shown themselves to be socially most powerful.

In sum, the great weakness of the historic movement that has laid claim to the title of liberalism and that has proclaimed its operating purpose to be that of securing and protecting the freedom of individuals—the great weakness of this movement has been its failure to recognize that the true and final source

of change has been, and now is, the corporate intelligence
embodied in science. The principle, as I have already said, cuts
in two directions. In so far as the attempts that are now being
made in the direction of organized social control and planned
economy ignore the rôle of scientific intelligence; in so far as
these attempts depend upon and turn for support to external
institutional changes effected for the most part by force, just so
far are they re-enstating reliance upon the method of external
authority that has always broken down in the past. For a time,
while in need of security and a sense and feeling of solidarity,
men will submit to authority of this kind. But if history shows
anything, it shows that the variable factors in individuals cannot be permanently suppressed or completely eradicated. The
principle of individual freedom expressed in the modern individualistic movement is deeply rooted in the constitution of
human beings. The truth embodied in it cannot die, no matter
how much force is brought down upon it. The tragedy of the
movement is that it misconceived and misplaced the source and
seat of this principle of freedom. But the attempt to eliminate
this principle on behalf of the assurance of security and attainment of solidarity by means of external authority is doomed to
ultimate defeat no matter what its temporary victories.

There is no need to dwell upon the enormous obstacles that
stand in the way of extending from its limited field to the larger
field of human relations the control of organized intelligence,
operating through the release of individual powers and capa-
bilities. There is the weight of past history on the side of those
who are pessimistic about the possibility of achieving this humanly desirable and humanly necessary task. I do not predict that
the extension will ever be effectively actualized. But I do claim
that the problem of the relation of authority and freedom, of
stability and change, if it can be solved, will be solved in this
way. The failure of other methods and the desperateness of the
present situation will be a spur to some to do their best to make
the extension actual. They know that to hold in advance of trial
that success is impossible is a way of condemning humanity to

that futile and destructive oscillation between authoritative power and unregulated individual freedom to which we may justly attribute most of the sorrows and defeats of the past. They are aware of the slow processes of history and of the unmeasured stretch of time that lies ahead of mankind. They do not expect any speedy victory in the execution of the most difficult task human beings ever set their hearts and minds to attempt. They are, however, buoyed by the assurance that no matter how slight the immediate effect of their efforts, they are themselves, in their trials, exemplifying one of the first principles of the method of scientific intelligence. For they are experimentally projecting into events a large and comprehensive idea by methods that correct and mature the method and the idea in the very process of trial. The very desperateness of the situation is, for such as these, but a spur to sustained, courageous effort.

9

LIBERTY AND SOCIAL CONTROL

I

TODAY THERE IS NO WORD MORE BANDIED ABOUT THAN LIBERTY. Every effort at planned control of economic forces is resisted and attacked, by a certain group, in the name of liberty. The slightest observation shows that this group is made up of those who are interested, from causes that are evident, in the preservation of the economic status quo; that is to say, in the maintenance of the customary privileges and legal rights they already possess. When we look at history in the large we find that the demand for liberty and efforts to achieve it have come from those who wanted to *alter* the institutional set-up. This striking contrast is a stimulus to thoughtful inquiry. What does liberty mean anyway? Why should the cause of liberty have been identified in the past with efforts at change of laws and institutions while at the present time a certain group is using all its vast resources to convince the public that change of economic institutions is an attack upon liberty?

Well, in the first place, liberty is not just an idea, an abstract principle. It is power, effective power to do specific things. There is no such thing as liberty in general; liberty, so to speak, at large. If one wants to know what the condition of liberty is at a given time, one has to examine what persons *can* do and what they *cannot* do. The moment one examines the question from the standpoint of effective action, it becomes evident that the demand for liberty is a demand for power, either for possession of powers of action not already possessed or for retention and expansion of powers already possessed. The present ado in behalf of liberty by the managers and beneficiaries of the existing economic system is immediately explicable if one views it as a demand for preservation of the powers they already possess. Since it is the existing system that gives them these powers, liberty is thus inevitably identified with the perpetuation of that system. Translate the present hullabaloo about liberty into struggle to retain powers already possessed, and it has a meaning.

In the second place, the possession of effective power is always a matter of the *distribution* of power that exists at the time. A physical analogy may make clear what I mean. Water runs downhill and electric currents flow because of *difference in potentials*. If the ground is level, water is stagnant. If on the level ocean, there are dashing waves, it is because there is another power operating, that of the winds, occasioned ultimately by a difference in the distribution of temperature at different points. There is no such thing physically as manifestation of energy or effective power by one thing except in relation to the energy manifested by other things. There is no such thing as the liberty or effective power of an individual, group, or class, except in relation to the liberties, the effective powers, of *other* individuals, groups, and classes.

Demand for retention of powers already possessed on the part of a particular group means, therefore, that other individuals and groups shall continue to possess only the capacities in and for activity which *they* already possess. Demand for increased power at one point means demands for change in the distribution of powers, that is, for less power somewhere else. You cannot discuss or measure the liberty of one individual or group of individuals without thereby raising the question of the effect upon the liberty of others, any more than you can measure the energy of a head water at the head without measuring the difference of levels.

In the third place, this relativity of liberty to the existing distribution of powers of action, while meaning that there is no such thing as absolute liberty, also necessarily means that wherever there is liberty at one place there is restraint at some other place. *The system of liberties that exists at any time is always the system of restraints or controls that exists at that time.* No one can *do* anything except in relation to what others can do and cannot do.

These three points are general. But they cannot be dismissed as mere abstractions. For when they are applied either in idea or in action they mean that liberty is always a *social* question, not an individual one. For the liberties that any individual actually has depends upon the distribution of powers or liberties that exists, and this distribution is identical with actual social arrangements, legal and political—and, at the present time, economic, in a peculiarly important way.

Return now to the fact that historically the great movements for human liberation have always been movements to change institutions and not to preserve them intact. It follows from what has been said that there have been movements to bring about a changed distribution of power to do—and power to think and to express thought is a power to do—such that there would be a more balanced, a more equal, even, and equitable system of human liberties.

The present movement for social control of industry, money and credit is simply a part of this endless human struggle. The present attempt to define liberty in terms of the existing distribution of liberty is an attempt to maintain the existing system of control of power, of social restraints and regimentations. I cannot go here into the nature and consequences of this system. If one is satisfied with it, let him support the conception of liberty put forth by, say, the Liberty League, which represents the present economic system. But let him not be fooled into thinking that the issue is liberty versus restraint and regimentation. For the issue is simply that of one system of control of the social forces upon which the distribution of liberties depends, versus some other system of social control which would bring about another distribution of liberties. And let those who are struggling to replace the present economic system by a cooperative one also remember that in struggling for a new system of social restraints and controls they are also struggling for a more equal and equitable balance of powers that will enhance and multiply the effective liberties of the mass of individuals. Let them not be jockeyed into the position of supporting social control at the expense of liberty, when what they want is another method of social control than the one that now exists, one that will increase significant human liberties.

It is nonsense to suppose that we do not have social control *now.* The trouble is that it is exercised by the few who have economic power, at the expense of the liberties of the many and at the cost of increasing disorder, culminating in that chaos of war which the representatives of liberty for the possessive class identify with true discipline.

II

It is constantly urged by one school of social thought that liberty and equality are so incompatible that liberalism is not a possible social philosophy. The argument runs as follows: If liberty is the dominant social and political goal then the natural diversity and inequality of natural endowments will inevitably work out to produce social inequalities. You cannot give free rein to natural capacities, so runs the argument, without producing marked inequality in cultural, economic, and political status as a necessary consequence. On the other hand, if equality is made the goal, there must, the argument continues, be important restrictions put upon the exercise of liberty. The incompatibility of liberty and equality is the rock, it is asserted, upon which liberalism is bound to founder. Consequently, the school of liberalism that identifies liberty with *laissez-faire* claims to be the only logical school of liberalism, and it is willing to tolerate any amount of actual social inequality provided it is the result of the free exercise of natural powers.

The original idea and ideal of democracy combined equality

and liberty as coordinate ideals, adding to them, in the slogan of the French Revolution, fraternity as a third coordinate. Both historically and actually the possibility of realization of the democratic ideal is conditioned, therefore, upon the possibility of working out in social practice and social institutions a combination of equality and liberty. As is proved by the present state of democracy in nominally democratic countries the problem is a practical one.

The formula of early democratic political liberalism was that men are born free and equal. Superficial critics have thought that the formula is peremptorily refuted by the fact that human beings are not born equal in strength and abilities or natural endowments. The formula, however, never assumed that they were. Its meaning is the same as that of the familiar saying that in the grave pauper and millionaire, monarch and serf, are equal. It was a way of saying that political inequality is the product of social institutions; that there is no "natural" inherent difference between those of one social caste, class, or status and those of another caste, class, or status; that such differences are the product of law and social customs. The same principle holds of economic differences; if one individual is born to the possession of property and another is not, the difference is due to social laws regulating inheritance and the possession of property. Translated into terms of concrete action, the formula means that inequalities of natural endowment should operate under laws and institutions that do not place permanent handicaps upon those of lesser gifts; that the inequalities in the distribution of powers, achievements, and goods that occur in society should be strictly proportionate to natural inequalities. In the present social arrangement, opportunities for individuals are determined by the social and family status of individuals; the institutional set-up of human relations provides openings to members of certain classes to the detriment of other classes. The challenge of progressive and liberal democracy can be stated in the familiar war-cry: Institutions and laws should be such as to secure and establish equality for all.

This formula expressed revolt against the existing institutions that automatically limited the opportunities of the mass of individuals. It was this revolt and the aspiration it embodied that was the essence of democratic liberalism in its earlier political and humanitarian manifestations. But the rise of machine-industry, controlled by finance-capitalism, was a force that was not taken into account. It gave liberty of action to those particular natural endowments and individuals that fitted into the new economic picture. Above all, the Industrial Revolution gave scope to the abilities involved in acquiring property and to the employment of that wealth in further acquisitions. The employment of these specialized acquisitive abilities has resulted in the monopoly of power in the hands of the few to control the opportunities of the wide masses and to limit their free activities in realizing their natural capacities.

In short, the common assertion of the mutual incompatability of equality and liberty rests upon a highly formal and limited concept of liberty. It overlooks and rules out the fact that the *actual* liberties of one human being depend upon the powers of action that existing institutional arrangements accord to other individuals. It conceives of liberty in a completely abstract way. The democratic ideal that unites equality and liberty is, on the other hand, a recognition that actual and concrete liberty of opportunity and action is dependent upon equalization of the political and economic conditions under which individuals are alone free *in fact,* not *in some abstract metaphysical way.* The tragic breakdown of democracy is due to the fact that the identification of liberty with the maximum of unrestrained individualistic action in the economic sphere, under the institutions of capitalistic finance, is as fatal to the realization of liberty for all as it is fatal to the realization of equality. It is destructive of liberty for the many precisely because it is destructive of genuine equality of opportunity.

The social philosophy of Thomas Jefferson is regarded as outmoded by many persons because it seems to be based upon the then existing agrarian conditions and to postulate the persistence of the agrarian régime. It is then argued that the rise of industry to a position superior to that of agriculture has destroyed the basis of Jeffersonian democracy. This is a highly superficial view. Jefferson predicted what the effects of rise of the economics and politics of an industrial régime would be, unless the independence and liberty characteristic of the farmer, under conditions of virtually free land, were conserved. His predictions have been realized. It was not agrarianism *per se* that he really stood for, but the kind of liberty and equality that the agrarian régime made possible when there was an open frontier. The early Jeffersonians, for example, held that national credit was a national asset and ought to be nationally controlled; they were bitterly opposed to the capture of national credit by private banking institutions. They were even opposed to financing wars by means of bonds and debts where the income accrued to private individuals, maintaining that wars should be paid for during the time they occur through taxation upon the incomes of the wealthy.

I refer to this particular instance merely by way of illustration, and to indicate how far away so-called Jeffersonian democracy has drifted from the original ideas and policies of any democracy whatsoever. The drift of nominal democracy from the conception of life which may properly be characterized as democratic has come about under the influence of a so-called rugged individualism that defines the liberty of individuals in the terms of the inequality bred by existing economic-legal institutions. In so doing, it puts an almost exclusive emphasis upon those natural capacities of individuals that have power to effect pecuniary and materialistic acquisitions. For our existing materialism, with the blight to which it subjects the cultural development of individuals, is the inevitable product of exaggeration of the economic liberty of the few at the expense of the all-around liberty of the many. And, I repeat, this limitation upon genuine liberty is the inevitable product of the inequality that arises and must arise under the operations of institutionally established and supported finance-capitalism.

III

The idea of civil liberties developed step by step as the ideals of liberalism displaced the earlier practices of political autocracy, which subordinated subjects to the arbitrary will of governmental authorities. In tradition, rather than in historic fact, their origin for English-speaking people is associated with the Magna Carta. Civil liberties were definitely formulated in the Bill of Rights adopted by the British Parliament in 1689 after the exile of the Stuarts and the final overthrow of dynastic government in that country. At the time of the revolt of the American colonies against the mother country many of the state constitutions embodied clauses very similar to those in the Bill of Rights. They were not contained in the Federal Constitution adopted at a time of reaction against the more radical revolutionary ideas, Hamilton being especially opposed to their inclusion. But in order to secure ratification by the several states, constitutional guarantees of civil rights were added in the first ten amendments in 1789. They contained, however, little more than what had become commonplaces of the rights of citizens in Great Britain. The only novel features in our constitutional provisions were the denial to government of the right of establishing religion and a greater emphasis upon the right of individuals to complete freedom in choice of a form of religious worship. The gist of the civil rights, constitutionally guaranteed to individuals, was freedom of the press, of peaceful assemblage and discussion, and of petition.

I have given this slight historic review because history throws much light on the present confused state of civil liberties. A consistent social philosophy of the various rights that go by this name has never existed. Upon the whole, the dominant philosophy has sprung from fear of government and of organized control, on the ground of their supposed inherent antagonism to the liberties of individuals. Hence, one theoretical justification of freedom of conscience, of choice of worship, of freedom of speech (which is what freedom of assembly amounts to practically) and of publication, has been based upon the theory of natural rights, rights that inhere in individuals prior to political organization and independent of political authority. From this point of view, they are like the rights of "life, liberty, and the pursuit of happiness" made familiar to us in the Declaration of Independence. They represent fixed and external limits set to political action.

This motif comes out most clearly in the last two articles of the amendments that form the Bill of Rights, articles which expressly reserve to the several states or to the people in general all powers not expressly granted by the Constitution to the Federal Government. The majority opinion in the A.A.A. decision used this clause of the Constitution as its authority for declaring the Agricultural Adjustment Act unconstitutional. On the face of things, there is no kinship between regulation of agriculture and the right, say, of free speech. But the two things have been brought together in the theory that there is an inherent opposition between political power and individual liberty.

The opposite strain in the theory of civil liberties is indicated by the contrast between the word "civil" on the one hand and the words "natural" and "political" on the other. The term *civil* is directly connected with the idea of citizenship. On this basis, civil liberties are those which belong to citizens as such and are different both from those which individuals are supposed to possess in a state of nature and from political rights such as the franchise and the right to hold office. Upon this basis, the justification for the various civil liberties is the contribution they make to the welfare of the community.

I have intimated that the present confused and precarious condition of civil liberties, even in nominally democratic countries like our own, is due to the conflict of these two opposed ideas of the basis and purpose of civil liberties. As social relations have become more complicated and the problem of maintaining social order becomes more difficult, it is practically inevitable that whatever the nominal theory be, *merely* individual claims will be forced to give way in practice to social claims. The individualistic and *laissez-faire* conception of civil liberties (say of free inquiry and free discussion) has been put forward to an extent which largely accounts for the ease with which nominally constitutional guarantees of civil liberties are violated in fact and are explained away by the courts. It is a commonplace that they go into discard when a nation is engaged in war. This is simply the crucial instance of the fact that *merely* individual claims will be lightly esteemed when they appear (or can be made to appear) in conflict with the general social welfare.

Moreover, civil liberties are never absolute nor is their precise nature in concrete situations self-evident. Only a philosophic anarchist holds, for example, that the freedom of speech includes the right to urge other men to engage in murder, arson, or robbery. Hence in the concrete, civil liberties mean what the courts construe them to mean. Courts, in all matters that have a general political or social bearing, are notoriously subject to social pressure and social currents, both those coming from without and those flowing from the education and political affiliations of judges. These facts give short shrift to civil liberties that are claimed upon a purely individualistic basis when judges are of the opinion that their exercise is dangerous to social ends which the judges set store by. Holmes and Brandeis are notable not only for their sturdy defense of civil liberties but even more for the fact that they based their defense on the indispensable value of free inquiry and free discussion to the normal development of public welfare, not upon anything inherent in the individual as such.

Anyone who views the situation impartially will not be surprised at the contradiction which is so marked in the conduct of liberals of the *laissez-faire* school. They constantly protest against any "interference" on the part of government with freedom of business enterprise, but are almost uniformly silent in the case of even flagrant violations of civil liberties—in spite of lip service to liberal ideas and professed adulation of the Constitution. The cause for the contradiction is obvious. Business interests have been and still are socially and politically dominant. In standing for *laissez-faire* liberalism in economic matters, these "liberals" are moving with the tide. On the other hand, only those individuals who are *opposing* the established order ever get into trouble by using the right to free inquiry and public discussion. In their case, the "liberals" who are vociferous against anything that looks like economic regimentation are content to tolerate intellectual and moral regimentation on the ground that it is necessary for the maintenance of "law and order."

No genuine believer in the democratic ideals of universal distribution of equal liberties will find it necessary to argue at large in behalf of the maximum possible of intellectual liberty in the fullest sense of that term. He knows that freedom of thought in inquiry and in dissemination of the conclusions of inquiry is the vital nerve of democratic institutions. Accordingly, I have not indulged in a general eulogy of civil liberties but have tried to show that the first step in rescuing them from their present uncertain and perilous state is to insist upon their social basis and social justification.

Invasions of civil liberties have grown in pretty much all directions since the first World War, in spite of alleged constitutional guarantees. The only hope for liberalism is to surrender, in theory and practice, the doctrine that liberty is a full-fledged ready-made possession of individuals independent of social institutions and arrangements, and to realize that social control, especially of economic forces, is necessary in order to render secure the liberties of the individual, including civil liberties.

IV

It is an interesting fact in the history of English words that the word *liberal* was applied to education even earlier than it was used to denote generosity and bountifulness. A liberal education was the education of a free man. Liberal subjects

were those fitted to be pursued by a free man and were opposed
to those subjects that were adapted to the training of mechanics.
This meant in fact that the liberal arts and a liberal education
were confined to persons who occupied a superior social status.
They belonged to gentlemen as distinct from the "lower classes."
It would be interesting to trace the effect of these ideas upon
school education. They influenced schooling even in this country. For the men of this country who prided themselves upon
being all free naturally took over for the staple of their subjects,
especially in secondary and higher education, just the subjects
which in the old country were thought to be suited to preparing
gentlemen for their higher walks of life.

However, my present point does not concern this story.
The idea of the *free* and *common* schools developed among us
on the ground that a nation of truly free men and women
required schools open to all and hence supported by public
taxation. Upon the whole, considerable progress has been made
in making schooling accessible to all, though of course it is still
true that the opportunity to take advantage of what is theoretically provided for all is seriously limited by economic status.
But what I am here concerned with is the meaning of liberalism
itself.

The meaning of liberalism has undergone many changes
since the word came into vogue not very much more than a
century ago. The word came into use to denote a new spirit that
grew and spread with the rise of democracy. It implied a new
interest in the common man and a new sense that the common
man, the representative of the great masses of human beings,
had possibilities that had been kept under, that had not been
allowed to develop, because of institutional and political conditions. This new spirit was liberal in both senses of the word.
It was marked by a generous attitude, by sympathy for the
underdog, for those who were not given a chance. It was part
of a widespread rise of humanitarian philanthropy. It was also
liberal in that it aimed at enlarging the scope of free action on
the part of those who for ages had had no part in public affairs
and no lot in the benefits secured by this participation.

Owing to the conditions that existed in the late eighteenth century and throughout the nineteenth century, liberalism soon, however, took on a limited and technical significance. The class that was most conscious of suffering from restrictions, most active in removing them, and best organized to fight against them consisted of those who were engaged in manufacturing industries and in commerce. On the one hand, the application of steam to production was revolutionizing the production and distribution of goods, opening new avenues to human energy and ambition, and supplying commodities more effectively than was possible under the system of production by hand. On the other hand, there existed a mass of regulations and customs, formed to a large degree in feudal times, that hampered and checked the expression of these new energies. Moreover, political power was mainly in the hands of landlords representing older agrarian habits of belief and action.

The liberalism of the industrial class took accordingly the form of political and legal struggle to do away with restrictions upon free manifestation of the newer economic activities. The restrictive and oppressive forces were those embodied in institutions that were readily identified with the government and with the state. Hence the slogan of organized liberalism was, "Let the government keep hands off industry and commerce. Its action in these spheres is preventing the growth of activities that are of the highest value to society. These new industrial activities furnish men with things they need more cheaply and in greater quantities than the old system did or could do. They encourage invention and stimulate progress. They promote energy and thrift by holding out to all the reward of their initiative, skill, and labor. The free exchange of goods binds men and nations together in ties of common interest and brings near the reign of harmony and peace throughout all mankind." Such were the claims.

Given the particular time and place in which the claims were made, they had their own justification. A great burst of energy accompanied the onset of the industrial revolution, and did so in many ways of creative action other than industrial production. But as the new social group won power, their doctrines hardened into the dogma of the freedom of the industrial entrepreneur from any organized social control. Because law and administration had been, at a turning point in history, the foe of the liberation of human energies, it was proclaimed that they were always the enemy of human liberty. The idea of hands off, practically sound under special circumstances, was stiffened into the dogma of *laissez-faire* "individualism." The new economic interests, much better organized than the earlier agrarian class, got an enormous grip upon the social forces.

Because the interests of the dominant economic class became anti-social in some of their consequences, the complete separation of the economic from the political (no government in business), isolated individualism, and the negation of organized social direction were put forward as eternal truths. Meantime, the generous sympathetic spirit characteristic of earlier liberalism was split off and confined to philanthropic movements; when it affected legislation and administration it confined itself to remedial measures for those at marked social disadvantage, leaving intact the system that produced the symptoms dealt with. In this country even these remedial measures were bitterly opposed by the dominant class, although that class would be their final residuary legatee, inasmuch as these measures would render the inherited system more endurable by the masses.

Consequently, that which began as a movement in the direction of greater liberty for expression of the energies of man and which was put forward as giving every individual new opportunities and powers, has become socially oppressive for the greater number of individuals. It has almost resulted in identifying the power and liberty of the individual with ability to achieve economic success—or, to put it in a nutshell, with ability to make money. Instead of being the means of promoting harmony and interdependence among peoples, it has proved, as it worked out, to be divisive: Let imperialism and war be the evidence.

The idea and ideal of more liberty for individuals and of the release of the potentialities of individuals, the enduring core of the liberal spirit, is as sound as ever it was. But the rise of business to a dominant position has, in fact, given anti-social liberty to the few; has identified rugged individualism with uncontrolled business activity, and has regimented the thought and conduct of multitudes. Meantime, the cause that brought about the immense rise in capacity to produce and to distribute, that which made possible the mass production of the factory and its mass distribution by transportation facilities, has been effectually captured for the benefit of the few. The cause of the release of productive energies was the rise of experimental science and its technological application. Physical machinery and trained technical ability have now reached a point where it is all but a commonplace that an era of material abundance and material security for all is possible, laying the material basis for the cultural flowering of human beings.

In consequence, the ends which liberalism has always professed can be attained only as control of the means of production and distribution is taken out of the hands of individuals who exercise powers created socially for narrow individual interests. The ends remain valid. But the means of attaining them demand a radical change in economic institutions and the political arrangements based upon them. These changes are necessary in order that social control of forces and agencies socially created may accrue to the liberation of all individuals associated together in the great undertaking of building a life that expresses and promotes human liberty.

10

THE FUTURE OF LIBERALISM

I

LIBERALISM AS A CONSCIOUS AND AGGRESSIVE MOVEMENT AROSE IN Great Britain as two different streams flowed into one.

One of these streams was the humanitarian and philanthropic zeal that became so active late in the eighteenth century and that in various forms is still a mighty current. It was expressed in the feeling that man is his brother's keeper and that the world is full of suffering and evil that are caused by failure to recognize this fact. In consequence of the failure, political and social institutions are horribly and tragically harsh and cruel in their effect upon the mass of men, women and children.

This humanitarian movement itself represents the conflux of many separate streams. There was, for example, the tremendous influence exerted by Rousseau, the real author of the doctrine of the forgotten man and the forgotten masses. His influence was quite as great in literature as in politics. It helped create the novel of the common man in England in the eighteenth century, a literary influence that found such vivid expression in the nineteenth century in the novels of Dickens.

Independent of Rousseau, but reinforced by his influence, there was a reaction against the importance attached by most eighteenth-century thought to "reason." Reason, it was felt if not argued, is a prerogative of a select few. The mass of men are influenced by feeling and instinct, and the hope of the

126

world lies in giving free play to the instinct of sympathy, rather than to logic and reason.

This new attitude found expression in the deification of the "man of sentiment" so characteristic of one period of English thought. The interest in the "noble savage" is another expression of the same attitude. Aside from the fact that he was supposed, in a wholly illusory way, to be independent and free from the constraints of convention and custom, he was idealized as the creature of instinct and emotion.

Another influence that finally joined in to form the humanitarian current was the religious. In England it was stimulated by the Wesleyan movement, with its peculiar appeal to the "lower" and neglected classes. But it affected the established church as well. Ardent, aggressive missionary zeal for saving the souls of men, especially those of the humble and poor, ran over into efforts to improve their condition by abolishing harsh and cruel inequalities.

The movement, instigated by religion, was active in attack upon slavery, upon the abuses of prison life, upon brutal and mechanical methods of administering charity, and, through the factory laws, upon the inhuman conditions of labor of women and children in mines and factories. In every one of these movements evangelical zeal was the motive force.

The other great stream that entered into the formation of liberalism sprang from the stimulus to manufacturing and trade that came from the application of steam to industry. The great intellectual leader of this movement was Adam Smith. His theories found practical reinforcement in the endeavor of manufacturers and traders to get free from the immense number of laws and customs that restricted the freedom of movement of laborers, that subjected the market price to prices legally fixed and that hampered freedom of exchange especially with foreign markets.

This mass of restrictions, that tended to strangle at birth the new infant industry, held over from agrarian feudalism and was kept in force by the influence of landed interests. Because the restrictive and oppressive conditions were embodied in law and because law was the voice of government in control of human action, government was taken to be the great enemy of liberty; interference with human industry engaged in satisfaction of human needs was taken to be the chief cause why progress was retarded and why a reign of harmony of interests and peace did not exist.

Freedom of production would, it was held, lead to the maximum stimulation of human effort and automatically direct abilities into the channels in which, in bringing most reward to the individual, they would also be most serviceable to society. Freedom of exchange would create an interdependence that would automatically create harmony of interests. The negative side of the doctrine, its opposition to governmental action in production and trade, came to full flower in the principle of *laissez-faire*: hands off on the part of government and the maximum of free activity on the part of producer and trader in the advancement of his own interests.

This historical summary is more than historical. It is indispensable to any understanding of liberalism as a social and political movement. For, while the two stream came together, they never coalesced.

Although the humanitarian movement expressed itself most actively in personal and voluntary effort, it was far from averse to employing governmental agencies to achieve its reforms. Most of them, in fact, like abolition of the slave trade, prison reform, removal of abuses attending the labor of women and children, could not be effected without some intervention on the part of government.

The whole movement toward what is known as social legislation with its slogan of social justice derives from this source and involves more and more appeal to governmental action. Hence there was from the beginning an inner split in liberalism. Any attempt to define liberalism in terms of one or the other of its two strains will be vehemently denied by those attached to the other strain.

Historically, the split was embodied in the person of one of the chief representatives of nineteenth-century liberalism, Jeremy Bentham. Whether he was aware of it or not, his leading principle, that of the greatest happiness of the greatest number, was derived from the philanthropic and humanitarian movement. But when it came to the realization of this goal, he ranked himself, with some exceptions, such as public health and public education, with *laissez-faire* liberalism.

He was strong for political action to reform abuses of judicial procedure, of lawmaking and methods of electing lawmakers, but he regarded the abuses to be corrected as the product of the failure of government in the past to confine itself to its proper sphere. When the abuses of governmental action by government were once removed, he believed that the free play of individual initiative and effort would furnish the sure road to progress and to producing the greatest happiness of the greatest number.

As I have indicated, the inner breach in liberalism has never been healed. On the Continent, so-called liberal parties have been almost universally the political representatives of big industry, banking and commerce. In Great Britain, true to the spirit of tradition and compromise so strong in English affairs, liberalism has been a mixture of the two strains, leaning now in one direction and now in another.

In the United States liberalism has been identified largely with the idea of the use of governmental agencies to remedy evils from which the less-fortunate classes suffer. It was "forward-looking" in the Progressive movement; it lies, nominally at least, behind Square Deals and New Deals. It has favored employer-liability acts, laws regulating hours and conditions of labor, anti-sweatshop legislation, supplementation of private charity by public relief and public works, generous appropriations for public schools, graded higher taxation of larger incomes and of inheritances; in general, when there has been a conflict between labor and employers it has sided with labor.

Its philosophy has rarely been clear cut. But so far as it has had a philosophy it has been that government should regularly intervene to help equalize conditions between the wealthy and the poor, between the overprivileged and the underprivileged. For this reason liberals of the other, or *laissez-faire*, school have always attacked it as pink socialism, as disguised radicalism; while at the present time the favorite charge is that it is instigated, of all places in the world, from Moscow.

As a matter of fact, up to this time in this country political liberalism has never attempted to change the fundamental conditions of the economic system or to do more than ameliorate the estate in which the mass of human beings live. For this reason liberalism at present is under more violent attack from radicals than from conservatives. In the mouth of radicals liberalism is a term of hissing and reproach.

In spite of the extreme clash, both schools of liberalism profess devotion to the same ultimate ideal and goal. The slogan of both schools is the utmost possible liberty of the individual. The difference between them concerns the province in which liberty and individuality are most important and the means by which they are to be realized.

One has only to read any outgiving of the adherents of *laissez-faire* liberalism to see that it is the liberty of the entrepreneur in business undertakings which they prize and which they come close to identifying with the heart of all liberty.

To the spokesmen of the Liberty League and to ex-President Hoover in his doctrine of rugged individualism, any governmental action that interferes with this particular kind of liberty is an attack upon liberty itself. The ruggedness, independence, initiative and vigor of individuals upon which they set chief store is that of the individuals who have come to the top in the existing economic system of finance capitalism. They are exposed to the charge of identifying the meaning of liberty and of rugged individualism with the maintenance of the system under which they have prospered.

The charge is given force by the fact that they have for the most part supported the system of protective tariffs, against which original simon-pure *laissez-faire* liberals directed some of their most violent attacks. The author of the phrase "rugged individualism" used the government to come to the aid of industry when it was in straits by means of the Reconstruction Finance Corporation, and, as far as I know, the opponents of governmental intervention made no protest at this flagrant case of governmental interference with the free course of private industry.

The most vocal spokesmen for this special form of liberty have never attacked land monopoly and, if they think at all about Henry George, they think of him as one of the subversive and dangerous radicals. They have themselves built up financial and industrial systems so concentrated as to be semi-monopolies or monopolies proper.

Liberals of the other school are those who point to things like those just mentioned and who assert that the system of industry for private profit without regard to social consequences has had in fact a most unfavorable effect upon the real liberty of the mass of individuals.

Their conception of what I called the province of liberty and individuality is broader and more generous than is that of those who come forward as the self-appointed champions of liberty. They think that liberty is something that affects every aspect and phase of human life—liberty of thought, of expression, of cultural opportunity—and that it is not to be had, even in the economic sphere, without a degree of security that is denied to millions by the present economic system.

They point out that industry, banking and commerce have reached a point where there is no such thing as merely private initiative and enterprise. For the consequences of private business enterprise affect so many persons and in such deep and enduring ways that all business is affected with a public interest. Since the consequences of business are social, society must itself look after, by means of increased organized control, the industrial and financial causes of these consequences.

There is, accordingly, no doubt in my own mind that laissez-faire liberalism is played out, largely because of the fruits of its own policies. Any system that cannot provide elementary security for millions has no claim to the title of being organized in behalf of liberty and the development of individuals. Any person and any movement whose interest in these ends is genuine and not a cover for personal advantage and power must put primary emphasis in thought and action upon the means of their attainment.

At present those means lie in the direction of increased social control and increased collectivism of effort. Humane liberalism in order to save itself must cease to deal with symptoms and go to the causes of which inequalities and oppressions are but the symptoms. In order to endure under present conditions, liberalism must become radical in the sense that, instead of using social power to ameliorate the evil consequences of the existing system, it shall use social power to change the system.

Radicalism in the minds of many, however, both among its professed adherents and its bitter enemies, is identified with a particular method of changing the system. To them, it means the change of the present system by violent overthrow. Radicalism of this sort is opposed to liberalism, and liberalism is opposed to it. For liberalism both by its history and by its own nature is committed to democratic methods of effecting social change.

The idea of forcing men to be free is an old idea, but by nature it is opposed to freedom. Freedom is not something that can be handed to men as a gift from outside, whether by old-fashioned dynastic benevolent despotisms or by new-fashioned dictatorships, whether of the proletarian or of the fascist order. It is something which can be had only as individuals participate in winning it, and this fact, rather than some particular political mechanism, is the essence of democratic liberalism.

The denial of the democratic method of achieving social control is in part the product of sheer impatience and romantic longing for a short-cut which if it were taken would defeat its own end. It is in part the fruit of the Russian revolution, oblivious of the fact that Russia never had any democratic tradition in its whole history and was accustomed to dictatorial rule in a way that is foreign to the spirit of every Western country. In part, it is the product of the capture of the machinery of democratic legislation and administration by the dominant economic power, known for short as plutocracy or "the interests."

Discontent with democracy as it operates under conditions of exploitation by special interests has justification. But the notion that the remedy is violence and a civil war between classes is a counsel of despair.

If the method of violence and civil war be adopted, the end will be either fascism, open and undisguised, or the common ruin of both parties to the struggle. The democratic method of social change is slow; it labors under many and serious handicaps imposed by the undemocratic character of what passes for democracy. But it is the method of liberalism, with its belief that liberty is the means as well as the goal and that only through the development of individuals in their voluntary cooperation with one another can the development of individuality be made secure and enduring.

II

The emphasis of earlier liberalism upon individuality and liberty defines the focal points of discussion of the philosophy of liberalism today. This earlier liberalism was itself an outgrowth, in the late eighteenth and nineteenth centuries, of the earlier revolt against oligarchical government, one which came to its culmination in the "glorious revolution" of 1688. The latter was fundamentally a demand for freedom of the taxpayer from government arbitrary action in connection with a demand for confessional freedom in religion by the Protestant churches. In the liberalism, expressly so called, demand for liberty and individual freedom of action came primarily from the rising industrial and trading class and was directed against restrictions placed by government, in legislation, common law and judicial action, and other institutions having connection with the political state, upon freedom of economic enterprise. In both cases, governmental action and the desired freedom were placed in antithesis to each other. This way of conceiving liberty has persisted; it was strengthened in this country by the revolt of the colonies and by pioneer conditions.

Nineteenth-century philosophic liberalism added, more or less because of its dominant economic interest, the conception of natural laws to that of natural rights of the Whig movement. There are natural laws, it held, in social matters as well as in physical, and these natural laws are economic in character. Political laws, on the other hand, are man-made and in that sense artificial. Governmental intervention in industry and exchange was thus regarded as a violation not only of inherent individual liberty but also of natural laws—of which supply and demand is a sample. The proper sphere of governmental action was simply to prevent and to secure redress for infringement by one, in the exercise of his liberty, of like and equal liberty of action on the part of others.

Nevertheless, the demand for freedom in initiation and conduct of business enterprise did not exhaust the content of earlier liberalism. In the minds of its chief promulgators there was included an equally strenuous demand for the liberty of mind, freedom of thought and its expression in speech, writing, print and assemblage. The earlier interest in confessional freedom was generalized, and thereby deepened as well as broadened. This demand was a product of the rational enlightenment of the eighteenth century and of the growing importance of science. The great tide of reaction that set in after the defeat of Napoleon, the demand for order and discipline, gave the agitation for freedom of thought and its expression plenty of cause and plenty of opportunity.

The earlier liberal philosophy rendered valiant service. It finally succeeded in sweeping away, especially in its home,

Great Britain, an innumerable number of abuses and restrictions. The history of social reforms in the nineteenth century is almost one with the history of liberal social thought. It is not then from ingratitude that I shall emphasize its defects, for recognition of them is essential to an intelligent statement of the elements of liberal philosophy for the present and any nearby future. The fundamental defect was its lack of perception of historic relativity. This lack is expressed in the conception of the individual as something given, complete in itself, and of liberty as a ready-made possession of the individual, only needing the removal of external restrictions in order to manifest itself. The individual of earlier liberalism was a Newtonian atom having only external time and space relations to other individuals, save in that each social atom was equipped with inherent freedom. These ideas might not have been especially harmful if they had been merely a rallying cry for practical movements. But they formed part of a philosophy and of a philosophy in which these particular ideas of individuality and freedom were asserted to be absolute and eternal truths; good for all times and all places.

This absolutism, this ignoring and denial of temporal relativity is one great reason why the earlier liberalism degenerated so easily into pseudo-liberalism. For the sake of saving time, I shall identify what I mean by this spurious liberalism, the kind of social ideas represented by the "Liberty League" and ex-President Hoover. I call it a pseudo-liberalism because it ossified and narrowed generous ideas and aspirations. Even when words remain the same, they mean something very different when they are uttered by a minority struggling against repressive measures and when expressed by a group that has attained power and then uses ideas that were once weapons of emancipation as instruments for keeping the power and wealth they have obtained. Ideas that at one time are means of producing social change assume another guise when they are used as means of preventing further social change. This fact is itself an illustration of historic relativity, and an evidence of the evil that

lay in the assertion by earlier liberalism of the immutable and
eternal character of their ideas. Because of this latter fact, the
laissez-faire doctrine was held by the degenerate school of liberals to express the very order of nature itself. The outcome was
the degradation of the idea of individuality until in the minds
of many who are themselves struggling for a wider and fuller
development of individuality, individualism has become a term
of hissing and reproach, while many can see no remedy for the
evils that have come from the use of socially unrestrained liberty in business enterprise, save change produced by violence.
The historic tendency to conceive the whole question of liberty
as a matter in which individual and government are opposed
parties has borne bitter fruit. Born of despotic government, it
has continued to influence thinking and action after government had become popular and *in theory* the servant of the
people.

I pass now to what the philosophy of liberalism would be
were its inheritance of absolutism eliminated. In the first place
such liberalism knows that an individual is nothing fixed, given
ready-made. It is something achieved, and achieved not in isolation, but with the aid and support of conditions, cultural and
physical, including in "cultural" economic, legal and political
institutions as well as science and art. Liberalism knows that
social conditions may restrict, distort and almost prevent the
development of individuality. It therefore takes an active interest in the working of social institutions that have a bearing,
positive or negative, upon the growth of individuals who shall
be rugged in fact and not merely in abstract theory. It is as
much interested in the positive construction of favorable institutions, legal, political and economic, as it is in the work of
removing abuses and overt oppressions.

In the second place, liberalism is committed to the idea of
historic relativity. It knows that the content of the individual
and freedom change with time; that this is as true of social
change as it is of individual development from infancy to
maturity. The positive counterpart of opposition to doctrinal

absolutism is experimentalism. The connection between historic relativity and experimental method is intrinsic. Time signifies change. The significance of individuality with respect to social policies alters with change of the conditions in which individuals live. The earlier liberalism in being absolute was also unhistoric. Underlying it there was a philosophy of history which assumed that history, like time in the Newtonian scheme, means only modification of external relations; that it is quantitative, not qualitative and internal. The same thing is true of any theory that assumes, like the one usually attributed to Marx, that temporal changes in society are inevitable—that is to say, are governed by a law that is not itself historical. The fact is that the historicism and the evolutionism of nineteenth-century doctrine were only half-way doctrines. They assumed that historical and developmental processes were subject to some law or formula outside temporal processes.

The commitment of liberalism to experimental procedure carries with it the idea of continuous reconstruction of the ideas of individuality and of liberty in intimate connection with changes in social relations. It is enough to refer to the changes in productivity and distribution since the time when the earlier liberalism was formulated, and the effect of these transformations, due to science and technology, upon the terms on which men associate together. An experimental method is the recognition of this temporal change in ideas and policies so that the latter shall coordinate with the facts instead of being opposed to them. Any other view maintains a rigid conceptualism and implies that facts should conform to concepts that are framed independently of temporal or historical change.

The two things essential, then, to thorough-going social liberalism are, first, realistic study of existing conditions in their movement, and, secondly, leading ideas, in the form of policies for dealing with these conditions in the interest of development of increased individuality and liberty. The first requirement is so obviously implied that I shall not elaborate it. The second point needs some amplification. Experimental method is not just messing around nor doing a little of this and a little of that in the hope that things will improve. Just as in the physical sciences, it implies a coherent body of ideas, a theory, that gives direction to effort. What is implied, in contrast to every form of absolutism, is that the ideas and theory be taken as methods of action tested and continuously revised by the consequences they produce in actual social conditions. Since they are operational in nature, they modify conditions, while the first requirement, that of basing them upon realistic study of actual conditions, brings about their continuous reconstruction.

It follows, finally, that there is no opposition in principle between liberalism as social philosophy and radicalism in action, if by radicalism is signified the adoption of policies that bring about drastic instead of piecemeal social changes. It is all a question of what kind of procedures the intelligent study of changing conditions discloses. These changes have been so tremendous in the last century, yes, in the last forty years, that it looks to me as if radical methods were now necessary. But all that the argument here requires is recognition of the fact that there is nothing in the nature of liberalism that makes it a milk-water doctrine, committed to compromise and minor "reforms." It is worth noting that the earlier liberals were regarded in their day as subversive radicals.

What has been said should make it clear that the question of method in formation and execution of policies is the central thing in liberalism. The method indicated is that of maximum reliance upon intelligence. This fact determines its opposition to those forms of radicalism that place chief dependence upon violent overthrow of existing institutions as the method of effecting desired social change. A genuine liberal will emphasize as crucial the complete correlation between the means used and the consequences that follow. The same principle which makes him aware that the means employed by pseudo-liberalism only perpetuate and multiply the evils of existing conditions makes him aware also that dependence upon sheer massed force as the means of social change decides the kind of conse-

PART II

Human Nature and Scholarship

I

CHALLENGE TO LIBERAL THOUGHT

THERE IS PROBABLY NO BETTER WAY TO REALIZE WHAT PHILOSO-
phy is about when it is living, not antiquarian, than to ask ourselves what criteria and what aims and ideals should control
our educational policies and undertakings. Such a question, if
it is systematically followed out, will bring to light things that
are morally and intellectually fundamental in the direction of
human affairs. It will disclose differences and conflicts that
are basic in society as it now exists. It will give concrete and
definite meaning to problems and principles that are remote
and abstract when they are presented in terms of philosophical
systems isolated from human needs and human struggles. For
this reason the present campaign of assault upon what is modern and new in education is to be welcomed even by those
who believe its tendency is thoroughly reactionary. It has to
be faced, and facing it will bring to light beliefs that have too
long been kept in the dark. For it is true in education as elsewhere that the Great Bad is the mixing together of things that
are contrary and opposed. The drawing of lines that is now going on will not only serve to clear up confusion in our educational estate but will tend to breathe life into the dead bones
of philosophy.

We are told that scientific subjects have been encroaching
upon literary subjects, which alone are truly humanistic. We
are told that zeal for the practical and utilitarian has resulted
in displacement of a liberal education by one that is merely
vocational, one that narrows the whole man down to that frac-
tion of his being concerned with making a living. We are told

143

that the whole tendency is away from the humane to the materialistic, from the permanently rational to the temporarily expedient—and so on. Now curiously enough it happens that some of us who disagree radically with the reasons given for criticizing our present system and equally radically with the remedy that is urged, agree that the present system (if it may be called a system) is so lacking in unity of aim, material, and method as to be something of a patchwork. We agree that an overloaded and congested curriculum needs simplification. We agree that we are uncertain as to where we are going and where we want to go, and why we are doing what we do.

In many details our criticisms of the present state of education do not differ widely from those of the critics whose fundamental premises and aims are in sharp opposition to ours. The standpoint from which criticisms are made and the direction in which reform is urged are, however, worlds apart. The issue is taking shape. We agree as to absence of unity. We differ profoundly from the belief that the evils and defects of our system spring from excessive attention to what is modern in human civilization—science, technology, contemporary social issues and problems. Rather we rest our own critical estimate on the present educational situation upon a belief that the factors that correspond to what is living in present society, the factors that are shaping modern culture, are either confusedly smothered by excessive attention to the old or are diverted into channels in which they become technical and relatively illiberal in comparison with what they would be if they were given the central position.

I begin then with the fact that we are now being told that a genuinely liberal education would require return to the models, patterns, and standards that were laid down in Greece some twenty-five hundred years ago and renewed and put into practice in the best age of feudal medievalism six and seven centuries ago. It is true that a theory of education using the word "liberal," as applied to an education having nothing to do with the "practical," was formulated in Greece. From Greece we inherit the tradition that puts "liberal" and "mechanical" education in sharp opposition to each other and that—a fact to be noted—identifies as mechanical anything and everything concerned with industry and useful commodities and services.

This philosophy was faithful to the facts of the social life in which it appeared. It translated into intellectual terms the institutions, customs, and moral attitudes that flourished in the life of Athens. As was proper, a liberal or free education was the education of a free man in the Athenian community. But this has to be placed alongside the fact, totally improper from the standpoint of modern democratic communities, that free citizens were few in number, and that their freedom had a large servile class as its substratum. The class that enjoyed the privileges of freedom and a liberal education was based upon precisely those considerations that modern liberation has steadily striven to get rid of. For a status fixed at and by birth, sex, and economic condition is just what democratic societies regard as *illiberal*. To the Greek philosopher, these differences were necessary; they were fixed "by nature." They were so established in social institutions that any other view seemed irrational even to the wisest men of the time.

This fact might well make us look with suspicion upon an educational philosophy which, at the *present* day, defines liberal education in terms that are the opposite of what is genuinely liberal. Vocational and practical education was illiberal in Greece because it was the training of a servile class. Liberal education was liberal in Greece because it was the way of life enjoyed by a small group who were free to devote themselves to higher things. They were free to do so because they lived upon the fruits of the labor of an industrially enslaved class. Moreover, industry was carried on by routine apprenticeship in ways that were handed down from parents to children.

That the models and patterns followed by craftsmen achieved a high degree of aesthetic development should not be permitted to blind us to this fact. For it marks a striking contrast with the conditions of modern industry. Methods of work are now the result of the continuous application of science. Inventions, themselves the result of application of science, are constantly encroaching upon ways of production that carry over routine and precedent. There was justification in existing conditions for the Greek who distinguished between activities that were the manifestation of rational insight or science and those that were the expression of irrational routine. But there is no excuse for such a view at the present time. There is now more natural science involved in the conduct of our industry than there is anything nearly resembling science in the conduct of our political and social affairs.

The problem of going ahead instead of going back is then a problem of liberalizing our technical and vocational education. The average worker has little or no awareness of the scientific processes embodied in the work he carries on. What he does is often to him routine and mechanical. To this extent the diagnosis the critics make of present vocational education is correct in too many cases. But their reactionary remedy involves fixation of just that which is bad in the present system. Instead of seeking an education that would make all who go to school aware of the scientific basis of industrial processes, they would draw the lines still more sharply between those who receive a vocational training, deliberately kept illiberal, and the much smaller number who enjoy a liberal education—after the Greek literary model. A truly liberal, and liberating, education would refuse today to isolate vocational training on any of its levels from a continuous education in the social, moral, and scientific contexts within which wisely administered callings and professions must function.

Not to base the materials and methods of the education that does this work upon intelligent selection and arrangement of what is growing and vital in the present, with deliberate omission of that which has served its time, is the sure way to perpetuate the confusion and conflicts of the world in which we now live. Exercise of intelligent courage to make education what it might be would result in an access of both confidence and the wisdom that would justify the confidence.

The situation is no better when we turn to the medieval version of the Greek theory of liberal education. The gulf between serf and landlord was too fixed in medieval society even to attract the attention of the most liberal-minded philosophers. It was accepted as a matter of course, or as "natural." In addition, medieval society had no political citizenship and no community life in the *civic* sense that was supreme in the Athenian city-state. Although words borrowed from Greek philosophy about liberal arts and education were profusely employed, their meanings had nothing in common with those of Athenian life. The important institution was the church, not the city-state. Consequently, in medieval thought the difference between the priest and the layman took the place occupied in Greek philosophical writings by the difference between freeman and artisan. The word *cleric* strikes the keynote of medieval culture in very much the same way that the word *citizen* sounds the keynote of Athenian life.

The result, so far as educational philosophy is concerned, explains how it is that the present reactionary movement is closer to the medieval model than to the Greek. The activity of the free Athenian citizen was directly concerned with the affairs and problems of a civic community in which theocratic interests and religious rites were a regular and subordinate part of the life of a secular and temporal community. Aristotle, moreover, taught that even free political life was not completely free from the taint of the practical. The only completely free life was that devoted to pursuit of science and philosophy. And nature, not the supernatural, was at the heart of ancient Greek philosophy.

To the Greek scientist-philosopher firsthand perception of nature, if not through the senses then through the "intellect," was the source of truth. Writings bequeathed by the past were used for the suggestions they contained, as materials to set forth alternative possibilities. They were never taken as final authority. The one thing forbidden was to permit the opinions of others to come between vision and the facts of nature. But in medieval culture that which had already been said, written down and transmitted by linguistic means from generation to generation, became *the* final authority. It is enough to cite the role of what are significantly known as "the Scriptures." I do not mean that there was not a great display of intellectual acuteness and sharpening of wits. But it was directed to the study, interpretation, adaptation, and organization of letters, of what was linguistically transmitted from previous learning. By and large these writings took the place nature itself had held in Greek philosophy and science. *They* constituted the world to be investigated.

Nevertheless, given the conditions of Europe at the time, this dependence upon letters as the medium of communication with past knowledge was practically necessary. To be liberal is all one with being liberating, with effecting a release of human powers. Failure to realize this is the source of one of the great errors of our neo-scholastics who suppose that the subject matter of a liberal education is fixed in itself. Linguistic arts and the written materials of the past exercised a liberating function in the Middle Ages as nothing else could have done. For all northern Europe was only just emerging from a state of barbarism. Historically speaking, it is practically impossible to see what effective tutor and guide the movement could have had save acquaintance with the products of the infinitely higher culture developed centuries before the Mediterranean basin. Language, letters, was the sole medium of contact with those products. Clerics were the sole class possessing both the mastery of linguistic tools and the moral authority to make them central in education.

Social and cultural conditions since the Middle Ages have undergone a great, a revolutionary, change. In spirit, we are nearer the culture of antiquity than we are to that of the medieval period. Great as is the change from a servile to a free basis in organization of social relations, it can be said with considerable truth that the change is in line with *principles* stated in Athens. The full significance of these principles could not be perceived by their authors because of the practical pressure exerted by social institutions. Historical illiteracy is thus the outstanding trait of those critics who urge return to the ideas of the Greek-medieval period as if the ideas of the two ages were the same because philosophers of the medieval period used some of the verbal formulas set forth by philosophers of the earlier period.

Language is still fundamentally important in education. Communication is the feature that definitely marks off man from other creatures; it is the condition without which culture would not exist. But the notion that language, linguistic skills and studies can be used for the same ends and by the same methods under contemporary conditions as in Greek, Alexandrian, or medieval times is as absurd in principle as it would be injurious in practice were it adopted. The attempt to reestablish linguistic skills and materials as the center of education, and to do it under the guise of "education for freedom" or a "liberal" education, is directly opposed to all that democratic countries cherish as freedom. The idea that an adequate education of any kind can be obtained by means of a miscellaneous assortment of a hundred books, more or less, is laughable when viewed practically. A five-foot bookshelf for adults, to be read, reread, and digested at leisure throughout a lifetime, is one thing. Crowded into four years and dealt out in fixed doses, it is quite another thing. In theory and basic aim, however, it is not funny. For it marks a departure from what is sound in the Greek view of knowledge as a product of intelligence exercised at first hand. It marks reversion to the medieval view of dependence upon the final authority of what others have found out—or supposed they had found out—and without the historical grounds that gave reason to the scholars of the Middle Ages.

The reactionary movement is dangerous (or would be if it made serious headway) because it ignores and in effect denies the principle of experimental inquiry and firsthand observation that is the lifeblood of the entire advance made in the sciences —an advance so marvelous that the progress in knowledge made in uncounted previous millenniums is almost nothing in comparison. It is natural enough that the chief advocates of the scholastic reaction should be literary men with defective scientific educations, or else theologians who are convinced in advance of the existence of a supernaturally founded and directed Institution, whose official utterances rank as fixed and final truths because they are beyond the scope of human inquiry and criticism.

Mr. Hutchins wrote as follows:*

"We know that there is a natural moral law, and we can understand what it is because we know that man has a nature, and we can understand it. The nature of man, which is the same everywhere, is obscured but not obliterated by the differing conventions of different cultures. The specific quality of human nature . . . is that man is a rational and spiritual being . . ."

By his inherent and necessary essence, then, man is the same in all ages, climes, and cultures. Nothing that can happen to him, or in the physical, biological, and social world of which man is a part, can make any difference to his nature. The principles that have authority over his conduct and his moral beliefs are therefore fixed and immutable. Moreover, they are perceived by a faculty independent of, and supreme over, the methods by which patient inquiry, with the aid of experimental observation, discovers natural facts of self, society, and the physical world.

There is nothing novel in this view. We are familiar with it from early childhood. It is a conventionally established part of a large portion of our training in family and Sunday school. Nevertheless, it is the expression of a provincial and conventional point of view, of a culture that is pre-scientific in the sense that science bears today. Men of at least equal penetra-

* Fortune, June, 1943.

tion (Aristotle himself, for example) with those now asserting the absolute uniformity of human nature and morals taught the same thing about natural objects. Astronomical and biological sciences were once as firmly based upon eternal uniformity as moral science and philosophy are now asserted to be. In astronomy, it was held that the higher heavens have always had and always will have, with everything in them, an unswerving circular movement. The teachings of present astronomical science would then have seemed like a proclamation of chaotic turmoil. In biology, the complete fixity and uniformity of species of plants and animals were taken to be the rational and necessary foundational truths for all scientific knowledge.

In short, the view now so confidently put forth about morals once prevailed in natural science. The foundation of both is that the uniform and unchangeable is inherently superior in perfection and truth to anything subject to change. From the standpoint of society, it is easy to understand the rise of this view. It is appropriate to societies ruled by custom—they fear change as the source of instability and disorder. It was also a natural view when observation was restricted by lack of instruments. Without the use of a telescope, variations in the positions of "fixed stars" could not be noticed. Changes of kind or species in plants and animals were observable only when monstrosities appeared. Belief in the eternal uniformity of human nature is thus the surviving remnant of a belief once universally held about the heavens and about all living creatures. Scientific method and conclusions have had little effect upon persons whose education is predominantly literary. Otherwise they would not continue to assert in one field a belief that science has abandoned everywhere else.

The group in question does not, however, oppose the teaching of science. Far from it. Their claim is that the subject matter of natural science is of subordinate importance; and that, when all is said and done, it belongs with the subjects whose value is technical, utilitarian, practical. Thereby they endorse and tend to confirm the split between natural means of authentic knowing, on the one hand, and everything having moral, ideal, and "spiritual" importance, on the other.

It is hard to see how any thoughtful person can view a split of this kind lightly. There was no such separation in Greek and medieval "science." All fundamental truths about the natural world and natural objects in their science concerned what was as eternal and unchanging as were moral ends and principles. In fact, Aristotle, the authority in the medieval period in respect to natural and temporal matters, expressly assigned to the subject matter of astronomy and biology a higher position in respect to complete constancy than to moral knowledge. For he observed the undoubted fact that moral practices and aims change from place to place and time to time.

In truth, the present-day alliance between those who appeal to Greek philosophy and those who appeal to medieval philosophy is tactical rather than basic. They are allies in a common dislike, co-dwellers in a Cave of Adullam. They have the same dislikes without having the same loyalty and goal. Greek science is indeed marked by traits that are supranatural from the standpoint of the present science of nature. Nevertheless, according to Greek science the subjects of science were profoundly natural and inherently reasonable. According to medieval theological philosophy, the basis of all ultimate moral principles is supernatural—not merely above nature and reason, but so far beyond the scope of the latter that they must be miraculously revealed and sustained.

Some of the theological fellow travelers of Mr. Hutchins make this point clear. For they characteristically introduce a complete division between political, civic, and social morality and personal morality. The former is *"natural"*; its virtues are directed toward "the good of civilization." The latter has to take into account "the *supratemporal* destiny" of man. The teaching of "natural morality" merely is likely to be influenced by "what are *called* the virtues of political life and civilization." It tends to neglect or disparage personal morality, which "is the root of *all* morality"—a morality, be it remembered, that is supernatural in origin and destination.

The dilemma in which liberal writers of this school find themselves is illustrated in the fact that they make a plea for an "integral humanism," and for avoidance of cleavage. They then set up a series of complete cleavages on their own account. There is one between man and the supernatural; one between the temporal and the eternal; one between humanity and divinity; one between the inner and the outer; and finally one between the civic and social (or things of this world generally) and the alleged supratemporal destiny of man—needing, of course, a special supernatural and infallible church to bridge the gulf.

From one point of view, these authors simply manifest the division and conflict characteristic of our present civilization. But in addition they recommend its systematic fixation as the cure of the evils that the cleavage occasions. At that, in view of what the two schools have in common, the one represented by our theological philosopher seems to have the advantage over its temporary partner. For they claim to speak for a divinely founded church, which is permanently directed from on high. When, therefore, the utterances of fallible human reason vary and when the merely civic moralities of different peoples conflict with one another, it can authoritatively point out *the* truth.

The issue raised in educational philosophy is thus significant as a manifestation of a cleft that now marks every phase and aspect of philosophy. It presents the difference between an outlook that goes to the past for instruction and for guidance, and one that holds that philosophy, if it is to be of help in the present situation, must pay supreme heed to movements, needs, problems, and resources that are distinctively modern. This latter view is often countered by caricaturing it. It is said to be based upon insensate love of novelty and change, upon devotion to the modern just because it happens to come later in the course of time. The actual state of the case, however, is that there are factors at work in contemporary life that are of transcendent value in promise, if not yet in achievement. They are experimental science and experimental method in the field of knowledge. This field includes a definite morale and ethic as well as definite conclusions about man and the world. The second modern factor is the democratic spirit in human relations. The third is technological control of the energies of nature in behalf of human ends. All three are closely linked. The revolution in natural science is the parent of inventions of instruments and processes that provide the substantial body of modern industrial technology. This fact is so obvious as to be undeniable—though there are some persons superficial enough to attribute the great advance in industry not to the methods and conclusions of modern science but to love of pecuniary power. What perhaps is not equally obvious is that the marvelous advance in natural science has come about because of the breaking down of the wall existing in ancient and medieval institutions between "higher" things of a purely intellectual and "spiritual" nature and the "lower" things of a "practical" and "material" nature.

For it is a historical fact, evident to all who are willing to look, that the change from relative sterility and stagnation to a career of fruitfulness and continued progress in science began when inquirers used the instruments and processes of socially despised industry as agencies by means of which to know nature. Then the change achieved in production of commodities and services was a great factor in breaking down feudal institutions. Substitution of easy communication in place of the isolation of peoples, groups, and classes has been an agency in bringing the democratic movement into existence.

I come back to the fact that we are living in a mixed and divided life. We are pulled in opposite directions. We have not as yet a philosophy that is modern in other than a chronological sense. We do not have as yet an educational or any other social institution that is not a mixture of opposed elements. Division between methods and conclusions in natural science and those prevailing in morals and religion is a serious matter, from whatever angle it be regarded. It means a society that is not unified in its most important concerns.

I do not understand that those who are urging return to the ancient foundation in morals and social institutions wish to return to earlier conditions in natural science; nor yet to abolish all modern inventions and appliances that are the fruit of experimental extension of science. But the logical and practical import of their scheme is simply to fixate the division, the split from which we suffer. The spirit and method of the pre-scientific period is to prevail in the "higher" sphere while science and technology are relegated to an inherently lower and separate compartment of life. Preaching, or else an external institutional authority, is to keep the latter in its place.

The one outstanding issue concerns, then, the direction in which we are to move. Are we compelled to hold that one method obtains in natural science and another, radically different, in moral questions? Scientific method is now finding its way into the psychological field; it is already at home in anthropological study. As the conclusions reached in these studies find their way into general acceptance, is a conflict between science and moral beliefs to replace the old conflict between science and what was taken to be religion? And the question is the more pertinent because the religion in question was also the expression of a pre-scientific stage of culture.

The issue as it offers itself in the educational field brings home in a vivid and striking manner this problem of the direction to be taken in philosophy. I do not mean that the question in philosophy is as momentous as the direction we are to take in our practical affairs—in education, industry, and politics. But the two are closely connected. The old metaphysical and theological philosophies reflected the social conditions in which *they* were formulated. By their translation into terms of reason, these conditions were given support. The traditional philosophies provided guidance in the direction taken by social movements. They strive to exercise these functions today. They succeed in so doing, however, only to the extent of introducing confusion and conflict.

I hope I have made it clear that I have no sympathy with the philosophy underlying the views I have been considering. But its active appearance on the scene is to be welcomed. Philosophy needed to be taken out of the hands of those who have identified it with barren intellectual gymnastic exercise and purely verbal analyses. Perhaps it took the severe jolt of the present reaction to bring philosophy back to man. At all events, the educational philosophy here discussed raises all the philosophical problems that now demand attention if philosophy is to have anything to say in the present crisis.

The issue of the immutable versus the changing involves the question of whether the method of inquiry and test that has wrought marvels in one field is to be applied so as to extend and advance our knowledge in moral and social matters. Is there an impassable gulf between science and morals? Or are principles and general truths in morals of the same kind as in science—namely, working hypotheses that on one hand condense the results of continued prior experience and inquiry, and on the other hand direct further fruitful inquiry whose conclusions in turn test and develop for further use the working principles used? Suppose it *were* true in the abstract that moral principles are as fixed and eternally uniform as they are said to be. Has anyone indicated even in the roughest way how they are then to be applied? At bottom the issue is drawn between dogmas (so rigid that they ultimately must appeal to force) and recourse to intelligent observation guided by the best wisdom already in our possession, which is the heart of scientific method.

Let me give one illustration of the application of scientific thinking to what was formerly regarded as an unchangeable absolute. It is drawn from the man who more than any other single person is the begetter in philosophy of an attitude and outlook distinctively American, Charles Peirce. The illustration is taken from a subject of crucial moral import, the meaning of truth. Over against the traditional view of truth as a fixed structure of eternal and unchanging principles already in our possession to which everything else should be made to conform, Peirce said that truth "is that concordance of an abstract statement with the ideal limit toward which endless investigation would tend to bring scientific belief." This concordance may be possessed even now and here by a scientific belief in case there is "confession of its inaccuracy and one-sidedness," since this "confession is an essential ingredient of truth." We have here, as in a nutshell, a statement of the profound difference that is made in a crucial instance between belief in fixity and in change. There is also the definite implication that change can mean continuous growth, development, liberation, and cooperation, while fixity means the dogmatism that historically has always exhibited itself in intolerance and brutal persecution of the dissenter and the inquirer. Faith in endlessly pursued inquiry and in an undogmatic friendly attiture toward present possessions (which is the spur to continued persistent effort) is treated by those whose education has failed to encompass the scientific spirit as a kind of systematic indifference and carelessness amounting to demoralization.

The very heart of political democracy is adjudication of social differences by discussion and exchange of views. This method provides a rough approximation to the method of effecting change by means of experimental inquiry and test: the scientific method. The very foundation of the democratic procedure is dependence upon experimental production of social change; an experimentation directed by working principles that are tested and developed in the very process of being tried out in action. Its operation is compromised, however, by the persistent influence of the very philosophy we are urged to fall back upon.

It is no mere accident that continental Europe, which is now the most disturbed portion of the world and the source of tragic disturbance everywhere else, is just that part that has stuck most closely to the educational philosophy we are now being urged to go back to. America must be looked upon as either an offshoot of Europe, culturally speaking, or as a New World in other than a geographical sense. To take the latter view is neither brash patriotic nationalism nor yet a brand of isolationism. It is an acknowledgment of work to be done. Europe has, at least till very recently, led the world in scientific achievement, and it will be a long time before America will rival what the Old World has accomplished in the plastic arts and in literature. But continental Europe in general and Germany in particular has been the home of the practices and the philosophy based on strict separation between science as technical and ever changing and morals conceived in terms of fixed, unchanging principles. If the name "New World" applies to the American scene, it is because we have the task of bringing into cooperative union the things that the philosophy and the education to which we are being urged to return have kept divided.

In short, the chief influence in retarding and preventing the conscious realization that will give unity and steadiness to the democratic movement is precisely the philosophy of dogmatic rigidity and uniformity. In consequence, the chief opportunity and chief responsibility of those who call themselves philosophers are to make clear the intrinsic kinship of democracy with the methods of directing change that have revolutionized science. In that way and only in that way can we be rid of the dualism of standards, aims, and methods—that is to say the very division from which we are now suffering. Technological industry is the creation of science. It is also the most widely and deeply influential factor in the practical determination of social conditions. The most immediate human problem of our age is to effect a transformation of the immense resources the new technology has put in our hands into positive instruments of human being. The contribution that the reactionary philosophy makes is to urge that technology and science are intrinsically of an inferior and illiberal nature!

What exists in social philosophy at the present time is

largely an abstract disputation between something called "individualism" and something called "socialism." But the problem is a concrete one. How shall this and that definite factory and field operation be made to contribute to the educative release and growth of human capacities, as well as to production of a large and reasonably cheap supply of material goods? The problem is one that, by its own terms, can be dealt with only by the continuous application of the scientific method of experimental observation and test. Those who feel in need of a specific example of the connection between science and morals, between "natural" facts and human values, will find it here.

A philosophy that glorifies the gulf between the "material" and the "spiritual," between immutable principles and social conditions in a state of rapid change, stands in the way of dealing effectively with this dominant issue. The solution of the issue will not, of course, take place in philosophy. But the opportunity of philosophy is to help get rid of intellectual habits that now stand in the way of a solution.

As far as school education is a part of the required practical means, educational theory or philosophy has the task and the opportunity of helping to break down the philosophy of fixation that bolsters external authority in opposition to free cooperation. It must contest the notion that morals are something wholly separate from and above science and scientific method. It must help banish the conception that the daily work and vocation of man are negligible in comparison with literary pursuits, and that human destiny here and now is of slight importance in comparison with some supernatural destiny. It must accept wholeheartedly the scientific way, not merely of technology, but of life in order to achieve the promise of modern democratic ideals.

2

THE REVOLT AGAINST SCIENCE

IT WOULD BE A WASTE OF TIME TO ARGUE THAT AT THE PRESENT time we are in the presence of a widespread revolt against science, for its presence is obvious in almost every field. In education it takes the form of setting the humanities up against the sciences, accompanied with the clamorous assertion that all the ailments and failures of the present school system—numerous and serious beyond a peradventure—are the result of subordination of the "humanities" to the sciences. And if I place quotation marks about the word *humanities* it is because the attack which is made in this field proceeds *from* teachers of literary subjects and proceeds *by* identification of the humane with the linguistic and literary.

Upon the side of theory, of pseudo-philosophy, the attack rests upon calling the sciences "materialistic" while literary subjects are identified with whatever is idealistic and "spiritual" in our traditions and institutions. This position rests back upon belief in the separation of man from nature. Man is taken not only as lord over nature but as lord in its oldest and most discredited sense—that of a despotic monarch supposed to rule by mere fiat. This separation, the most fundamental of all forms of isolationism, completely ignores the daily interests and concerns of the great mass of human beings which are bound up in the most intimate way with the conditions of nature they have to face—conditions which so largely affect their welfare and destiny as human beings. Anyone who will allow himself to observe the spectacle offered to view by the great mass of human beings in the matter of making and having a decent

160

living alone will be aware of the monstrous insolence of identification of the humanities with linguistics and literatures.

The fact, however, that the identification is made, and that the indictment of the sciences is then made to depend upon it, is intensely illuminating. It spotlights the background of the revolt against science; it delineates the genuinely human values and ends at stake, and points to the only road which leads to a genuine and not a sham advancement of humanism. With reference to the background, with reference to the source of the revolt, it points straight to those who have "authority" against movements which threaten their supremacy by ushering in a new, wider and more humane order. Fundamentally, the attack proceeds from representatives of those who have enjoyed the power of control and regulation of other human beings because of the existing setup in political, ecclesiastical and economic institutions. Superficially, and more vocally, it proceeds from teachers who find that their place and prestige in the educational system is being impaired, and who innocently, that is ignorantly, do the work of campfollowers.

It will be found significant as well as interesting to compare the present revolt against science with the earlier movement that bears the name of "Conflict of Science and Religion." In that earlier warfare, attacks upon science hinged upon certain general conclusions reached by the sciences, first in astronomical and finally in biological science. The attacks centered upon the destructive doctrinal effect of the new conclusions upon beliefs that had been established in a primitive stage of human history, and that, in the course of intervening millennia, had become invested with all kinds of intellectual, institutional and emotional sanctions.

It can hardly be said that the scientific doctrines won a complete victory. "Fundamentalism" is still rife in both Roman Catholic and Protestant denominations. But upon the whole the climate of opinion became adjusted to the new views. Attacks upon them are now of sectarian rather than of general social importance. The present revolt against science goes

deeper than the earlier one—and this in spite of victories won
by scientific men in the intervening period. We no longer have
a battle between a new set of beliefs in special matters and old
ones which had endeared themselves to the human heart. The
attack upon science is now an attack upon the attitude, the
standpoint, the methods, which are science, with especial reference to their bearing upon human institutional problems, focussing on the supreme issue of who and what shall have authority
to influence and to give direction to life.

I shall not attempt here to criticize the underlying philosophy used to provide justification for the attack upon science
whenever anyone ventures to apply scientific methods and
results beyond the technical "material" now so charitably allotted to it—provided, of course, it doesn't dare to trespass
upon the moral domain of humane concerns. I want rather to
point out some of the factors which confer a show of justification upon the attacks made upon science as "materialistic," and
upon its materialism as hostile to the humane values. We are
all familiar with the distinction commonly drawn between
"pure" and "applied" science. I do not intend to repeat here a
point which I have repeatedly made elsewhere—namely, that
the sharp division which is made is an intellectual relic from the
time when, in Aristotle's phraseology, "theory" had to do with
things which were supreme because divine and eternal, and
"practice" had to do with things that were merely mundane,
things at worst menial and at best earth-bound and transient.

I want rather to call attention to the fact that however good
may be the grounds a small class of intellectuals have for keeping pure and applied science apart, the great mass of people
come in contact with "science" *only* in its applications. Science
to them *is* what it means in their life day by day; the consequences it has on their daily occupations, the uses, enjoyments
and limitations of use and enjoyment that mark their lives in
homes, neighborhoods and factories; on their work and in failures to get work.

"Applied" science means, then, somewhat quite different to

them from what it means to the philosopher who is engaged in making distinctions. It means something quite different from what it means to the inventor who is engaged in translating mathematical-physical formulae into machines and other power devices. For it doesn't mean to him technology in the abstract; it means technology *as it operates under existing political-economic-cultural conditions.* Here and not in science, whether pure or abstract, is where materialism as the enemy of the humane is found; and here, not elsewhere, is where attacks should be directed.

When those who pridefully label themselves humanists, guardians of the moral and ideal interests of mankind, begin to attack the habits and institutions which cause the technological applications of science to work with harshness on such vast portions of the population, limiting alike their education and their other opportunities for a generous human life, transforming the potential instruments of security into devices for producing mass-insecurity, shall we have reason for believing that their concern for humane values is honest, instead of a device, deliberate or innocent, for maintaining some form of institutionalized class interest. *Human is as human does.*

3

THE RELATION OF SCIENCE AND PHILOSOPHY
AS THE BASIS OF EDUCATION

EMPIRICAL AND EXPERIMENTAL PHILOSOPHY HAS NO QUARREL
with science, either in itself or in its application to education.
On the contrary, scientific conclusions and methods are the
chief ally of an empirical philosophy of education. For according to empirical philosophy, science provides the only means
we have for learning about man and the world in which he
lives. Some have thought that this fact makes philosophy unnecessary. They have supposed that the admission that science
is supreme in the field of knowledge covers the whole ground
of human experience. The elimination does rule out *one* kind
of philosophy, namely, that which held that philosophy is a
higher form of knowledge than the scientific kind, one which
furnishes knowledge of ultimate higher reality. But it does not
follow from the elimination of this particular type of philosophy
that philosophy itself must go.

It would follow if man were simply and only a knowing
being. But he is not. He is also an acting being, a creature with
desires, hopes, fears, purposes and habits. To the average person
knowledge itself is of importance because of its bearing upon
what he needs to do and to make. It helps him in clarifying his
wants, in constructing his ends and in finding means for realizing them. There exist, in other words, values as well as known
facts and principles, and philosophy is concerned primarily with
values—with the ends for the sake of which man acts. Given the
most extensive and accurate system of knowledge, and man is

still faced with the question of what he is going to do about it and what he is going to do with the knowledge in his possession.

In this matter of the connection of what is known with values, science is an ally of an empirical philosophy against absolute philosophies which pretend that fixed and eternal truths are known by means of organs and methods that are independent of science. The objection to this position is not merely theoretical. The practical objections to it are that it strengthens appeal to authority and promotes controversies which cannot be settled by the use of the methods of inquiry and proof that have been worked out in the sciences. The only remaining alternative is the use of coercion and force, either openly or covertly through falling back on customs and institutions as they happen to exist. There is no great danger that the present-day revival in some quarters of Greek and medieval philosophies of eternal first principles will make much headway as a theoretical philosophy. There is always danger that such philosophies will have practical influence in reinforcing established social authority that is exercised in behalf of maintenance of the *status quo.* Against this danger, an experimental philosophy stands in firm alliance with the methods by which the natural sciences arrive at warranted truths.

The philosophy of education is not a poor relation of general philosophy even though it is often so treated even by philosophers. It is ultimately the most significant phase of philosophy. For it is through the processes of education that knowledge is obtained, while these educational processes do not terminate in mere acquisition of knowledge and related forms of skill. They attempt to integrate the knowledge gained into enduring dispositions and attitudes. It is not too much to say that education is *the* outstanding means by which union of knowledge and the values that actually work in actual conduct is brought about. The difference between educational practices that are influenced by a well-thought-out philosophy, and practices that are not so influenced is that between education conducted with some clear idea of the ends in the way of ruling attitudes of desire and purpose that are to be created, and an education that is conducted blindly, under the control of customs and traditions that have not been examined or in response to immediate social pressures. This difference does not come about because of any inherent sacredness in what is called philosophy, but because any effort to clarify the ends to be attained is, as far as it goes, philosophical.

The need for such systematic clarification is especially urgent at the present time. Applications of natural science have made an enormous difference in human relations. They have revolutionized the means of production and distribution of commodities and services. They have effected an equally great change in communication and all the means for influencing the public opinion upon which political action depends. These applications decide, more than any other force or set of forces, the conditions under which human beings live together and under which they act, enjoy and suffer. Moreover, they have produced communities that are in a state of rapid change. Wherever the effect of the applications of science has been felt, human relations have ceased to be static. Old forms have been invaded and often undermined, in the family, in politics and even in moral and religious habits as well as in the narrower field of economic arrangements. Almost all current social problems have their source here. Finally, ends and values that were formed in the pre-scientific period and the institutions of great power that were formed in the same period retain their influence. Human life, both individually and collectively, is disturbed, confused and conflicting.

Either the instrumentalities of education will ignore this state of affairs and the schools will go their own way, confining themselves for the most part to providing standardized knowledge and forms of skill as ends in themselves, modified only by concessions to temporary social pressures, or they will face the question of the relation of school-education to the needs and possibilities of the social situation. If the latter problem is faced, then there arise problems of the re-adaptation of materials of the curriculum, methods of instruction and the social organization of the school. A philosophy of education can not settle once for all how these problems shall be resolved. But it can enforce perception of the nature of these problems, and can give suggestions of value as to the only ways in which they can satisfactorily be dealt with. Administrators and teachers who are imbued with the ideas can test and develop them in their actual work so that, through union of theory and practice, the philosophy of education will be a living, growing thing.

I come back, then, to the question of the alliance of empirical pragmatic philosophy with science against both a philosophy of truths and principles that are alleged to be superior to any that can be ascertained by empirical methods of science, and also against dogmatic authority, custom, routine and the pressure of immediate circumstances. Science used in the educational field can ascertain the actual facts, and can generalize them on the basis of relations of cause and effect. It can not itself settle the value of the consequences that result from even the best use of more economical and effective methods as causes of effects produced. The consequences have to be evaluated in the light of what is known about social problems, evils and needs. But without the knowledge of actual conditions and of relations of cause and effect, any values that are set up as ends are bare ideals in the sense in which "ideal" means utopian, without means for its realization.

I shall mention two or three matters in which the need for cooperation between philosophy and science is especially intimate. Since scientific method depends upon first-hand experimentally controlled experiences, any philosophic application of the scientific point of view will emphasize the need of such experiences in the school, as over against mere acquisition of ready-made information that is supplied in isolation from the students' own experience. So far, it will be in line with what is called the "progressive" movement in education. But it will be an influence in counteracting any tendencies that may exist in progressive education to slur the importance of continuity in the experiences that are had and the importance of organization. Unless the science of education on its own ground and behalf emphasizes *subject-matters* which contain within themselves the promise and power of continuous growth in the direction of organization, it is false to its own position as scientific. In cooperation with a philosophy of education, it can lend invaluable aid in seeing to it that the chosen subject-matters are also such that they progressively develop toward formation of attitudes of understanding the world in which students and teachers live and towards forming the attitudes of purpose, desire and action which will make pupils effective in dealing with social conditions.

Another point of common interest concerns the place in the schools of the sciences, especially the place of the habits which form scientific attitude and method. The sciences had to battle against entrenched foes to obtain recognition in the curriculum. In a formal sense, the battle has been won, but not yet in a substantial sense. For scientific subject-matter is still more or less segregated as a special body of facts and truths. The full victory will not be won until every subject and lesson is taught in connection with its bearing upon creation and growth of the kind of power of observation, inquiry, reflection and testing that are the heart of scientific intelligence. Experimental philosophy is at one with the genuine spirit of a scientific attitude in the endeavor to obtain for scientific method this central place in education.

Finally, the science and philosophy of education can and should work together in overcoming the split between knowledge and action, between theory and practice, which now affects both education and society so seriously and harmfully. Indeed, it is not too much to say that institution of a happy marriage between theory and practice is in the end the chief meaning of a science and a philosophy of education that work together for common ends.

4

RELIGION, SCIENCE AND PHILOSOPHY

MR. BERTRAND RUSSELL BEGINS HIS IMPORTANT BOOK WITH THE statement that "Science and religion are both aspects of social life." * Few, I suppose, would question this statement as far as religion is concerned. It is often ignored with respect to science. For the latter is currently treated as if it were an abstract intellectual pursuit having at most but accidental and external contacts with social forces and institutions. Yet the historic conflict of religion and science since the sixteenth century, the theme of Mr. Russell's work, cannot be understood save as full heed is given to the proposition Mr. Russell puts at the forefront of his discussion. For, ultimately, the conflict is between two opposed conceptions of the authority by which beliefs are to be formed and regulated, the beliefs in question affecting every phase of life from care of the body to moral endeavor.

The need for authority is a constant need of man. For it is the need for principles that are both stable enough and flexible enough to give direction to the processes of living in its vicissitudes and uncertainties. Libertarians have often weakened their case by the virtual assumption that authority in every form and mode is the great enemy. In making this assumption, they play directly into the hands of those who insist upon the necessity of some external and dogmatic authority, whether ecclesiastical or political or a mixture of both. The underlying problem of recent centuries is the question of whether and how scientific method, which is the method of intelligence in experimental action, can provide the authority that earlier centuries

* *Religion and Science.*

sought in fixed dogmas. The conflict of science and religion is one phase of this conflict.

Indeed, the history of man is largely a history of the blind struggles of mankind to satisfy the need for authoritative direction in the conduct of life. It is the story of the places in which men have thought they found the seat of authority. It has been a blind struggle because men did not know what they were after, and in consequence have grasped at whatever the accidents of history and of social conditions have placed in a condition of temporary control. The history is thus one of recurrent disappointments and kaleidoscopic shifts. Until the rise of scientific method, the one constant thing amid all the changes was that the seat of authority was placed outside the patient and cumulative inquiries of intelligence, in some institution from which final principles and rules were supposed to emanate. In its early beginnings, the men who committed themselves to inquiry and experimentation were not aware of the import of what they were doing. They were moved chiefly by avid curiosity and by impatience with the ignorance and confusion they found about them. But in view of the fact that their efforts carried with them an ultimate change in the seat of authority, there is no cause for wonder in the spectacle of the struggle which has gone on in every domain of belief since the seventeenth century. Perhaps the chief cause for surprise is that the struggle has not been even more bitter and that science has won as many victories as it has.

Were it not for the depth and scope of the issue involved, the report which Mr. Russell gives of the conflicts in astronomy, in biology, in medicine, in psychology and morals, would be enormously depressing. For it is largely a record of stupidities that in the light of present knowledge seem incredible and of recurring evidence of inability to learn from past defeats as the conflict moved on from one terrain to another. When the record is viewed as one of the growing development of human intelligence out of an animal-like stage with its predominance of emotional fantasy and brute power, the story is exhilarating rather than depressing. Or it would be such were it not for a matter which is the unifying motif of Mr. Russell's book. As he says in the early pages of his volume, "The rise of new religions in Russia and Germany, equipped with new means of missionary activity provided by science, has again put the issue in doubt, as it was at the beginning of the scientific epoch." As he says toward the close, "The threat to intellectual freedom is greater in our day than at any time since 1660; but it does not now come from the Christian churches. It comes from governments, which, owing to the modern danger of chaos and anarchy, have succeeded to the sacrosanct character formerly belonging to the ecclesiastical authorities." And again, "The newer religions are taking the place of Christianity, and repeating the errors of which Christianity has repented."

This state of affairs is the poignant issue raised by Mr. Russell's book. It is that which I propose to consider. The detailed contents of Mr. Russell's book are accessible to all; his lucidity and felicity of expression are ever the despair of lesser writers, and in this volume he has almost surpassed himself. The material in the way of facts is freely drawn from Andrew D. White's monumental *Warfare of Science with Theology* and Lecky's hardly less monumental *History of Rationalism in Europe*. The material, however, is compressed and presented in sharp relief. Each phase of the conflict is made to stand out in clear perspective. It is unnecessary to give a synopsis or a paraphrase. But the issue raised is, in my judgment, the most momentous the world faces at present. By all the signs of the times it is one that is going to grow in intensity and widen in area in coming years.

The question, as I see it, is twofold. What is the cause of the sudden decline of faith in the method of free, experimental inquiry and of the recrudescence of dogmatic authorities, backed by physical force? The other question is: What has human society to gain from accepting the method of science as authoritative in the beliefs that direct human action—accepting it, that is, not nominally but in operative action? The two questions point different ways. But I do not see how we can tell what science might do for us unless we first have some notion of its seeming eclipse, almost collapse, coming after a time, not so far long ago, when it seemed to be triumphant all along the line. Why is it, then, that after a period of great technical success, the position of science is so subordinate and so precarious over so much of the world? For I see no escape from either one or other of two alternatives. Either the method of intelligence is perpetually doomed to relative impotence because it is a feeble part of human nature in comparison with habit, emotion, and the impulses of some to power and of others to subjection; or else there are special causes for the present decline in the authority of science.

The historical causes for the decline of science are found in large measure in the fact intimated in an earlier sentence when I spoke of the *technical* successes of science. Mr. Russell justly distinguishes between the scientific temper and the scientific technique. The former is "cautious, tentative, and piecemeal; it does not imagine that it knows the whole truth, or even at its best knowledge is wholly true. It knows that every doctrine needs emendation sooner or later, and that the necessary emendation requires freedom of investigation and freedom of discussion." It starts from observed facts, not with fixed general truths from which particular truths can be deductively derived. It arrives at its general rules through experimental observation of many individual occurrences, and it employs general rules when arrived at as working hypotheses, not as eternal and immutable truths. In the course of time, different hypotheses are sufficiently confirmed by observed facts to become theories, and these theories converge to form a still more extensive generalization. But while theologies, from the most primitive to the most elaborate systems, start from general principles, assured in part by "pure reason" and in part by revelation from ultimate divine authority, scientific generalizations are conclusions and are conclusions that are subject to revision as inquiry proceeds. "Knowledge ceases to be a mental mirror of the universe and becomes a practical tool in the manipulation of matter."

Scientific technique, as distinguished from the scientific temper, is concerned with the methods by which matter is manipulated. It is the source of special technologies, as in the application of electricity to daily life; it is concerned with immediate fruits of a practical kind in a sense in which *practical* has a special and technical meaning—power stations, broadcasting, lighting, the telephone, the ignition system of automobiles. "The practical experts who employ scientific technique, and still more the government and large firms which employ the practical experts, acquire a quite different temper from that of men of science—a temper full of a sense of limitless power, of arrogant certainty, and of pleasure in manipulation of even human material."

What these facts, which seem to me to be undeniable, show is that, after all, the scientific temper, the method of intelligent experiment, made but little progress even during the period when it was not only winning technical triumphs but was displacing earlier dogmatic beliefs about the heavens, about the human body, about the origin and growth of vegetable and animal forms. Science took effect in modifying beliefs on a multitude of special matters. It displaced beliefs that were fruit of early emotional fancies which by the accidents of history had become embodied in scriptures and incorporated in the structure of the creeds that were to be accepted if the individual soul was to be saved. It also revolutionized, through its technological applications, industry and commerce, affecting the details of daily work, recreation, domestic economy, and comfort. But when the history of the victories of science is examined, its triumphs are found to be confined to these special fields, save for a relatively small group of working men of science.

"Science," in other words, is still something that a group of persons, called scientists, do; something they do in laboratories, observatories, and places of special research. It is far from being the temper of mind with which human beings individually and collectively approach the problems that confront them. It is so far from this goal that the surface of the working dispositions of men has hardly been touched. The ground is barely scratched.

The prestige of science is due for the most part not to general adoption of its temper of mind but to its material application. The inherent idealism of the scientific temper is submerged, for the mass of human beings, in the use and enjoyment of the material power and material comforts that have resulted from its technical applications.

To a considerable extent this outcome is explicable. In the perspective of history, scientific method is a newcomer on the scene. It is an infant struggling with adults generated and nourished through the long millennia of life on earth. Moreover, it came to men who were for the most part almost starved and made its appeal to them on the basis of the promise of power and ease that it held out.

The rapid development of the material side of scientific technique cannot be understood save as it is viewed in the perspective formed by this background. Appetites that had been choked, desires that had been smothered, were brought into lively action when men began to enjoy the fruits of the inventions made possible by science. The new force of the latter was in direct ratio to men's previous impotence to satisfy their wants. Society in general (and not merely a few persons here and there) exemplifies the situation of the *nouveaux riches*. Most individuals, to be sure, have not enjoyed any large participation in the milk and honey of the promised land. But there are few who have not been affected by the lure science in its technical applications has held out.

What has been said, however, is but the negative aspect of the case. The positive aspect is the essential capture of the technical resources of the new science; first, by industry controlled by finance-capital, and then by political nationalism. The recent menace of what Mr. Russell terms the new religions to the temper of science, to its free, tentative, and experimental method and its substitution of working hypotheses for immutable and eternal truths, is, after all, but the climacteric expression of forces that have been at work all during the period when science was winning its technical and material victories.

The bursting into bloom of a new way of thinking and action ever comes as a surprise. For we never know just what we are doing till its critical consequences force themselves upon us. But we may be sure that in spite of the suddenness of the emergence of new forms, their incubating forces have long been operating underground.

This is not the place for a disquisition upon nationalism and economic capitalism. But a reference to a phrase contained in a sentence already quoted from Mr. Russell is decidedly in place. The phrase is "the modern danger of chaos and anarchy." This danger springs from the uncontrolled operation of our economic system on one hand and of our political nationalism on the other. It is a real danger because it is the necessary product of the union of economic and political forces. The peril of anarchy and chaos, which is not a mere threat but a present fact, is a new urgent demand for the manifestation of the principle of authority. Because science was not ready to meet the demand, we have the old appeal to external dogmatic authority. The appeal is old; it is in accord with the established precedents of history for most of its course. The form of its expression is new and terrific. For it has all the resources of the technical applications of science at its command. The danger of chaos that springs from war, as a product of political nationalism, is met by mobilizing the resources of science to prepare for greater wars. The danger of anarchy and chaos that arises from economic dislocation and insecurity is met by dictatorships that seize control of all the processes of industrial life in the interest of one class or another. Both performances are dependent upon the use of techniques that science has brought into being. Both are dependent upon an exploitation, by means of technical facilities generated by science, of emotion and imagination. The outcome justifies Mr. Russell in calling the movements new religions. They have their established dogmatic creeds, their fixed rites and ceremonies, their central institutional authority, their distinction between the faithful and the unbelievers, with persecution of heretics who do not accept the true faith.

It is this situation which to my mind makes the issue of the social place and work of science so momentous and so urgent. We are in danger lest the only way out that will occur to men, even to us here in this country, will be the lining up of one creed and institution against the other and a consequent new type of religious war. I do not mean that in this country the issue will necessarily take the form of direct conflict between the forces that constitute fascist and communist dictatorships. But chaos and anarchy are with us. And every failure to meet the situation by the use of the patient and experimental method of intelligence means the strengthening of appeal to some form of external and dogmatic authority to bring seeming order out of chaos. The disposition to make war and call it peace did not die out in the age of Tacitus. It has only assumed new forms. There are already among us groups of "intellectuals" who are fostering the external authoritarian doctrine and who are ready to become the official philosophers of the movement.

For the question is one that concerns philosophy as well as science. And at this point I am compelled, reluctantly, to part company with Mr. Russell. The portions of Mr. Russell's exposition that are most definitely philosophical in import are found in his chapters on soul and body, cosmic purpose, and science and ethics. My divergencies do not concern the conclusion reached as far as they bear upon the traditional conceptions of religion; they have to do with the philosophical conceptions put forth in connection with the discussion. The present essay does not offer the time and place for an excursion into the philosophy of perception and of value, and I should not go into the matter at all if it did not seem to me to have a bearing upon the main issue with which Mr. Russell is so deeply and justly concerned.

The point at issue is concerned with the "privacy" of perception and experience generally, and with the "subjectivity" of value, the two doctrines being intimately connected with one another. Mr. Russell believes that "seeing," perception generally, is a private event and that "each person's experience is private to himself." No two persons can see or remember or experience

exactly the same thing; since physical science consists of inferences from what is perceived and remembered, "the data of
physics, when closely examined, have the same kind of privacy
as those of psychology," while it is added that those of psychology may have the same kind of "quasi-publicity" that belongs to those of physics. The reason given by Mr. Russell is
that when we say we perceive an object, say, the sun, the object
is only a remote cause, and what we perceive is dependent upon
the intervening medium and upon certain processes in the body,
especially the brain. I am unable to see what this has to do
with the privacy of perception or with its "mental" character.
The argument would seem to show that perception is a complex objective event taking place in the objective world through
the interaction of a variety of conditions. It is more a complex
event than that which we call, say, the shining of the sun. But
save by carrying over without question the conclusions of traditional dualistic psychology I cannot see how it is different save
in the complexity of its conditioning factors. Moreover, its very
complexity is the ground of our ability to make certain inference
as to the part that different objects—"sun," "medium," and
"nervous system"—play in its production. As for the argument
that experience is private because no two persons have exactly
the same experience, I suppose it is also true that exactly the
same physical event does not occur twice. But unless individuality of occurrence is defined in advance to *mean* being
private, a purely verbal matter, I do not see how the rich
diversity of existence proves its privacy.

As I have said, I should not have engaged in these comments
if they did not have a direct bearing upon the question of the
social function of science. It is difficult, it seems to be logically
impossible, to unite a plea for its authority in determination of
the beliefs that hold men together in conjoint action with the
doctrine of the inherent privacy of its procedures and conclusions. If the latter doctrine were substantiated, we should have
to accept it, whatever its unfortunate social consequences. But
if it is not valid and yet is accepted, it tends to strengthen the

idea that in a conflict of private views we must have recourse to
external authority and force in order to effect a semblance of
communal order. The issue involved comes out even more
clearly in the case of the nature of value in its connection with
morals.

According to Mr. Russell, "Ethics contains no *statements*,
whether true or false, but consists of desires of a certain general
kind." Disagreement about what is good or bad is, then, of the
nature of a difference in tastes. To call something a good or
positive value is one way of saying, "I like it," as in another area
I may like oysters: to call it bad is not to make an objective
statement, but a statement about one's personal and subjective
attitude. I do not doubt that ethical theories are often put forth
that are in fact elaborate "rationalizations" of private and group
likes and dislikes; I do not doubt that a desire is a condition of
our being aware that something is a value, and possibly also
one causal condition among others of anything's *being* a value.
But there is a long road from even the latter position to the
doctrine that good is identical with that which we like. For
likings and desires are natural events. While they have conditions, they are not identical with their causal conditions, and
certainly not with one of them in isolation. Mr. Russell says
something that is profoundly true when he says that "it is by
cultivation of large and generous desires through intelligence,
happiness and freedom from fear, that men can be brought to
act more than they do at present in a manner that is consistent
with the general happiness of mankind." But I doubt whether
this statement is consistent with the doctrine of the complete
"subjectivity" of desires and values, or whether it means *merely*
that Mr. Russell, in common with a few other persons, happens
to like "large and generous desires" better than he likes certain
other desires. For the argument assumes that desires have objective conditions and objective consequences.

While it is true, as Mr. Russell says in the same passage, that
it is not ethical theory which produces the sort of desires that
are needed, it is theoretically conceivable that there should be

ethical theory that concerns itself scientifically and objectively with the causal conditions and the concrete consequences of this and that desire. The practical difficulties in the way are immense. Only a slight beginning has been made. But were the enterprise pursued, it would develop, as it matures, techniques for dealing with human nature as we now have them for physical nature. These techniques would not consist in manipulation from without because they would demand coöperative voluntary responses for their realization. Such a science and technique are not conspicuous for their absence. To follow this train of thought would, I believe, throw a flood of light upon the existing comparatively slight influence of the scientific temper and the enormous influence of scientific techniques because of the material power, comfort, and ease they afford. It is an oft-told story that physical science is indefinitely advanced beyond the human and moral sciences. Knowledge of the relation of means and consequences with respect to human desires and purposes, comparable to the knowledge we have of physical causes and effects, is the only way in which to bring social knowledge and actions to anything approaching what already exists in physical knowledge and power.

5

WHAT IS SOCIAL STUDY?

IN THE NEW PROPER EMPHASIS UPON SOCIAL STUDIES, THE PRIMARY
problem, it seems to me, is to determine the scope and range
of the subject-matter designated by "social." More definitely, the
question is: how far that which is social can be separated and
treated by itself, and how far the "social" is a limiting function
of the subject-matter of all studies—what philosophers might
call a category by which all materials of learning are to be interpreted. There is, of course, a restricted sense in which it is correct enough to isolate social materials. Questions of family life,
of politics and economics, of war and peace, are obviously social
questions. The problem I am raising is how far such materials
can be understood and be educative in the full sense without a
background of study of matters which lie outside of the social
as thus limited.

No one would deny, I suppose, that many political questions
at the present time have economic roots. Issues of the relation
of capital and labor, of concentration and distribution of wealth,
of economic security and unemployment, occupy the attention
of our legislative bodies. They are primarily economic questions
but they find their way into political action because their impact upon human relations and their public consequences are
intense and widespread. Can the student stop when he has
traced these political themes to their economic sources? Or does
understanding of the economic situation demand going further?

It would probably be admitted on all hands that the present
economic situation is a historical development, and that while

180

present facts may be amassed in quantities, the information thus gained needs to be placed in an historic setting if it is to be intelligently grasped and used. Many, perhaps all, of the economic questions have also definitely geographical aspects. The problem of the farmer comes to mind, for example, and that of the railways as means of distribution of products. So does that of soil conservation and reforestation. The question of the distribution of population, of congestion in industrial and commercial centers, is another aspect of the same general question. Careful studies show that in recent years there have been a number of great regional migrations which have left certain large regions in a state of relative desolation while the burdens of relief, hospitalization, etc., have been greatly increased in the areas to which they have gone. That miners live and work where there are mines and lumbermen work where there are still forests, as well as that farmers live on farms, and that certain centers are what they are because of facilities of transportation and need for reshipment of products, are obvious facts. But they raise the question how far are social studies to be conducted in the light of fundamental geographic and physiographic knowledge?

The reference that was made in an earlier paragraph to the historic context of economic questions suggests in turn the scientific background. The industrial and commercial change which has taken place in the world in the last century, in the past forty years, is the product of the great change which has taken place in physical, chemical and, more recently, biological science. The prime factor in the economic and political history of this period is what is known as the industrial revolution. The story of that revolution is the story of new technologies, in the production and distribution of goods, which are themselves the result of a scientific revolution. Any vital comprehension of existing economic and political issues demands insight into processes and operations that can be grasped only through understanding of fundamental physical and chemical operations and laws. I will not press the point further, though it might be extended into the subjects of literature, the fine arts and mathematics. The obvious objection that may be made to what has been said is that if it is accepted it swells the social studies beyond all limits; that they have so many ramifications and absorb so much of other studies that teacher and student alike are confronted with an unwieldy, unmanageable mass. The objection, when it is analyzed, brings us to the other aspect of the educational question.

When I asked how far the social is, from an educational point of view, the limiting function of all the studies, the question I had in mind was whether such subjects as, for example, the history, geography and natural science already mentioned can be isolated, so as to be treated as independent subjects; or whether from the beginning and constantly they should be treated in their social bearings and consequences—consequences in the way, on one side, of problems and on the other side of opportunities. The human and cultural is after all the embracing limit to which all other things tend. In the higher reaches of school education there must, of course, be provision for training of experts and specialists. In them, a certain amount of relative separation of subjects from their social context and function is legitimate. But it is a fair question whether society is not suffering even here because the expert specialists have not the educational background which would enable them to view their special skills and knowledge in connection with social conditions, movements and problems.

But the particular point I would make is that in any case we have carried the isolation of subjects from their social effects and possibilities too far down the educational scale. From the psychological and moral standpoint it may be urged that for most boys and girls the material of studies loses vitality, becomes relatively dead, because it is separated from situations, and that much of the need which is felt at the present time for resorting to extraneous devices to make subjects interesting or else to coerce attention is a necessary effect of this isolation. Natural docility leads to acceptance. But underneath, there is the subconscious questioning, "What does all this mean? What is it for? What do the studies signify outside of the schoolroom or do they belong only there?"

The problem of congestion of studies and diversion of aims with resulting superficiality is a pressing one today. The progressive and the reactionary agree in this one thing on the negative side. Both insist that there is lack of unity of aim, that there is dispersion and confusion. As far as I can see, the one hope of obtaining the desired unification is that which has been suggested. The natural focus, the assembling point, of the various studies is their social origin and function. Any other scheme of unification and correlation seems to me artificial and doomed to only transitory success. Progressive education has reached a point where it is looking for a lead which will give coherence and direction to its efforts. I believe it will find it here and that in the end emphasis upon social studies as a separate line of study may only add to the confusion and dispersion that now exist! Not because they are not important, but precisely because they are so important that they should give direction and organization to all branches of study.

In conclusion, I want to say that in my judgment what has been said has a definite bearing upon what is called indoctrination, or, if one prefer, teaching, with respect to preparation for a different social order. Social studies as an isolated affair are likely to become either accumulations of bodies of special factual information or, in the hands of zealous teachers, to be organs of indoctrination in the sense of propaganda for a special social end, accepted enthusiastically, perhaps, but still dogmatically. Young people who have been trained in all subjects to look for social bearings will also be educated to see the causes of present evils. They will be equipped from the sheer force of what they have learned to see new possibilities and the means of actualizing them. They will be indoctrinated in its deeper sense without having had doctrines forced upon them.

6

DOES HUMAN NATURE CHANGE?

I HAVE COME TO THE CONCLUSION THAT THOSE WHO GIVE DIFFER-
ent answers to the question I have asked in the title of this
article are talking about different things. This statement in itself,
however, is too easy a way out of the problem to be satisfactory. For there is a real problem, and so far as the question is a
practical one instead of an academic one, I think the proper
answer is that human nature *does* change.

By the practical side of the question, I mean the question
whether or not important, almost fndamental, changes in the
ways of human belief and action have taken place and are
capable of still taking place. But to put this question in its
proper perspective, we have first to recognize the sense in which
human nature does not change. I do not think it can be shown
that the innate needs of men have changed since man became
man or that there is any evidence that they will change as long
as man is on the earth.

By "needs" I mean the inherent demands that men make
because of their constitution. Needs for food and drink and for
moving about, for example, are so much a part of our being that
we cannot imagine any condition under which they would cease
to be. There are other things not so directly physical that seem
to me equally engrained in human nature. I would mention as
examples the need for some kind of companionship; the need
for exhibiting energy, for bringing one's powers to bear upon
surrounding conditions; the need for both coöperation with and
emulation of one's fellows for mutual aid and combat alike; the
need for some sort of aesthetic expression and satisfaction; the
need to lead and to follow, etc.

184

Whether my particular examples are well chosen or not does not matter so much as does recognition of the fact that there are some tendencies so integral a part of human nature that the latter would not be human nature if they changed. These tendencies used to be called instincts. Psychologists are now more chary of using that word than they used to be. But the word by which the tendencies are called does not matter much in comparison to the fact that human nature has its own constitution.

Where we are likely to go wrong, after the fact is recognized that there is something unchangeable in the structure of human nature, is the inference we draw from it. We suppose that the manifestation of these needs is also unalterable. We suppose that the manifestations we have got used to are as natural and as unalterable as are the needs from which they spring.

The need for food is so imperative that we call the persons insane who persistently refuse to take nourishment. But what kinds of food are wanted and used are a matter of acquired habit influenced by both physical environment and social custom. To civilized people today, eating human flesh is an entirely unnatural thing. Yet there have been peoples to whom it seemed natural because it was socially authorized and even highly esteemed. There are well-accredited stories of persons needing support from others who have refused palatable and nourishing foods because they were not accustomed to them; the alien foods were so "unnatural" they preferred to starve rather than eat them.

Aristotle spoke for an entire social order as well as for himself when he said that slavery existed by nature. He would have regarded efforts to abolish slavery from society as an idle and utopian effort to change human nature where it was unchangeable. For according to him it was not simply the desire to be a master that was engrained in human nature. There were persons who were born with such an inherently slavish nature that it did violence to human nature to set them free.

The assertion that human nature cannot be changed is heard when social changes are urged as reforms and improvements of existing conditions. It is always heard when the proposed changes in institutions or conditions stand in sharp opposition to what exists. If the conservative were wiser, he would rest his objections in most cases, not upon the unchangeability of human nature, but upon the inertia of custom; upon the resistance that acquired habits offer to change after they are once acquired. It is hard to teach an old dog new tricks and it is harder yet to teach society to adopt customs which are contrary to those which have long prevailed. Conservatism of this type would be intelligent, and it would compel those wanting change not only to moderate their pace, but also to ask how the changes they desire could be introduced with a minimum of shock and dislocation.

Nevertheless, there are few social changes that can be opposed on the ground that they are contrary to human nature itself. A proposal to have a society get along without food and drink is one of the few that are of this kind. Proposals to form communities in which there is no cohabitation have been made and the communities have endured for a time. But they are so nearly contrary to human nature that they have not endured long. These cases are almost the only ones in which social change can be opposed simply on the ground that human nature cannot be changed.

Take the institution of war, one of the oldest, most socially reputable of all human institutions. Efforts for stable peace are often opposed on the ground that man is by nature a fighting animal and that this phase of his nature is unalterable. The failure of peace movements in the past can be cited in support of this view. In fact, however, war is as much a social pattern as is the domestic slavery which the ancients thought to be an immutable fact.

I have already said that, in my opinion, combativeness is a constituent part of human nature. But I have also said that the manifestations of these native elements are subject to change because they are affected by custom and tradition. War does not exist because man has combative instincts, but because social conditions and forces have led, almost forced, these "instincts" into this channel.

There are a large number of other channels in which the need for combat has been satisfied, and there are other channels not yet discovered or explored into which it could be led with equal satisfaction. There is war against disease, against poverty, against insecurity, against injustice, in which multitudes of persons have found full opportunity for the exercise of their combative tendencies.

The time may be far off when men will cease to fulfill their need for combat by destroying each other and when they will manifest it in common and combined efforts against the forces that are enemies of all men equally. But the difficulties in the way are found in the persistence of certain acquired social customs and not in the unchangeability of the demand for combat.

Pugnacity and fear are native elements of human nature. But so are pity and sympathy. We send nurses and physicians to the battlefield and provide hospital facilities as "naturally" as we change bayonets and discharge machine guns. In early times there was a close connection between pugnacity and fighting, for the latter was done largely with the fists. Pugnacity plays a small part in generating wars today. Citizens of one country do not hate those of another nation by instinct. When they attack or are attacked, they do not use their fists in close combat, but throw shells from a great distance at persons whom they have never seen. In modern wars, anger and hatred come after the war has started; they are effects of war, not the cause of it.

It is a tough job sustaining a modern war; all the emotional reactions have to be excited. Propaganda and atrocity stories are enlisted. Aside from such extreme measures there has to be definite organization, as we saw in the two World Wars, to keep up the morale of even non-combatants. And morale is largely a matter of keeping emotions at a certain pitch; and unfortunately fear, hatred, suspicion, are among the emotions most easily aroused.

I shall not attempt to dogmatize about the causes of modern wars. But I do not think that anyone will deny that they are social rather than psychological, though psychological appeal is highly important in working up a people to the point where they want to fight and in keeping them at it. I do not think, moreover, that anyone will deny that economic conditions are powerful among the social causes of war. The main point, however, is that whatever the sociological causes, they are affairs of tradition, custom, and institutional organization, and these factors belong among the changeable manifestations of human nature, not among the unchangeable elements.

I have used the case of war as a typical instance of what is changeable and what is unchangeable in human nature, in their relation to schemes of social change. I have selected the case because it is an extremely difficult one in which to effect durable changes, not because it is an easy one. The point is that the obstacles in the way are put there by social forces which do change from time to time, not by fixed elements of human nature. This fact is also illustrated in the failures of pacifists to achieve their ends by appeal simply to sympathy and pity. For while, as I have said, the kindly emotions are also a fixed constituent of human nature, the channel they take is dependent upon social conditions.

There is always a great outburst of these kindly emotions in time of war. Fellow feeling and the desire to help those in need are intense during war, as they are at every period of great disaster that comes home to observation or imagination. But they are canalized in their expression; they are confined to those upon our side. They occur simultaneously with manifestation of rage and fear against the other side, if not always in the same person, at least in the community generally. Hence the ultimate failure of pacifist appeals to the kindly elements of native human nature when they are separated from intelligent consideration of the social and economic forces at work.

William James made a great contribution in the title of one of his essays, *The Moral Equivalents of War*. The very title conveys the point I am making. Certain basic needs and emotions are permanent. But they are capable of finding expression in ways that are radically different from the ways in which they now currently operate.

An even more burning issue emerges when any fundamental change in economic institutions and relations is proposed. Proposals for such sweeping change are among the commonplaces of our time. On the other hand, the proposals are met by the statement that the changes are impossible because they involve an impossible change in human nature. To this statement, advocates of the desired changes are only too likely to reply that the present system or some phase of it is contrary to human nature. The argument *pro* and *con* then gets put on the wrong ground.

As a matter of fact, economic institutions and relations are among the manifestations of human nature that are most susceptible of change. History is living evidence of the scope of these changes. Aristotle, for example, held that paying interest is unnatural, and the Middle Ages reëchoed the doctrine. All interest was usury, and it was only after economic conditions had so changed that payment of interest was a customary and in that sense a "natural" thing, that usury got its present meaning.

There have been times and places in which land was held in common and in which private ownership of land would have been regarded as the most monstrous of unnatural things. There have been other times and places when all wealth was possessed by an overlord and his subjects held wealth, if any, subject to his pleasure. The entire system of credit so fundamental in contemporary financial and industrial life is a modern invention. The invention of the joint stock company with limited liability of individuals has brought about a great change from earlier facts and conceptions of property. I think the need of owning something is one of the native elements of human nature. But it takes either ignorance or a very lively fancy to suppose that the system of ownership that exists in the United

States in 1946, with all its complex relations and its interweaving with legal and political supports, is a necessary and unchangeable product of an inherent tendency to appropriate and possess.

Law is one of the most conservative of human institutions; yet through the cumulative effect of legislation and judicial decisions it changes, sometimes at a slow rate, sometimes rapidly. The changes in human relations that are brought about by changes in industrial and legal institutions then react to modify the ways in which human nature manifests itself, and this brings about still further changes in institutions, and so on indefinitely.

It is for these reasons that I say that those who hold that proposals for social change, even of rather a profound character, are impossible and utopian because of the fixity of human nature confuse the resistance to change that comes from acquired habits with that which comes from original human nature. The savage, living in a primitive society, comes nearer to being a purely "natural" human being than does civilized man. Civilization itself is the product of altered human nature. But even the savage is bound by a mass of tribal customs and transmitted beliefs that modify his original nature, and it is these acquired habits that make it so difficult to transform him into a civilized human being.

The revolutionary radical, on the other hand, overlooks the force of engrained habits. He is right, in my opinion, about the indefinite plasticity of human nature. But he is wrong in thinking that patterns of desire, belief, and purpose do not have a force comparable to the momentum of physical objects once they are set in motion, and comparable to the inertia, the resistance to movement, possessed by these same objects when they are at rest. Habit, not original human nature, keeps things moving most of the time, about as they have moved in the past.

If human nature is unchangeable, then there is no such thing as education and all our efforts to educate are doomed to failure. For the very meaning of education is modification of native human nature in formation of those new ways of thinking, of feeling, of desiring, and of believing that are foreign to raw human nature. If the latter were unalterable, we might have training but not education. For training, as distinct from education, means simply the acquisition of certain skills. Native gifts can be trained to a point of higher efficiency without that development of new attitudes and dispositions which is the goal of education. But the result is mechanical. It is like supposing that while a musician may acquire by practice greater technical ability, he cannot rise from one plane of musical appreciation and creation to another.

The theory that human nature is unchangeable is thus the most depressing and pessimistic of all possible doctrines. If it were carried out logically, it would mean a doctrine of predestination from birth that would outdo the most rigid of theological doctrines. For according to it, persons are what they are at birth and nothing can be done about it, beyond the kind of training that an acrobat might give to the muscular system with which he is originally endowed. If a person is born with criminal tendencies, a criminal he will become and remain. If a person is born with an excessive amount of greed, he will become a person living by predatory activities at the expense of others; and so on. I do not doubt at all the existence of differences in natural endowment. But what I am questioning is the notion that they doom individuals to a fixed channel of expression. It is difficult indeed to make a silk purse out of a sow's ear. But the particular form which, say, a natural musical endowment will take depends upon the social influences to which he is subjected. Beethoven in a savage tribe would doubtless have been outstanding as a musician, but he would not have been the Beethoven who composed symphonies.

The existence of almost every conceivable kind of social institution at some time and place in the history of the world is evidence of the plasticity of human nature. This fact does not prove that all these different social systems are of equal value, materially, morally, and culturally. The slightest observation shows that such is not the case. But the fact in proving the changeability of human nature indicates the attitude that should be taken toward proposals for social changes. The question is primarily whether they, in special cases, are desirable or not. And the way to answer that question is to try to discover what their consequences would be if they were adopted. Then if the conclusion is that they are desirable, the further question is how they can be accomplished with a minimum of waste, destruction, and needless dislocation.

In finding the answer to this question, we have to take into account the force of existing traditions and customs; of the patterns of action and belief that already exist. We have to find out what forces already at work can be reinforced so that they move toward the desired change and how the conditions that oppose change can be gradually weakened. Such questions as these can be considered on the basis of fact and reason.

The assertion that a proposed change is impossible because of the fixed constitution of human nature diverts attention from the question of whether or not a change is desirable and from the other question of how it shall be brought about. It throws the question into the arena of blind emotion and brute force. In the end, it encourages those who think that great changes can be produced offhand and by the use of sheer violence.

When our sciences of human nature and human relations are anything like as developed as are our sciences of physical nature, their chief concern will be with the problem of how human nature is most effectively modified. The question will not be whether it is capable of change, but of how it is to be changed under given conditions. This problem is ultimately that of education in its widest sense. Consequently, whatever represses and distorts the processes of education that might bring about a change in human dispositions with the minimum of waste puts a premium upon the forces that bring society to a state of deadlock, and thereby encourages the use of violence as a means of social change.

7

NATURE IN EXPERIENCE

THE TOPIC UNDER CONSIDERATION IS CAPABLE OF TWO INTERPRE-
tations. When it was communicated to me I took it to mean
that the subject for discussion was the relation between the
theory of experience and the theory of nature. But it also became clear that the topic could be interpreted broadly so that
anything I have written concerning either nature or experience
is open for consideration. I had then to decide how should I plan
my statement. I have adopted the first of the two versions. It
has the advantage of enabling me to centralize what I have to
say, since I should otherwise have to disperse what I have to say
over a large variety of topics. It has the disadvantage that it
may seem to show lack of respect for some quite important
criticisms that are passed over, and perhaps that of accepting as
sound the interpretations upon which the criticisms rest.

In this dilemma the finally decisive consideration was that
the course which enables me to introduce more unity and organization serves also to focus attention upon a problem which is
so central in philosophy that it must be met and dealt with by
all schools. The matter of perspectives is basic in the issue of the
connection between nature and experience. I find that with respect to the hanging together of various problems and various
hypotheses in a perspective determined by a definite point of
view, I have a system. In so far I have to retract disparaging
remarks I have made in the past about the need for system in
philosophy.

The peculiar importance in philosophy of a point of view and
of the perspective it institutes is enhanced by the fact that a

fairly large number of alternative points of view have been
worked out in the history of philosophy in terms of the ways in
which the world looks from them; that is to say, in terms of the
leading categories by which the things of the world are to be
understood. The significations attached to words and ideas
which recur in practically every system tend to become fixed
till it seems as if no choice were left, save to give the names (and
the problems to which they relate) the import sanctioned by
some one or other past philosophic point of view. In the degree
in which a philosophy involves a shift from older points of view
and from what is seen in their perspectives, both its author and
those to whom he addresses himself find themselves in difficulties. The former has to use words that have meanings fixed
under conditions of more or less alien points of view and the
latter have to engage in some kind of imaginative translation.

The bearing of this general remark upon the present theme
has to do first of all with the word 'experience' and the allied
word 'empiricism.' There is a long tradition of empiricism in
the story of philosophy; upon the whole the tradition is particularistic and nominalistic, if not overtly sensationalistic, in
its logic and ontology. When empiricism has escaped from the
limits thereby set, it has, upon the whole, been through making
human experience the broken but still usable ladder of ascent
to an absolute experience, and there has been a flight to some
form of cosmic idealism. Presentation of a view of experience
which puts experience in connection with nature, with the cosmos, but which would nevertheless frame its view of experience
on the ground of conclusions reached in the natural sciences,
has trouble in finding ways of expressing itself which do not
seem to lead into one or the other of these historically sanctioned alternative perspectives.

There is a circularity in the position taken regarding the connection of experience and nature. Upon one side, analysis and
interpretation of nature is made dependent upon the conclusions of the natural sciences, especially upon biology, but upon

a biology that is itself dependent upon physics and chemistry. But when I say 'dependent' I mean that the intellectual instrumentalities, the organs, for understanding the new and distinctive material of experienced objects are provided by the natural sciences. I do *not* mean that the material of experienced things *qua* experienced must be translated into the terms of the material of the physical sciences; that view leads to a naturalism which denies distinctive significance to experience, thereby ending in the identification of naturalism with mechanistic materialism.

The other aspect of the circle is found in the fact that it is held that experience itself, even ordinary gross macroscopic experience, contains the materials and the processes and operations which, when they are rightly laid hold of and used, lead to the methods and conclusions of the natural sciences; namely, to the very conclusions that provide the means for forming a theory of experience. That this circle exists is not so much admitted as claimed. It is also claimed that the circle is not vicious; for instead of being logical it is existential and historic. That is to say, if we look at human history and especially at the historic development of the natural sciences, we find progress made from a crude experience in which beliefs about nature and natural events were very different from those now scientifically authorized. At the same time we find the latter now enable us to frame a theory of experience by which we can tell *how* this development out of gross experience into the highly refined conclusions of science has taken place.

I come now to certain topics and criticism to be dealt with on the basis of the idea of this circular relation. The most inclusive criticism of my friend Morris Cohen is suggested, I think, by the word "anthropocentric" in the title of his paper; it is expressed in the saying that my absorption in human experience prevents me from formulating any adequate theory of non-human or physical nature. In short, it is held that the fact—which is not denied to be a fact—that experience involves a human element limits a philosophy that makes experience primary to human affairs as its sole material; hence it does not admit of propositions about such things as, say, the origin of life on earth or the events of geological ages preceding the advent of man and hence, of necessity, human experience.

Now there is a problem here which every empirical philosophy must meet; it can evade the challenge only to its own damage. Yet the problem is not confined to empiricism; the existence of experience is a fact, and it is fact that the organs of experience, the body, the nervous system, hands and eyes, muscles and senses, are means by which we have access to the non-human world. It would seem then as if the philosophy which denies that it is possible for experienced things and processes to form a road into the natural world must be controlled by an underlying postulate that there is a breach of continuity between nature and man and hence between nature and human experience. At all events, a fundamental question is raised. Is experience itself natural, a doing or manifestation of nature? Or is it in some genuine sense extra-natural, sub-natural or supernatural, something superimposed and alien? At all events, this is the setting in which I shall place and interpret some of the more basic criticisms passed upon my views.

(1) There are traits, qualities, and relations found in things experienced, in the things that are typically and emphatically matters of human experience, which do not appear in the objects of physical science; namely, such things as immediate qualities, values, ends. Are such things inherently relevant and important for a philosophical theory of nature? I have held that philosophical empiricism must take the position that they are intrinsically pertinent. I have written (and Cohen has quoted): "It is as much a part of the real being of atoms that they give rise in time, under increasing complications of relationships, to qualities of blue and sweet, pain and beauty, as that they have, at a certain cross-section of time, extension, mass or weight." Now whether this statement is correct or false, it is simply an illustration of what any theory must hold which sees things in

the perspective determined by the continuity of experience with nature.[1]

I also wrote that domination of man by desire and reverie is as pertinent to a philosophical theory of nature as is mathematical physics. The point of this statement is also truistic, given the point of view of the continuity of experience with nature. It certainly is not countered by the statement that "For the understanding of the general processes of nature throughout time and space, the existence of human reverie and desire is surely not as illuminating as are considerations of mathematical physics." For the whole point of the passage is that qualities of experienced things that are not the least bit illuminating for the understanding of nature in physical science are as important for a philosophy of nature as the thing most illuminating, namely mathematical physics—a view, as I have said, which any theory making experience continuous with nature is bound to hold.

This point gains more general philosophical significance because of the fact that qualities and values, which are not traits of the objects of natural science as these are now ascertained to be, were once completely fused with the material of what was taken to be science. The whole classic cosmology or theory of nature is framed in this sense. It is the progress of natural science itself that has destroyed this cosmology. As the history of modern philosophy proves, this destruction brought about that crisis which is represented by the bifurcation expressed in the dualistic opposition of subjective and objective, mind and matter, experience and nature. The problem involved is one which all philosophies alike must face. Any one view, such as the one I have set forth, can be intelligently criticized only from the standpoint of some alternative theory, while theories of bifurcation have their own difficulties and troubles, as the

---

[1] "Giving rise to" implies no particular theory as to causal determination, and the word "atom" is used illustratively. The point made would be the same if at some time in the future natural science abandoned the atomic theory and put something else in the place of atoms.

history of modern thought abundantly proves.[2] Affirmation of the continuity of experience with nature has its difficulties. But they are not grasped nor the theory refuted by translating what it says into terms of a theory which assumes that the presence of the human factor in experience precludes getting from experience to the non-human or physical.

(2) The passage which has been cited about the "real being" of the atom contains an explicit contrast between nature as judged in a short-time span or "cross-section" and in a long temporal span—one long enough to cover the emergence of human beings and their experiences. In order to be understood, what I have said about genesis and function, about antecedents and consequences, has to be placed in the perspective suggested by this emphasis upon the need of formulating a theory of nature and of the connections of man *in* (not *to*) nature on the basis of a temporal continuum.

What is basically involved is that some changes, those for example which terminate in the things of human experience, form a *history*, or a set of changes marked by development or growth. The dichotomy of the old discussion as to whether antecedents or ends are of primary importance in forming a theory of nature is done away with when growth, development, history is taken to be primary. Genesis and ends are of equal importance, but their import is that of terms or boundaries which delimit a history, thereby rendering it capable of description. The sentence before the one about the atom reads, for example, as follows: "For knowledge, 'cause' and 'effect' have a partial and truncated being"; the paragraph as a whole is

[2] While Cohen, it seems to me, has somewhat overstated my opposition to Greek and medieval philosophy, it is just the fact of the enormous change that has taken place in the method and conclusions of natural science which is the ground of my insistence upon need for a radical change in the theory of nature and of knowledge. Upon this point, it seems to me that it is rather Cohen than myself who fails to attach sufficient importance to physical science in its relation to philosophy. Piety to classic thought is an admirable trait; but a revolution in the physical constituents of nature demands considerable change in cosmological theory, as change in the method of inquiry demands reconstruction *in* (though not *of*) logic.

devoted to criticizing the notion that causal conditions have a "reality" superior to that of outcomes or effects. It is argued that the prevalent view which attributes superior rank to them results from hypostatizing a *function*: the function of causal conditions as means of control (ultimately, the *sole* means of control) is converted into a direct ontological property. Moreover, the chapter of which the paragraph is a part is devoted to showing that while Existence as process and as history involves "ends," the change from ancient to modern science compels us to interpret ends relatively and pluralistically, because as limits of specifiable histories.

Of the many special points which follow from this basic element in my theory of the connection of experience with nature—as itself an historical outcome or 'end,' I shall here deal with only one. In what I have said about meanings my critic finds an undue importance attached to consequences; in what I say (in a discussion devoted to a special problem) about the background of Greek philosophy he finds an equally one-sided importance attached to genesis. That in discussion of one particular history the emphasis with respect to a particular problem falls upon results, and in another history discussed in respect to another particular problem, emphasis falls upon antecedents, involves no inconsistency. With respect to consequences in their connection with meaning and verification I have repeatedly and explicitly insisted upon the fact that there is no way of telling what the consequences are save by discovery of antecedents, so that the latter are necessary and yet are subordinate in function.[3]

(3) Another aspect of the perspective determined by the point of view expressed in the continuity of nature and experience concerns the relation of theory and practical ends, particularly of physical science and morals. It is about this point, unless I am mistaken, that the fundamental criticisms of Cohen cluster,

[3] My use of the compound word "genetic-functional" to describe what I regard as the proper method of philosophy is, then, directly linked to the position taken regarding the temporal continuum.

since the passages upon which the criticisms are based are interpreted in another perspective than that in which they are stated. The fact that I have, quite consistently and persistently, as far as I am aware, insisted that inquiry should follow the lead of its subject-matter [4] and not be subordinated to any end or motive having an external source, is less important than the fact that any other view would be contradictory to my main theses regarding (i) the place of the natural sciences in the formation of the ends and values of practical life, and (ii) the importance of the experimental method of the natural sciences as the model for the sciences involving human practice, or the social and moral disciplines.

The view I have put forward about the nature of that to which the adjective "physical" applies is that, while it is arrived at by following out clews given in directly experimental matter, it constitutes the *conditions* upon which all the qualities and terminal values, the consummations, of experience, depend. Hence those things which are physical are the sole means that exist for control of values and qualities. To read anything extraneous into them, to tamper in any way with the integrity of the inquiry of which they are the product, would thus be to nullify the very function in terms of which the *physical* as such is defined. I have even gone so far as to ascribe the backwardness of the human, the practical, sciences in part to the long period of backwardness of the physical sciences themselves and in part to the refusal of moralists and social scientists to utilize the physical, especially the biological, material that is at their disposal.

[4] I would call attention to one passage, found on pp. 67–68 of *The Quest for Certainty* (cf. p. 228). The text states the nature of the ambiguity in the word "theoretical" which is the source of misunderstanding, the confusion of the attitude of the *inquirer* with the nature of the *subject-matter* inquired into. It is explicitly said that the former must be theoretical and cognitive, purged of personal desire and preference, marked by willingness to subordinate them to the lead of subject-matter. But it is also said that only inquiry itself can determine whether or not *subject-matter* contains practical conditions and qualities. To argue from the strictly theoretical character of the motives of the inquirer, from the necessity for "disinterested curiosity," to the nature of that investigated is a kind of "anthropocentricism" of which I should not wish to be guilty.

(4) These considerations bring me to my view regarding the nature and function of philosophy, a point which I think will be found crucial for the interpretation, and hence the criticism, of the passages upon which Cohen bases his view that I have pretty systematically subordinated inquiry, reflection, and science to extraneous practical ends. For speaking of *philosophy* (not of science) I have constantly insisted that since it contains value-considerations within itself, indispensable to its existence as philosophy—in distinction from science—it has a "practical," that is a *moral* function, and I have held that since this element is inherent, the failure of philosophies to recognize and make explicit its presence introduces undesirable properties into them, leading them on one side to make claims of being purely cognitive, which bring them into rivalry with science, and on the other side to neglect of the field in which they may be genuinely significant, that of possible guidance of human activity in the field of values.

The following passage is fairly typical of what I have said: "What would be its [philosophy's] office if it ceased to deal with the problem of reality and knowledge at large? In effect, its function would be to facilitate the fruitful interaction of our cognitive beliefs, our beliefs resting upon the most dependable methods of inquiry, with our practical beliefs about the values, the ends and purposes, that should control human action in the things of large and liberal human import." [5] Now whether this view of the nature of philosophic as distinct from distinctively scientific inquiry is correct or incorrect, the following points are so involved that the view cannot be understood without taking them into account: (i) It is one aspect of the general position of the experiential continuum constituted by the interaction of different modes of experienced things, in this case of the scientific and the moral; (ii) it gives philosophy a subject-matter distinct from the subject-matter of science and yet inherently connected with the latter, namely, the bearing of the conclusions reached in science ("the most dependable methods

[5] *The Quest for Certainty*, 10.

of inquiry") upon the value-factors involved in human action; (iii) there is no subordination of the results of knowledge to any preconceived scheme of values or predetermined practical ends (such as fixes the usual meaning of "reform"), but rather emphasis upon the reconstruction of existing ends and values in behalf of more generous and liberal human activities.

Now whether this view of philosophy is right or wrong (and my critic says nothing about what he takes to be the subject-matter and function of philosophy in connection with, or distinction from, that of science), if what is said about philosophy is taken to be said about science or about reflection in general, the meanings which result will be justly exposed to all the criticisms passed upon them.[6] It is perhaps significant that Cohen himself virtually recognizes the presence of the human and moral factor in philosophy as distinct from science. For the "resignation" which he finds to be the lesson taught by a just theory of nature is surely a human and moral factor; it remains such even if I have overemphasized the traits of courage and active responsibility, as I may have done in view of the fact that resignation and the purely consolatory office of philosophy have received more than enough emphasis in the historical tradition. But I have also pointed out that the classic or catholic version of that tradition recognizes that this lesson of passive resignation is not final; that it has to be supplemented by a divine institution which undertakes the positive function of

[6] It often happens in addition that what is said about a particular type of philosophic system, in a context which qualifies what is said, is taken by Cohen absolutely, without qualification. For example, if the reader will consult the passage (*The Influence of Darwin*, 298–299) containing the words "luxury," "nuisance," etc., it will be seen that instead of referring to philosophy in general or even to a particular historical school or schools—much less to impartial inquiry —it is qualified by a succession of "ifs." And the passage which says (*Creative Intelligence*, 60) that philosophy is of account only if it affords guidance to action, occurs in a paragraph dealing with the grounds for the difference between the popular and the professional reception of "pragmatism," not in a statement of my own view, although the idea that philosophy is love of wisdom as distinct from love of knowledge and that "philosophy is the guide of life" is not peculiarly new nor peculiarly a product of pragmatism.

guidance, and that in so far the practical logic of the situation is with the Church rather than with traditional philosophy which is minus institutional support and aid. As far as I am concerned the issue is between a theory of experience in nature which renders experienced things and operations impotent, and a theory which would search for and utilize the *things in experience* that are capable of progressively providing the needed support and guidance.[7] Finally, while I am grateful and deeply appreciative of Cohen's approval of my personal liberalism, I must add not only that this liberalism is definitely rooted in the very philosophy to which he takes exception, but that any theory of activity in social and moral matters, liberal or otherwise, which is not grounded in a comprehensive philosophy seems to me to be only a projection of arbitrary personal preference.

I come now, rather belatedly, to the criticisms of my other friendly critic, Ernest Hocking. If I grasp aright the point of view from which his criticisms are made, it does not involve the postulate of separation of experience from nature that is found in Cohen's criticisms, but rather a point of departure similar to mine. In that respect, Cohen's paper involves a criticism of Hocking as well as of me, and reciprocally. The trouble with my views lies, then, according to Hocking, in the account I have given of experience, primarily in my failure to give its due place and weight to thought in relation to knowledge and to the world of reality. I am grateful to Hocking for his explicit recognition of the place given in my theory of knowledge to thought and theory, to his recognition that in my theory "the scientific process is intellectualized to the last limit." His conclusion that, since I have done this, I am logically bound to go farther and take the position that "the more thought, the more reality," thus has a relevancy to my position not possessed by

[7] Since readers cannot be expected to look up all quotations made from my writings, I will say that the sentence about the capacity of man to shape his own destiny is part of a passage about the atmosphere of the eighteenth-century thought which put forth the doctrine of the indefinite perfectibility of man. My own view is much more qualified.

criticisms based upon the notion that I have adopted the depreciatory view of thought, theory, and abstraction characteristic of traditional nominalistic empiricism.

(1) However, in criticizing sensational and particularistic empiricism and in insisting upon the indispensable rôle of thought and theory in the determination of scientific objects, I have not gone so far as to deny the really indispensable rôle of observed material and the processes of observation. On the contrary, I have criticized traditional rationalism, not indeed for pointing out the necessary operational presence of thought, but for its failure to recognize the essential rôle of observation to bring into existence that material by which objects of thought are tested and validated—or the contrary—so as to be given something more than a hypothetical status. I quote from Hocking the following passage, speaking of such things as atoms and electrons: "Dewey will not say that I observe them, but only that I think them. I agree. But is the atom then less real than the chair?" My view more completely stated is that *at present* atom and electron are objects of thought *rather* than of observation. But, instead of denying the necessity of observed material, or even the possibility of observation of objects that are atomic in the scientific sense, I have held that the theoretical value of the atom consists in its ability, as a hypothesis or *thought*, to direct observations experimentally and to coördinate their results. The mere observation of something which if it were observed by a physicist would be an atom is not, however, observation of an atom as a *scientific object* unless and only in so far as it meets the requirements of definition which has been attained by a set of systematic inferences, that is, of the function to which the name thought is given. The place of differential equations in the formulation of the atom as a scientific theoretical and hypothetical object is undeniable. But the equations as far as atoms as *existences* are concerned (in distinction from their function in facilitating and directing further inferences) state conditions to be satisfied by any observed material if it is to be warrantably asserted to *be* atomic.

(2) The formulation of the conditions to be satisfied takes a form which prescribes operations that are to be performed in instituting and interpreting observations. This fact leads to consideration of what Hocking says about operations. *If* thought and its object *as* object of thought were as complete and final apart from any connection with observed things as Hocking assumes them to be, then the operational view of scientific objects would indeed hang idly and unsupported in the void. To place, as Hocking does, interest in the entities of differential equations in opposition to interest in operations is to overlook, it seems to me, the fundamental thesis of operationalism; namely that these entities, as far as physics, including mathematical physics, is concerned, *are* formulations of operations to be performed in obtaining specified observed materials, and determining whether or not that material answers to or satisfies certain conditions imposed upon it if it is to merit the name of a certain scientific object, atom, electron, or whatever. As I have frequently said, a given scientific person may occupy himself exclusively with the mathematical aspect of the matter, and do so fruitfully as far as the historic development of a science is concerned. But this fact taken by itself is not decisive about the actual place and function of the mathematical material.

(3) I come now to another criticism of Hocking's, connected with the "reality" part of his saying "the more thought, the more reality." My criticism of Hocking's criticism has up to this point concerned only the first part of his sentence. It amounts to saying that while he has not disrupted the continuity of experience with nature, he has, to my mind, broken off one aspect of experience, namely thought, from another aspect, that of perception. Further consequences of this artificial breach seem to me to be found in what he says about "reality." It is quite true, as he says, that one meaning of reality is the "independent being upon which other things depend"; and he finds this independent being in "the content of true judgment," a saying which seems to me to express in an almost flagrantly

emphatic way the isolation of one mode of experience and its material from other modes and *their* things. For he goes on to say that Nature, as the content of true judgment or the object of perfect thought in its capacity of measure of knowledge, is the independent reality of which experience is the dependent derivative.

Now reality is, I fear, more than a double-barrelled word. Its ambiguity and slipperiness extend beyond the two significations which Hocking mentions in such a way as to affect the interpretation of 'independence' and 'dependence' in the view taken by him. For there is a definitely pragmatic meaning of 'dependence' and 'derivation,' which affects the meaning of that most dangerous of all philosophical words, "reality." The objects of knowledge, when once attained, exercise, as I have already said, the function of *control* over other materials. Hence the latter in so far depend for their status and value upon the object of knowledge. The idea of the ether was dropped when it ceased to exercise any office of control over investigations. The idea of quanta has increased its rôle because of its efficacy and fertility in control of inquiries. But this interpretation of dependence is strictly functional. Instead of first isolating the object of knowledge or judgment and then setting it up in its isolation as a measure of the "reality" of other things, it connects the scientific object, genetically and functionally, with other things without casting the invidious shadow of a lesser degree of reality upon the latter.

(4) This consideration brings me to the fourth point in Hocking's paper upon which I shall comment. It is of course true that I have emphasized the temporal continuity of inquiry, and in consequence the dependence of conclusions reached at a given time upon the methods and results of previous investigations, and their subjection to modification in subsequent inquiries. But, as far as I can see, the idea that this view indefinitely defers possession and enjoyment of stable objects to the end of an infinite progression applies rather to Hocking's position than to mine. That is, if I held that thought is the only

valid approach to "reality" and that the latter is the content of a perfect judgment, I should be troubled by the question of the worth, from the standpoint of reality, of all my present conclusions.

But I do not see that the question arises within the perspective of my own point of view. For in the latter, instead of there being isolation of the material of knowledge, there is its continual interaction with the things of other forms of experience, and the worth (or "reality") of the former is to be judged on the basis of the control exercised by it over the things of noncognitive experiences and the increment of enriched meaning supplied to them. Even from the standpoint of knowledge by itself, inquiry produces such cumulative verification and stability that the prospect of future modification is an *added* value, just as in all other affairs of life those accomplishments that open up new prospects and new possibilities are enhanced, not depressed, by their power in this respect. But what is even more important is that, from the standpoint of the continuous interaction of the things of different modes of experience, the final test of the value of "contents of judgment" now attained is found not in their relation to the content of some final judgment, to be reached at the close of an infinite progression, but in what is done in the living present, what is done in giving enriched meaning to other things and in increasing our control over them.

Criticisms are the means by which one is enabled to take, at least in imagination, a new point of view, and thus to re-see, literally to review and revise, what fell within one's earlier perspective. If I have succeeded now in making my views clearer to others than I have managed to do in my previous writings, it is because my critics have made their import clearer to myself. For that I am grateful to them.

PART III

Value and Thought

I

LOGICAL CONDITIONS OF A SCIENTIFIC TREATMENT OF MORALITY

SEC. 1 · *The Use of the Term "Scientific"*

THE FAMILIAR NOTION THAT SCIENCE IS A BODY OF SYSTEMATIZED knowledge will serve to introduce consideration of the term "scientific" as it is employed here. The phrase "body of systematized knowledge" may be taken in different senses. It may designate a property which resides inherently in arranged facts, apart from the ways in which the facts have been settled upon to be facts, and apart from the way in which their arrangement has been secured. Or, it may mean the intellectual activities of observing, describing, comparing, inferring, experimenting, and testing, which are necessary in obtaining facts and in putting them into coherent form. The term should include both of these meanings. But since the static property of arrangement is dependent upon antecedent dynamic processes, it is necessary to make explicit such dependence. We need to throw the emphasis in using the term "scientific" first upon methods, and then upon results through reference to methods. As used in this article, "scientific" means regular methods of controlling the formation of judgments regarding some subject-matter.

The transition from an ordinary to a scientific attitude of mind coincides with ceasing to take certain things for granted and assuming a critical or inquiring and testing attitude. This transformation means that some belief and its accompanying statement are no longer taken as self-sufficing and complete in themselves, but are regarded as *conclusions*. To regard a statement as a conclusion means (1) that its basis and ground lie outside of itself. This reference beyond itself sets us upon the search for prior assertions which are needed in order to make this one, *i.e.*, upon inquiry. (2) Such prior statements are considered with reference to their bearings or import in the determination of some further statement, *i.e.*, a consequent. The meaning or significance of a given statement lies, logically, in other statements to which we are committed in making the one in question. Thus we are set upon reasoning, the development of the assertions to which a particular assertion or view commits and entitles us. Our attitude becomes scientific in the degree in which we look in both directions with respect to every judgment passed; first, checking or testing its validity by reference to possibility of making other and more certain judgments with which this one is bound up; secondly, fixing its meaning (or significance) by reference to its use in making other statements. The determination of *validity* by reference to possibility of making other judgments upon which the one in question depends, and the determination of *meaning* by reference to the necessity of making other statements to which the one in question entitles us, are the two marks of scientific procedure.

So far as we engage in this procedure, we look at our respective acts of judging not as independent and detached, but as an interrelated system, within which every assertion entitles us to other assertions (which must be carefully deduced since they constitute its meaning) and to which we are entitled only through other assertions (so that they must be carefully searched for). "Scientific" as used in this article thus means the possibility of establishing an order of judgments such that each one when made is of use in determining other judgments, thereby securing control of their formation.

Such a conception of "scientific," throwing the emphasis upon the inherent logic of an inquiry rather than upon the particular form which the results of the inquiry assume, may serve to obviate some of the objections which at once suggest themselves when there is mention of a science of conduct. Unless this conception is emphasized, the term "science" is likely to suggest those bodies of knowledge which are most familiar to us in physical matters; and thus to give the impression that what is sought is reduction of matters of conduct to similarly physical or even quasi-mathematical form. It is, however, analogy with the method of inquiry, not with the final product, which is intended. Yet, while this explanation may preclude certain objections, it is far, in the present state of discussion, from removing all objections and thus securing a free and open field. The point of view expressely disclaims any effort to reduce the statement of matters of conduct to forms comparable with those of physical science. But it also expressly proclaims an identity of logical procedure in the two cases. This assertion will meet with sharp and flat denial. Hence, before developing the logic of moral science, it is necessary to discuss the objections which affirm such an inherent disparity between moral judgments and physical judgments that there is no ground in the control of the judging activity in one case for inferring the possibility of like control in the other.

SEC. 2 · *The Possibility of Logical Control of Moral Judgments*

In considering this possibility, we are met, as just indicated, by an assertion that there is something in the very nature of conduct which prevents the use of logical methods in the way they are employed in other recognized spheres of scientific inquiry. The objection implies that *moral* judgments are of such character that nothing can be systematically extracted from one of them which is of use in facilitating and guaranteeing the formation of others. It denies, from the logical side, the continuity of moral experience. If there were such continuity, any one judgment could be dealt with in such a way as to make of it a conscious tool for forming other judgments. The ground of denial of continuity in moral experience rests upon the belief that the basis and justifying principle of the ethical judgment is found in transcendental conceptions, viz., considerations which do not flow from the course of experience as that is judged in terms of itself, but which have a significance independent of the course of experience as such.

The assertion of such logical disparity assumes a variety of forms, all coming back to pretty much the same presupposition. One way of putting the matter is that ethical judgments are immediate and intuitive. If this be true, an ethical judgment cannot be considered a conclusion; and hence there can be no question of putting it into orderly intellectual (or logical) relations with other like judgments. A merely immediate judgment is, by the nature of the case, incapable of either intellectual rectification or of intellectual application. This view finds expression in popular consciousness in the notion that scientific judgments depend upon reason, while moral valuations proceed from a separate faculty, conscience, having its own criteria and methods not amenable to intellectual supervision.

Another way of affirming radical disparity is that scientific judgments depend upon the principle of causation, which of necessity carries with it the dependence of one phenomenon upon another, and thus the possibility of stating every fact in connection with the statement of some other fact; while moral judgments involve the principle of final cause, of end and ideal. Hence to endeavor to control the construction and affirmation of any content of moral judgment by reference to antecedent propositions is to destroy its peculiar moral quality. Or, as it is popularly expressed, ethical judgment is ethical just because it is not scientific; because it deals with norms, values, ideals, not with given facts; with what *ought* to be, estimated through pure spiritual aspiration, not with what *is*, decided after investigation.

Pretty much the same point of view is expressed when it is said that scientific judgments, as such, state facts in terms of sequences in time and of co-existences in space. Wherever we are dealing with relations of this sort, it is apparent that a knowledge of one term or member serves as a guide and check in the assertion of the existence and character of the other term or member. But moral judgments, it is said, deal with actions which are still to be performed. Consequently in this case characteristic meaning is found only in the qualities which exist *after* and by means of the judgment. For this reason, moral judgment is often supposed to transcend anything found in past experience; and so, once more, to try to control a moral judgment through the medium of other judgments is to eliminate its distinctive ethical quality. This notion finds its popular equivalent in the conviction that moral judgments relate to realities where freedom is implicated in such a way that no intellectual control is possible. The judgment is considered to be based, not upon objective facts, but upon arbitrary choice or volition expressed in a certain sort of approval or disapproval.

I have no intention of discussing these points in their full bearing. I shall reduce them to a single logical formulation, and then discuss the latter in its most general significance. The justification of the single statement, as a formulation of the objections just set forth (and of other like ones), will not be attempted, for further discussion does not turn upon that point. When generalized, the various statements of the logical gulf between the moral judgment and the scientific reduces itself to an assertion of two antinomies: one, the separation between the universal and the individual; the other, between the intellectual and the practical. And these two antinomies finally reduce themselves to one: Scientific statements refer to *generic conditions* and relations, which are therefore capable of complete and objective statement; ethical judgments refer to an *individual act* which by its very nature transcends objective statement. The ground of separation is that scientific judgment is universal, hence only hypothetical, and hence incapable of relating to acts, while moral judgment is categorical, and thus individualized, and hence refers to acts. The scientific judgment states that where some condition or set of conditions is found, there also is found a specified other condition or set of conditions. The moral judgment states that a certain end has categorical value, and is thus to be realized without any reference whatsoever to antecedent conditions or facts. The scientific judgment states a connection of conditions; the moral judgment states the un-conditioned claim of an idea to be made real.

This formulation of the logic of the problem under con-sideration fixes attention upon the two points which are in need of discussion. First: Is it true that scientific judgment deals with contents which have, in and of themselves, a universal na-ture—that its whole significance is exhausted in setting forth a certain connection of conditions? Secondly: Is it true that the attempt to regulate, by means of an inellectual technique, moral judgments—which, of course, are thoroughly individualized—destroys or in any way lessens distinctively ethical value?

In discussing the two questions just propounded, I shall endeavor to show: First, that scientific judgments have all the logical characteristics of ethical judgments; since they refer (1) to individual cases, and (2) to acts. I shall endeavor to show that the scientific judgment, the formulation of a connection of condition, has its origin, and is developed and employed for the specific and sole purpose of freeing and reinforcing acts of judgment that apply to unique and individual cases. In other words, I shall try to show that there is no question of eliminat-ing the distinctive quality of ethical judgments by assimilating them to a different logical type, found in so-called scientific judgments; precisely because the logical type found in recog-nized scientific judgments is one which already takes due account of individualization and activity. I shall, then, secondly, endeavor to show that individualized ethical judgments require for their control generic propositions, which state a connection of relevant conditions in general (or objective) form; and that it is possible to direct inquiry so as to arrive at such universals. And finally, I shall briefly set forth the three typical lines along which the construction of such generic scientific proposi-tions must proceed, if there is to be a scientific treatment of ethics.

Sec. 3 · *Nature of Scientific Judgments*

The proposition that scientific judgments are hypothetic because they are universal is almost commonplace in recent logical theory. There is no doubt that there is a sense in which this proposition states an unquestioned truth. The aim of science is law. A law is adequate in the degree in which it takes the form, if not of an equation, at least of formulation of constancy, of relationship, or order. It is clear that any law, whether stated as formulation of order or as an equation, conveys, in and of itself, not an individualized reality, but a certain connection of conditions. Up to this point there is no dispute. When, however, it is argued that this direct and obvious concern of science with generic statements exhausts the logical significance of scientific method, certain fundamental presuppositions and certain fundamental bearings are ignored; and the logical question at issue is begged. The real question is not whether science aims at statements which take the form of universals, or formulae of connection of conditions, but *how* it comes to do so, and *what it does with* the universal statements after they have been secured.

In other words, we have, first, to ask for the logical import of generic judgments. Accordingly, not questioning the importance of general formulae as the objective content of the sciences, this section will endeavor to show that such importance lies in the development of "sciences" or bodies of generic formulae as instrumentalities and methods of controlling individualized judgments.

1. The boast and pride of modern science is its distinctly empirical and experimental character. The term "empirical" refers to origin and development of scientific statements out of concrete experiences; the term "experimental" refers to the testing and checking of the so-called laws and universals by reference to their application in further concrete experience. If this notion of science be correct, it shows, without further argument, that generic propositions occupy a purely intermediate position. They are neither initial nor final. They are the bridges by which

we pass over from one particular experience to another; they are individual experiences put into such shape as to be available in regulating other experiences. Otherwise scientific laws would be only intellectual abstractions tested on the basis of their own reciprocal consistencies; and the trait which is supposed to demarcate science from medieval speculation would at once fade away.

Moreover if the generic character of propositions of physical and biological sciences were ultimate, such propositions would be entirely useless from a practical point of view; they would be quite incapable of practical application because they would be isolated from intellectual continuity with the particular cases to which application is sought. No amount of purely deductive manipulation of abstractions brings a resulting conclusion any nearer a concrete fact than were the original premises. Deduction introduces in regular sequence new ideas, and thus complicates the general content. But to suppose that by complicating the content of a proposition we get nearer the individual of experience is the fallacy at once of mediaeval realism and of the ontological argument for the existence of God. No range of synthesis of universal propositions in chemistry, physics, and biology would (if such propositions were logically self-sufficing) assist us in building a bridge or in locating the source of an epidemic of typhoid fever. If, however, such propositions and their deductive synthesis are to be interpreted in the sense of the manufacturing and employing of intellectual tools for the express purpose of facilitating our individual experiences, the outcome is quite other.

The empirical origin, the experimental test, and the practical use of the statements of science are enough of themselves to indicate the impossibility of holding to any fixed logical division of judgments into universal as scientific, and individual as practical. It suggests that what we term science is just the forging and arranging of instrumentalities for dealing with individual cases of experience—cases which, if individual, are just as unique and irreplaceable as are those of moral life. We might even say that the very fact which leads us upon a superficial view into believing in the logical separation of the generic judgment from the individual, viz., the existence of a large and self-contained body of universal propositions, is proof that as to some individual experiences we have already worked out methods of regulating our reflective transactions with them, while for another phase of experience this work remains to be done; *i. e.*, is the problem of current ethical science.

The consideration of the technique by which the desired end of control is accomplished does not belong here. It suffices to note that the hypothetic judgment is a most potent instrumentality. If we inhibit the tendency to say, "This, A, is B," and can (1) find ground for saying, "Wherever there is *mn* there is B," and can (2) show that wherever there is *op* there is *mn*, and (3) have a technique for discovering the presence of *op* in A, we shall have warrant for identifying This, A, as B, even if all the outward and customary traits are lacking, and even if this A, presents certain traits which, without the mediation of a generic proposition, would have inevitably led us to identify it as C. Identification, in other words, is secure only when it can be made through (1) breaking up the unanalyzed This of naïve judgment into determinate traits, (2) breaking up the predicate into a similar combination of elements, and (3) establishing uniform connection between some of the elements in the subject and some in the predicate. All judgments of everyday life, and indeed all judgments in such sciences as geology, geography, history, zoölogy, and botany (all sciences that have to do with historic narration or with description of space co-existences), come back ultimately to questions of identification. Even judgments in physics and chemistry, in their ultimate and concrete form, are concerned with individual cases. Of all the sciences, mathematics alone [1] is concerned with pure general

[1] If it were necessary for the purpose of this argument, it could of course be shown that reference to individual cases is involved in all mathematics. Within mathematical science, symbols (and diagrams are symbols) are individual objects of just the same logical nature as are metals and acids in chemistry and as are rocks and fossils in geology.

propositions—hence the indispensable significance of mathematics as a *tool* for all judgments of technology and of the other sciences. It also is true in all the arts, whether commercial, professional, or artistic, that judgments reduce themselves to matters of correct identification. Observation, diagnosis, interpretation, and expert skill all display themselves in transactions with individual cases as such.

2. Thus far we have seen that the importance of generic statements in science is no ground for assuming a disparity in their logic from that of a scientific treatment of conduct. Indeed, since we have found that generic propositions originate, develop, and find their test in control of individual cases, the presumption is of similarity rather than of dissimilarity. Can we extend the parallelism farther? Does it apply equally well to the other characteristic trait of ethical judgment, viz., its reference to an act?

Just as modern logic has seized upon the hypothetic and universal character of scientific statements, relegating their bearing upon individual judgments into the background (but in truth so relegating them only because that bearing is always taken for granted), so modern logic has emphasized the aspect of content in judgment at the expense of the act of judging. I shall now try to show, however, that this emphasis also occurs because reference to act is so thoroughly taken for granted that it is possible to ignore it—that is, fail to give it explicit statement. I shall try to show that every judgment must be regarded as an act; that, indeed, the individual character of judgment proper, which has just been brought out, means, in final analysis, that the judgment is a unique act for which there is no substitute.

Our fundamental point is the control of the content or meaning which is asserted in any given judgment. How can such control be obtained? So far we have spoken as if the content of one judgment might be elaborated simply by reference to the content of another—particularly as if the content of an individual judgment, a judgment of identification, might be secured by reference to the content of a universal or hypothetic proposition. In truth, there is no such thing as control of one content by mere reference to another content as such. To recognize this impossibility is to recognize that the control of the formation of the judgment is always through the medium of an act by which the respective contents of both the individual judgment and of the universal proposition are selected and brought into relationship to each other. There is no road open from any generic formula to an individual judgment. The road leads through the habits and mental attitudes of the one engaged in judging. The universal gets logical force, as well as existence, only in the acts by which it is invented and constructed as a tool and then is employed for the purpose for which it was intended.

I shall accordingly try to show that activity shows itself at every critical point in the formation of judgment: (*a*) that it shows itself in the genesis of the generic or universal employed; (*b*) that it shows itself in the selection of the particular subject-matter which is judged; and (*c*) that it shows itself in the way in which the validity of the hypothesis is tested and verified, and the significance of the particular subject-matter determined.

a) So far we have assumed the possibility of building up and selecting for use some generic principle which controls the identification reached in an individual case. We cannot, that is to say, regulate judgments of the type, "This is typhoid," or, "That is Bela's comet," unless we have certain generic concepts, which are defined as connection of particular conditions, and unless we know when and how to select from the stock of such concepts at our disposal the particular one required. The entire science considered as a body of formulae having coherent relations to one another is just a system of possible predicates—that is, of possible standpoints or methods to be employed in qualifying some particular experience whose nature or meaning is not clear to us. It furnishes us with a set of tools from which choice has to be made. The choice, of course, depends upon the needs of the particular facts which have to be discriminated and identified in the given case—just as the carpenter decides, on the basis of what he is going to do, whether he will take a hammer, a saw, or a plane from his tool-chest. One might as well suppose that the existence of possible candidates for office, plus the mathematically possible combinations and permutations of them, constitutes an election of one of them to office, as to suppose that a specific judgment follows from even an ideally exhaustive system of general principles. The logical process includes, as an organic part of itself, the selection and reference of that particular one of the system which is relevant to the particular case. This individualized selection and adaptation is an integral portion of the logic of the situation. And such selection and adjustment is clearly in the nature of an action.

Nor must we fail to make clear that we are concerned, not with selecting and adapting a ready-made universal, but with the *origin* of the universal wholly for the sake of just such adaptation. If individual cases in experience never gave us any difficulty in identification, if they never set any problem, universals would simply not exist, to say nothing of being used. The universal is precisely such a statement of experience as will facilitate and guarantee the valuation of individualized experiences. It has no existence, as it has no check of validity, outside of such a function. In some cases where science has already made considerable headway, we may, without error, speak as if universals were already at hand, and as if the only question were which one of them to pick out and employ. But such a way of speaking must not blind us to the fact that it was only because of the need of some more objective way of determining given cases that a universal ever originated and took on form and character. Did not the universal develop as medium of conciliation in just the same sort of situation of conflict as that in which it finds its use, such use would be absolutely arbitrary, and consequently without logical limit. The activity which selects and

employs is logical, not extra-logical, just because the tool selected and employed has been invented and developed precisely
for the sake of just such future selection and use.[2]

b) The individualized act (or choice) in judgments of
identification shows itself not only in selection from a body of
alternatives of the specific predicate required, but in the determination of the "This," or subject, as well. Students of logic
are familiar with the distinction between the fact of particularity and the qualifications or distinguishing traits of a particular
—a distinction which has been variously termed one between the
"That" and the "What," or between "This" and "Thisness."[3]
Thisness refers to a quality which, however sensuous it be (such
as hot, red, loud), may yet in its own meaning belong equally
well to a large number of particulars. It is something a presentation *has*, rather than what it just *is*. Such a variety of applications is involved in the very notion of quality. It makes all
qualities capable of consideration as degrees. It is responsible
for the ease with which names of qualities transform themselves
into abstract terms, blue into blueness, loud into loudness, hot
into heat, etc.

The particularity, or better, singularity, of the judgment is
constituted by the immediate demonstrative reference of the

[2] The point of view which is here presented is, of course, distinctly pragmatic. I am not quite sure, however, of the implications of certain forms of
pragmatism. They sometimes seem to imply that a rational or logical statement
is all right up to a certain point, but has fixed external limits, so that at critical
points recourse must be had to considerations which are distinctly of an irrational
or extra-logical order, and this recourse is identified with choice and "activity."
The practical and the logical are thus opposed to each other. It is just the
opposite which I am endeavoring to sustain, viz., that the logical is an inherent
or organic expression of the practical, and hence is fulfilling its own logical basis
and aim when it functions practically. I have no desire to show that what we
term "science" is arbitrarily limited by *outside* ethical considerations; and that
consequently science cannot intrude itself into the ethical sphere; but precisely
the contrary, viz., that just because science is a mode of controlling our active
relations with the world of experienced things, ethical experience is supremely in
need of such regulation. And by "practical" I mean only regulated change in
experienced values.

[3] This distinction in recent logic has been brought out with great force and
clearness by BRADLEY, *Principles of Logic* (London, 1883), pp. 63-7.

"This."[4] This demonstrative character means a preferential selection; it is a matter of action. Or, from the psychological side, the sensory quality becomes specific only in motor response. Red, blue, hot, etc., as immediate experiences, always involve motor adjustments which determine them. Change the kind of motor adjustment and the quality of the experience changes; diminish it and the quality relapses more and more into indefinite vagueness. The selection of any particular "This" as the immediate subject of judgment is not arbitrary, however, but is dependent upon the end involved in the interest which is uppermost. Theoretically, any object within the range of perception, or any quality or any element of any one object, may function as the "This," or the subject-matter to be determined in judgment. Purely objectively, there is no reason for choosing any one of the infinite possibilities rather than another. But the aim in view (which, of course, finds its expression in the predicate of the judgment) gives a basis for deciding what object or what element of any object is logically fit. The implication of selective activity is thus an organic part of the logical operation, and not an arbitrary practical addition clapped on after the logical activity as such is complete. The very same interest which leads to the building up and selection of the universal leads to the constructive selection of the immediate data or material with reference to which the universal is to be employed.[5]

c) The experimental character of all scientific identification is a commonplace. It is so commonplace that we are apt to overlook its tremendous import—the unconditional necessity of overt activity to the integrity of the logical process as such.

[4] It is hardly necessary to point out that the article "the" is a weakened demonstrative, and that the pronouns, including "it," all have demonstrative reference.

[5] Hence in accepting Bradley's distinction between "This" and "Thisness" we cannot accept the peculiar interpretation which he gives it. According to his way of looking at it, no strictly *logical* connection is possible between "This" and "Thisness." "Thisness" alone has logical significance; the "This" is determined by considerations entirely beyond intellectual control; indeed, it marks the fact that a reality lying outside of the act of judging has broken in upon, or forced itself into, a region of logical ideas or meanings, this peculiar and coercive irruption being an essential attendant of the *finite* extremely limited character of our experience.

As we have just seen, an act is involved in the determination of both the predicate, or the interpreting meaning, and of the ".This," or fact to be identified. Were not both of these acts correlatives in a larger scheme of change of value in experience, they would both be arbitrary; and their ultimate appropriateness or adaptation to each other would be a sheer miracle. If one arbitrary act of choice reached forth to lay hold of some predicate from out the whole system of possible qualifications, while another act of choice, entirely independent in origin, reached out to seize a given area from the whole possible region of sense-perceptions, it would be the sheerest accident if the two selections thus made should fit into each other, should play into each other's hands.

But if one and the same end or interest operates in regulating both selections, the case stands quite otherwise. In such case, the experimental activity of verification is the carrying on of precisely the same purpose which found expression in the choice of subject and predicate respectively. It is in no sense a third process, but is the entire activity which we have already considered in two partial but typical aspects. The choice of meaning or predicate is always made with reference to the individual case to be interpreted; and the constitution of the particular objective case is always colored throughout by the point of view or idea with reference to which it is to be utilized. This reciprocal reference is the check or test continuously employed; and any particular more obvious experimental activity of verification means simply that conditions are such that the checking process is rendered overt.

I have now endeavored to show that if we take scientific judgment in its only ultimate form, viz., that which indentifies or discriminates an individualized portion of experience, judgment appears as an act of judging; the act showing itself both in the selection and determination of the subject and the predicate, and in the determination of their values with reference or in respect to each other, and hence in deciding as to truth and validity.

Since in the discussion I have used a terminology which is

hardly self-explanatory, and have introduced a variety of statements which to many will appear, in the present state or condition of logical discussion, to need rather than to afford support, I may point out that the force of the argument resides in matters capable of complete empirical confirmation. The truth or falsity of the conclusion reached depends upon these two notions:

First, every judgment is in its concrete reality an act of attention, and, like all attention, involves the functioning of an interest or end and the deploying of habits and impulsive tendencies (which ultimately involve motor adjustments) in the service of that interest. Hence it involves selection as regards both the object of attention and the standpoint and mode of "apperceiving" or interpreting. Change the interest or end, and the selected material (the subject of the judgment) changes, and the point of view from which it is regarded (and consequently the kind of predication) changes also.

Second, the abstract generalizing propositions of science have developed out of the needs of such individualized judgments or acts of attention; they have assumed their present form —that is, developed their characteristic structures or contents— as instrumentalities for enabling an individual judgment to do its work most effectively; that is to say, to accomplish most surely and economically the end for which it is undertaken. Consequently the value or validity of such concepts is constantly checked through a use which, by its success and failure, passes upon the competency of general principles, etc., to serve the regulative function for which they are instituted.[6]

So far as the scientific judgment is identified as an act, all

---

[6] It might check the prevalent tendency to draw sharp lines between philosophy as merely normative and the sciences as merely descriptive to realize that all generic scientific propositions, all statements of laws, all equations and formulae, are strictly normative in character, having as their sole excuse for being, and their sole test of worth, their capacity to regulate descriptions of individual cases. And the view that they are shorthand registers, or abstract descriptions, confirms instead of refuting this view. Why make a shorthand and abstract statement if it does not operate instrumentally in first-hand dealings with reality?

a priori reason disappears for drawing a line between the logic of the material of the recognized sciences and that of conduct. We are thus free to proceed, if we can find any positive basis. The recognition that the activity of judging does not exist in general, but is of such a nature as to require reference to an initial point of departure and to a terminal fulfilment, supplies exactly this positive ground. The act of judging is not merely an active experience at large, but one which requires specific motivation. There must be some stimulus which moves to performing this particular sort of act rather than some other. Why engage in that particular kind of activity that we call judging? Conceivably some other activity might be going on—the sawing of wood, the painting of a picture, the cornering of the wheat market, the administering of reproof. There must be something outside the most complete and correct collection of intellectual propositions which induces to engage in the occupation of judging rather than in some other active pursuit. Science furnishes conditions which are to be used in the most effective execution of the judging activity, *if* one means to judge at all. But it presupposes the If. No theoretical system can settle that the individual shall at a given moment judge rather than do something else. Only the whole scheme of conduct as focusing in the interests of an individual can afford that determining stimulus.

Not only must a practical motive be found for the use of the organized scientific system, but a similar motive must be found for its correct and adequate use. The logical value of any intellectual proposition, its distinctively logical significance as distinct from existence as mere *ens rationis*, depends upon practical, and ultimately upon moral, considerations. The interest must be of a kind not only to move the individual to judge, but to induce him to judge critically, bringing into use all necessary precautions and all available resources which may insure the maximum probability of truth in the conclusion. The system of science (employing the term "science" to mean an organized intellectual content) is absolutely dependent for logical worth upon a moral interest: the sincere aim to judge truly. Remove such an interest, and the scientific system becomes a purely aesthetic object, which may awaken emotional response in virtue of its internal harmony and symmetry, but which has no logical import. If we suppose, once more, that it is a case of identification of typhoid fever, it is the professional, social, and scientific interests of the physician which lead him to take the trouble and pains to get all the data that bear upon the forming of judgment, and to consider with sufficient deliberateness as to bring to bear the necessary instrumentalities of interpretation. The intellectual contents get a logical function only through a specific motive which is outside of them barely as contents, but which is absolutely bound up with them in logical function.

If the use made of scientific resources, of technique of observation and experiment, of systems of classification, etc., in directing the act of judging (and thereby fixing the content of the judgment) depends upon the interest and disposition of the situation, we have only to make such dependence explicit, and the so-called scientific judgment appears definitely as a moral judgment. If the physician is careless and arbitrary because of overanxiety to get his work done, of if he lets his pecuniary needs influence his manner of judgment, we may say that he has failed both logically and morally. Scientifically he has not employed the methods at command for directing his act of judging so as to give it maximum correctness. But the ground for such logical failure lies in his own habit or disposition. The generic propositions or universals of science can take effect, in a word, only through the medium of the habits and impulsive tendencies of the one who judges. They have no *modus operandi* of their own.[7]

[7] So far as I know, MR. CHARLES S. PIERCE was the first to call attention to this principle, and to insist upon its fundamental logical import (see *Monist*, Vol. II, pp. 534–6, 549–56). Mr. Pierce states it as the principle of continuity: A past idea can operate only so far as it is physically continuous with that upon which it operates. A general idea is simply a living and expanding feeling, and habit is a statement of the specific mode of operation of a given mental continuum. I have reached the above conclusion along such diverse lines that, without in any way minimizing the priority of Mr. Pierce's statement, or its more generalized logical character, I feel that my own statement has something of the value of an independent confirmation.

The possibility of a distinctively moral quality attaching to an intellectual activity is due to the fact that there is no particular point at which one habit begins and others leave off. If a given habit could become entirely isolated and detached, we might have an act of judging dependent upon a purely intellectual technique, upon a habit of using specialized skill in dealing with certain matters, irrespective of any ethical qualifications. But the principle of the continuum is absolute. Not only through habit does a given mental attitude expand into a particular case, but every habit in its own operation may directly or indirectly call up any other habit. The term "character" denotes this complex continuum of interactions in its office of influencing final judgment.

SEC. 4 · *The Logical Character of Ethical Judgment*

We now recur to our original proposition: Scientific treatment of any subject means command of an apparatus which may be used to control the formation of judgments in all matters appertaining to that subject. We have done away with the *a priori* objection that the subject matter to which recognized scientific judgments apply is so unlike that with which moral judgments are concerned that there is no common denominator. We are now free to revert to the original question: What are the differentiating logical conditions of a scientific treatment of conduct? Every sort of judgment has its own end to reach; and the instrumentalities (the categories and methods used) must vary as the end varies. If in general we conceive the logical nature of scientific technique, of formulae, universals, etc., to reside in their adaptation to guaranteeing the act of judging in accomplishing a purpose, we are thereby committed to the further proposition that the logical apparatus needed varies as the ends to be reached are diverse. If, then, there is anything typically distinctive in the end which the act of ethical judging has to subserve, there must be equally distinctive features in the logic of its scientific treatment.

The question thus recurs to the characteristic differential features of the ethical judgment as such. These features readily present themselves if we return to those cases of scientific identification in which ethical considerations become explicit. There are cases, we saw, in which the nature of the identification—and its consequent truth or falsity—is *consciously* dependent upon the attitude or disposition of the judger. The term "consciously" differentiates a peculiar type of judgment. In all cases of individual judgment there is an act; and in all cases the act is an expression of interest, and thus of habit, and finally of the whole body of habit or character. But in many cases this implication of character remains a presupposition. It is not necessary to take notice of it. It is part of the practical conditions of making a judgment; but is no part of the logical conditions, and hence is not called upon to enter into a content—a conscious objectification in the judgment. To regard it as a practical instead of a logical condition means that while it is necessary to *any* judgment, the one act of judgment in question requires it no more than any other. It affects all *alike*; and this very impartiality of reference is equivalent to no reference at all as regards the truth or falsity of the particular judgment. Judging in such cases is controlled by reference to conditions of another quality than those of character; its presented data are judged in terms of objects of the same order or quality as themselves. Not only is there no conscious inclusion of interest and disposition within the content judged, but there is express holding off, inhibition, of all elements proceeding from the judger. From the standpoint of judgments of this type, such elements are regarded as logically merely subjective, and hence as disturbing factors with respect to the attainment of truth. It is no paradox to say that the activity of the agent in the act of judging expresses itself in effort to prevent its activity from having any influence upon the material judged. Accordingly through such judgments "external" objects are determined, the activity of the judger being kept absolutely neutral or indifferent as to its reference. The same idea is expressed by saying that the operation of motive and character may be presupposed, and thence left out of account, when they are so uniform in their exercise that they make no difference with respect to the *particular* object or content judged.

But whenever the implication of character, the operation of habit and interest, is recognized as a factor affecting the quality of the specific object judged, the logical aim makes it necessary to take notice of this fact by making the relationship an explicit element of content in the subject-matter undergoing judgment. When character is not an indifferent or neutral factor, when it qualitatively colors the meaning of the situation which the judger presents to himself, a characteristic feature is introduced into the very object judged; one which is not a mere refinement, homogeneous in kind with facts already given, but one which transforms their significance, because introducing into the very content judged the standard of valuation. In other words, character as a practical condition becomes *logical* when its influence is preferential in effect—when instead of being a uniform and impartial condition of any judgment it is, if left to itself (or unstated), a determinant of *this* content-value of judgment rather than that. Put from the other side, in the "intellectual" judgment, it makes no *difference* to character *what* object is judged, so be it the one judged is judged accurately; while in the moral judgment the nub of the matter is the difference which the determination of the content as this or that effects in character as a necessary condition of judging *qua* judging.

The express reference to disposition makes the object an active object, viz., a process defined by certain limits—given facts on one side and the same facts as transformed by agency of a given type on the other. The object judged is active, not "external," because it requires an act of judging, not merely as antecedent, but as a necessary element in its own structure. In judgments of the distinctively intellectual type, the assumption is that such activity as is necessary to effect certain combinations and distinctions will keep itself outside the material judged, retiring as soon as it has done its work in bringing together the elements that belong together and removing those that have no business. But in the ethical judgment the assumption is in the contrary sense; viz., that the situation is made what it is through the attitude which finds expression in the very act of judging. From the strictly logical standpoint (without reference, that is, to overtly moral considerations) the ethical judgment thus has a distinctive aim of its own; it is engaged in judging a subject-matter, in whose determination the attitude or disposition which leads to the act of judging is a factor.

It follows immediately that the aim of the ethical judgment may be stated as follows: Its purpose is to construct the *act* of judgment as itself a complex objective content. It goes back of the judging act as that is employed in distinctively intellectual processes, and makes its quality and nature (as distinct from its form—a question for psychology) an object of consideration. Just because character or disposition is involved in the material passed in review and organized in judgment, character is determined by the judgment. This is a fact of tremendous ethical significance; but here its import is not ethical, but logical. It shows that we are dealing, from the strictly logical point of view, with a characteristic type of judgment—that in which the conditions of judging activity are themselves to be objectively determined. The judger is engaged in judging himself; and thereby in so far is fixing the conditions of all further judgments of any type whatsoever. Put in more psychological terms, we may say the judgment realizes, through conscious deliberation and choice, a certain motive hitherto more or less vague and impulsive; or it expresses a habit in such a way as not merely to strengthen it practically, but as to bring to consciousness both its emotional worth and its significance in terms of certain kinds of consequences. But from the logical standpoint we say that the judger is consciously engaged in constructing as an object (and thereby giving objective form and structure to) the controlling condition of every exercise of judgment.

Sec. 5 · *The Categories of a Science of Ethics*

The ethical judgment is one which effects an absolutely reciprocal determination of the situation judged, and of the character or disposition which is expressed in the act of judging. Any particular moral judgment must necessarily reflect within itself all the characteristics which are essential to moral judgment *ueberhaupt*. No matter how striking or how unique the material of any particular ethical experience, it is at least an ethical experience; and as such its consideration or interpretation must conform to the conditions involved in the very act of judging. A judgment which institutes the reciprocal determination just described has its own characteristic structure or organization. The work that it has to do gives it certain limiting or defining elements and properties. These constitute the ultimate Terms or Categories of all ethical science. Moreover, since these terms are reflected in every moral experience that is in course of judgment, they do not remain formal or barren, but are instruments of analysis of any concrete situation that is subjected to scientific scrutiny.

The distinctively intellectual judgment, that of construing one object in terms of other similar objects, has necessarily its own inherent structure which supplies the ultimate categories of all physical science. Units of space, time, mass, energy, etc., define to us the limiting conditions under which judgments of this type do their work. Now, a type of judgment which determines a situation in terms of character, which is concerned with constructing what may be termed indifferently an active situation or a consciously active agency, has a like logical title to the standpoints and methods as the tools, which are necessary to its task. Ethical discussion is full of such terms: the natural and the spiritual, the sensuous and the ideal, the standard and the right, obligation and duty, freedom and responsibility, are samples. The discussion and use of these terms suffer, however, from a fundamental difficulty. The terms are generally taken as somehow given ready-made and hence as independent and isolated things. Then theory concerns itself, first, with debating as to whether the categories have validity or not; and, secondly, as to what their specific significance is. The discussion is arbitrary precisely because the categories are not taken as limiting terms; as constituent elements in a logical operation which, having its own task to perform, must have the means or tools necessary for its successful accomplishing. Consequently the primary condition of a scientific treatment of ethics is that the fundamental terms, the intellectual standpoints and instrumentalities used be discussed with reference to the position they occupy and the part they play in a judgment of a peculiar type, viz., one which brings about the reciprocal objective determination of an active situation and a psychical disposition.

When the categories receive the fate which is meted out to them in current discussion, when they are taken up in accidental because isolated ways, there is no method of controlling formation of judgment regarding them. Consequently other judgments which depend upon their use are in an increasing measure uncontrolled. The very tools which are necessary in order that more specific judgments may work economically and effectively are only vaguely known as to their own structure and modes of operation. Naturally they are bungled in employ. Because categories are discussed as if they had some ready-made independent meaning, each of its own, there is no check upon the meaning which is assigned to any one of them, and no recognized standard for judging the validity of any. Only reference to a situation within which the categories emerge and function can furnish the basis for estimation of their value and import. Otherwise the definition of basic ethical terms is left to argumentation based upon opinion, an opinion which snatches at some of the more obvious features of the situation (and thereby may always possess some measure of truth), and which, failing to grasp the situation as a whole, fails to grasp the exact significance of its characteristic terms. Discussion, for instance, about what constitutes the ethical standard—whether conduciveness to happiness, or approximation to perfection of being

—must be relatively futile, until there is some method of determining by reference to the logical necessity of the case what *anything* must be and mean in order to be a standard at all. We lack a definition of standard in terms of the essential conditions of the ethical judgment and situation. Such a definition of standard would not indeed give us an off-hand view of the make-up of moral value such as might be utilized for forming moral precepts, but it will set before us certain conditions which any candidate for the office of moral standard must be capable of fulfilling; and will thereby serve as an instrument in criticizing the various claimants for the position of standard, whether these offer themselves in generic theory or in the affairs of concrete conduct. Similarly, theorists have been attempting to tell what the ideal of man is, what is *summum bonum*, what is man's duty, what are his responsibilities, to prove that he is possessed or not possessed of freedom, without any regulated way of defining the content of the terms "ideal," "good," "duty," etc. If these terms have any verifiable proper meaning of their own, it is as limiting traits of that type of judgment which institutes the reciprocal identification of mental attitude in judging and subject- matter judged. An analysis of the make-up of judgment of this type must reveal all the distinctions which have claim to the title of fundamental ethical categories. Whatever element of meaning reveals itself as a constituent part of such a judgment has all the claim to validity which moral experience itself possesses; a term which is not exhibited within such an analysis has no title to validity. The differential meaning of any one of the terms is dependent upon the particular part it plays in the development and termination of judgments of this sort.

Sec. 6 · *Psychological Analysis as a Condition of Controlling Ethical Judgments*

If it be true that a moral judgment is one in which the content finally affirmed is affected at every point by the disposition of the judger (since he interprets the situation that confronts him in terms of his own attitude), it follows at once that one portion of the generic theory necessary for adequate control of individual moral judgments will consist in an objective analysis of disposition as it affects action through the medium of judgment. Everyone knows, as simple matter of fact, that a large part of existing treatises on morals are filled with discussions concerning desirable and undesirable traits of character—virtues and vices; with conscience as a function of character; with discussions of intention, motive, choice, as expressions of, and as ways of forming, character. Moreover, a concrete discussion of freedom, responsibility, etc., is carried on as a problem of the relationship of character to the media of action. The reciprocal determination, already set forth, of character and the content judged shows that such discussions are not mere practical desiderata, nor yet a mere clearing up of incidental points, but integral portions of any adequate ethical theory.

If character or disposition reflects itself at every point in the constitution of the content finally set forth in judgment, it is clear that control of such judgment depends upon ability to state, in universalized form, the related elements constituting character an objective fact.[8] Our particular judgments regarding physical things are controlled only in so far as we have, independent of and prior to any particular emergency in experience, a knowledge of certain conditions to be observed in judging every physical object as physical. It is through reference to such laws, or statements of connected conditions, that we get the impartiality or objectivity which enables us to judge in a particular crisis unswerved by purely immediate considerations. We get away from the coercive immediacy of the experience, and into a position to look at it clearly and thoroughly. Since

---

[8] Of course, the terms "object" and "objective" are used in a logical sense, not as equivalent to "physical," which denotes simply one form which the logical object may take. Dr. Stuart's article on "Valuation as a Logical Process" in *Studies in Logical Theory* (The University of Chicago Press, 1903) may be referred to for a discussion of the study of the logical significance of the term "object" and its bearing upon the objectivity of economic and ethical judgments.

character is a fact entering into any moral judgment passed, ability of control depends upon our power to state character in terms of generic relation of conditions, which conditions are detachable from the pressure of circumstance in the particular case. Psychological analysis is the instrument by which character is transformed from its absorption in the values of immediate experience into an objective, scientific fact. It is indeed, a statement of experience in terms of its modes of control of its own evolving.

Even popular consciousness is aware of many ways in which active dispositions modify judgment in a moral sense; and is accustomed to take advantage of its knowledge to regulate moral judgments. A score of proverbs could be collected expressing ways in which psychological attitudes affect moral valuation. The ideas in such statements as the following are commonplaces to the plain man: Habit, wont, and use dull the power of observation; passion blinds and confuses the power of reflection; self-interest makes the judger alert to certain aspects of the situation judged; impulse hurries the mind on uncritically to a conclusion; ends, ideals, arouse, when contemplated, emotions that tend to fill consciousness, and which, as they swell, first restrict and then eliminate power of judgment. Such statements, which might be indefinitely increased, are not only popularly known, but are commonly used in formation of a kind of hygiene of moral action.

Psychology proper differs from the aggregate of such statements through setting forth *how* various dispositions operate in bringing about the effects attributed to them. Just what are the various distinguishable mental attitudes and tendencies? How do they hang together? How does one call forth or preclude another? We need an inventory of the different characteristic dispositions; and an account of how each is connected, both in the way of stimulation and inhibition, with every other. Psychological analysis answers this need. While it can answer this need only through development of scientific constructs which present themselves in experience only as results of the psychological examination, yet it is true that the typical attitudes and dispositions are familiar as functions of every-day experience. It is equally true that even the most atomic psychology employs generalized statements about the ways in which certain "states of consciousness" or elements (the constructs referred to) regularly introduce certain other "states." The theory of association is, indeed, just a generalization concerning an objective sequence of elements which reflects to the psychologist the sequence of attitudes or dispositions which are found in the immediate course of experience. In particular the sensationalists not only admit but claim that the association of other states of consciousness with states of pleasure and pain have uniform tendencies which may be reduced to universal propositions; and which may be employed to formulate principles exhibited in all conduct. If such is the case with psychological atomism, every step toward recognition of a more organized, or inherently complex, mental structure multiplies the number and range of possible propositions relating to connection of conditions among psychic states—statements which, if true at all, have exactly the same logical validity that is possessed by any "physical law." And in so far as these "states" are symbols of the attitudes and habits which operate in our immediate experience, every such proposition is at once translatable into one regarding the way in which character is constituted—just the type of generic statement required by a scientific ethics.

Psychology of course does not aim at reinstating the immediate experience of the individual; nor does it aim at describing that experience in its immediate values, whether aesthetic, social, or ethical. It reduces the immediate experience to a series of dispositions, attitudes, or states which are taken as either conditions or signatures of life-experience. It is not the full experience-of-seeing-a-tree it is concerned with, but the experience reduced by abstraction to an attitude or state of perception; it is not the concrete getting angry, with all its personal and social implications, but anger as one species of a generic mental disposition known as emotion. It is not concerned with a concrete judgment as such—to say nothing of moral judgment. But psychological analysis finds in experience the typical attitudes it deals with, and only abstracts them so that they may be objectively stated.

Every statement of moral theory which purports to relate to our moral consciousness sets forth relations whose truth must ultimately be tested through psychological analysis—just as every judgment regarding a special physical phenomenon must finally satisfy certain generic conditions of physical reality set forth in physical analysis.

Psychological analysis does not, for example, set before us an end or ideal actually experienced, whether moral or otherwise. It does not purport to tell us *what* the end or ideal is. But psychological analysis shows us just what forming and entertaining an end means. Psychological analysis abstracts from the concrete make-up of an end, as that is found as matter of direct experience, and because of (not in spite of) that abstraction sets before us having-an-end in terms of its conditions and its effects, that is, in terms of taking other characteristic attitudes which are present in other experiences.

Hence purely psychologic propositions are indispensable to any concrete moral theory. The logical analysis of the process of moral judgment, setting forth its inherent organization or structure with reference to the peculiar logical function it has to accomplish, furnishes the categories or limiting terms of ethical science, and supplies their formal meaning, their definition. But the logical category, say, of end or ideal becomes concrete only as some individual has actually experience of and with ends—and this involves the act or attitude of forming and entertaining them. So the category of standard becomes more than a possible intellectual tool only as some individual actually engages in an experience concerned with right and wrong, and which, when viewed objectively, is regarded as a judgment. The entertaining of ends, the adjudging of values—such acts are character-phenomena. Considered in abstraction from their immediate matter in experience, viz., just as acts, states, or dispositions, they are character-phenomena as these present themselves to psychological analysis. Even to consider any experience, or any phase of an experience, as an ideal is to reflect upon that experience; it is to abstract and to classify. It involves passing judgment *upon* an experience; something beyond the concrete experiencing. It is, as far as it goes, psychological analysis—that is, it is a process of exactly the same order and implying just the same distinctions and terms as are found in psychological science. But the latter, in making abstraction and classification conscious processes, enables us to control them, instead of merely indulging in them.

Hence it is futile to insist that psychology cannot "give" the moral ideal, and that consequently there must be recourse to transcendental considerations—to metaphysics. Metaphysics, in the sense of a logical analysis of that type of judgment which determines the agent and the content of judgment in complete reciprocity to each other, may "give" the ideal—that is, it may show how the form or category of ideal is a constitutive element in this type of judgment, and hence has whatever of validity attaches to this mode of judging. But such a logical analysis is far from transcendental metaphysics; and in any case we thus obtain only the category of ideal as a standpoint or terminus of a *possible* moral judgment. There is no question here of ideal as immediately experienced. Only living, not metphysics any more than psychology, can "give" an ideal in this sense. But when ethical theory makes statements regarding the importance of ideals for character and conduct, when it lays stress upon the significance of this, rather than that, kind of ideal, it is engaged in setting forth general relations of conditions; and there is absolutely no way of testing the validity of such statements with respect to their claim of generality or objectivity save by an analysis of mental dispositions which shows what is meant by having-an-ideal in terms of its antecedents and consequences. If any general statement whatsoever can be made about ideals, it is because the mental attitude corresponding to conceiving an ideal can be abstracted, and placed in a certain connection with attitudes which represent abstracts of other experiences. To have an ideal, to form and entertain one, must be a fact, or else ideals are absolute non-existence and non-sense. To discuss what it is to have an ideal is to engage in psychological analysis. If the having-an-ideal can be stated in terms of sequence with other similar attitudes, then we have a psychological generic statement (or "law") which can be employed as a tool of analysis in reflecting upon concrete moral experiences, just as the "law" of falling bodies is of use in controlling our judgment of pile-drivers, the trajectory of shells, etc. The possibility of *generalized propositions* regarding any character-phenomenon stands and falls with the possibility of psychological analysis revealing regular association or coordination of certain tendencies, habits, or dispositions with one another. Hence the continued reiteration that psychology as a natural science deals only with facts, while ethics is concerned with values, norms, ideals which *ought* to be whether they exist or no, is either aside from the point, or else proves the impossibility of making any general statements, metaphysical as well as practical and scientific, about such matters.

SEC. 7 · *Sociological Analysis as a Condition of Controlling Ethical Judgments*

We revert once more to our fundamental consideration: the reciprocal determination in moral judgment of the act of judging and the content judged. As we have just seen, adequate control of an act as determining a content involves the possibility of making character an object of scientific analysis—of stating it as a system of related conditions or an object complete in itself—a universal. We have now to recognize the converse, viz., that we can control the judgment of the act, hence of character as expressed in act, only as we have a method of analyzing the *content* in itself—that is, in abstraction from its bearings upon action.

The ethical problem needs to be approached from the point

of view of the act as modifying the content, and of the content as modifying the act; so that, on one hand, we require, prior to a particular moral crisis, a statement in universal terms of the mechanism of the attitudes and dispositions which determine judgment about action; while, on the other hand, we need a similar prior analysis and classification of the situations which call forth such judgment. Which portion of the scientific apparatus we bring most prominently into play in any given case depends upon the circumstances of that case as influencing the probable source of error. If the situation or scene of action (by which we mean the conditions which provoke or stimulate the act of moral judging) is fairly familiar, we may assume that the source of error in judgment lies in the disposition which is back of the experience—that if we can only secure the right motive on the part of the judger, the judgment itself will be correct. In other cases circumstances are reversed. We can fairly presuppose or take for granted a right attitude on the part of the judger; the problematic factor has to do with the interpretation of the situation. In this case what is needed for right judgment is a satisfactory knowledge of the "facts of the case." Given that, the existing motive will take care of the rest. It is this latter aspect of the matter that we now have to discuss.

The only way in which the agent can judge himself as an agent, and thereby control his act—that is, conceive of himself as the one who is to do a certain thing—is by finding out the situation which puts upon him the necessity of judging it in order that he may decide upon a certain course of action. As soon as a conclusion is reached as to the nature of the scene of action, a conclusion is also reached as to what the agent is to do, and this decides in turn what sort of an agent he is to be. The merely intellectual judgment may be marked off as one in which a content or object is fixed in terms of some other object or content, homogeneous in worth, and where accordingly it is a necessary part of the procedure to suppress participation in judging of traits which proceed from, or refer to, the disposition of the judger. But judgments which are ethical (not merely

intellectual) make no such abstraction. They expressly and positively include the participation of the judger in the content
judged, and of the object judged in the determination of the
judger. In other words, the object judged or situation constructed in moral judgment is not an external object, cold, remote, and indifferent, but is most uniquely, intimately, and
completely the agent's own object, or is the agent *as object*.

Such being the case, what is required in order to form such
a judgment of the scene or conditions of action as will facilitate
the most adequate possible construing of the agent? I reply: A
social science which will analyze a content as a combination of
elements in the same way that psychological analysis determines an act as a set of attitudes. It is assumed that the situation
which calls forth distinctively moral judgment is a social situation, which accordingly can be adequately described only
through methods of sociological analysis. I am aware that (even
admitting the necessity of some sort of scientific interpretation
of the scene of action) it is something of a jump to say that such
science must be sociological in character. The logical gap could
be covered only by carrying the discussion of the categories of
moral judgment to the point where their social value would explicitly show itself. Such analysis is apart from my present purpose. Here I need only recur to the proposition of the reciprocal determination, in the ethical judgment, of the judger and
the content judged, and suggest that this idea requires in its
logical development the conclusion that, since the judger is
personal, the content judged must ultimately be personal too—
so that the moral judgment really institutes a relationship between persons, relationship between persons being what we
mean by "social."

But in any case, some way of getting an objective statement
of the situation, a statement in terms of connection of conditions, is necessary. Certain descriptive sciences are necessary
and in many cases no one would deny that elements of associated life enter into the facts to be described. But even if it
be admitted that the scene is social, this characterization does

not exhaust the description. Any scene of action which is social is *also* cosmic or physical. It is also biological. Hence the absolute impossibility of ruling out the physical and biological sciences from bearing upon ethical science. If ethical theory require, as one of its necessary conditions, ability to describe in terms of itself the situation which demands moral judgment, any proposition, whether of mechanics, chemistry, geography, physiology, or history, which facilitates and guarantees the adequacy and truth of the description, becomes in virtue of that fact an important auxiliary of ethical science.

In other words, the postulate of moral science is the continuity of scientific judgment. This proposition is denied by both the materialistic and transcendental schools of philosophy. The transcendental school draws such a fixed line between the region of moral and of cosmic values that by no possibility can propositions which refer to the latter become auxiliary or instrumental with respect to the former. The fact that advance of physical and biological science so profoundly modifies moral problems, and hence moral judgments, and hence once more moral values, may serve as an argument against transcendental ethics—since, according to the latter, such obvious facts would be impossibilities. Materialism denies equally the principle of continuity of judgment. It confuses continuity of method, the possibility of using a general statement regarding one object as a tool in the determination of some other, with immediate identity of subject-matter. Instead of recognizing the *continuity* of ethical with other forms of experience, it wipes out ethical experience by assimilating it not simply with reference to logical method, but in its own ontological structure, to another form of objects defined in judgment—that is, the physical form. If it is once recognized that *all* scientific judgments, physical as well as ethical, are ultimately concerned with getting experience stated in objective (that is, general) terms for the sake of the direction of further experience, there will, on the one hand, be no hesitation in using any sort of statement that can be of use in the formation of other judgments, whatever be their topic or reference; and, on the other hand, there will be no thought of trying to explain away the *distinctive* traits of any type of experience. Since human life is continuous, the possibility of using any one mode of experience to assist in the formation of any other is the ultimate postulate of *all* science—non-ethical and ethical alike. And this possibility of use, of application, of instrumental service, makes it possible and necessary to employ "materialistic" science in the construction of ethical theory, and also protects in this application ethical values from deterioration and dissolution.

In conclusion, it may avoid misapprehension if I say that the considerations set forth in this paper do not involve any pedantic assumption regarding the necessity of using science, or logical control, in any particular instance of moral experience. The larger part, infinitely the larger part, of our concrete contact with physical nature takes place without conscious reference to the methods, or even the results, of physical science. Yet no one questions the fundamental importance of physical science. This importance discovers itself in two ways:

First, when we come to peculiarly difficult problems (whether of interpretation or of inventive construction), physical science puts us in possession of tools of conscious analysis and of synthesis. It enables us to economize our time and effort, and to proceed with the maximum probability of success to solution of the problem which confronts us. This use is conscious and deliberate. It involves the critical application of the technique and already established conclusions of science to cases of such complexity and perplexity that they would remain unsolved and undealt with, were it not for scientific resources.

In the second place, physical science has a wide sphere of application which involves no *conscious* reference whatsoever. Previous scientific methods and investigations have taken effect in our own mental habits and in the material dealt with. Our unconscious ways of apprehending, of interpreting, of deliberating, are saturated with products of prior conscious critical science. We thus get the benefit, in our intellectual commerce with particular situations, of scientific operations which we have forgotten, and even of those which we individually have never performed. Science has become incarnate in our immediate attitude toward the world about us, and is embodied in that world itself. Every time that we solve a difficulty by sending a telegram, crossing a bridge, lighting the gas, boarding a railroad train, consulting a thermometer, we are controlling the formation of a judgment by use of so much precipitated and condensed science. Science has pre-formed, in many of its features, the situation with reference to which we have to judge; and it is this objective delimitation and structural reinforcement which, answering at every point to the conformation of habit, most assists intelligence in the details of its behavior.

There is every reason to suppose that the analogy holds with reference to a science of conduct. Such a science can be built up only through reference to cases which at the outset need explicit critical direction in judgment. We need to know what the social situation is in which we find outselves required to act, so that we may know what it is right to do. We need to know what is the effect of some mental disposition upon our way of looking at life and thereby upon our conduct. Through clearing up the social situation, through making objective to ourselves our own motives and their consequences, we build up generic propositions: statements of experience as a connection of conditions, that is, in the form of objects. Such statements are used and applied in dealing with further problems. Gradually their use becomes more and more habitual. The "theory" becomes a part of our total apparatus. The social situation takes on a certain form or organization. It is pre-classified as of a certain sort, as of a certain genus and even species of this sort; the only question which remains is discrimination of the particular variety. Again, we get into the habit of taking into account certain sources of error in our own disposition as these affect our judgments of behavior, and thereby bring them sufficiently under control so that the need of conscious reference to their intellectual formulation diminishes. As physical science has brought about an organization of the physical world along with an organization of practical habits of dealing with that world, so ethical science will effect an organization of the social world and a corresponding organization of the mental habits through which the individual relates himself to it. With this clearing up of the field and organs of moral action, conscious recourse to theory will, as in physical cases, limit itself to problems of unusual perplexity and to constructions of a large degree of novelty.

Summary

1. By "scientific" is meant methods of control of formation of judgments.

2. Such control is obtained only by ability to abstract certain elements in the experience judged, and to state them as connections of conditions, *i. e.*, as "objects," or universals.

3. Such statements constitute the bulk of the recognized sciences. They are generic propositions, or laws, put, as a rule, in the hypothetic form if M, then N. But such generic propositions are the instruments of science, not science itself. Science has its life in judgments of identification, and it is for their sake that generic propositions (or universals, or laws) are constructed and tested or verified.

4. Such judgments of concrete identification are individualized, and are also acts. The presence of action as a logical element appears indirectly in (a) the selection of the subject, (b) the determination of the predicate, and (c) most directly in the copula—the entire process of the reciprocal forming and testing of tentative subjects and predicates.

5. Judgments are "intellectual" in logical type so far as this reference to behavior may be presupposed, and thereby not require to be consciously set forth or exposed. This happens whenever the action involved is impartial in its influence upon the quality of the content judged. Judgments are "moral" in

logical type so far as the presence of activity in affecting the content of judgment is seen consciously to affect itself—or whenever the reciprocal determination of activity and content becomes itself an object of judgment whose determination is a prerequisite for further successful judgments.

6. Control of moral judgment requires ability to constitute the reciprocal determination of activity and content into an "object." This has three phases: First, a statement of the limiting forms of that type of judgment which is concerned with construing an activity and a content in terms of each other. The limiting terms of such a type of judgment constitute the characteristic features, or categories, of the object of ethical science, just as the limiting terms of the judgment which construes one object in terms of another object constitute the categories of physical science. A discussion of moral judgment from this point of view may be termed "The Logic of Conduct." Second, an abstraction of the activity, which views it as a system of attitudes or dispositions involved in having experiences, and states it (since a system) as an object constituted by definite connections of diverse attitudes with the attitude of judging—viz., the science of psychology. Third, a similar abstraction of the "content," which views it as a system of social elements which form the scene or situation in which action is to occur, and with reference to which, therefore, the actor is to be formed—viz., sociological science.

7. The whole discussion implies that the determination of objects as objects, even when involving no conscious reference whatever to conduct, is, after all, for the sake of the development of further experience. This further development is change, transformation of existing experience, and thus is *active*. So far as this development is intentionally directed through the construction of objects as objects, there is not only active experience, but *regulated activity, i. e.*, conduct, behavior, practice. Therefore, all determination of objects as objects (including the sciences which construct physical objects) has reference to change of experience, of experience as activity; and, when

this reference passes from abstraction to application (from negative to positive), has reference to conscious control of the nature of the change (*i. e.*, deliberate change), and thereby gets ethical significance. This principle may be termed *the postulate of continuity of experience.* This principle, on the one hand, protects the integrity of the moral judgment, revealing its supremacy and the corresponding instrumental or auxiliary character of the intellectual judgment (whether physical, psychological, or social); and, upon the other, protects the moral judgment from isolation (*i. e.*, from transcendentalism), bringing it into working relations of reciprocal assistance with all judgments about the subject-matter of experience, even those of the most markedly mechanical and physiological sort.

2

VALUATION JUDGMENTS AND IMMEDIATE QUALITY

THERE IS MUCH IN MR. PHILIP B. RICE'S RECENT ARTICLE IN THE *Journal of Philosophy* with which a neo-empiricist is happy to agree.[1] He will agree, on the critical side, with opposition to the metaphysical "realism" that locates the "objectivity" of value in "objects" that are so called because of lack of any connection whatever with human behavior. He will agree also with the opposition to those views which admit a human factor in values, but which interpret it in such a way that the result is sceptical denial of the possibility of any genuine judgments about them. These agreements are based upon those positive aspects of Mr. Rice's paper which (1) identify the problem of the possibility of genuine judgments of value with the problem of the possibility of reaching conclusions about value that are capable of providing guidance to life-behavior; and (2) which identify the "objectivity" of judgments with verifiability by empirical evidence. The view that value-judgments are "objective" for the same reason that other judgments are accepted as valid because, that is, they are verifiable by the hypothetico-inductive method,[2] is that upon which the neo-empiricist stands.

I

The greater one's satisfaction with these points of Mr. Rice's article, the greater, however, will be one's disappointment that

---

[1] "Objectivity" in Value Judgments, Vol. XL (1943), pp. 5–14.

[2] *Op. cit.*, p. 12. In view of this emphasis upon verifiability, it seems a matter of regret that no allusion is made to the articles by Dr. Lepley dealing with this point.

Mr. Rice introduces an element of "subjectivity" which is reached by a different method and depends upon a different kind of criterion than that used in defining "objectivity." The method and criterion are so fundamentally different that they cease to be correlative. For *subjective* is defined in terms of a special order of Being, viz., one that is directly open to observation only by one person, and by a special kind of knowing called "introspection," or "*self*-knowledge"—an order of Being which accordingly is "inner" and "private." It is defined, then, by falling back upon an assumption of a certain sort of epistemological-metaphysical "reality" while "obective," on the other hand, is defined on the basis of evidential support depended upon in all scientific inquiry. Not only does Mr. Rice use a method and criterion that are explicitly rejected in the case of "objectivity," but he further complicates matters by holding that this introspective approach to a private and inner material provides a special kind of verifying evidence with respect to valuation judgments, a kind which can and should be *added on* to the evidence supplied by common and public observation, such as is used in arriving at non-valuation propositions—a view which renders the "subjective" itself "objective" on the basis of the definition given of objectivity!

Before dealing with this latter matter, I shall say something about the definition of "subjectivity" that would be arrived at on the basis of parity of reasoning and criterion with that used in the case of "objectivity." It would run something as follows: Propositions (judgments, beliefs, or whatever) are *subjective* when they are produced by causal conditions which fail to possess genuine evidential capacity and verifying power, but which nevertheless are taken at the time to possess them and hence to provide acceptance and assertion of the propositions in question. The only "assumption" in this definition is the empirically verifiable fact that all beliefs, right and wrong, valid and invalid, have concrete causal conditions which, under the given circumstances, *produce* judgments, but which in some cases are conditions that warrant or justify the proposition that is generated, while in other cases they are found not to be such as to furnish justifying ground. Epistemological philosophers make a great ado about illusions, hallucinations, forms of insanity. But science proceeds on the basis that there are concrete conditions for their occurrence, and that these conditions are capable of being detected and eliminated, or discounted, as far as capacity to produce acceptance of a given proposition and belief is concerned. It was perhaps "natural" in a backward state of science to lump together concrete and specifiable conditions of error and mistake under the general and supposedly unanalyzable assumption of "a subject," as a name for a general peculiar order of Being. But scientific inquiry has progressed by searching for and detecting specific concrete conditions which are subject to exactly the same kind of public observation and test as are the conditions that warrant and justify sound and valid propositions (judgments, beliefs, or whatever). It is the peculiarity of Mr. Rice's view of evaluative judgments that he has completely rejected the epistemological-metaphysical assumption in the case of "objectivity" while retaining it in the case of the "subjective." The consistent empirical view is that viewed as *events,* as occurrences, the *subjective* and *objective* are both of the same nature. They differ (and differ basically) with respect to the capacity of their respective causal conditions to serve as valid *grounds*—in their ability, that is, to stand up in the exercise of the verifying evidential function.

II

Mr. Rice offers no direct evidence or argument for holding to the existence of material that is private and inner and hence (by its very nature) accessible directly only to observation by a "self" which is single, exclusive, and non-public and non-social. He engages, however, in a discussion of another view whose defects are supposed to provide ground for the position he takes. As this other view is attributed to me, consideration of it may have the disadvantage of seeming to be purely an argument *pro domo*. But I hope the discussion will turn out, as it develops, to deal with two points of much more than personal importance. One of them concerns the matter of subjectivity; the other concerns the capacity of a "value experience" (as described by Mr. Rice) to serve as supplementary or "plus" evidence in verification of value-*judgments*.

Mr. Rice attributed to me, quite correctly, the view that evaluative judgments are conclusions of inquiries into the "conditions and results of experienced objects." He also points out, quite correctly, that this view is equivalent to holding that "objectivity" resides in "the publicly observable conditions and consequences of value-experiences." And he further states that I am moving in the right direction in seeking objectivity in the evidence for value judgments. The trouble is that I do not go far enough with respect to what is evidential and verifying material. My "social behaviorism leads [me] to ignore one very important kind of evidence, namely, that concerning the immediate quality of the experience of value itself."[3] This statement does not of itself expressly assert that this "immediate quality" is private and subjective. In so far, it is possible to discuss the question of the evidential value of an immediately experienced quality apart from the question of its alleged subjective nature.

Mr. Rice's statement that "value-judgments are concerning the immediate quality of the experience of value itself," is joined to a statement that since I *admit* "that 'liking' or 'enjoyment' is a constituent of the value experience itself," it is the more strange that I ignore the evidential and verifying force of the experience of liking and enjoyment.[4]

Now I do a good deal more than hold that qualitative "enjoyment," "satisfaction," is a *constituent* of the experienced material which the valuation judgment is about or "is concerning." I hold that it is the *entire* material that judgment is about.

[3] *Op. cit.*, pp. 9–10.
[4] P. 9. The word "admits" is not italicized in Mr. Rice's text. My reason for italicizing will be readily gathered from what follows.

But it is an essential part of my view of valuation judgments that the satisfaction, liking, enjoyment, they are about is not itself a *value* save in a figurative way, a way illustrated in the figure of speech in which a man is called a candidate. For it is not asserted that he is inherently and *per se* a *candidate,* but that he is one in connection with an on-going course of events of which a future election is an indispensable part—that is, in a prospective reference. And so an enjoyment is called a *value* with reference to being potentially the material for an evaluative judgment, or in connection with events still to occur. This designation is innocent as a figure of speech; it confuses the entire issue when taken literally.

The strange part of Mr. Rice's criticism of my view is that he himself explicitly insists upon the prospective reference of an evaluation judgment as far as its "objectivity" is concerned— and I fail to see how any statement can be regarded as a *judgment* unless it lays claim to objectivity in the sense of evidential support. The following considerations quoted from Mr. Rice's article certainly read as if they were in complete harmony with my view that the mere enunciation that something, as a matter of fact, is enjoyed or liked is not a *judgment* of the value of what is enjoyed. For in defining "objectivity" (without a claim to which, as I have just said, no form of words can be termed *judgment*) he says expressly that an ethical judgment is *not* a simple descriptive judgment concerning present or past fact, but "is a *predictive* judgment concerning the *potentialities* of human nature as well as its actuality." And he explicitly states that to say an act, *x*, is good refers to it not in isolation, but in connection with a whole system or "pattern of interests"; and that it has "objectivity," in case it will promote the *pattern* of interests "in the long run . . . to a greater extent than any feasible alternative"; [5] and that *x* has objectivity because it refers "to something *beyond my desire or liking at the moment.*" And while he does not go further than say that my emphasis

[5] *Op. cit.,* p. 11, my italics.

upon "conditions and consequences" is "in the right direction," he does not indicate on what basis alternative possibilities can be compared and investigated with respect to connection with a system of interests save on the ground of "conditions and consequences."

III

What then is the difference between us? Why does Mr. Rice find my view to be seriously defective, since he agrees with the two main points of my theory as to *judgments* that are evaluations, namely, as to the points (1) that the problem of *objectivity* of such judgments amounts to the problem of whether intelligent guidance of the course of life-conduct is possible, and (2) that *objectivity* is possible because value-judgments concern a set, system, or pattern of interests, beyond the immediate occurrence of a given liking or satisfaction? As far as I can make out, the difference is two-fold. My critic holds that the occurrence of a liking or satisfaction affords an added or "plus" verifying *evidence*; and he holds that since what is liked is qualitative, it is subjective in the sense of being directly open only to *self*-observation or introspection, or is private and inner. I take up first his view that the immediate quality of a satisfaction is a necessary part of the *evidence* that the satisfaction is a value. This view seems quite incompatible with Mr. Rice's doctrine that the question of value has to do with the connection of a satisfaction with a system of interests, involving the future and a comparison of alernative acts with respect to their integrative function.

Hence the force of his statement that my "social behaviorism leads me to ignore one very important kind of evidence, namely, that concerning the immediate quality of the experience of value itself" seems to rest upon an equivoke. I am so far from "ignoring" it that, according to my view, the entire valuation process is precisely and exclusively about or concerning this quality in its immediate occurrence. And the statement of Mr. Rice himself to the effect that valuation is not a description of what has happened, but is *predictive in reference,* reads like an explicit endorsement of the same doctrine. The equivoke consists in taking evidence *concerning* an immediately experienced quality to be identical with evidence *supplied* by that very immediate qualitative satisfaction (enjoyment, liking) although its *doubtful* status with respect to its connection with a whole pattern of interests is the occasion and the ground for a valuation-*judgment!* The equivoke is clear in the assumption made in the following passage. He says that since "Dewey admits that 'liking' or 'enjoyment' is a constituent of the value experience itself . . . it would seem to be a grave sin of omission for an empiricist to exclude this phase of the act from study when seeking evidence for valuations" (p. 9). The clear implication is that the exclusion of an immediately experienced quality from possession of *evidential and verifying function in judgment* is equivalent to excluding it from all recognition or attention whatever—although in fact this phenomenon is precisely that which judgment is about, or "is concerning" in the attempt to determine its standing *qua* value! And when he says, as a criticism of my view, that "in no other field do we rule out attention to the phenomenon under study itself, to concentrate exclusively upon its conditions and results" (p. 9), it seems to me clear that there is an illicit transfer from the problem of the *evidential* force and function of a given phenomenon over to the fact that a liking has taken place: A transfer that is illicit because it unwittingly substitutes possession of evidential force for the fact of the bare occurrence of that which evokes and demands judgment with respect to its value-status. It is not easy to understand why and how an inquiry, in the case of a given event, into *its* conditions and results is a case of ruling out attention to it. So much for the question of the evidential worth, with respect to determination of value, of the bare occurrence of an event which as an event is undeniably immediately *qualitative.*

IV

I turn now to the other question, the assumption of Mr. Rice that since what is enjoyed is immediately qualitative it is therefore "subjective." For there is no doubt that it is this assumption that leads him to believe that definition in terms of causes and effects, conditions and consequences, is only a partial definition, being confined to factors admittedly "objective" in Mr. Rice's, as well as my own, sense of the word. I point out that in my general doctrine about judgment and verification *situation* is the key word, and that a situation is held to be *directly and immediately qualitative.* And it is held that a situation evokes inquiry, terminating in *judgment,* when it is *problematic* in its immediate quality, because of confusing, conflicting, relatively disordered qualities. Hence any inquiry which is evoked is successful in the degree in which further observation succeeds in discovering facts by means of which inquiry terminates in an ordered, unified situation (as immediately qualitative as the original problematic situation). What is discovered in effecting this kind of transformation from one type of quality to another constitutes its *verifying* status with respect to any theory of hypothesis that is involved in the conduct of observations: the hypothetico-inductive method to which reference was earlier made.

Since the present matter of discussion does not concern the truth of my theory but its nature, I content myself with a single quotation. A transformed qualitative situation is said to be the *end* of inquiry "in the sense in which 'end' means '*end-in-view*' and in the sense in which it means 'close.' " [6]

Now Mr. Rice gives no argument at all in support of his position that the immediate qualitative material of liking (satisfaction, enjoyment) is *subjective.* Apparently he takes it to be self-evident. But Mr. Rice holds that the reason my theory is defective is because I hold that valuation judgments are determined in terms of "conditions and consequences," thus leaving

[6] *Logic: The Theory of Inquiry,* p. 158.

out of account evidence supplied by material which is "subjective." Hence it is more than pertinent for me to point out that, according to my theory, while the initial problematic situation and the final transformed resolved situation are equally immediately qualitative, no situation is subjective nor involves a subject-object relation. While this fact shows that my theory is at the opposite pole from "ignoring" qualitative immediacy, its pertinence here lies in the fact that if Mr. Rice wishes to engage in relevant criticism of my theory he should give arguments in support of his view that qualities, at least in the case of phenomena of liking and satisfaction, are open to direct inspection or observation only by an act of introspection or "self-observation" of material which is inherently "inner and private." And he should give reasons for holding that the events which provide the primary datum are (1) not of the nature of *situations*, and/or (2) that there is satisfactory evidence for holding that situations with respect to their qualitative immediacy are "subjective" instead of being prior to, neutral to, and inclusive of, any distinction and relation that can be legitimately instituted between subject and object. For *denial* of the primacy and ultimacy of this relation (supposed to be the inherent epistemological-metaphysical basis and background from which philosophical theory must proceed) is the basic feature of my general theory of knowledge, of judgment and verification, my theory of value-judgments being but a special case of this general theory.

And in calling my theory on this matter a special case of my *general* theory I intend to call attention to the fact that I have denied that as judgments, or in respect to method of inquiry, test, and verification, value-judgments have any peculiar or unique features. They differ from other judgments, of course, in the specific material they have to do with. But in this respect inquiries and judgments about potatoes, cats, and molecules differ from one another. The genuinely important difference resides in the fact of the much greater *importance with respect to the conduct of life-behavior* possessed by the special subject-matter of so-called value-judgments. For in comparison with the deep and broad *human* bearing of their subject-matter, the subject-matter of other judgments is relatively narrow and technical.

V

I am grateful to Mr. Rice not only for his agreement, as far as it goes, with some of the main tenets of my theory, but for the opportunity his article gives me for making clear any actual position on the secondary and derived nature of the "subject-object" distinction and relation, and the primary character of situations that are completely neutral to this distinction and relation, for the latter, in my view, is intermediate, transitive, and instrumental in the transformation of one type of imme-diately qualitative situation into a situation of another type in respect to ordering and arrangement of qualities, but of the same type with respect to its immediate qualitative nature, which is neither subjective, nor objective, nor a relation of the two.

I am grateful because I have come increasingly to the con-clusion that failure to grasp my view on this matter and its fundamental position in my discussion of special topics is the chief factor in producing misapprehension of my view of many special topics I have discussed. A recent article in the *Journal of Philosophy* by Mr. Brotherston is in point. Entitled "The Genius of Pragmatic Empiricism"[7] it sets out by saying this theory holds that "the subject-object relation . . . [obtains] in a field of common sense and scientific procedure which at the very beginning of enquiry is given as an on-going concern" (p. 14). Representatives of the theory have made, according to him, an advance in showing that there is no explicit awareness of this relation until reflective analysis sets in. But they have made the mistake of not expressly pointing out that it is there from the beginning, with primacy attached to the "subject" factor. Now

[7] Vol. XL (1943), pp. 14–21 and pp. 29–39.

whether or not we *should* have taken this view, it is in fact so different from that we have taken that it may be called "the *evil* genius" of pragmatic empiricism.[8]

I now recur to the matter of the connection of immediate quality with value-judgments. The view that the bare occurrence of *any* kind of satisfaction is evidence of value seems to me to involve a relapse into that prescientific method which Peirce called the method of *congeniality*. Nor is it at all clear to me how a quality said to be private and inner can be added on to qualities which are public to form an evidential whole. Such an addition or joining seems to be something like a contradiction *in adjecto*. But these considerations are not at all incompatible with the fact that marked satisfaction, amounting at times to positive excitement, may qualify situations in which terminate judgments of value are *verified by evidential facts*. But the quality of a satisfaction that arises because of attainment of adequate verification is *toto coelo* different from the quality of a satisfaction that happens to occur independent of evidence as to its status *qua* value. One of the main benefits of a genuine education in use of scientific method is that it produces immediate sensitiveness to the difference between these two kinds of satisfaction.

[8] Another article by A. F. Bentley on "Truth, Reality, and Behavioral Fact" states the actual position correctly, and in particular effects a correction of Mr. Brotherston's misconception of James's "neutral entities" (the *Journal of Philosophy*, Vol. XL, 1943, pp. 169–187. I may refer to an earlier article of mine, "How is Mind to be Known," *ibid.*, Vol. XXXIX (1942), pp. 29–35. In an earlier article of mine, "The Objectivism-subjectivism of Modern Philosophy" (*ibid.*, Vol. XXXVIII, 1941, pp. 533–542), I fear I did not make it sufficiently clear that in speaking of organic and environmental factors as conditions of a situation, what is meant is that they are conditions of the *occurrence* of situations, the distinction when made in respect to *production* being the chief factor in aiding us to bring the quality of situations (in which the relation does not obtain) under purposive regulation.

3

FURTHER AS TO VALUATION AS JUDGMENT [1]

I AM GRATEFUL TO MR. RICE FOR GIVING ME FURTHER OPPOR-
tunity to clear up points in my view which I have failed to
make sufficiently clear in the past. I shall in my present attempt
confine myself to two leading theses put forth by Mr. Rice.
One of them is that there are certain events which are intrinsically of such a nature that they can be observed only "introspectively," or by the single person or self in whom they occur,
such events being so "sequestered and idiosyncratic" as to be
private and, psychologically, "subjective." The second proposition is that in spite of their subjective intrinsic nature they are
capable of being used as evidence in the case of judgments of
value along with facts of a public and "objective" nature, thus
being logically "objective" although subjective in existence. [2]

I

The first of these two propositions concerns a question of
fact. The fact involved is of such a fundamental nature that it

[1] The present paper is called out by the article of Professor Rice on *Types
of Value Judgment,* the *Journal of Philosophy,* Vol. XL (1943), pp. 533-543.
I add here the remark that while I occasionally use the words "valuation judgments," I regard the phrase as pleonastic, *valuation* being judgment. (*Valuing,*
as I pointed out long ago, is an ambiguous word standing both for judgment or
evaluation and for direct liking, cherishing, relishing, holding dear, etc.) Since
Mr. Rice in his present paper attributes to me an identification of what I called
neo-empiricism—to distinguish it from traditional sensationalist empiricism—and
scientific method with "instrumentalism," I also add the remark that the only
identification I made was—and is—with the "hypothetico-inductive method."

[2] There is a third point in Mr. Rice's paper which, apparently, gives its
caption to his article. It is sufficiently independent of the points just mentioned
to merit consideration on its own account and, accordingly, is not touched upon
in this reply.

has no more bearing upon or connection with the logical question of the evidence that validity supports judgments of valuation than it has with a multitude of other philosophic questions.
I shall discuss it, then, *as* a question of fact, noting, however,
that in Mr. Rice's view the fact, as he interprets it, plays an
important part in judgments about "values." Mr. Rice holds
that such events as "shapes, colors, overt movements" have
qualities which are open to observation on equal terms by a
number of observers, and hence are public and "objective" in
their mode of existence. In contrast with such events stand
events such as "muscular sensations," thoughts not uttered or
enacted, feelings having affective tone, etc. The latter can be
observed only by a single person, or "introspectively," and
hence are private, subjective. It is expressly held that "both
the occurrence and the quality of these events can be directly
observed only by the individual in whose organism they are
occurring." Physiologically, they are said to be conditioned by
proprioceptors and interoceptors, while events of a public and
"objective" nature are conditioned by exteroceptors.

There is one difficulty in discussing this question of fact.
The kind of event whose character is in dispute cannot, by
definition, be had by any two observers in common, and hence
not by Mr. Rice and myself. Mr. Rice accordingly refers me,
quite logically, to "my own" (exclusively my own) "joys, pains,
and secret thoughts" for evidence of the existence of privately
observed events. Now the bald statement that while I recognize
the existence of such events as Mr. Rice gives examples of, I do
not find them to be "private" or inner as observed and known,
does not carry discussion far; it seems rather to leave it at a
dead end.

The matter at issue may, however, be approached indirectly. Mr. Rice objects to my characterizing his position as
"epistemological-metaphysical." I gave no reasons for that characterization. For I did not intend it to apply in any invidious
way to Mr. Rice's view. On the contrary, I intended it to apply
to a traditional and still generally accepted doctrine which

originated and developed in modern epistemological discussions, and which is "metaphysical" in the sense that it has to do with the inherent nature of two kinds or orders of existence. Since Mr. Rice accepts and promulgates the view, if I understand him aright, that there are two such orders, one psychological and "individual," the other not, I used the characterization in question.[3]

In any case, I wish to repeat my expression of gratitude to Mr. Rice for giving me an opportunity to state my position on this matter as explicitly as possible, since, as I remarked in my earlier article, failure to grasp my actual view seems to account for misapprehension of many points in my general philosophical theory. In this restatement of my view, I begin by stating the conclusion I have arrived at. It is as follows: The undeniable *centering* of the events which are the more immediate condition of the occurrence of events in the way of observation and of knowledge generally, within a particular organism, say that of John Smith, has been taken as proof that the resulting *observation* is itself "individual." I believe further that this conversion of a condition of the occurrence of an event into an inherent and intrinsic property of the event itself (that of observation) is not due to anything in the facts, but is derived from the holdover of an earlier doctrine, of pre-scientific and largely theological origin, of an individual soul as the knower—even though the "soul" part has been thinned down into "mind," "consciousness," or even that supposedly scientific *Ersatz,* the brain of a single organism.

I do not deny, in other words, that the immediate or last conditions of the *occurrence* of a pain, say of a toothache, and

[3] This matter is somewhat complicated in Mr. Rice's last paper by the fact that he freely refers to "subjective" and "objective" as *aspects;* aspects it would seem of "experience," which is taken to have two sides or faces, *x,* one private and one public. I should still regard this view as "metaphysical" in the sense of involving generalizations of the highest degree of generality about the nature of what exists. In any case, since I cannot suppose that Mr. Rice is hedging in using the word "aspects," the word seems to need explanation. Mr. Rice's discussion of "muscular sensations, secret thoughts, feelings of affective tone," seems to treat them as events on their own account.

the immediate and last conditions of the occurrence of an event in the way of knowing a given event *as* a toothache, are *centered* in particular organic bodies. But I do deny that causal conditions of the *occurrence* of an event are *ipso facto* qualities or traits of the event. I hold that they are extrinsic to the event itself although strictly relevant to its occurrence. And I also hold that while the temporally and spatially terminal conditions of an observation are *centered* in a particular organism, they are not *located* under the skin of the organism. For events outside the skin as well as under it are directly involved in the production of either a pain or an observation of it *as* pain.

I begin with the last point. In making a distinction between what I have called the *centering* of an event and its *location,* I have nothing recondite in mind. Every event that takes place has a certain extensive durational and spatial spread, as long and as wide as all the interacting conditions involved. Environmental conditions are surely as much a part of the occurrence of a toothache as are organic conditions; to *know* the event *as* the toothache it actually is depends on knowledge of the former. The sole difference that exists between environmental conditions and organic conditions is that the former occupy a relatively initial place and the latter a relatively terminal position in the series of occurrences forming a single total event. The operative presence of both environing and organic conditions, on equal terms, is found in events Mr. Rice terms "private" as it is in those he calls "public." The notion that language in the cases when it is not heard by others (is not "uttered or enacted") is on that account private in origin, occurrence, and quality is so extreme that it is hard for me to believe that it is held by any except extreme solipsists. Moreover, if the fact that certain occurrences center in a particular organism justifies the conclusion that the event thus conditioned is private and "subjective," the doctrine that colors and overt movements *as perceived* are also private seems logically to follow. Mr. Rice has corrected my impression that he holds qualities *as such* to be "subjective." But I think the logic of the matter as far as concerns the grounds for holding that *all* qualities are subjective is with those who make no difference between perceived colors and perceived pains.

As far as the logic of the matter is concerned, why not hold that *all events* have an exclusive, sequestered, private, self-centered aspect? A fire, for example, does not occur at large. It takes place in a particular house and may be confined to a single house: that is, according to the logic employed in behalf of the subjectivistic doctrine, it is "individual." All, except confirmed panpsychists, who hold that this fact does not render the fire subjective while a similar fact causes the perception of a toothache to be private, seem to have a responsibility for indicating the difference in the two cases—pan-psychists not having that responsibility because they use the same logic all the way through.

Finally, and most conclusively, the qualified and restricted relative sense in which a pain-event, say, may properly be said to be *centered,* with respect to its occurrence, in a particular organism has nothing to do with *observational knowledge* of it *as* pain and *as* the pain of a toothache. The fact that under ordinary conditions someone else can see "my own" teeth much more readily than I can will not, I suppose, be taken to prove that after all what is seen by him belongs to him in a "private" way. Nor will the fact that I cannot, under ordinary conditions, see the back of my own head be taken to militate against the fact that, after all, it is the back of "my own" head that is involved. Nor will the fact that from where I now sit I can observe certain things not observable by others from the positions they now occupy be taken as evidence that the things in question are private and subjective.

The examples I have chosen will, presumably, call out the retort that the conditions of perception and non-perception in the cases cited are wholly extrinsic, not affecting the nature or quality of the things perceived. Exactly so. My position is that the causes why a toothache is "felt" directly by one and not by another human being are of a similar extrinsic kind, not at all affecting the observed nature of the event as pain and as pain of a toothache. We are brought back to the matter of the distinction between conditions for the occurrence of a given event and the observed qualities of that event.

We have to *learn* to see, hear, and to feel when "feeling" is taken to mean an identification and demarcation of an event as having the qualities that define it as a kind of event—as happens in the case of identifying and distinguishing an event as pain and as toothache. It is to be hoped, though not too confidently asserted, that, in another generation or so, facts ascertained in biology, anthropology, and other sciences will displace the influence now exerted upon theories of observation and knowledge by doctrines that were framed before the sciences attained anything approaching their present estate. As things now stand, much that still passes as sound psychological knowledge is the result of the seeping in of doctrines it was "natural" enough to hold in earlier conditions, but which are now scientifically nullified.

In recurring to the confusion of events which, in a relative and restricted sense, are conditions of the occurrence of an event with the properties of that event as observed, I mentioned that under ordinary circumstances we do not perceive our own teeth or the backs of our own heads. Nevertheless it is easily "done with mirrors." In principle, though not in practical ease, the same thing holds in the case of a toothache. In case a certain grafting of the proprioceptor nerve tissues of two organisms could be successfully effected (and events as strange as this have actually taken place) there would exist the conditions for observation on equal terms by different observers—the criterion for that which is said to be "public."

And in connection with the other point, that perception and observation are affairs of identifying and distinguishing an event as *such-and-such,* Mr. Rice evinces a sound sense of fact in his admission that a perception based upon knowledge of the public kind—as in the case of observation by a dentist—is more likely to be valid than the observation of one with less technical knowledge, even though the conditions of occurrence of what is observed happen to center in the organism of the latter. In fact this admission on the part of Mr. Rice comes so close to taking the view I have been presenting that the matter might be left there.

I add, however, that I believe detailed examination of the case represented by "muscular sensations" would prove especially instructive. At what time and under what circumstances was it that the existence of qualities, which, on the physiological side, are mediated by changes of the nervous tissues in muscular structures, was first detected? I believe that the facts of the case would show that instead of their presence being an affair of direct and easy observation on the part of the one in whose organism the immediately conditioning events take place, it was an affair, at the outset, of a conclusion reached by knowledge of other facts—a hypothetical conclusion which was then tested by setting up special conditions (in principle like the use of a mirror in perceiving the back of one's own head) that enabled direct observation to be made.

I add also that examination of the case of language, whether uttered or "secret," would supply, in my judgment, evidence that is all but crucial. That language is something *learned,* and learned under social or public conditions, hardly needs argument. If we eliminate the influence exerted by traditional doctrines owing their present currency to the force of tradition rather than to scientifically ascertained facts, we shall, I believe, have no difficulty in accepting the view that instead of their first being "thoughts" which are private and which become public by being clothed externally in language, it is by language, by communication, that events otherwise dumb become possessed of "meanings" which, when they are studied in a cut-off way, are called "thoughts." I can imagine that this reference to language deciding the meanings *"pain, toothache"* will seem irrelevant to Mr. Rice. The issue is too large to argue at length here. But the question at issue is accessibility to *observation.* To defend the position of irrelevancy it would be necessary to show that observation of an event as *such-and-such* is possible without use of characteristics determined publicly in language, and/or that conditions without which an event cannot occur are not relevant to its characterization.[4]

II

The previous section concerns a matter of fact. While the conclusion reached affects the theory of valuation, it affects it only in the way in which it bears upon discussion of any philosophic topic. Its discussion takes up as much space as is given it in the present paper because the question raised and the

[4] Mr. Rice was kind enough to send me a copy of his rejoinder, published in the same issue, to this article. Accordingly I append a few brief comments bearing upon the foregoing section. (1) I began the present article by saying that the first thesis of Mr. Rice which I should criticize is the view of the *"intrinsic,"* and *"unique,"* inaccessibility of certain events to public (i.e., dual or plural) observation. For I understood Mr. Rice to hold to the *intrinsic* character of the inaccessibility of certain events to dual observation. And I do not find in his rejoinder any disavowal of this position. It is retracted, however, if I understand him, in one case, a case usually cited as typical, that of the pain of a toothache. But, if I understand him, there is still not the retraction of the view of *intrinsic* inaccessibility which seems to follow. (2) My point was that cases like this one proved that the number of observers to whom a given event is observable is an *extrinsic* matter, just as with the fact that *under present conditions* I am the only observer to whom events in the room where I am now writing are "accessible." (3) I was so far from attributing to Mr. Rice the view that *he* bases *his* distinction between public and private events upon the causal conditions of their occurrence," that I pointed out that his failure to do so was a case of his regarding inaccessibility under specifiable conditions of time and place as *intrinsic* and absolute—if I understand the words "intrinsic" and "unique" correctly. (4) Hence, instead of taking the position that "external relations can not be used as the 'defining properties' of events" (and of classes of events), my argument is that spatial-temporal *differences* in such "external relations" make the entire difference between the events and classes of events set *intrinsically* apart by Mr. Rice. So that the distinction is as *extrinsic* as is my inability to see, under *usual* space-time conditions, the back of my own head. (5) I am not sure whether Mr. Rice intended to attribute to me the view that I base the distinction between the classes of events in question "on their centering in the organism." But to avoid the possibility of misunderstanding, I add that I do not. On the contrary, my point is that *all* events in the way of observations are *centered* in an organism, while *all* events, those Mr. Rice calls private as well as those he calls public, extend, spatially and temporally, far beyond the skin of the organism in which they come to a head. This consideration adds to the relevancy of reference to language in the matter of observation in which an event is characterized as *such-and-such*.

criticisms made in previous articles seem to make it necessary. The conclusion I have reached appears at first sight to have left, as far as I am concerned, the question having to do with evidence for valuation in a total *impasse*. For if there are no "subjective" events of the kind indicated, then of course subjective events are not evidential with respect either to valuation or anything else.

The actual question, with respect to valuations, however, is not disposed of in this rather cavalier manner. I do not deny the existence of the kind of *subject-matter* which is called private and inner by Mr. Rice. On the contrary, we agree that this kind of material (whether subjective or objective) is that which valuations are about or concern. The question as to the evidential status for judgment of this material is accordingly still before us. The logical issue as distinct from that of fact needs discussion. Moreover, in his last article Mr. Rice has given illustrations that help define the issue.

Let me begin, then, by repeating as emphatically as possible that the occurrence of events in the way of prizing, cherishing, admiring, relishing, enjoying, is not in question. Nor is their primary importance for human life in any way depreciated; the events are what make life worth having. Nor is it held that they *must* be taken out of their qualitative immediacy and be subjected to judgment. On the contrary, my thesis, as respects valuation, is that only when conditions arise that cause doubt to arise as to their value (not their occurrence) are they judged. There is no single word that covers the entire range of events of the kind mentioned. It is convenient to use a single word to save constant repetition of things admired, enjoyed, liked, held dear, relished, cherished; this list being far from covering their entire range. I shall use the word "the enjoyeds." I use that term rather than "enjoyments" because it emphasizes the fact that actual events are involved; we do not enjoy enjoyments, but persons, scenes, deeds, works of art, friends, conversations with them, and ball games and concertos, to mention Mr. Rice's illustrations.

In his original article, Mr. Rice criticized my view that valu-ation-judgments proceed by placing the enjoyeds in the context (provided of course by inquiry) of conditions that produce them and consequences that result from them. Mr. Rice did not deny that this operation furnishes evidence, but charged me with neglecting the evidence which is supplied by the very occurrence of the enjoyeds. In fact he even went so far as to imply that I paid no attention to their occurrence in my pre-occupation with conditions and consequences. My reply was that so far from neglecting this fact, my theory holds that such are the events the *subject-matter* of valuations; but that since their unsettled or dubious state *qua* value is precisely that which calls out judgment, it is an equivoke to treat them, *in their bare occurrence,* as capable of providing evidence.

In his present reply, Mr. Rice cites the case of a toothache, saying that its immediately dis-enjoyed qualities may, and often do, furnish part of the evidence for the judgment of value: " 'I ought to visit a dentist,' or—though with less initial probability —'I ought to have a cavity filled.' " He continues "The ache is not, as Mr. Dewey seems to hold, merely a 'dubious' element in the situation, but, together with my previous knowledge of similar situations, it constitutes *prima facie* evidence for these value judgments." I do not know just what Mr. Rice has in mind by saying that I seem to hold that the ache is "merely a dubious element in the situation." I do not, however, suppose that he means to impute to me the view that its existence is in doubt. So I repeat that *if* there is a pause for valuation-judgment, it is because there is some doubt, in the total situation, of just what it indicates as to what it is better to do; what *should* or ought to be done. And I insert the *if* because it is by no means neces-sary that judgment intervene. One having the ache may make it a rule to visit a dentist; the event in question then operates as a direct stimulus—and unfortunately many persons react just by standing an ache until it ceases.

The nub of Mr. Rice's position, however, is found in the sentence containing the phrase "together with," in saying that the qualities of the ache provide, *along with previous knowledge*, evidence. Now there is a meaning of the words "together with" in which the statement made seems just as sensible and evident to me as it does to Mr. Rice. But this meaning is just not that which Mr. Rice gives the words. "Together with" is an ambiguous phrase. Mr. Rice gives it the meaning his own theory requires; that it is itself evidence as far as it goes, evidence which is then *added on* to evidence supplied by previous knowledge of a similar situation. My understanding of the words is that which, I believe, would occur to one independent of any theory. When the event of an enjoyed is judged with respect to estimating its value, its occurrence *qua* value is passed upon by means of taking it out of its isolated occurrence and bringing it into connection with the other facts, primarily those supplied by memory-knowledge of what has happened in the past in similar situations. By being viewed "together with" such facts, judgment is formed as to what the event indicates to be better or as to what should be. From my point of view, then, the meaning Mr. Rice gives the phrase repeats the equivoke with which he was charged in my previous article.

Mr. Rice's sense for facts leads him, even so, to qualify the evidential status of the event; he calls it *"prima facie* evidence," and goes on to speak of the need of "further evidence" being sought for to confirm (or, I suppose, perhaps to refute) evidence that is only *prima facie.* My point is that this further evidence is "together with" the enjoyed in question in precisely the same sense in which the knowledge of previous situations is together with it: the means of determining a valuation of it.

Mr. Rice gives some further examples of the same general type, referring to valuations regarding events to happen in the future. He says in the case of a judgment that it will be enjoyable to go to a Beethoven concerto or a ball game between the Dodgers and the Reds, "it is in part because I remember that similar occasions in the past have been accompanied by enjoyment, and because I discover introspectively that my imaginative rehearsal of the probable experience ahead of me is now accompanied by relish." No one can doubt that evidence supplied by the fact that similar events in the past have proved enjoyable is good evidence of the fact that, under like conditions, the same sort of event will be enjoyed in the future. Instead of proving Mr. Rice's contention that the present relish of the prospect is *added* evidence it goes to show that evidence provided by *other* events is summoned to pass upon the quality *qua* value, of the relish in question. I repeat that I don't hold that valuation-judgment *must* intervene. One may react directly by going to the ball park or the concert hall. Unless perchance Mr. Rice holds that every case of an enjoyed is, *ipso facto*, also a case of occurrence of a valuation-judgment, what are the conditions which according to him, evoke judgment of an enjoyed event in case there is no doubt as to its status *qua* value?

But the reader can analyze for himself the examples cited by Mr. Rice, and decide whether they are in fact instances that what is directly enjoyed are cases of providing additional, even *prima facie*, evidence in *judgments* regarding value, or whether the evidence to which it is said to be *added* is in fact that which decides the *value* of an enjoyed event. And if we were engaged merely in controversy and not in discussion of an issue, I would add that introduction of the phrase *prima facie* is itself a sufficient indication that the latter of the two alternatives describes the facts of the case.

4

SOME QUESTIONS ABOUT VALUE

WHEN I ANALYZE THE DISCOURAGEMENT I HAVE EXPERIENCED lately in connection with discussion of value, I find that it proceeds from the feeling that little headway is being made in determining the questions or issues fundamentally involved rather than from the fact that the views I personally hold have not received general approval. The clear-cut quality of the recent paper by Dr. Geiger [1] moves me to try to do something by way of clarifying underlying issues, with only that degree of attention to answers and solutions as may serve to make the nature of the questions stand out. I do not suppose that any formulation of questions which I can make will be uninfluenced by the answers I would give them. But if others will state the issues that seem to *them* to be basic, perhaps discussion of solutions will be more fruitful in the way of approach to agreement than has been the case. [2]

I begin with a preliminary rough listing.

I. What connection is there, if any, between an attitude that will be called prizing or holding dear and desiring, liking, interest, enjoying, etc.?

II. Irrespective of which of the above-named attitudes is taken to be primary, is it by itself a *sufficient* condition for the existence of values? Or, while it is a necessary condition, is a further condition, of the nature of *valuation* or *appraisal*, required?

[1] "Can We Choose between Values?" the *Journal of Philosophy*, Vol. XLI, pp. 292–298.

[2] I should add that no attempt is made to list all the questions upon which division in conclusions rests. The view that gives value a *transcendent* character has been omitted, so what is said will not appeal to those who hold that view.

III. Whatever the answer to the second question, is there anything in the nature of appraisal, evaluation, as judgment or/and proposition, that marks them off, with respect to their logical or their scientific status, from other propositions or judgments? Or are such distinctive properties as they possess wholly an affair of their subject-matter—as we might speak of astronomical and geological propositions without implying that there is any difference between them *qua* propositions?

IV. Is the scientific method of inquiry, in its broad sense,[3] applicable in determination of judgments and/or propositions in the way of valuations or appraisals? Or is there something inherent in the nature of values as subject-matter that precludes the application of such method?

I

It cannot be assumed that the meaning of the words "prizing" and "desiring" (or of any of the words of the first question) is evident on their face. To attempt to define them all is impossible and unnecessary. The word "prizing" is here used to stand for a *behavioral* transaction. If its force is reduced from overt action to an *attitude*, then the attitude or disposition in question must be understood to be taken toward things or persons, and as having no shadow of meaning if it be isolated from that which it is *towards*. Equivalent names would be nourishing, caring for, looking out after, fostering, making much of, being loyal or faithful to, clinging to, provided these words are taken in an active behavioral sense. If this meaning belongs to "prizing," then the first question concerns the connection (or lack of connection) which holds between the way of behaving that is specified and such states, acts, or processes, as "desiring," "liking," "interest," "enjoying," *no matter how the latter are defined*.

[3] The phrase "in its broad sense" is inserted to make it clear that "scientific" is not assumed in advance to signify reduction to physical or biological terms, but, as is the case with scientific investigations of concrete matters generally, leaves the scope of the subject-matter to be determined in the course of inquiry.

That is to say, *if* the latter words are given a behavioral description, the problem is that of the connections sustained to one another by various attitudes or dispositions which are homogeneous in dimension, since all are behavioral. It might, for example, be held that, since what is called *prizing, holding dear,* is a way of behaving tending to maintain something in factual (space-time) existence, *interest* stands for an enduring, or long-time-span, disposition of this nature, one which holds together in system a variety of acts otherwise having diverse directions. *Desire* might then be the behavioral attitude that arises when prizings are temporarily blocked or frustrated, while *enjoying* would be the name for the consummatory phase of prizing.[4] If, however, *desire, interest,* etc., are given a non-behavioral meaning, then it seems that they must stand for something "internal," "mentalistic," etc. In this case, the issue at stake would be a choice between a view which holds that *valuing* is basically a mode of behavior that serves to keep in being a thing that exists independently of being valued, and the view that some kind of a mental state or process suffices to generate value as an uniquely complete product.

Upon the first-mentioned view, "prizing" (as here understood) has definite biological roots, such as, for example, are manifest in the behavior of a mother bird in nourishing its young or of a mother-bear in attacking animals that threaten her young. The intensity of the "prizing" involved is then measured by the amount of energy that goes into the nourishing or the protecting behavior. Upon this view there is always an event or thing having existence independently of being prized (or valued) to which the quality or property of "value" is added under specified conditions of space-time. From the view that the desire, liking, interest, or whatever, that generates value is solely "internal" or "mental," it seems to follow that if the value in question is then attached to an event or object (something in

---

[4] The word "might" is used in the text to indicate that the particular descriptions given are intended to serve as sample illustrations of homogeneous behavioral interpretation, not as finalities.

space-time), it is because of an external more or less accidental association. For if desire or liking is an "internal" state complete in itself, then the fact that it hits upon or bears upon, say, a diamond, or a young woman, or holding an official position, is assuredly so external as to be relatively a matter of accident.

II

Another issue that seems to be basic in current literature concerns the question of the connection or lack of connection between *valuing* and *valuation* in the sense of *evaluating*. Do values come into existence (no matter how they are understood and accounted for) apart from and prior to anything whatever in the way of an evaluating condition? In case they do so arise, what is the relation of subsequent evaluations to a value having prior existence? *How* does a valuation supervene? And *why* does it supervene—that is to say, what is its function, if any?

The statements in the foregoing paragraph are based upon belief that examination of current discussions will show that some hold that nothing having the properties of value can arise save as some factor of appraisal, of measuring and comparing, enters in; while others hold that values may and do exist apart from any operation of this latter sort so that valuation is always wholly *ex post facto* as far as existence of values is concerned.

It is true, I think, that holding dear and valuing are used interchangeably. As far as usage goes, this fact might seem on its face to point to valuing being complete apart from evaluating. But the fact that valuation and valuing are also often used as synonyms is enough to give pause to such a conclusion. Appraisers in the field of taxation, for example, are said to value real estate, and there are expert appraisers in almost every field having to do with buying and selling property. And it is just as true that they *fix* value as it is that they pass upon it. The underlying issue here is whether "value" is a noun standing for something that is an entity in its own right or whether the word is adjectival, standing for a property or quality that belongs, under specifiable conditions, to a thing or person having existence independently of being valued. If the first view is adopted, then to say that a diamond, or a beloved person, or holding an official position, has or is a value, is to affirm that a connection somehow has been set up between two separate and unlike entities. If the second view is held, then it is held that a thing in virtue of identifiable and describable events, has acquired a quality or property not previously belonging to it. As a thing previously hard becomes soft when affected by heat, so, on this view, something previously indifferent takes on the quality of value when it is actively cared for in a way that protects or contributes to its continued existence. Upon this view, a value-quality loses the quasi-mystical character often ascribed to it, and is capable of identification and description in terms of conditions of origin and consequence, as are other natural events.[5]

When it was suggested above that *appraising* (*evaluating*) is often used interchangeably with *valuing*, there was no intention of intimating that there is no difference between the direct behavioral operation of holding dear and such operations as valuations of real estate and other commodities. There is a decided difference. The point in calling attention to the fact of common usage is two-fold. It definitely raises the question of the relation of *valuation* and *value* to one another. Does *valuation* affect or modify things previously valued in the sense of being held dear (desired, liked, enjoyed), or does a valuation-proposition merely communicate the fact that a thing or person has in fact been held dear (liked, enjoyed, esteemed)? If the latter, what is the function of deliberation? Is it or is it not true that at times questions arise as to whether things previously highly esteemed (desired, liked, etc.) *should* be so viewed and treated? In the latter case, it would seem that reflective inquiry

---

[5] If this line of interpretation were carried out, it would indicate that the appearance of value-quality is genetically and functionally continuous, not only with physiological operations that protect and continue living processes, but with physical-chemical interactions that maintain stability amid change on the part of some compounds.

(deliberation) is engaged in for the sake of determining the value-status of the thing or person in question.

The other point in calling attention to occasional interchangeable use of *valuing* and *valuation* is to raise the question whether the undeniable difference between direct valuing and the indirectness of evaluation is a matter of *separation* or of *emphasis*. If there is in direct valuing an element of recognition of the properties of the thing or person valued as *ground* for prizing, esteeming, desiring, liking, etc., then the difference between it and explicit evaluation is one of emphasis and degree, not of fixed kinds. *Ap-praising* then represents a more or less systematized development of what is already present in *prizing*. If the valuing is *wholly* a-rational, if there is nothing whatever "objective" as its ground, then there is complete separation. In this case the problem is to determine whether valuation (i) is simply a "realistic" apprehension of something already completely there, or (ii) is simply a verbal communication of an established fact but not in any sense a proposition, or (iii) if it does enter at all into formation of subsequent valuings, how does it manage to do so.

III

The third problem grows quite directly out of the one just considered. It may be stated as follows: Is there anything unique or distinctive about valuation-propositions *as propositions?* (If they merely enunciate to others facts already in existence, this question does not arise, since such communications are, *ipso facto*, not *propositions*. Outright statements that valuation-propositions *qua* propositions and not just because of their subject-matter are of a distinctive kind are not usual in the literature that discusses the subject of value. But positions are frequently taken and topics introduced that do not seem to have any meaning unless that position has been assumed without explicit statement. I give one typical example.

Articles frequently appear that discuss the relation of *fact* and *value*. If the subject discussed under this caption were the relation of value-facts to *other* facts, there would not be the assumption of uniqueness just mentioned. But anyone reading articles devoted to discussion of this issue will note that it is an issue or problem just because it is held that propositions about values are somehow of a unique sort, being *inherently* marked off from propositions about facts. I can think of nothing more likely to be clarifying in the present confused state of the subject than an explicit statement of the *grounds* upon which it is assumed that propositions about values are *not* propositions about space-time facts, together with explicit discussion of the *consequences* of that position. If a question were raised about the relation of geological propositions to astronomical propositions, or of meteor-propositions to comet-propositions, it would not occur to anyone that the "problem" was other than that of the connection between two sets of facts. It is my conviction that nothing would better clarify the present unsatisfactory state of discussion of value than definite and explicit statement of the reasons why the case is supposed to be otherwise in respect to value.

IV

Of late, there has appeared a school of theorists insisting with vigor that genuine propositions (and/or judgments) about values are impossible, because the latter have properties that render them wholly recalcitrant to cognitive treatment. In brief, this school holds the verbal expressions about values are of the nature of exclamations, expressing only the dominant emotional state of the one from whom the ejaculation issues. The ejaculation may be verbally extended into a sentence expressing a desire or liking or an interest. But, so it is said, the only question of a cognitive or intellectual nature that can be raised is whether the verbal expression in question (whether it be a shorter ejaculation or an expanded sentence) actually expresses the emotional state of the speaker or is meant to mislead others by concealing or distorting his actual state.

The practical import of this position may be inferred from

the fact that according to it differences as to value can not be adjudicated or negotiated. They are just ultimate facts. In the frank words of one who has taken this position, serious cases of ultimate difference can be settled, if at all, only by "bashing in of heads." I shall not ask here how far this view carries to its logical conclusion the view that some "internal" or mentalistic state or process suffices to bring value-events into existence. I limit myself to pointing out that at the present time serious differences in valuing are in fact treated as capable of settlement only by recourse to force and in so far the view in question has empirical support. This is the case in recourse to war between nations, and in less obvious and complete ways, in domestic disputes between groups and in conflict of classes. In international relations short of war, the view is practically taken in acceptance of an ultimate difference between "justiciable" and "non-justiciable" disputes.

It can not be denied that this particular question is of immense practical import. Using the word "bias" without prejudice, I think it may be stated as follows: Are value-facts biasfacts of such intensity and exclusiveness as to be unmodifiable by any possible consideration of grounds and consequences? The question at issue is not whether some values are now actually treated as if they were of this kind. It is whether the cause of their being so treated inheres in them as value-facts or is a cultural-social phenomenon. If the latter is the case, they are capable of modification by socio-cultural changes. If the former is the case, then differences in valuing which are of serious social importance can not be brought within the scope of investigation so as to be settled in a reasonable way. They may not always lead to open conflict. But if not it will be because it is believed that the latter will not be successful, or will be too costly, or that the time is not ripe, or that some more devious method will accomplish a wished-for triumph more effectively.

This fourth question is evidently connected with those previously discussed. If valuing consists *wholly* and exclusively of something inherently recalcitrant to inquiry and adjudication, then it must be admitted that it can not rise about the brute-animal level—save with respect to the *means* most likely to secure its victory over conflicting valuations and values. But if, in answer to the third question, it is decided that there is some element or aspect of valuation on "objective" grounds in every case of prizing, desiring, etc., etc., then it is possible that this element or aspect may itself become so prized, desired, and enjoyed that it will gain in force at the expense of the brute and non-rational factor.

In this connection it seems worthy of note that those writers who hold to the completely a-rational character of valuing begin by accepting the "internal" mentalistic theory of value, and then proceed to endow this quasi-gaseous stuff with powers of resistance greater than are possessed by triple-plate steel. While the four questions that have been formulated are those which seem to me to be more or less openly expressed in current discussion, the fact I have just stated leads me to raise, on my own account, another question which does not often appear in the literature on value, and which, nevertheless, may be more fundamental than those which do appear. Are values and valuations such that they can be treated on a psychological basis of an allegedly "individual" kind? Or are they so definitely and completely socio-cultural that they can be effectively dealt with only in that context? [6]

[6] Since the above text was written, I find this question explicitly raised as basic to economic theory, in the book of Ayres, *The Theory of Economic Progress*, especially pp. 73–85, 90, 97.

5

THE AMBIGUITY OF "INTRINSIC GOOD" [1]

THE POINT I WISH TO MAKE CONCERNS A CERTAIN AMBIGUITY IN the word "intrinsic" as applied to *good* and other subjects of philosophic discussion. Sometimes it is used to designate that which is *essential* in the sense of the "formal cause" of Aristotle. It is then opposed to "existential" as a designation for what is temporal and spatial, but not necessary and universal. I shall introduce the discussion by reference to verbal usage, but not with the intention of ascribing any legislative capacity to such usage. The particular usage I have in mind is that of the words "intrinsic" and "inherent." One who consults the *Oxford Dictionary* finds that the words are sometimes employed as synonyms in a way which gives *intrinsic* the force of standing for that which belongs to the very nature or essence of a thing. For example, the third definition of "intrinsic" reads: "Belonging to a thing in itself, or by its very nature; inherent, essential; proper; 'of its own.'" There is obviously involved in this definition an acceptance of the logico-metaphysical doctrine that some qualities belong to some entities necessarily, permanently, and universally, in distinction from qualities that are "possessed" only contingently and occasionally. A definition of "inherent" found in the same dictionary makes this signification explicit: "Existing in something as a permanent attribute or

[1] These pages would not have been written without the stimulus received from Barnett Savery's recent paper on "Intrinsic Good," published in the *Journal of Philosophy*, Vol. XXXIX (1942), pp. 234–244. In fact, I should look upon the present paper as a development of some points made in his article, were it not that I might thereby seem to make him responsible for conclusions not implied in what he has said.

quality; . . . belonging to the intrinsic nature of that which is spoken of."

So far there is no question of ambiguity. But under the very definition of "intrinsic" that has been quoted there is cited as an illustration the following passage from a writing of John Locke's: "The intrinsic value of silver considered as money, is that estimate which common consent has placed upon it." This "estimate" is evidently a mutable and contingent affair, varying with time and place. It has nothing to do with a value belonging to silver because of its own inherent and permanent nature or essence. In the language of Aristotle, it designates an "accidental" quality, one which varies as spatial and temporal conditions vary.

Mr. Savery's article quotes from G. E. Moore two definitions or descriptions of intrinsic good.[2] That one which says that to call a good intrinsic is to affirm that it would be a good thing for it to exist "even if it existed quite alone" does not appear to go beyond the existential or non-essential signification. This fact quite justifies the remark of Mr. Savery that this definition "is apparently harmless." But Moore also says that the question whether a good can be said to be intrinsic "depends solely upon the intrinsic nature of the thing in question."

Suppose instead of the quality "good" we take such a quality as "white." If I say that the quality "white" belongs intrinsically to the paper upon which I am writing, since it would still belong to it if the paper existed quite alone in the world, I do not see that I am saying any more than that the quality does in fact belong to the paper, no matter how it came to belong to it. "Intrinsic" in this sense does not go beyond assertion of a brute matter of space-time existence. In this signification, I should say that *all* qualities whatever are "intrinsic" to the things they qualify at the time and place of the occurrence of the latter—provided only the things in question do genuinely "have" them. If, however, I were to say that the quality "white" belongs to this paper because of the "intrinsic nature" of the paper, I should be using "intrinsic" in quite another sense.

[2] *Op. cit.*, p. 235.

Now in the case in which the applicability of "good" is said to depend upon the "intrinsic nature" of the thing in question, there is no doubt which of the two senses of the ambiguous word is involved. What unfortunately is not so evident is that the ambiguity of the word has the effect of shifting the issue. Instead of the question of whether or not some event or existence actually has the quality "good," independently of how it came to have it, we have a transfer of the question to the general metaphysical-logical issue of intrinsic natures or essences. The whole problem of the intrinsic nature of "good" is thus made to depend upon another problem, one directly associated with the doctrine of indwelling immutable natures or essences.

I do not propose to discuss the validity of the latter doctrine. It is obviously within the rights of any one writing on the subject to use that doctrine in defining "good" in discussion of ethical problems. But I submit that in every such case it should be made clear to the reader that the moral definition is made on the ground of a wider logico-metaphysical doctrine, and that its validity depends upon the validity of the latter doctrine—which accordingly requires independent justification in order to prove the validity of the moral doctrine of "good" which is put forth.

Without going into the larger issue, one may, I suppose, assume that some writers on morals distinguish between what I have called the existential and the essential significations of a quality as intrinsic by holding that, in its non-moral use, "good" is equivalent to a satisfaction or an enjoyment that actually exists as a quality of some event at a given time or place, it is "intrinsic" simply in the sense that the thing in question actually has or "owns" that quality at that time and place. *Moral* good on the other hand, it may be held, *is* moral precisely because of the permanent nature or essence of what is characterized as "good."

I do not question that this is a tenable position. But if it is taken it certainly needs argumentative support. For there are alternative positions. By way of indicating the need for explicit statement and explicit defense, I mention one alternative. It may be held that the moral issue regarding a good as a satisfaction or enjoyment arises only when such enjoyments have become problematic and arouse reflective inquiry. In this case, the contrast in question is to be regarded not as a contrast between something good only in an "extrinsic" or accidental sense and that which is good because of an eternal and universal nature, but as a contrast between a good which is *immediately* such and one determined as good upon *reflection* covering an extensive number of existing cases. I am not arguing here that such is the case. I am pointing to a possible alternative definition in order to indicate the necessity for explicit formulation and explicit justification of a certain view of "intrinsic good," so as to make sure that it does not ultimately rest upon an ambiguity of the word "intrinsic" in connection with a metaphysical position which is left unstated.

6

BY NATURE AND BY ART

I

CURRENT PHILOSOPHICAL THEORIES OF KNOWLEDGE ARE STRANGELY
neglectful of the implications and consequences of the revolution that has taken place in the actual subject-matter and methods of scientific knowledge. In substance, this revolution may
be said to be one from knowledge that is such "by nature" to
scientific subject-matter which is what it is because it is "by art."
The classic scheme, following Aristotle, held that the subject-
matter of science, as the highest grade of knowledge, is what
it is because of certain inherent forms, essences, or natures.
These indwelling and constitutive natures are eternal, immutable, and necessary. It followed that in the Greek-medieval
system all *sciences,* from astronomy to biology, were concerned
with species or kinds, which are immutably the same and
eternally separated from one another by the fixed natures
forming their inherent essences or Being.

Other forms of knowledge, such as were called sense-perception and opinion, were also what they were by the nature of
their inherent Beings; or, more strictly, by the unchangeable
and incorrigible partiality or defect of Being which marked
them. For over against fixed and eternal species constituted by
inherent essential forms were the things that change; things
that are generated and perish. Alteration, modifiability, muta-
bility, are *ipso facto* proof of instability and inconstancy. These
in turn are proof of lack of Being in its full sense. It is because
of lack, or privation, of self-contained and self-sufficient Being

286

that some things are variable and transient, now one thing and now another. The lack of inherent natures or essences is equivalent to dependence upon circumstances that are external, this dependence upon what is outside being manifested in their variability. In classic terminology, science is concerned with "formal causes," that is, with inherent natures which "cause" things to be *what* they are. Sense-knowledge and opinion are inferior forms of knowledge concerned with things which by their natures are so mutable that knowledge of them is itself unstable and shifting—as in the case of things touched, heard, seen.

It should not be necessary to dwell upon the fact that, according to what is now science, what the ancient scheme relegated to an inferior position, namely, efficient and material "causes," constitutes the only legitimate subject-matter of natural science, acceptance of the view that essential forms or natures are its subject-matter, accounting for the sterility of science during the period before the scientific revolution occurred. According to the ancient doctrine, the subject-matter of sense-knowledge and opinion on one side, and of science on the other, are forever separated by a gulf that is impassable for the reason that it is cosmological and ontological—that is, due to the very "being" of the subjects involved. In what now constitutes science, the difference is methodological. For it is due to *methods of inquiry*, not to inherent natures. Potentially the subject-matters of sense and opinion are science in the making; they are its raw material. Increased maturity of the procedures and techniques of inquiry will transform their material into scientific knowledge. On the other side, there is no subject-matter of the scientific kind which is eternally the same and not subject to improvement with further development of efficacy in inquiry-procedures.

The scientific revolution, which put science upon the road of steady advance and ever increasing fertility, is connected with substitution of knowledge "by art" for that said to be "by nature." The connection is not remote nor recondite. The arts are concerned with production, with generation, with doing and making. They fall, therefore, within the domain of things which in the classic scheme are mutable, and of which, according to that scheme, scientific knowledge is impossible. According to the present conduct of science and according to its conclusions, science consists of knowledge of *orders of change*. While this fact marks a complete departure from the classic view, it does not suffice of itself to justify calling scientific knowledge an art, though it provides a condition without which that designation is not warranted; for it completely breaks down the grounds upon which a fixed and impassable line was originally drawn between the subject-matters of science and of art. For it connects science with change. The consideration that completes the ground for assimilating science to art is the fact that assignment of scientific status in any given case rests upon facts which are experimentally produced. Science is now the product of operations deliberately undertaken in conformity with a plan or project that has the properties of a working hypothesis. The value or validity of the latter is tested, as in the case of any art, by what happens in consequence of the operations it instigates and directs. Moreover, science is assimilated to the conditions defining an art by the fact that, as in the case of any industrial art, production of relevant and effective consequences depends upon use of artificially designed appliances and apparatus as means of execution of the plan that directs the operations which are undertaken.

II

It is an old and familiar story that "nature" is a word of many senses. One of its senses has been mentioned. According to it, the nature of that which is undergoing investigation, say combustion, electricity, or whatever, is the subject-matter of scientific generalizations. We still use the expression "the nature" of something or other in this sense, though, I imagine, with decreasing frequency. But when we do use it in this sense, its meaning is radically different from that possessed by the same expression in the classic scheme. For it no longer designates a fixed and inherent essence, or Being, that makes facts to *be* what they are. Instead, it signifies an order of connected changes, an order which is found to be fruitfully effective in understanding and dealing with particular changes. The difference is radical.[1]

Another meaning of "nature" is *cosmological*. The word is used to stand for the world, for the universe, for the sum total of facts which actually and potentially are the subject of inquiry and knowledge. With respect to this sense of "nature," ancient philosophy has an important advantage over the general tenor of modern philosophy. For while modern philosophy is conformable to actual scientific practice in eliminating an ontological difference, or a difference in kinds of Being, between the eternal and the changing, it has, unfortunately, tended to substitute for this difference one equally fixed between supposed subjective and objective orders of Being.[2] "Unfortunately" is in fact too mild and neutral a word. For the net effect has been to set up a seat and agency of knowing over against Nature as that known. Hence the "knower" becomes in effect extra-natural. Historically, the facts of the case are easily explainable. For while in the Greek version mind, in both its sensible and its rational operations, was a culminating manifestation or terminal "end," of natural facts, in the medieval version (out of which modern theory grew without outgrowing some of its major tenets) soul and mind took on definitely supernatural traits. These traits, in a more or less attenuated form, reappear in the extra-natural knowing "subject" of modern philosophy as that is set over against the natural world as "object."

To complete the statement of the terms of the question

---

[1] It may be remarked in passing that the *old* sense of the "nature" of a thing still prevails in discussion of moral and social subjects; and this fact may explain the continued stagnation and infertility of inquiry in these fields.

[2] Virtual synonyms are "mental" and "physical" orders, and "personal" and "impersonal," taken as separate and opposed with reference to their inherent stuffs or subject-matters.

under discussion, it is necessary to note explicitly the sense of "nature" and "natural" in which they contrast with "art" and "artificial." For in the cosmological sense of nature, the saying of Shakespeare holds to the effect that nature is made better by no mean but nature makes that mean; in the third sense of natural (that just mentioned), science is definitely and conclusively a matter of art, not of nature.

We most readily lay hold of the meaning of this statement by presenting to ourselves a picture of an astronomical observatory or a physical laboratory. And we have to include as part of the picture the rôle of collections of books and periodicals, which operate in the most intimate and vital working connection with the other means by which science is carried on. For the body of printed matter is what enables the otherwise highly restricted material of immediate perception to be linked with subject-matters having an indefinitely wide spatial and temporal range. For only in fusion with book-material does what is immediately present take on scientific status, and only in fusion with the latter does the former cease to be "theoretical" in the hypothetical sense of that word. For only as culturally transmitted material with its deep and wide scope is anchored, refreshed, and tested continually through *here-and-now* materials provided by direct experimental observations, does it become a warranted part of authentic science.

A further qualification has to be added to complete the statement that science, with respect to both method and conclusions, is an art. For there is a sense in which every form of knowledge is an affair of art. For all knowledge, even the most rudimentary, such as is attributable to low-grade organisms, is an expression of skill in selection and arrangement of materials so as to contribute to maintenance of the processes and operations constituting life. It is not a metaphorical expression to say that at the very least all animals know *how,* in virtue of organic structure and physiological processes in connection with transcuticular conditions, to do things of this sort. When, then, it is said that science, as distinct from other modes of knowledge, is an art, the word "art" is used with a differential property. The operations of *search* that constitute the art or skill marking other modes of knowledge develop into re-search.

A more concrete qualification of the art which constitutes scientific knowledge is its dependence upon *extra-organic* appliances and instrumentalities, themselves artificially devised. The scientific revolution may be said to have been initiated when investigators borrowed apparatus and processes from the industrial arts and used them as means of obtaining dependable scientific data. The use of the lens was of itself almost enough to revolutionize the science of astronomy. As we look back, we note that the bulk of early knowledge was in fact built up through the pursuit of industrial and mechanical arts. The low social status of artisans (in which class were included sculptors, architects, painters of pictures, musicians, in fact all producers save those working with words) was "rationalized" in the doctrine of the inherently inferior state of all knowledge of this kind. At best, it was "empirical" in the disparaging sense of that word. Fundamentally, the scientific revolution consisted of transformation of "empirical" into *experimental*. The transformation was effected, historically, by adoption, as means of obtaining scientific knowledge, of devices and processes previously employed in industry to obtain "material" ends—in that sense of "material" which identifies "matter" with the menial and servile. After a period in which natural knowledge progressed by *borrowing* from the industrial crafts, science entered upon a period of steady and ever-accelerated growth by means of deliberate invention of such appliances on its own account. In order to mark this differential feature of the art which is science, I shall now use the word "technology." [3]

Because of technologies, a circular relationship between the

[3] While a number of writers have brought forward the facts which are involved in this view, Dr. Clarence Ayres, as far as I am aware, was the first one explicitly to call science a mode of technology. It is probable that I might have avoided a considerable amount of misunderstanding if I had systematically used "technology" instead of "instrumentalism" in connection with the view I put forth regarding the distinctive quality of science as knowledge.

arts of production and science has been established. I have
already spoken of the dependence of science as now conducted
upon the use of appliances and processes such as were once
confined to the "utilitarian" and "practical" ends to which a
subordinate and "base" status was attributed socially and morally. On the other hand, before the application in a return
movement of science in the industrial arts, production was a
routine affair. It was marked by imitation and by following
established models and precedents. Innovation and invention
were accidental rather than systematic. Application of scientific
conclusions and methods liberated production from this state—
a state justifying use of the adjective "empirical" in its disparaging sense. Through incorporation into the arts of production of the methods and conclusions of science, they are capable of becoming "rational" in the honorific sense of that word.
The phrase "rationalization of production" states a fact. Indeed,
it may be said that the distinction between science and other
technologies is not intrinsic. It is dependent upon cultural conditions that are extrinsic to both science and industry. Were it
not for the influence exerted by these conditions, the difference
between them would be conventional to the point of being
verbal. But as long as some technologies are carried on for
personal profit at the expense of promotion of the common
welfare, the stigma of "materialism" will continue to be attached
to industrial technologies, and the honorific adjective "idealistic" will be monopolized by the technology which yields
knowledge—especially if that knowledge is "pure"—that is, in
the classic view, uncontaminated by being put to "practical"
use.

III

Valuable instruction concerning a number of mooted problems in the theory of knowledge may be derived from the
underlying principles of the prior discussion. One of them, perhaps the most obvious on the surface, is the fact that many

classifications and distinctions which have been supposed to be inherent or intrinsic to knowing and knowledge are in fact due to socio-cultural conditions of a historical, and therefore temporal and local, sort. There is the fact (upon which I have dwelt at length in previous writings) of the arbitrary and irrelevant nature of the sharp line drawn in the classic philosophical tradition between "theoretical" and "practical" knowledge. The gulf that was supposed to separate them is in fact merely a logical corollary of the view that the proper subject of scientific knowledge is eternal and immutable. The connection of science with change and the connection of the methods of science with experimental production of change have completely vitiated this doctrine. The infertility of natural knowledge before adoption of the experimental method is attributable, in large measure, to the fact that ancient and medieval science took the material of ordinary observation "as is"; that is, in lumps and chunks as given "naturally" in a ready-made state. In consequence, the only treatment to which it could be subjected was dialectical.

What is not so obvious upon the surface is that a theory of knowledge based upon the conduct and conclusions of science does away, once and for all, with the fixed difference supposed to exist between sense-knowledge and rational-knowledge. The sensory aspect of knowledge is strictly an *aspect*. It is distinguishable in intellectual analyses that are undertaken for special purposes. But it is not, as it was long taken to be, a special kind of knowledge, nor yet a separate component in knowledge. It is that aspect of the system of knowledge, in and by which knowledge extending across an indefinitely extensive spatial and temporal range of facts is anchored and focalized in that which is *here-and-now*. Without demonstrated anchorage of this sort, any system, no matter how well organized with respect to internal consistency, is "theoretical" in the sense of being hypothetical. On the other hand, the "rational" aspect of knowledge is constituted by the corpus of extant knowledge which has been constituted by prior inquiries and which is so organized as to be communicable—and hence applicable to results of further inquiry by which the old system is corrected and extended.

The principle underlying these special matters is that the legitimate subject-matter of a *theory* of knowledge consists of *facts* that are known at a given time, with, of course, the proviso that the procedures by which this body of knowledge has been built up are an integral part of it. This view of the grounds of a competent theory of knowledge stands in open opposition to that which underlies the *epistemological* theory: the postulate, namely, that no subject-matter is entitled to be called knowledge until it has been shown to satisfy conditions that are laid down prior to any case of actual knowledge and independently of any conclusion reached in the course of the inquiries by which knowledge in the concrete is arrived at. The completeness of the opposition between the two postulates may be judged from the following consideration. Upon the ground of the first postulate subject-matter is entitled to the name of knowledge when it is determined by the methods of inquiry, test, verification, and systematic arrangement, or organization, which are factually employed in the sciences. Upon the other basis, the antecedent conditions apply to any and every case, good, bad, and indifferent. Hence they are of an entirely different order from the facts of actual investigation, test, and verification, which warrant use of the name "knowledge" in its honorific sense in actual instances.

It was then inevitable, from the standpoint of logic, that the epistemological approach culminated in the Kantian question: How is knowledge possible anyway (*ueberhaupt*)? If the question were put with reference to the "possibility" of any other subject under investigation, the *existence* of the subject-matter under inquiry would be the starting point. It suffices, for example, to show that cancer exists for the question as to its possibility to be simply the question of the specific conditions of an *actuality*. Only in the case of knowledge is it supposed that the question of its "possibility" is one which puts actuality into total doubt until certain universal antecedent conditions have been laid down and shown to be satisfied.

In the case of cancer, for example, the question of possibility means that our knowledge is still in a doubtful and indeterminate state, so that research is going on to discover the characteristic properties, conditions, and consequences of facts whose actual existence sets the problem. Yet strangely enough (strangely, provided, that is, historical-cultural facts are left out of account) the dogmatic and contradictory assumption that there exists knowledge of the conditions of knowledge prior to and conditioning every specific instance of knowledge arrogated to itself the name of a *critical* theory of knowledge!

IV

I do not propose to discuss further this contradiction, beyond saying that the contradiction will be obvious to anyone who views the matter in terms of the facts of knowledge, instead of in terms supplied by the history of philosophical systems viewed in isolation from other cultural events. I propose rather to set forth some of the historical-cultural conditions which generated in general the epistemological assumption of prior conditions to be satisfied; and which, in particular, led to the "subject-object" formula about these conditions. One of the influential factors consists of the conditions existing when the scientific revolution took place. It is hardly possible to over-emphasize the fact that these conditions were those of revolt, not merely against long accepted intellectual doctrines, but also against customs and institutions which were the carriers of these doctrines, and which gave them a support extraneous to their own constituents. Because of causes which are psychologically adequate, if not factually so, the word "social" has come to be regarded as applicable to that which is institutionally established and which exerts authority because of this fact. The adjective "individual" is identified on this basis with that which marks a departure from the traditionally and institutionally established, especially if the departure is of a quality involving revolt and a challenge to the rightful authority of tradition and custom.

These conditions were fully and strikingly present at the time of the rise of modern science. Every book on the history of philosophy mentions the fact that the philosophical literature of the fifteenth and subsequent centuries is marked by treatises, essays, tractates, that deal with the methods to be adopted and pursued if scientific knowledge is to be actually obtained. The negative aspect of these new ventures is assault, overt or implicit, upon all that had long been accepted as science. There was in effect, if not openly, an assertion that currently accepted subject-matter was hardly more than a systematized collection of errors and falsities. The necessity of radically new procedures of assault upon existing "science" was uniformly treated as an affair of *method*. It was because of the *methods* habitually used and sanctioned that existing "science" was stagnant, and so far removed from its proper mark—understanding of nature. Other documents upon right methods may not have used the words of Francis Bacon's *Novum Organum*, much less endorsed its precepts. But they were at one with him in proclaiming the necessity of a complete break with traditional methods and in stark opposition to the tenets of the *Organon* of Aristotle.

If the movement of protest, revolt, and innovation that was expressed in these documents and put in practice in the new astronomy and "natural philosophy" had been confined to "science" in its technical and isolated aspect, there would not have been the crisis that actually occurred. The facts constituting what is called "the conflict of science with religion"—or theology—clearly and convincingly prove that the movement of innovation, protest, and revolt was not so confined. The new science was treated as morally heretical and as a dangerous menace to the very foundations of a stable and just social order. Upon the Continent, especially, it was treated as rebellion against divinely established authority. In a more fundamental way than in the ecclesiastic movement named Protestantism, it was a protest against established foundations in morals and religion. Its opponents made this point clear when its proponents failed to do so.

Stated in slightly different terms, the subject-object formulation of the conditions to be satisfied before any subject-matter has a right to the honorable title of "knowledge" has to be viewed in vitally intimate connection with those movements in political and economic institutions which popularly bear the name "individualism." For, as has been already remarked, any departure from traditions and customs that are incorporated in and backed by institutions having firmly established authority is regarded as "individual" in a non-social and *anti*-social sense by the guardians of old forms in church and state. Only at a later time, when it is possible to place events in a long historic perspective, instead of in the short-time crowded and broken perspective of what is immediately contemporary, can so-called "individualism" be seen to be as "social" in origin, content, and consequences as are the customs and institutions which are in process of modification.

In this cultural situation, the fact that philosophers as unlike as Descartes and Berkeley both refer to the seat and agent of knowledge as "I" or an "ego," a personal self, has more than casual significance. This reference is especially significant as evidence of the new climate of opinion just because no attempt at justification accompanied it. It was taken to be such an evident matter that no argument in its behalf was called for. References and allusions of this kind are the forerunners of the allegedly "critical" attempt of Kant to frame an account of the conditions of knowledge in terms of a "transcendental ego," after Hume had demonstrated the shaky character of the "empirical" self as the source and agent of authentic knowledge.

If we adopt the customary course of isolating philosophies in their historical appearance, which is their actuality, from other socio-cultural facts, if we treat the history of philosophy as something capable of being understood in the exclusive terms of documents labeled philosophical, we shall look at the outstanding feature of modern philosophy as one of a conflict between doctrines appealing to "sense-experience" as ultimate authority and theories appealing to intuition and reason, a conflict reaching a supposed solution in the Kantian reconciliation of the *a priori* and the *a posteriori*. When these philosophies are placed in their cultural context, they are seen to be partners in a common movement, both schools being in revolt against traditional science in its methods, premises, and conclusions, while both schools are engaged in search for a new and different seat of intellectual and moral authority. There are indeed significant differences between the two schools. But when these are historically viewed, they appear as differences of emphasis, one school inclining to the "conservative" phase of cultural institutions, and the other school to the "progressive" or radical phase.

While those aspects of the new science which express initiative, invention, enterprise, and independence of custom (on the ground that customs are more likely to be distorting and misleading than helpful in attaining scientific knowledge) are necessary conditions for generation of the subject-object formulation, they are far from being its sufficient condition. Unquestioned persistence of fundamental tradition controlled protest against other customs. Medieval institutions centered in belief in an immaterial soul or spirit. This belief was no separate item. It permeated every aspect of life. The drama of the fall, the redemption, and the eternal destiny for weal or woe, of the soul was all-controlling in the accepted view of the creation and history of the universe and of man. Belief in the soul was so far from being just an intellectual tenet that poignant emotion and the deepest and most vivid images of which man is capable centered about it. The church that administered the concerns of the soul was in effect the dominant educational and political institution of the period.

Secularizing movements gradually undermined the monopoly of authority possessed by the church. Although interests of a natural type did not supersede supernatural interests, they tended to push them out of a central into a peripheral position.

But supernatural concerns retained such force in moral and religious matters that the theory of knowledge was routed through the channels they had worn after the *facts* of science were wearing a natural channel. This roundabout channel seemed, because of the force of habit, more "natural" than any indicated by the facts of science. The enormous gap between knowledge-facts and epistemological theory which marks modern philosophy was instituted.

In spite of revolt and innovation, the hold of the belief in the soul as knowing subject upon the attitudes which controlled the formation of the theory of knowledge was so firm that it could not be broken until the institutions, upon which the belief in its concrete validity depended had undergone definite degeneration.

Revolt and innovation were sufficient, however, to bring to explicit and emphatic statement one aspect of the Christian doctrine of the soul, an aspect which was kept covert and hidden in the dominant institutionalism of the Middle Ages. This aspect was the *individual* or singular nature of the subject of sin, redemption, punishment, and reward. Protestantism insisted upon making this aspect of the Christian position overt and central in religious matters. The writers who were concerned with the new science performed a similar task in the theories of knowledge they promulgated. The hold of the old doctrine, even upon those most indifferent to its theological phases, is shown in the persistence of belief in an immaterial mind, consciousness, or whatever, as being the seat and agent of knowledge. The influence of the belief upon the new science, even with its fundamental revolt and innovation, is exhibited in identification of the subject and agent of sound knowledge with "individuals" who had freed themselves from the perverting and deadening effect of custom and tradition. Even today those who deny in words that mind and consciousness are organs of knowledge, replacing them with an organic body or with the nervous system of the organism, attribute to the latter an isolation from the rest of nature (including transmitted and communicated culture) which is much more than reminiscent of the lonely isolation of the medieval soul.

It took more than the undeniable but negative fact of the gradual attenuation and decay of the importance once attached to the soul as seat of knowledge to effect an adequate elimination. The new movement of science had to achieve, on the ground of its own methods and conclusions, a positive conquest of those aspects of natural fact that deal with life and human history before complete elimination could occur. Only during the last hundred years (less than that in fact) have the sciences of biology, cultural anthropology, and history, especial of "origins," reached a stage of development which places man and his works squarely within nature. In so doing they have supplied the concrete and verified positive facts that make possible and imperatively demand formation of a systematic theory of knowledge, in which the facts of knowledge are specified or described and organized exactly as are the facts of the sciences which are the relevant subject-matter of a theory of knowledge. Only in this way will the facts of our knowledge-systems and those of the theory of knowledge be brought into harmony with one another, and the present glaring discrepancy between them be done away with.

7

HOW IS MIND TO BE KNOWN?

ALL INTERESTED IN PHILOSOPHY WILL AGREE THAT THE QUESTION "What is mind and the mental?" is an important one. They will agree notwithstanding the great difference in conclusions that are arrived at. Some recent discussions of the topic have suggested to me that perhaps it is desirable, if only as a temporary expedient, to raise the question of how the problem of the nature of mind is to be approached—the question, that is, of the way in which the nature of the mental can be *known*. In offering this suggestion I do not intend to suggest anything of the nature of *epistemological* inquiry into the possibility of knowledge, but simply the general question of the method to be used, as one might raise the question of the most effective method of inquiry with respect to any subject-matter.

Asking about the question of method of knowing may serve to explain some of the differences now existing in the views that are held as to the nature of the mental. For it is evident that certain doctrines about the nature of the mental rest upon a virtual assumption that the only method that is at all appropriate is that of *introspection*; and of introspection in the sense in which that word has a signification radically different from the meaning borne by *observation* in connection with everything except the "mental."

The existence of another possible method and something about the character of that other method is suggested by the earlier meaning of the word "introspection." For it was originally used as a synonym for inspection, examination, looking into something, usually with the understanding that the thing

301

looked into was one's own conduct from a moral point of view. It is doubtless true that the fact that one's own conduct was the thing looked into, played a part in development of the later sense of the word in which "introspection" came to stand for an alleged act of immediate and intuitive knowledge of mind or of consciousness. But nevertheless the earlier and later significations are in sharp contrast. The careful thoroughgoing investigation of the moral character of acts performed, which is what is designated by earlier usage, implies in a definite way that the moral nature of those acts is *not* properly known at the time they are committed, but is something demanding reflective examination.[1]

It was the accepted postulate of ancient and medieval knowledge that *certainty* is an essential property of anything entitled to be called knowledge in its full sense, so that inferred or discursive conclusions depend for their status as knowledge on being derived by inherently necessary true procedures from premises that are immediately and self-evidently known to be true. Modern physical science destroyed the grounds upon which rested the special propositions that had previously been taken to be ultimate first truths and to be the premises upon which the proof of truth of all other scientific truths depended. Nevertheless, the postulate of inherent connection of certainty with knowledge remained. It is a commonplace of the history of modern thought that immediate facts of consciousness, or "mental facts," were appealed to to provide the supposedly required unshakable and indubitable first truths without which there is no possibility of inferring other true propositions. One interesting illustration may be cited. Early modern philosophy retained the belief in the self-evident truth of mathematical definitions and axioms which was common to Greek and medieval philosophy. But the change in physical science furnished no

---

[1] It is perhaps worth noting that a somewhat similar change took place in the significations of *conscience* and *consciousness*. *Con-scious*, and *conscire*, originally meant *to know with another,* and *conscire alii* and *conscire sibi* were both legitimate expressions. "To know with one's self" meant, without doubt, private or unshared knowledge. But it did *not* mean knowledge of something intrinsically private.

logical warrant that truths which are self-evident *qua* mathematical are validly applicable to *physical* phenomena. Hence the necessity (exemplified alike in Descartes and Kant in spite of their other differences) of finding something completely certain in "consciousness" or "mind" that gives solid warrant to the application.

Persons who are fond of quoting Santayana's remark about the difference between knowing a thing and being it by taking complete possession of it, as if knowing were a kind of eating, and those who accept that principle, irrespective of Santayana's endorsement, will be aware of the existence of the radical contrast existing in methods employed in knowing the "mental." For the epistemological doctrine lying back of belief in immediate and certain knowledge of the mental is that in the case of the mental *to be and to be known* are one and the same thing. Indirect approach through more or less prolonged inquiry, with use of formation of hypothesis and by experimental observation, may be required for knowing everything else. But in the case of the mental, so it is assumed, the objects or events to be known are self-revealing, self-disclosing. To have them is to know them.

There are dialectical difficulties in the position. How do we know, apart from comparison and contrast with other subject-matters, that the particular objects or events in question are *mental?* What possible meaning does the word "mental," or even the word "consciousness," have in case the events they are supposed to designate are so unique that no identification with or discrimination from anything else is involved? I am not concerned to follow up this dialectical difficulty. I mention it as a way of calling emphatic attention to the fact that knowledge of *everything else* involves institution of *connections* through operations of comparison and discrimination by means of which connections are discovered. This is the contrasted method of knowing the nature of mind and the mental which is so frequently ignored as to justify raising the question to which this article is devoted.

The statement, often made, to the effect that the particular, individual, unique, can not be known is ambiguous until further qualified. It may mean that it cannot be known in its capacity of being particular, or that it cannot be known in any way or fashion. The first of these two meanings is consistent with the view that knowledge involves description in terms of traits of connection constituting a kind. In this sense, the immediate qualities that are *had* and which knowledge of the "mental" is *about* or is *of*, are like the immediate qualities of any event in its particularity of occurrence.[2] For the events which when known are called, say, fire, fever, fight, or by another common noun, are particular in their immediacy of occurrence. In the latter capacity they have no characteristics in common with other occurrences in *their* particularity. If awareness were conferred upon an event, as a Leibnizian monad, it could be said that the qualities of which the event is aware, are *private*; the word "private" being here a strict synonym for "particular." If the same logical method were employed as in the case of the doctrine of the immediate and intuitive self-knowledge of the "mental," an event could then be said to have knowledge of its own qualities, and to be the only existence able to know its "own" states and processes.

This fanciful endowment of events is indulged in as a way of calling attention to that difference between having and knowing (and being known) which characterizes every event in its particularity of occurrence. When, for example, it is said that my toothache is private, is immediately known by me, and is completely inaccessible to every one else, there is just one element in the statement capable of empirical verification. And that element has nothing to do with "knowing." It is a verifiable fact that your *having* a toothache is quite a different event from *my* having it. It does not follow that you know that *what* you have is a toothache any differently from the way in which

[2] It is obvious that "mental" and "mind" designate *kinds*. I pass over the dialectical difficulty involved in the inconsistency of this trait with their alleged uniqueness, since it is probably another form of that previously mentioned—the difficulty of knowing something to be mental without comparison with and discrimination from other things.

any one else knows it. As a matter of fact, the dentist probably knows the nature of toothache, the special location and other characteristics of *this* toothache, much better than does the one who *has* it. And the "privacy" of what is had seems to depend upon physical conditions rather than upon anything intrinsic to its nature. There is good ground for believing that were our techniques further advanced, nerve-graftings might enable me to feel or have a toothache whose immediate locus is in the jaw of your head—just as by means of radio we hear a sound originating indefinitely far away.

There are, in short, such things as enjoyments and sufferings which are "private" in occurrence. That they are *known* in any way different from the way in which we know sounds, colors, etc., seems to be a dictum resting upon an epistemological theory, not upon any evidence specifically relevant to the case. Moreover, the privacy of enjoyments and sufferings in their occurrence seems to describe a *social* fact—as much so as in the case of a miser who has and gloats over a "private" store of gold. I ran across the following in a book I read recently: "The private individual privately setting forth his will by marking a private ballot." It needs no argument to show that ability to cast a private or secret ballot is a publicly determined matter, and an arrangement believed to be socially desirable. The "private individual" who is mentioned in the sentence quoted is able to cast a ballot only when publicly determined conditions of age, citizenship, registration, etc., have been satisfied. Similarly, emphasis upon "private initiative" in business is a mark of a certain *social* regime, is urged by those who support it as a social policy because of alleged social benefits. One can even go so far as to say that the *significance* of the recognition that enjoyments and suffering are privately *had*, is a matter of social morals. For it is an accompaniment of the rather recent development of humanitarianism and of philanthropy which goes beyond racial and credal limits. The currency of the doctrine which mistakenly converts the event of having into a unique mode of knowing can be said to be a confused product of an "individualistic" *social* movement in politics and economics.

One retort to what I am saying is that it completely overlooks the primary mode of knowledge called *acquaintance*. My argument, however, is far from ignoring the fact of acquaintance. I shall not repeat here what I have said elsewhere about the intimate connection of acquaintance with knowing *how* to make appropriate active responses to an event, as in having a speaking acquaintance with a foreign language, or being acquainted with John F. Exbury. It suffices here to point out the difference between acquaintance-knowledge and any knowledge that makes scientific or philosophical claims for itself. Human beings were well acquainted with torrid heat and frigid cold, with various diseases, with stones, plants, and animals, long before they had anything approaching what now alone passes for scientific knowledge. As the case of Greek and medieval "science" proves, the belief that scientific knowledge is of the same order as acquaintance kept actual science in leading-strings for centuries. Personally, I doubt whether one could even be acquainted with the things he enjoys and undergoes, any more than with milk, oak trees, or neighbors, unless he got beyond what he *has* by means of operations of comparison and discrimination, which result in giving the things in question a general or public status. But the point I am making as to the difference between acquaintance and the kind of knowledge of the mental that could be entitled to recognition in philosophy or psychology is independent of this belief of mine.

Any theory of the nature of the mental which depends for its validity upon postulation of a special mode of knowing, one applying to that particular object and to nothing else, would, I believe, be regarded with highly suspicious eye were it not for the currency of a special type of epistemology. Given that currency, the case for antecedent suspicion is countered by what, upon examination, turns out to be a special case of reasoning in a closed circle. It is said in effect that the peculiar, the extraordinarily peculiar, nature of mind requires an equally peculiar, unique procedure by which to know it. Since, however, the doctrine of the completely unique nature of the mental rests upon an assumption of the way in which it is known, the argument is not exactly convincing.

If the nature of the phenomena termed mental is to be known in the way in which other immediately present unique qualities, such as this *hot*, this *cold*, this *red*, are known, then the "mental" stands pretty well at the opposite pole from things that are known with a slight amount of mediation. To know scientifically what red color is, an extensive field of knowledge, factual and theoretical, is a necessary condition. Carefully tested ideas of the nature of light had to be attained, and they were found to involve a tested theory about electro-magnetism. I need not go into further detail to illustrate the point about the indirect character of knowledge of a particular quality immediately *had* in experience. While I am not here concerned to try to tell what are the distinctive characteristics that describe the mental, I am suggesting that in order to discover the nature of the mental, we might have to begin with the best conclusions that have been reached about behavior from the standpoint of biology, and then utilize all that is known about the modifications produced in such behavior by the complex of conditions constituting culture, including communication or language.

C. I. Lewis, in his article "Some Logical Considerations concerning the Mental" [3] uses at least nine times the phrase "behavioral [behavioristic] and [or] brain states." He thus identifies, without argument, the behavioral account of the mental with description in terms of the brain. Hence it is probably well to state that *behavior*, as I use the word in the previous paragraph, even on the biological level (without reference to behavior as it is culturally constituted), includes a great deal more than "brain events." Indeed, I have difficulty in seeing how any one can give an intelligible account of cerebral behavior unless that limited mode of behavior is itself descriptively determined

[3] This JOURNAL, Vol. XXXVIII (1941), pp. 225–233.

in connection with the whole scheme of what is known about behavior in its widest biological sense—a sense in which inter-action with environmental conditions is included. There is one passage, as against nine of the kind just mentioned, in which Mr. Lewis speaks of "brain facts or facts of physical behavior." Even if "or" is here used to express an alternative instead of a synonym, the adjective "physical" constitutes a limitation of the behavioral approach which will be accepted only by "be-haviorists" who subordinate their account of behavior to episte-mological considerations.

The last paragraphs are introduced only to illustrate the fact that to *know* mind, in distinction from just *having* qualities that are "mental," one has to go to things that are *not* mind nor mental and to translate qualities that immediately occur into a set of connections between events. The idea of method which they are intended to illustrate is one which stands, as has been indicated, at the opposite pole to the method of complete and indubitable immediate knowledge—a method that eliminates, once for all, the need for reflection and inquiry. Since it is the question of method I am raising, I shall not say anything here about the conclusions as to the nature of mind to which use of the method of systematic investigation might lead us. It is, however, pertinent to say that much more in the way of positive results has already been attained than is indicated anywhere in this article.

8

THE OBJECTIVISM-SUBJECTIVISM OF MODERN PHILOSOPHY

I

IN HIS *Adventures of Ideas,* WHITEHEAD WRITES AS FOLLOWS: "It is customary to contrast the objective approach of the ancient Greeks with the subjective approach of the moderns. . . . But whether we be ancients or moderns we can deal only with things, in some sense, experienced." [1] Since I agree fully with this statement, my only comment is that it involves repudiation of the view that approach through experience is *ipso facto* subjective. There is a further statement of Whitehead's which I wish to use as a peg from which to hang some remarks of my own, as preachers use a text. "The difference between ancients and moderns is that the ancients asked what have we experienced and the moderns asked what can we experience." [2] I propose to develop the distinction between "what *has* been" and "what *can* be" experienced, in explanation of the difference between ancient and modern philosophy, in a way that has no authorization in Whitehead's treatment. In fact, my development is in a direction contrary to what Whitehead goes on to say. For that reason I feel the more bound to say that the particular interpretation he gives the distinction commands, within the limits set by the point he is making, my full assent. For he is concerned to show how the notion of experience was narrowed by the criteria set up by some moderns for judging what

[1] P. 287.
[2] *Op. cit.,* p. 288.

309

can be experienced. There can be no doubt as to the existence of this criterion, nor as to its restrictive consequence.

The limitation is due, as Whitehead justly says, to two errors. "The first error is the assumption of a few definite avenues of communication with the external world, the five sense-organs. This leads to the pre-supposition that the search for data is to be narrowed to the question, what data are directly provided by the activity of the sense-organs. . . . The second error is the presupposition that the sole way of examining experience is by acts of conscious introspective analysis." [3] When applied to such writers as Locke and Hume on one side and Kant on the other side nothing could be truer than these statements. The outcome was a definite and, to my mind, disastrous narrowing of the field of experience. Upon the face of the matter, then, the view I am going to advance seems to be contradicted by facts. For what I wish to say is that ancient philosophy is the one which is restricted, since it could not venture beyond what had already been accomplished in the way of experienced things—using "things" to designate activities and institutions as well as "objects," while modern experience is expansive since it is marked off by its constant concern for potentialities of experience as yet unrealized, as is shown, for example, in its interest in discovery and invention. In consequence what *can* be experienced stands for something wider and freer than what *has* been experienced.

II

There is an undeniable discrepancy involved in admitting the justice of what Whitehead says about the way in which the idea of what "can be experienced" was used to narrow the experiential field and the position I am here taking. As to the views about experience literally expressed by modern philosophers of both the experiential and the *a priori* schools, I have

[3] *Op. cit.*, p. 269 and p. 290. Cf. the following from p. 269, "Warping has taken the form of constant reliance upon sensationalist activity as the basis of all experimental activity."

no desire to explain away the discrepancy. What I intend to point out is that the spirit and direction of modern philosophy is of quite another sort, since it has been occupied with breaking down fixed barriers, with novelty, expansion, growth, potentialities previously unforeseen; in short, with an open and "infinite" world instead of the closed and finite world of the Greeks. If this statement does not apply to the general movement and implicit intent of modern philosophy, we are faced with a much greater discrepancy than the one just mentioned: that between the actual tendencies of modern experience and the philosophy that has been produced on the ground of this experience.

Accordingly, I do not think it is a necessary part of my task to account for the view nominally taken by modern philosophers about what *can* be experienced. At the same time, I do not believe the paradox is as great as it seems to be on the surface. The very fact that modern philosophy has been concerned with conditions of experience which lie beyond the range of what *has been* experienced in the past made it peculiarly sensitive to the existence of certain barriers to their acceptance and realization; namely, the barriers that are products of past culture and are sanctioned by the philosophy which reflected that culture. In behalf of their own interest in the prospective, in possible expansion, philosophers were obliged to assail the beliefs and habits which stood in the way. They needed a criterion and method for carrying on their battle. In short, the positive side of modern philosophy, what I have called its spirit and direction of movement, was such as to give great importance to the negative work that had to be done. The readiest instrumentality of destructive criticism was identification of valid beliefs with those authorized by experience when experience is reduced to material of direct observation; namely, to simple ideas, impressions, sense data. The incompatibility of this reduction to the positive faith which animated the modern philosophers was concealed from view by their intense belief that if only obstructions inherited from the past were once done away with, the forces inhering in experience would carry men forward. Even more instructive than what was explicitly said about experience is the revolution that took place as to the respective outlooks of "experience" and "reason." In ancient philosophy, experience stood for the habits and skills acquired by repetition of particular activities by means of selection of those which proved successful. It was a limiting principle, while reason, insight into reasons, was emancipatory of the bonds that were set by acquired habits. Francis Bacon and his experiential followers took exactly the opposite view. The "rational," when disassociated from personal experience, was to them the lifeless, the secondhand. Personal "experience," irrespective of any technical definition, was the means of initiation into living realities and provided the sole assurance of entering pastures that were fertile as well as fresh. Empiricism and liberalism were allies; the possibility of growth, of development, idealization of change as progress, were all, whether rightly or wrongly, connected with faith in experience. Technically, or in strict formal logic, the *tabula rasa*, the blank sheet of paper, view of mind to be written upon by "external" impressions, should have led to the conclusion that human beings are passive puppets. Actually, the feeling that if hampering and restrictive traditions and institutions could be got rid of, firsthand experience would ensure that men could and would go ahead, was the dominant factor.

III

If we consider Greek thought in an analytical way, we shall be persuaded, in any event, that from its own standpoint it can not be called *objective*. If the term is used, it is from our own present standpoint; that is, on the ground of the contrast of Greek thought with subjectivistic tendencies of modern philosophy, tendencies which, however, could not be identified as such, were it not that the distinction between the cosmological and the psychological, the "objective" and the "subjective," had been consciously made and become current. And it is precisely this distinction which does not appear in Greek thought. "Being" was set over against becoming, the latter containing an element of non-being or imperfection; the everlasting, immutable, and immortal were marked off from the transitory, and mortal imitations or images were set over against their originals. But the nearest approach to anything like the modern distinction of subjective-objective was between that which is by *nature* and that which is by *institution* or *convention*.

What may be truly said of ancient philosophy in contrast with modern is that it is naïve, using that word to designate a condition in which the distinction between the subjective and the objective is not made. Since naïveté suggests freshness and directness of approach, due to absence of artificial sophistication, one may apply the word "naïve" eulogistically to Greek philosophy. Of the Greek attitude, we could say that it fused qualities we now distinguish, were it not that fusion suggests prior differentiation, and it is just this antecedent differentiation that is lacking. In every characteristic expression of the Greek genius, the qualities we call emotional and volitional, and hence attribute to persons, are used to clothe things that we call physical and lacking in such qualities. The atomists, literally interpreted, are an exception to this statement. But one has only to read Lucretius (or Santayana today), and to reflect upon what is known regarding Democritus, to see that their interest in cosmology was a moral interest rather than a scientific one in the modern sense. In all influential and widely held ancient cosmologies, the physical world was marked by qualitative and teleological traits which modern physics has stripped away. Until this stripping had taken place there was no ground for anything like sharp opposition of the animate and inanimate; the human and the non-human; the "subjective" and "objective." In the matter of accounting for human traits in terms of generic cosmological qualities, there is no difference between Plato and Aristotle on one side and Democritus on the other.

There is a positive point involved in the foregoing negations. Greek philosophy moved and had its being in and among the things, the subjects, of *direct* experience, the world in which we human beings act, suffer, and enjoy. There is no particular point in saying their attitude was *animistic*, as if they had *first* discriminated certain qualities as psychic and personal and had *then* projected them into an "external" and purely physical (in our sense) world. As a contemporary writer has said in a criticism of the idea about animism entertained by such writers as Tylor, Spencer, and Lang:

> Our present day dichotomy of *behavior* has isolated two types: the type directed toward things, which follows strictly a cause and effect sequence; and the type directed toward persons, which runs the gamut from love to manipulation. . . . Animism considered as *behavior* is nothing more than this; properly speaking, it is only the expression of a state of mind that has not made our distinction between *behavior* toward persons and behavior toward things, but which brings the whole field under one rubric, treating the entire external world according to the pattern learned in dealing with fellow beings.[4]

The fact that philosophers refined and systematized what is involved in this habitual attitude does not militate against the other fact that they retained it intact as far as its fundamental moral and qualitative implications are concerned. Until the type of physical science which we call modern had become established, what alternative did philosophy have save to describe the world in terms of basic properties of the material of direct experience? If we did not have an alternative in the *pou sto* provided for us by present-day physical science, we too should "naturally" describe the world in teleological and qualitative terms. Any other procedure would strike us as artificial and arbitrary. I was strongly reminded of this fact in reading recently a book by a writer deeply imbued with the spirit of

---

[4] Article, by Ruth Benedict, on "Animism" in the *Encyclopaedia of the Social Sciences*, Vol. I, p. 66. I have italicized "behavior" in order to emphasize the point made.

classic Greek philosophy. He uniformly refers to "philosophies of experience" in a disparaging tone. But, as uniformly, his own account of Nature is couched in moral and poetic terms appropriate only to Nature as it is directly presented in experience and inappropriate to Nature as disclosed to us in physics.

IV

For the purpose of the present article, the point of the foregoing is the necessity of distinguishing between the things of *direct* experience (which may also be called everyday experience if the latter word is extended to include the relatively extraordinary experiences of poets and moral seers), and something else. What name shall be given to this something else? It may be called *physical* subject-matter in the sense of material of the physical sciences. But this name only makes the *problem* more precise; it offers no solution. And here I recur to the special postulate of this particular discussion: The postulate, namely, that "whether we be ancients or moderns, we can deal only with things, *in some sense,* experienced." From the standpoint of this postulate, the problem is to discover *in terms of an experienced state of affairs* the connection that exists between physical subject-matter and the common-sense objects of everyday experience. Concern for the *conditions* upon which depend the activities, enjoyments, and sufferings, constituting direct experience, is an integral part of that very experience when it is marked by faith in the possibility of its own indefinite expansion. The hypothesis here offered is that physical subject-matter represents in its own distinctive nature the *conditions* upon which rest the having, and the averting, of things in direct experience. What other method of getting outside and beyond the things of direct experience is conceivable save that of penetration to the conditions upon which they depend?

It is a commonplace that the sole method of controlling the occurrence of specific events—whether as to production or prevention—is by means of knowledge of their connections.

It is also a commonplace that modern science, as distinct from ancient, is occupied with determination of such conditions, and also that their discovery has been attended with creation of all sorts of technologies by means of which the area of things experienced and experienceable has been indefinitely widened. Every student of philosophy knows that Greek philosophy subordinated its account of things in terms of "efficient" causation to the account of them in terms of "formal" and "final" causation: that is, it was concerned with stating, by means of definition and classification, *what* things are and *why* they are so (in terms of the ends they serve), rather than with the quite subordinate question of *how* they come into being. The habit of viewing the history of philosophy in isolation from the state of culture in which philosophical theories are produced explains why this undeniable fact has not been linked to the fact that technologies for production and prevention of specifiable objects did not then exist; at least, not outside of certain arts and crafts which, in any case, were products of past experiences, or of what *had* been experienced, not of scientific insight. Under these circumstances, the part of intelligent persons was to make as much as possible of characters, of natures, or essences, that "make things to be *what* they *are*" in their own alleged non-relational or "inherent" being. The connections of space, time, motion, that are so important in modern science could not possibly have appeared to be of more than secondary significance until the use of these connections in making possible a control of experience had been demonstrated in experience.

It is not a new discovery that the word "object" is highly ambiguous, being used for the sticks and stones, the cats and dogs, the chairs and tables of ordinary experiences, for the atoms and electrons of physics, and for any kind of "entity" that has logical subsistence—as in mathematics. In spite of the recognized ambiguity, one whole branch of modern epistemology is derived from the assumption that in the case of at least the first two cases, the word "object" has the same general meaning. For otherwise the subject-matter of physics and the things of everyday experience would not have presented themselves as rivals, and philosophy would not have felt an obligation to decide which is "real" and which is "appearance," or at least an obligation to set up a scheme in which they are "reconciled." The place occupied in modern philosophy by the problem of the relation of so-called "scientific objects" and "common-sense objects" is proof, in any case, of the dominating presence of a distinction between the "objective" and the "subjective" which was unknown in ancient philosophy. It indicates that at least in the sense of awareness of an ever-present problem, modern philosophy is "objective-subjective," not just subjective. I suggest that if we gave up calling the distinctive material of the physical sciences by the name "objects" and employed instead the neutral term "scientific subject-matter," the genuine nature of the problem would be greatly clarified. It would not of itself be solved. But at least we should be rid of the implication which now prevents reaching a solution. We should be prepared to consider on its merits the hypothesis here advanced: namely, that scientific subject-matter represents the *conditions* for having and not-having things of direct experience.

Genuinely complete empirical philosophy requires that there be a determination *in terms of experience* of the relation that exists between physical subject-matter and the things of direct perception, use, and enjoyment. It would seem clear that historic empiricism, because of its commitment to sensationalism, failed to meet this need. The obvious way of meeting the requirement is through explicit acknowledgment that direct experience contains, as a highly important direct ingredient of itself, a wealth of *possible* objects. There is no inconsistency between the idea of direct experience and the idea of objects of that experience which are as yet unrealized. For these latter objects are directly experienced *as* possibilities. Every plan, every prediction, yes, every forecast and anticipation, is an experience in which some non-directly experienced object is directly experienced *as a possibility*. And, as previously suggested, modern experience is marked by the extent to which directly perceived, enjoyed, and suffered objects are treated as signs, indications, of what has *not* been experienced in and of itself, or/and are treated as means for the realization of these things of possible experience. Because historic empirical philosophy failed to take cognizance of this fact, it was not able to account for one of the most striking features of scientific method and scientific conclusions—preoccupation with generality as such.

For scientific methods and scientific subject-matter combine highly abstract or "theoretical" considerations with directly present concrete sensible material, and the generality of conclusions reached is directly dependent upon the presence of the first-named type of considerations. Now in modern philosophy, just as scientific "objects" have been set over against objects in direct experience, thereby occasioning the *ontological* problem of modern philosophy (the problem of where "reality" is to be found), so identification of the experiential with but one of the two factors of the method of knowing has created the *epistemological* problem of modern philosophy: the relation of the "conceptual" and "perceptual"; of sense and understanding. In terms of our hypothesis, the distinction and the connection of the distinguished aspects rests upon the fact that what *is* (has been) experienced is of cognitive importance in connection with what *can* be experienced: that is, as evidence, sign, test, of forecast, anticipation, etc., while, on the other hand, there is no way of valid determination of objects of possible experiences save by employing what *has* been experienced, and hence is sensible. Anticipation, foresight, prediction, depend upon taking what is "given" (what has indubitably been experienced) as ominous, or of prospective reference. This is a speculative operation, a wager about the future. But the wager is subject to certain techniques of control. Although every projection of a possible object of experience goes beyond what has been experienced and is in so far risky, this fact does not signify that every idea or projected possibility has an equal claim. Techniques of observation on one side and of calculation (in its broad sense) on the other side have been developed with a view to effective cooperation. Interactivity *of the two factors* constitutes the method of science. Were it not for the influence of the inertia of habit it would be fairly incredible that empiricists did not long ago perceive that material provided by direct sense-perception is limited and remains substantially the same from person to person and from generation to generation. Even when we take into account the additional sense data furnished by artificial instruments, the addition bears no proportionate ratio to the expansion of the subject-matter of the sciences that is constantly taking place. Were it not that "rationalist" theories of knowledge are in no better case with respect to accounting for increase in scientific knowledge (which is its most striking trait in modern times), the marked impotency of sensationalist empiricism would long ago have effected its disappearance.

V

I have presented the more difficult aspect of my position and argument first. Few persons, I take it, would be rash enough to deny that an *actual* experience of a definite thing depends upon the operation of factors which have to be distinguished from those of *physical* subject-matter. It is better at first to refer to these latter factors denotatively, rather than to apply the word "subjective." From the denotative point of view, no one will deny that an experience of light involves an optical apparatus and not simply the existence of certain physical vibrations and quanta, and similarly with experiences of sound, temperature, solidity, etc. In the logical sense of "objectivity," these organic conditions are as objective as those described in physics. The organism is one "object" among others. However, the function of organic factors is so distinctive that it has to be discriminated. When it is discriminated, it is seen to be so different in kind from that of physical subject-matter as to require a special name. As a candidate for the name, "subjective" has one great disadvantage, namely, its traditional use as a name for some sort of existential stuff called psychical or mental. It has, on the other hand, the advantage of calling attention to the particular agency through which the function is exercised: a singular organism, an organism that has been subjected to acculturation, and is aware of itself as a social subject and agent.

The difference in function is, in any case, the important matter. Physical subject-matter consists of the conditions of *possible* experiences in their status *as* possible. It does not itself account for any actual experience. It is general and remote. Objects of direct experience are singular and are here and now. The "subjective" factor (using the word to designate the operations of an accultured organism) is, like "objective" (physical subject-matter) a *condition* of experience. But it is *that* condition which is required to convert the conditions of *kinds* of objects, which as kinds represent generic possibilities, into *this* object. Since every actual or direct experience is of some *this*, here and now, it is imperative to distinguish this type of condition from the type supplied by generic "objective" subject-matter. Greek thought failed to recognize the existence of this "subjective" factor as a condition of positive control. It took account of it only as a ground for indiscriminate scepticism. Or, when convention and institution were regarded as more important than "nature" (as it was by one Greek school) it was because nature was regarded as so crude, raw, wild, that the most arbitrary escape from it was better than subjection to nature. What is not sufficiently noted is that definite differentiation of personal-social factors in their functions in production of things of experience is now part of the technique of controlling the experienced presence of objects; with further advance of behavioral psychology it will become of constantly increased importance. The old stock-in-trade of wholesale scepticism, namely, dreams, illusions, hallucinations, the effect of organic defects, of beliefs locally current, is now in practical fact a positive resource in the management of experience.

I hope what has been said will at least serve to explain the title I have given this article. It is true that modern philosophy is "subjective" as ancient philosophy was not.

In its concern with what *can* be experienced whether or not it *has* been experienced, it has systematically taken account of the operation of *specific* personal-social factors. But it is equally true that modern philosophy has been "objective" in a way in which ancient philosophy was not. It is impossible to make sense of the problems with which modern philosophy has been pre-occupied unless this fact is recognized in its full force. The outstanding defect of modern philosophy is that these problems have taken form by means of setting the two sets of conditions in opposition to one another. This fact is explicable only in terms of the projection into the modern situation of certain heritages from the earlier philosophy which originated in and reflects a different state of culture. Philosophy will become *modern* in a pregnant sense only when the "objectivism-subjectivism" involved is seen to be one of coöperative interaction of two distinguishable sets of conditions, so that knowledge of them *in their distinction* is required in order that their interaction may be brought under intentional guidance. Without such knowledge, intelligence is inevitably held down to techniques for making mechanical permutations and combinations of things that *have* been experienced, and mankind is dependent upon accident for introduction of novelty. The fact that mankind is still far from realization of the power contained in its ability to distinguish certain conditions of experience as physical and others as socio-psychological is true enough. This fact indicates the special responsibility of philosophy today.

9

INQUIRY AND INDETERMINATENESS OF SITUATIONS

I AM INDEBTED TO MR. MACKAY FOR THE OPPORTUNITY TO COR-
rect some wrong impressions about my theory of inquiry,
especially as to the meaning of "indeterminate" in connection
with it.[1] While I hope I may be able to say something of a
clarifying kind, study of his paper has led me to believe, for
reasons that will appear later, that the difference between us
goes much deeper than the special difficulties he points out. If
I am correct in this belief, my reply to Mr. Mackay's questions
and criticisms would have to take up issues more fundamental
than those he brings up, and my article would be different from
the one his paper evokes.

Two questions are raised by Mr. Mackay. Since he says that
his second question, that concerning an alleged material flaw
in my analysis, is probably the ground for his first charge, that
of vagueness, and since I agree with him that such is the case,
I begin with the second, "the more serious difficulty." Mr.
Mackay introduces his discussion by asking the following question: "What does it mean to say that *the existential conditions*
in a problematic situation are indeterminate?" That the crux of
Mr. Mackay's difficulty and criticism has to do with the use of
the word "existential" is shown not only by his use of italics but
is explicitly stated in the next sentences. "Assuming that the
situation is indeterminate, proleptically, with respect to its
eventual issue, Mr. Dewey seems to suppose that the antecedent

---

[1] D. S. Mackay, *What Does Mr. Dewey Mean by an "Indeterminate Situation"?*, the *Journal of Philosophy*, Vol. XXXIX (1942), pp. 141–148.

conditions must also be existentially indeterminate on the ground that the issue is itself an existential and not a merely intellectual affair. *But the issue, while still pending and in the future, is an ideal or intellectual affair, an affair of meanings, an anticipated possibility"* (p. 145, italics not in original text). Consequently, he charges me, apparently on the ground of a statement made by me in another book in discussing another topic, of "conversion of eventual functions into antecedent existence"; of "reading the *indeterminate* character of an eventual function, *before* its fulfilment, back into a causal antecedent reality." He makes the same criticism in other language when he says that I confuse an experienced quality of indeterminateness which is purely *cognitive* (that of the eventual issue *before* accomplishment) with the *practical* and *operational* indeterminateness of the experienced quality of the original antecedent situation.

The sentence stating that an eventual issue before fulfilment is reached, or while still future, is ideal or intellectual, and hence a non-existential affair, is, then, the crux of Mr. Mackay's position. It is the only ground adduced for the charge brought against me. This fact makes it the more extraordinary that Mr. Mackay offers no argument or evidence in support of the proposition. Usually such a course signifies that the writer regards the statement as self-evident, or at least as obvious beyond reasonable doubt. But if this is the case here, Mr. Mackay believes, and believes it to be self-evident as a general proposition, that whatever is in the future is merely intellectual and non-existential. I hesitate to ascribe to Mr. Mackay the idealistic metaphysics according to which the future and future events, even when they are so bound up with what is going on at a given date as to be the issue or outcome of the latter, are merely ideal and non-existential. But in case that is his view, I must say it is the opposite of mine, and there is no ground whatever for interpreting what I have said in terms of his belief.

There is another possible explanation, one which, upon the whole, seems the more probable. Mr. Mackay may suppose that *my theory as a whole* commits me logically to acceptance of the proposition he makes, so that it expresses my actual position, which, however, I have in my confusion covered up and virtually denied. Even so, it seems to me astonishing that no evidence is given and no passages of my logical theory are alluded to in support of ascription to me of such a view.

Usually it would be extremely difficult to reply to or even discuss a thesis left in such a vague state. But in this particular case it happens to be a simple matter to point out that the view in question—the premise, be it recalled, of which the charge of basic confusion is the conclusion—goes contrary to my whole theory of inquiry; and to such an extent, moreover, as to make nonsense of the theory. I should have supposed that the general tenor of my theory of inquiry would have been made clear by the definition of inquiry which Mr. Mackay himself quotes in his article. An eventual situation which is the "controlled or directed transformation" of an original indeterminate situation would, I should have supposed, be seen to possess, necessarily, the *existential* nature of the original situation. If, however, the fact that such is the nature of my position does not appear from this definition of inquiry, the doctrine that the original indeterminate situation and the eventual resolved one are precisely *initial and terminal phases* of one and the same existential situation, is involved in every chapter of my *Logic* in treating every problem taken up.[2]

Proof of the statement I have just made would, in order to be completely adequate, obviously involve giving a resumé of the entire text of my *Logic*. Since this course is out of the question and in view of the fact that Mr. Mackay cites no specific evidence in support of the view he ascribes to me, I confine my

[2] In the course of his article Mr. Mackay makes, also without supporting evidence or reference, the following statement about the resolved final stage of the situation under inquiry: "Its determinateness belongs to the context and not to the content of the knowledge, or warranted assertibility, to which the inquiry leads." In my view the determinateness of the final phase of the situation undergoing inquiry is not only the *content* of knowledge, but it provides the *definition* of knowledge, as far as that determinateness is the outcome or "issue" of the operations constituting the inquiry.

remarks on the view I actually hold to one general and one special point—a point, however, which is a special case of the general theory. As to my general position, I believe the following passage, in its context and as a sample of many other passages to the same effect, shows that my view treats the original and the eventual situation as the two existential ends, initial and terminal, of one and the same existential situation: "The transformation [accomplished in inquiry] is existential and hence temporal. The pre-cognitive unsettled situation can be settled only by modification of its constituents. . . . The temporal quality of inquiry means, then, something quite other than that the process of inquiry takes time. It means that the objective subject-matter of inquiry undergoes modification." [3]

The existentiality of the situation from beginning to end is, indeed, so directly and so intimately bound up with every part of my discussion of inquiry that I almost hesitate to quote a special passage. To learn that my treatment is capable of being understood in precisely an opposite sense is a discouraging experience. But this completely contrary interpretation is contained in the sole reference made by Mr. Mackay to my fundamental "doctrine of the continuum of inquiry," when, instead of treating it as a temporal existential continuum, he says "it succeeds only in confusing the two kinds of indeterminateness without bridging the gap between them"—one kind being, of course, the non-existential indeterminateness *he* attributes to the eventual resolved situation, and the other kind the "practical operational" indeterminateness he supposes I give to the original situation—depending, moreover, as is shown later, upon its indeterminateness being taken by him in a merely privative sense. In this connection, Mr. Mackay's reference to "*causal* antecedent situation" makes it pertinent to mention that one chapter of my *Logic* contains a detailed criticism of the "antecedent-consequent" interpretation of the causal relation, and an exposition of

[3] *Logic: The Theory of Inquiry,* p. 118. Emphasis upon the necessity of experiment for competent inquiry and denial of the *mentalistic* nature of "thinking," because of the necessity or performance of overt operation, are mentioned in the context of this passage.

the view that it functions in inquiry as the means of instituting temporal "historic" continuity.

The more special point to which I call attention is a particular case of the general proposition set forth. The idea that the eventual situation is ideational (instead of being the existential issue or outcome of the existential transformation of the situation which in its first phase was indeterminate) makes nonsense of the very theory developed in my *Logic* regarding the nature of *ideational*. An *anticipation* of the eventual issue *is* an *idea*; such anticipation of a *possible* outcome defines being an *idea*; and (according to my view) such anticipations are necessary factors in effecting the *existential* transformation which it is the business of inquiry to accomplish: these propositions are indeed parts of my theory. But it is equally a part of my theory that the idea, or anticipation of *possible* outcome, must, in order to satisfy the requirements of controlled inquiry, be such as to indicate an operation to be *existentially* performed, or is a means (called *procedural*) of effecting the existential transformation without which a problematic situation cannot be resolved. Moreover, in my account of ideas it is expressly stated, at some length, that the *validity* of the idea, as an anticipation of eventual resolved existential situation, is *tested* by the contribution which performance of the operation prescribed by it makes to the institution of the final determinate phase. Exactly the same kind of interpretation is also given of the logical import of observed *data*, as the *material* means of effecting the needed existential transformation. That Mr. Mackay might object to my actual theory even more strenuously than he does to the one he thinks I hold, I can well understand. But that fact does not affect the irrelevancy of the view ascribed to me as the ground of the criticisms he actually sets forth.

II

In dealing with the difficulty due to *vagueness* in my idea of indeterminateness, I wish first to state that in one point mentioned by Mr. Mackay I was guilty of a loose use of language of a kind that readily leads to misunderstanding. I am glad of the occasion given me by Mr. Mackay's paper to correct my mistake. In a passage cited by Mr. Mackay I used the term *"doubtful"* in connection with the pre-inquiry situation, and used it as if it were a synonym for the indeterminateness I attribute to that pre-inquiry situation. Doubting is, obviously, correlative with inquiring. The fact that my misuse in this particular case did not bear at all upon the particular issue then under discussion may have been a factor in producing my carelessness but is no excuse for it.

Mr. Mackay's discussion of the second point makes it clear that he regards the *indeterminateness* of the antecedent situation as purely *privative*. He speaks of it as signifying "a felt *lack* of knowledge"; as the *"absence"* of certain characteristics that are to be *eventually* determined by means of *further* inquiry" (italics not in original text). His belief in the merely privative character of *indeterminate* in this connection is shown also in his quotation from James of the *toto coelo* difference between feeling of an absence and absence of a feeling. This view is also involved in his treatment of the indeterminateness of the original situation as "practical" and "operational." In this matter again Mr. Mackay's treatment does not enable a reader to judge whether he thinks his interpretation is "self-evident," in the nature of the case, or is a necessary logical implication of my theory. As far as his discussion is concerned, the statement is an *ipse dixit*. Accordingly, I can only say that as far as my own view is concerned, assertion of the negative or privative character of the original situation inverts my position. According to me, it is positive and intrinsic and in *that* capacity it evokes and directs the inquiry that attempts to effect existential transformation into an eventual determinate situation. What is said about "situation" applies in full force to the situation which is *indeterminate* in quality. "A situation is a whole in virtue of its immediately pervasive quality. . . . The pervasively qualitative is also unique; it constitutes each situation an *individual* situation, indivisible and induplicable. . . . Without its controlling presence, there is no way to determine the relevancy, weight or coherence of any designated distinction or relation." [4] The "controlling presence" of the *uniquely* pervasive indeterminate quality of the situation provides the direction which Mr. Mackay's criticism finds to be absent—and which, of course, *is* absent if the indeterminateness in question is a mere lack or absence, a deprivation. If, however, Mr. Mackay holds that the original situation is indeterminate in a purely negative sense, it is *he* who seems committed to the view that sheer ignorance, if felt, is capable of evoking effective inquiry. It is my denial of that view, my belief that only intrinsic, positive indeterminateness of a unique character is capable of bringing inquiry into existence, which provides the ground for my assertion that doubting and doubts which are not formulations of an initial distinctive existential indeterminateness are pathological, to the extent at least of being captious, arbitrary, self-made.

Mr. Mackay suggests that it is possible that my use of a number of words as synonyms of "indeterminate," as applied to the initial antecedent situation, increases rather than lessens the vagueness of that term. As for myself, I wish that I had enough poetic or dramatic capacity to multiply the words used still further. For no word can describe or convey a *quality*. This statement is, of course, as true of the quality *indeterminate* as it is of the qualities *red, hard, tragic,* or *amusing.* The words used can at best only serve to produce in hearer or reader an experience in which the quality mentioned is directly had or experienced. There was enough novelty in the view developed in my *Theory of Inquiry* to cause me to appreciate the difficulty that would take place in the having of the kind of situation that would give the word "indeterminate" realized meaning in the sense in which I used it. Accordingly, I spoke of some situations (those which evoke and direct inquiry) as perplexed, troubled, unsettled, open, imbalanced, in the hope that some adjective

[4] *Op. cit.,* p. 68.

might induce readers to call up for themselves the kind of situation to which the word "indeterminate" is applied in connection with inquiry. I might also have used, possibly I have at times used, such words as insecure, precarious, even *uncertain*, not indeed in its cognitive sense but in the sense in which it is said that a man's footing is unsure. How far the "vagueness" involved in use of a name that designates a quality is, in a given case, a matter of lack of proper skill of evocation on the part of the one who uses the word, and how far it is a matter of declining to have a situation which would give the designation its intended import—a refusal due as a rule to habits previously formed— cannot be decided on general principles. But I hope the variety of words I have used and suggested will at least protect the quality involved from being taken to be negative and privative.[5]

III

Were it not for the light shed upon the matter by Mr. Mackay's interpretation of *indeterminate* as sheer lack and absence, I would be completely at a loss in understanding what is meant by the concluding portion of Mr. Mackay's paper—especially as he again confines himself to making statements without adducing evidence, or support by reference to any specific passages in my writings. Given a belief that what is meant by *indeterminate* is purely privative, *and given also* the reading of that belief into what I have said in dealing with values, ends, standards, policies, I can begin, somewhat faintly, to understand how Mr. Mackay could connect my "liberalism" with "freedom of indifference," and could make his other charges. As matters stand, I can only express a hope that Mr. Mackay will in another article produce grounds derived from what is actually stated in

---

[5] On pages 68–70 of *Logic: The Theory of Inquiry*, in connection with the word "sitation" I have said something about the fact that in certain cases words, and discourse generally, can serve only as *invitations* to a reader or hearer which the latter may accept or refuse. What is there said is peculiarly applicable to the "indeterminate" under discussion.

my writings on social philosophy for the view he takes of the latter.

In the absence of anything of this sort, I confine myself to one remark. I am pretty well used to having my writings on value, and on social topics generally, criticized as based upon an extremely exaggerated view of *intelligence*—that word being, in my use of it, a short name for competent inquiry at work. Mr. Mackay's line of criticism has at least the stimulating quality of novelty. Definition of values and of freedom in terms of extended social use of the method of intelligence is a doctrine of the way in which (the *only* way in which as I see the matter) deep-seated confusions and conflicts, which now prevail and which hamper and prevent attainment of values and of effective or positive freedom, may be progressively overcome.

10

PROPOSITIONS, WARRANTED ASSERTIBILITY, AND TRUTH

I PROPOSE IN WHAT FOLLOWS TO RESTATE SOME FEATURES OF THE theories I have previously advanced on the topics mentioned above. I shall shape this restatement on the basis of ascriptions and criticisms of my views found in Mr. Russell's *An Inquiry into Truth and Meaning*. I am in full agreement with his statement that "there is an important difference between his views and mine, which will not be elicited unless we can understand each other." [1] Indeed, I think the statement might read "We cannot understand each other unless important differences between us are brought out and borne in mind." I shall then put my emphasis upon what I take to be such differences, especially in relation to the nature of propositions; operations; the respective force of antecedents and consequences; tests or "verifiers"; and experience, the latter being, perhaps, the most important of all differences because it probably underlies the others. I shall draw contrasts which, in the interest of mutual understanding, need to be drawn for the purpose of making my own views clearer than I have managed previously to do. In drawing them I shall be compelled to ascribe certain views to Mr. Russell, without, I hope, attributing to him views he does not in fact hold.

I

Mr. Russell refers to my theory as one which "substitutes 'warranted assertibility' for truth." [2] Under certain conditions, I

[1] *Op. cit.*, p. 401.
[2] *Op. cit.*, p. 362. This interpretation is repeated on p. 401, using the words "should take the place of" instead of "substitutes."

should have no cause to object to this reference. But the conditions are absent; and it is possible that this view of "substitution" as distinct from and even opposed to *definition*, plays an important rôle in generating what I take to be misconceptions of my theory in some important specific matters. Hence, I begin by saying that my analysis of "warranted assertibility" is offered as a *definition* of the nature of knowledge in the honorific sense according to which only *true* beliefs are knowledge. The place at which there is pertinency in the idea of "substitution" has to do with *words*. As I wrote in my *Logic: The Theory of Inquiry*, "What has been said helps explain why the term "warranted assertibility" is preferred to the terms *belief* and *knowledge*. It is free from the ambiguity of the latter terms." [3] But there is involved the extended analysis, given later, of the nature of assertion and of warrant.

This point might be in itself of no especial importance. But it is important in its bearing upon interpretation of other things which I have said and which are commented upon by Mr. Russell. For example, Mr. Russell says, "One important difference between us arises, I think, from the fact that Dr. Dewey is mainly concerned with theories and hypotheses, whereas I am mainly concerned with assertions about particular matters of fact." [4] My position is that something of the order of a theory or hypothesis, a meaning entertained as a *possible significance* in some actual case, is demanded, if there is to be *warranted* assertibility in the case of a particular matter of fact. This position undoubtedly gives an importance to ideas (theories, hypotheses) they do not have upon Mr. Russell's view. But it is not a position that can be put in opposition to assertions about matters of particular fact, since, in terms of my view, it states the *condi-*

[3] *Logic*, p. 9. Perhaps in the interest of clearness, the word "term" should have been italicized. The ambiguities in question are discussed in previous pages. In the case of *belief*, the main ambiguity is between it as a state of mind and as *what* is believed—subject-matter. In the case of *knowledge*, it concerns the difference between knowledge as an outcome of "competent and controlled inquiry" and knowledge supposed to "have a meaning of its own apart from connection with, and reference to, inquiry."

[4] *Op. cit.*, p. 408.

tions under which we reach warranted assertibility about particular matters of fact.[5]

There is nothing peculiarly "pragmatic" about this part of my view, which holds that the presence of an *idea*—defined as a possible significance of an existent something—is required for any assertion entitled to rank as knowledge or as true; the insistence, however, that the "presence" be by way of an existential operation demarcates it from most other such theories. I may indicate some of my reasons for taking this position by mentioning some difficulties in the contrasting view of Mr. Russell that there are propositions known in virtue of their own immediate direct presence, as in the case of "There is red," or, as Mr. Russell prefers to say, "Redness-here."

(i) I do not understand how "here" has a self-contained and self-assured meaning. It seems to me that it is void of any trace of meaning save as discriminated from *there*, while *there* seems to me to be plural; a matter of manifold *theres*. These discriminations involve, I believe, determinations going beyond anything directly given or capable of being directly present. I would even say, with no attempt here to justify the saying, that a theory involving determination or definition of what is called "Space" is involved in the allegedly simple "redness here." Indeed, I would add that since any adequate statement of the matter of particular fact referred to is "redness-here-now," a scientific theory of *space-time* is involved in a fully warranted assertion about "redness-here-now."

(ii) If I understand Mr. Russell aright, he holds that the ultimacy and purity of basic propositions is connected with (possibly is guaranteed by) the fact that subject-matters like "redness-here" are of the nature of perceptual experiences, in which perceptual material is reduced to a direct *sensible* presence, or a *sensum*. For example, he writes: "We can, however, in theory, distinguish two cases in relation to a judgment such as

[5] As will appear later, the matter is inherently connected with the proper interpretation of *consequences* on my theory, and also with the very fundamental matter of *operations,* which Mr. Russell only barely alludes to.

'that is red'; one, when it is caused by what it asserts, and the other, when words or images enter into its causation. In the former case, it must be true; in the latter it may be false." However, Mr. Russell goes on to ask: "What can be meant when we say a 'percept' causes a word or sentence? On the face of it, we have to suppose a considerable process in the brain, connecting visual centres with motor centres; the causation, therefore, is by no means direct." [6] It would, then, seem as if upon Mr. Russell's own view a quite elaborate physiological theory intervenes in any given case as condition of assurance that "redness-here" is a true assertion. And I hope it will not appear unduly finicky if I add that a theory regarding causation also seems to be intimately involved.

Putting the matter on somewhat simpler and perhaps less debatable ground, I would inquire whether what is designated by such words as "sensible presence" and "sensa" is inherently involved in Mr. Russell's view. It would seem as if some such reference were necessary in order to discriminate *"redness-here"* from such propositions as *"this ribbon is red,"* and possibly from such propositions as *"hippogriff-here."* If reference to a sensum *is* required, then it would seem as if there must also be reference to the bodily sensory apparatus in virtue of whose mediation a given quality is determined to be a *sensum*. It hardly seems probable to me that such knowledge is any part of the datum as directly "here"; indeed, it seems highly probable that there was a long period in history when human beings did not institute connection between colors and visual apparatus, or between sounds and auditory apparatus; or at least that such connection as was made was inferred from what happened when men shut their eyes and stopped up their ears.

The probability that the belief in certain qualities as "sensible" is an inferential matter is increased by the fact that Mr. Russell himself makes no reference to the presence of the bodily *motor* element which is assuredly involved in "redness-here"; —an omission of considerable importance for the difference be-

[6] *Op. cit.,* p. 200.

tween our views, as will appear later. In view of such considerations as these, any view which holds that all complex propositions depend for their status *as knowledge* upon prior atomic propositions, of the nature described by Mr. Russell, seems to me the most adequate foundation yet provided for complete scepticism.

The position which I take, namely, that all knowledge or warranted assertion depends upon inquiry and that inquiry is, truistically, connected with what is questionable (and questioned) involves a sceptical element, or what Pierce called "fallibilism." But it also provides for *probability*, and for determination of degrees of probability in rejecting all intrinsically dogmatic statements, where "dogmatic" applies to *any* statement asserted to possess inherent self-evident truth. That the only alternative to ascribing to some propositions self-sufficient, self-possessed, and self-evident truth is a theory which finds the test and mark of truth in *consequences* of some sort is, I hope, an acceptable view. At all events, it is a position to be kept in mind in assessing my views.

II

In an earlier passage Mr. Russell ascribes certain views to "instrumentalists" and points out certain errors which undoubtedly (and rather obviously) exist in those views—as *he* conceives and states them. My name and especial view are not mentioned in this earlier passage. But, aside from the fact that I have called my view of propositions "instrumental" (in the particular technical sense in which I define propositions), comment on the passage may assist in clarifying what my views genuinely are. The passage reads:

There are some schools of philosophy—notably the Hegelians and the instrumentalists—which deny the distinction between data and inference altogether. They maintain that in all our knowledge there is an inferential element, that knowledge is an organic whole, and that the test of truth is coherence rather than conformity with "fact." I do not deny an element of truth in this view, but I think that, if taken as a whole truth, it renders the part played by perception in knowledge inexplicable. It is surely obvious that every perceptive experience, if I choose to notice it, affords me either new knowledge which I could not previously have inferred, or, at least, as in the case of eclipses, greater certainty than I could have previously obtained by means of inference. To this the instrumentalist replies that any statement of the new knowledge obtained from perception is always an interpretation based upon accepted theories, and may need subsequent correction if these theories turn out to be unsuitable.[7]

I begin with the ascription to instrumentalists of the idea that "in all our knowledge, there is an inferential element." This statement is, from the standpoint of my view, ambiguous; in one of its meanings, it is incorrect. It is necessary, then, to make a distinction. If it means (as it is apparently intended to mean) that an element due to inference appears in *propria persona*, so to speak, it is incorrect. For according to my view (if I may take it as a sample of the instrumentalists' view), while to infer something is necessary if a warranted assertion is to be arrived at, this inferred somewhat never appears *as such* in the latter; that is, in knowledge. The inferred material has to be checked and tested. The means of testing, required to give an inferential element any claim whatsoever to be *knowledge* instead of conjecture, are the data provided by observation— and *only* by observation. Moreover, as is stated frequently in

---

[7] *Op. cit.*, p. 154. To clear the ground for discussion of the views advanced in the passage quoted in the text, and as a means of shortening my comments, I append a few categorical statements, which can be substantiated by many references to "instrumentalist" writings. Instrumentalists do *not* believe that "knowledge is an organic whole"; in fact, the idea is meaningless upon their view. They do *not* believe the test of truth is coherence; in the operational sense, stated later in this paper, they hold a correspondence view.

my *Logic: The Theory of Inquiry*, it is necessary that data (provided by observation) be *new*, or different from those which first suggested the inferential element, if they are to have any value with respect to attaining knowledge. It is important that they be had under as many different conditions as possible so that data due to *differential* origins may supplement one another. The necessity of both the distinction and the coöperation of inferential and observational subject-matters is, on my theory, the product of an analysis of scientific inquiry; this necessity is, as will be shown in more detail later, the heart of my whole theory that knowledge is warranted assertion.

It should now be clear that the instrumentalist would not dream of making the kind of "reply" attributed to him. Instead of holding that *"accepted* theories" are always the basis for interpretation of what is newly obtained in perceptual experience, he has not been behind others in pointing out that such a mode of interpretation is a common and serious source of wrong conclusions; of dogmatism and of consequent arrest of advance in knowledge. In my *Logic*, I have explicitly pointed out that one chief reason why the introduction of experimental methods meant such a great, such a revolutionary, change in natural science, is that they provide data which are new not only in detail but in *kind*. Hence their introduction compelled new kinds of inference to new kinds of subject-matters, and the formation of new types of theories—in addition to providing more exact means of testing old theories. Upon the basis of the view ascribed to instrumentalists, I should suppose it would have been simpler and more effective to point out the contradiction involved in holding, on one side, that the instrumentalist has no way of discovering "need for further correction" in accepted theories, while holding, on the other side, that all accepted theories are, or may be, "unsuitable." Is there not flat contradiction between the idea that "any statement of new knowledge obtained by perception is always an interpretation based upon accepted theories," and the view that it may need subsequent correction if these theories prove "unsuitable"?

How in the world, upon the ground of the first part of the supposed "reply" of the instrumentalist, could any theory once "accepted" ever be shown to be unsuitable?

I am obliged, unfortunately, to form a certain hypothesis as to how and why, in view of the numerous and oft-repeated statements in my *Logic* of the *necessity* for distinguishing between inferential elements and observational data (necessary since otherwise there is no approach to warranted assertibility), it could occur to anyone that I denied the distinction. The best guess I can make is that my statements about the necessity of hard data, due to experimental observation and freed from all inferential constituents, were not taken seriously because it was supposed that upon my theory these data themselves represent, or present, *cases of knowledge*, so that there must be on my theory an inferential element also in them. Whether or not this is the source of the alleged denial thought up by Mr. Russell, it may be used to indicate a highly significant difference between our two views. For Mr. Russell holds, if I understand him, that propositions about these data are in some cases instances of knowledge, and indeed that such cases provide, as basic propositions, the models upon which a theory of truth should be formed. In my view, they are not cases of *knowledge*, although propositional formulation of them is a *necessary* (but not sufficient) condition of knowledge.

I can understand that my actual view may seem even more objectionable to a critic than the one that has been wrongly ascribed to me. None the less, in the interest of understanding and as a ground of pertinent criticism, it is indispensable that this position, and what it involves, be recognized as fundamental in my theory. It brings me to what is meant, in my theory, by the instrumental character of a proposition. I shall, then, postpone consideration of the ascription to me of the view that propositions are true if they are instruments or tools of successful action till I have stated just what, on my theory, a proposition is. The view imputed to me is that "Inquiry uses 'assertions' as its tools, and assertions are 'warranted' insofar as they produce the desired result." [8] I put in contrast with this conception the following statement of my view:

> Judgment may be identified as the settled outcome of inquiry. It is concerned with the concluding objects that emerge from inquiry in their status of being *conclusive*. Judgment in this sense is distinguished from *propositions*. The content of the latter is intermediate and representative and is carried by symbols; while judgment, as finally made, has *direct* existential import. The terms *affirmation* and *assertion* are employed in current speech interchangeably. But there is a difference, which should have linguistic recognition, between the logical status of intermediate subject-matters that are taken for use in connection *with what they lead to as means,* and subject-matter which has been prepared to be final. I shall use *assertion* to designate the latter logical status and *affirmation* to name the former. . . . However, the important matter is not the words, but the logical properties characteristic of different subject-matters.[9]

Propositions, then, on this view, are what are affirmed but not asserted. They are means, instrumentalities, since they are the operational agencies by which *beliefs* that have adequate grounds for acceptance are reached as *end* of inquiry. As I have intimated, this view may seem even more objectionable than is the one attributed to me, i.e., the one which is not mine. But in any case the difference between the instrumentality of a *proposition* as means of attaining a grounded *belief* and the instrumentality of a *belief* as means of reaching certain "*desired* results," should be fairly obvious, independently of acceptance or rejection of my view.

[8] *Op. cit.,* pp. 401–402.
[9] *Logic: The Theory of Inquiry,* p. 120 (not all italics in original). The word "logical," as it occurs in this passage, is, of course, to be understood in the sense given that term in previous chapters of the volume; a signification that is determined by connection with operations of inquiry which are undertaken because of the existence of a problem, and which are controlled by the conditions of that problem—since the "goal" is to resolve the problem which evokes inquiry.

Unless a critic is willing to entertain, in however hypothetical a fashion, the view (i) that *knowledge* (in its honorific sense) is in every case connected with inquiry; (ii) that the conclusion or end of inquiry has to be demarcated from the intermediate means by which inquiry goes forward to a warranted or justified conclusion; that (iii) the intermediate means are formulated in discourse, i.e., as propositions, and that as means they have the properties appropriate to means (viz., relevancy and efficacy—including economy), I know of no way to make my view intelligible. If the view is entertained, even in the most speculative conjectural fashion, it will, I think, be clear that, according to it, truth and falsity are properties only of that subject-matter which is the *end*, the close of the inquiry by means of which it is reached. The distinction between true and false conclusions is determined by the character of the operational procedures through which propositions about data and propositions about inferential elements (meanings, ideas, hypotheses) are instituted. At all events, I cannot imagine that one who says that such things as hammers, looms, chemical processes like dyeing, reduction of ores, when used as means, are marked by properties of fitness and efficacy (and the opposite) rather than by the properties of truth-falsity, will be thought to be saying anything that is not commonplace.

IV

My view of the nature of propositions, as distinct from that held by Mr. Russell, may be further illustrated by commenting upon the passage in which, referring to my view concerning changes in the matter of hypotheses during the course of inquiry, he writes: "I should say that inquiry begins, as a rule, with an assertion that is vague and complex, but replaces it, when it can, by a number of separate assertions each of which is less vague and less complex than the original assertion." [10] I remark in passing that previous observations of this kind by

[10] *Op. cit.*, p. 403.

Mr. Russell were what led me so to misapprehend his views as to impute to him the assumption "that *propositions* are the subject-matter of inquiry"; an impression, which, if it were not for his present explicit disclaimer, would be strengthened by reading, "When we embark upon an inquiry we assume that *the propositions about which we are enquiring* are either true or false." [11] Without repeating the ascription repudiated by Mr. Russell, I would say that upon my view "propositions are *not* that about which we are inquiring," and that as far as we do find it necessary or advisable to inquire about them (as is almost bound to happen in the course of an inquiry), it is not their truth and falsity about which we inquire, but the relevancy and efficacy of their subject-matter with respect to the problem in hand. I also remark, in passing, that Mr. Russell's statement appears to surrender the strict two-value theory of propositions in admitting that they may have the properties of being vague-definite; complex-simple. I suppose, however, that Mr. Russell's reply would be that on his view these latter qualities are derivative; that the first proposition is vague and complex because it is a mixture of some (possibly) true and some (possibly) false propositions. While dialectically this reply covers the case, it does not seem to agree with what happens in any actual case of analysis of a proposition into simpler and more definite ones. For this analysis always involves modification or transformation of the terms (meanings) found in the original proposition, and not its division into some true and some false propositions that from the start were its constituents although in a mixture.

Coming to the main point at issue, I hold that the first propositions we make as means of resolving a problem of any marked degree of difficulty are indeed likely to be too vague and coarse to be effective, just as in the story of invention of other instrumentalities, the first forms are relatively clumsy, uneconomical, and ineffective. They have then, as means, to be replaced by others which are more effective. Propositions are vague when, for example, they do not delimit the problem sufficiently to in-

[11] *Op. cit.*, p. 361. My italics.

dicate what kind of a solution is relevant. It is hardly necessary to say that when we don't know the conditions constituting a problem we are trying to solve, our efforts at solution at best will be fumbling and are likely to be wild. Data serve as tests of any idea or hypothesis that suggests itself, and in this capacity also their definiteness is required. But, upon my view, the degree and the quality of definiteness and of simplicity, or elementariness, required, are determined by the problem that evokes and controls inquiry. However the case may stand in epistemology (as a problem based upon a prior assumption that knowledge is and must be a relation between a knowing subject and an object), upon the basis of a view that takes knowing (inquiry) as it finds it, the idea that simplicity and elementariness are *inherent* properties of propositions (apart from their place and function in inquiry) has no meaning. If I understand Mr. Russell's view, his test for the simple and definite nature of a proposition applies indifferently to all propositions and hence has no indicative or probative force with respect to any proposition in particular.

Accepting, then, Mr. Russell's statement that his "problem has been, throughout, the relation between events and propositions," and regretting that I ascribed to him the view that "propositions are the subject-matter of inquiry," I would point out what seems to be a certain indeterminateness in his view of the relation between events and propositions, and the consequent need of introducing a distinction: *viz.*, the distinction between the problem of the relation of events and propositions *in general,* and the problem of the relation of a *particular* proposition to the *particular* event to which it purports to refer. I can understand that Mr. Russell holds that certain propositions, of a specified kind, are such direct effects of certain events, and of nothing else, that they "must be true." But this view does not, as I see the matter, answer the question of how we know that *in a given case* this direct relationship actually exists. It does not seem to me that his theory gets beyond specifying the kind of case *in general* in which the relation between an event, as causal antecedent, and a proposition, as effect, is such as to confer upon instances of the latter the property of being true. But I cannot see that we get anywhere until we have means of telling *which* propositions in particular *are* instances of the kind in question.

In the case, previously cited, of *redness-here*, Mr. Russell asserts, as I understand him, that it is true when it is caused by a simple, atomic event. But how do we know in a given case whether it is so caused? Or if he holds that it *must* be true because it *is* caused by such an event, which is then its sufficient verifier, I am compelled to ask how such is known to be the case. These comments are intended to indicate both that I hold a "correspondence" theory of truth, and the sense in which I hold it—a sense which seems to me free from a fundamental difficulty that Mr. Russell's view of truth cannot get over or around. The event *to be* known is that which operates, on his view, as cause of the proposition while it is also its verifier; although the proposition is the sole means of knowing the event! Such a view, like any strictly epistemological view, seems to me to assume a mysterious and unverifiable doctrine of pre-established harmony. How an event can be (i) what-is-to-be-known, and hence by description is unknown, and (ii) what is capable of being *known* only through the medium of a proposition, which, in turn (iii) in order to be a case of knowledge or be true, must correspond to the to-be-known, is to me *the* epistemological miracle. For the doctrine states that a proposition is true when it conforms to that which is not known save through itself.

In contrast with this view, my own view takes correspondence in the operational sense it bears in all cases except the unique epistemological case of an alleged relation between a "subject" and an "object"; the meaning, namely, of *answering*, as a key answers to conditions imposed by a lock, or as two correspondents "answer" each other; or, in general, as a reply is an adequate answer to a question or a criticism—as, in short, a *solution* answers the requirements of a *problem*. On this view, both partners in "correspondence" are open and above board, instead of one of them being forever out of experience and the other in it by way of a "percept" or whatever. Wondering at how something in experience could be asserted to correspond to something by definition outside experience, which it is, upon the basis of epistemological doctrine, the sole means of "knowing," is what originally made me suspicious of the whole epistemological industry.[12]

In the sense of correspondence as operational and behavioral (the meaning which has definite parallels in ordinary experience), I hold that my *type* of theory is the only one entitled to be called a correspondence theory of truth.

V

I should be happy to believe that what has been said is sufficiently definite and clear as to the nature and function of "consequences," so that it is not necessary to say anything more on the subject. But there are criticisms of Mr. Russell's that I might seem to be evading were I to say nothing specifically about them. He asserts that he has several times asked me what the goal of inquiry is upon my theory, and has seen no answer to the question.[13] There seems to be some reason for inferring

[12] In noting that my view of truth involves dependence upon consequences (as his depends upon antecedents, not, however, themselves in experience), and in noting that a causal law is involved, Mr. Russell concludes: "These causal laws, if they are to serve their purpose, must be 'true' in the very sense that Dr. Dewey would abolish" (*op. cit.*, p. 408). It hardly seems unreasonable on my part to expect that my general theory of truth be applied to particular cases, that of the truth of causal laws included. If it was unreasonable to *expect* that it would be so understood, I am glad to take this opportunity to say that such is the case. I do not hold in this case a view I have elsewhere "abolished." I *apply* the general view I advance elsewhere. There are few matters with respect to which there has been as much experience and as much testing as in the matter of the connection of means and consequences, since that connection is involved in all the details of every occupation, art, and undertaking. That warranted assertibility is a matter of probability in the case of causal connections is a trait it shares with other instances of warranted assertibility; while, apparently, Mr. Russell would deny the name of knowledge, in its fullest sense, to anything that is not certain to the point of infallibility, or which does not ultimately rest upon some absolute certainty.
[13] *Op. cit.*, p. 404.

that this matter is connected with the belief that I am engaged in *substituting* something else for "truth," so that truth, as he interprets my position, not being the goal, I am bound to provide some other goal. A person turning to the Index of my *Logic: The Theory of Inquiry* will find the following heading: "Assertibility, warranted, as end of inquiry." Some fourteen passages of the text are referred to. Unless there is a difference which escapes me between "end" and "goal," the following passage would seem to give the answer which Mr. Russell has missed:

> Moreover, inference, even in its connection with test, is not logically final and complete. The heart of the entire theory developed in this work is that the resolution of an indeterminate situation is the end, in the sense in which "end" means *end-in-view* and in the sense which it means *close*.[14]

The implication of the passage, if not in its isolation then in its context, is that inquiry begins in an *indeterminate* situation, and not only begins in it but is controlled by its specific qualitative nature.[15] Inquiry, as the set of operations by which the situation is resolved (settled, or rendered determinate) has to discover and formulate the conditions that describe the problem in hand. For *they* are the conditions to be "satisfied" and the determinants of "success." Since these conditions are existential, they can be determined only by observational operations; the operational character of observation being clearly exhibited in the experimental character of all scientific determination of data. (Upon a non-scientific level of inquiry, it is exhibited in the fact that we *look* and see; *listen* and hear; or, in general terms, that a motor-muscular, as well as sensory, factor is involved in any perceptual experience.) The conditions discov-

[14] *Logic: The Theory of Inquiry*, pp. 157–158.
[15] *Logic*, p. 105. "It is a unique doubtfulness" that not only evokes the particular inquiry, but as explicitly stated "exercises control" over it. To avoid needless misunderstanding, I quote also the following passage: "No situation which is *completely* indeterminate can possibly be converted into a problem having definite constituents" (*Ibid.*, p. 108).

ered, accordingly, in and by operational observation, constitute the *conditions of the problem* with which further inquiry is engaged; for data, on this view, are always data of some specific problem and hence are not given ready-made to an inquiry but are determined in and by it. (The point previously stated, that propositions about data are not cases of knowledge but means of attaining it, is so obviously an integral part of this view that I say nothing further about it in this connection.) As the problem progressively assumes definite shape by means of repeated acts of observation, possible solutions suggest themselves. These possible solutions are, truistically (in terms of the theory), *possible* meanings of the data determined in observation. The process of reasoning is an elaboration of them. When they are checked by reference to observed materials, they constitute the subject-matter of *inferential* propositions. The latter are means of attaining the goal of knowledge as warranted assertion, not instances or examples of knowledge. They are also operation in nature since they institute new experimental observations whose subject-matter provides both tests for old hypotheses and starting-points for new ones or at least for modifying solutions previously entertained. And so on until a determinate situation is instituted.

If this condensed statement is taken in its own terms and not by first interpreting its meaning in terms of some theory it doesn't logically permit, I think it will render unnecessary further comment on the notion Mr. Russell has ascribed to me: the notion, namely, that "a belief is warranted, if as a tool, it is useful in some activity, i.e., if it is a cause of satisfaction of desire," and that "the only essential result of successful inquiry is successful action." [16]

In the interest of mutual understanding, I shall now make some comments on a passage which, if I interpret it aright, sets forth the nature of Mr. Russell's wrong idea of my view, and which also, by implication, suggests the nature of the genuine difference between our views:

[16] *Op. cit.*, pp. 404, 405.

If there are such occurrences as "believings," which seems undeniable, the question is: Can they be divided into two classes, the "true" and the "false"? Or, if not, can they be so analyzed that their constituents can be divided into these two classes? If either of these questions is answered in the affirmative, is the distinction between "true" and "false" to be found in the success or failure of the effects of believings, or is it to be found in some other relation which they may have to relevant occurrences? [17]

On the basis of other passages, such as have been quoted, I am warranted in supposing that there is ascribed to me the view that "the distinction between 'true' and 'false' is to be found in the success or failure of the effects of believings." After what I have already said, I hope it suffices to point out that the question of truth-falsity is *not*, on my view, a matter of the effects of *believing*, for my whole theory is determined by the attempt to state what conditions and operations of inquiry *warrant* a "believing," or justify its assertion as true; that propositions, as such, are so far from being cases of believings that they are means of attaining a warranted believing, their worth as means being determined by their pertinency and efficacy in "satisfying" conditions that are rigorously set by the problem they are employed to resolve.

At this stage of the present discussion, I am, however, more interested in the passage quoted as an indication of the difference between us than as a manifestation of the nature of Mr. Russell's wrong understanding of my view.[18] I believe most decidedly that the distinction between "true" and "false" is to be found in the relation which *propositions*, as means of inquiry,

<hr />

[17] *Op. cit.* p. 405.

[18] I venture to remark that the words "wrong" and "right" as they appear in the text are used unintentionally instead of the words "false" and "true"; for, according to my view, understanding and misunderstanding, conception and misconception, taking and mis-taking, are matters of propositions, which are not final or complete in themselves but are used as means to an end—the resolution of a problem; while it is to this resolution, as *conclusion* of inquiry, that the adjectives "true" and "false" apply.

"have to relevant occurrences." The difference between us concerns, as I see the matter in the light of Mr. Russell's explanation, the question of *what* occurrences *are* the relevant ones. And I hope it is unnecessary to repeat by this time that the relevant occurrences on my theory are those existential consequences which, in virtue of operations existentially performed, satisfy (meet, fulfill) conditions set by occurrences that constitute a problem. These considerations bring me to my final point.

VI

In an earlier writing, a passage of which is cited by Mr. Russell, I stated my conclusion that Mr. Russell's interpretation of my view in terms of satisfaction of personal desire, of success in activities performed in order to satisfy desires, etc., was due to failure to note the importance in my theory of the existence of indeterminate or problematic situations as not only the source of, but as the control of, inquiry. A part of what I there wrote reads as follows:

> Mr. Russell proceeds first by converting a doubtful *situation* into a personal doubt. . . . Then by changing doubt into private discomfort, truth is identified [upon my view] with removal of this discomfort . . . [but] "Satisfaction" is satisfaction of the conditions prescribed by the problem.

In the same connection reference is made to a sentence in the Preface in which I stated, in view of previous misunderstandings of my position, that consequences are only to be accepted as tests of validity "*provided* these consequences are operationally instituted." [19]
Mr. Russell has made two comments with reference to these

[19] The original passage of mine is found in Vol. I of the *Library of Living Philosophers*, p. 571. It is also stated as one of the conditions, that it is necessary that consequences be "such as to resolve the specific problem evoking the operations." Quoted on p. 571 of the *Library* from p. iv, of the Preface of my *Logic*.

two explicitly stated conditions which govern the meaning and function of consequences. One of them concerns the reference to the consequences being "operationally instituted." Unfortunately for the cause of mutual understanding, it consists of but one sentence to the effect that its "meaning remains to me somewhat obscure." Comment upon the other qualification, namely, upon the necessity of "doubtful" problematic, etc., being taken to be characteristic of the "objective" situation and not of a person or "subject," is, fortunately, more extended:

> Dr. Dewey *seems* to write as if a doubtful situation could exist without a personal doubter. I cannot think that he means this; he cannot intend to say, for example, that there were doubtful situations in astronomical and geological epochs before there was life. The only way in which I can interpret what he says is to suppose that, for him, a "doubtful situation" is one which arouses doubt, not only in some one individual, but in any normal man, or in any man anxious to achieve a certain result, or in any scientifically trained observer engaged in investigating the situation. *Some* purpose, i.e., *some* desire, is involved in the idea of a doubtful situation.[20]

When the term "doubtful situation" is taken in the meaning it possesses in the context of my general theory of experience, I *do* mean to say that it can exist without a personal doubter; and, moreover, that "personal states of doubt that are not evoked by, and are not relative to, some existential situation are pathological; when they are extreme they constitute the mania of doubting. . . . The habit of disposing of the doubtful as if it belonged only to *us* rather than to the existential situation in which we are caught and implicated is an inheritance from subjectivistic psychology." [21] This position is so intimately and fundamentally bound up with my whole theory of "experience" as behavioral (though not "behavioristic" in the technical sense

[20] *Op. cit.*, p. 407.
[21] *Logic*, p. 106.

that the word has assumed), as interactivity of organism and environment, that I should have to go into a restatement of what I have said at great length elsewhere if I tried to justify what is affirmed in the passage quoted. I confine myself here to one point. The *problematic* nature of situations is definitely stated to have its source and prototype in the condition of imbalance or disequilibration that recurs rhythmically in the interactivity of organism and environment—a condition exemplified in hunger, not as a "feeling" but as a form of organic behavior such as is manifested, for example, in bodily restlessness and bodily acts of search for food. Since I cannot take the space to restate the view of experience of which the position regarding the existential nature of the indeterminate or problematic situation is one aspect (one, however, which is logically involved in and demanded by it), I confine myself to brief comments intended to make clearer, if possible, differences between my position and that of Mr. Russell. (i) All experiences are interactivities of an organism and an environment; a doubtful or problematic situation is, of course, no exception. But the energies of an organism involved in the particular interactivity that constitutes, or *is*, the problematic situation, are those involved in an ordinary course of living. They are *not* those of doubting. Doubt can, as I have said, be legitimately imputed to the organism only in a *secondary* or derived manner. (ii) "Every such interaction is a temporal process, not a momentary, cross-sectional occurrence. The situation in which it occurs is indeterminate, therefore, with respect to its *issue*. . . . Even were existential conditions unqualifiedly determinate in and of themselves, they are indeterminate [are such in certain instances] in *significance*: that is, in what they import and portend in their interaction with the organism." [22] The passage should throw light upon the sense in which an existential organism is existentially implicated or involved in a situation as interacting with environing conditions. According to my view, the sole way in which a "normal person" figures is that such a person investigates only in the actual

[22] *Logic*, pp. 106–107.

presence of a problem. (iii) All that is necessary upon my view is that an astronomical or geological epoch be an actual constituent of some experienced problematic situation. I am not, logically speaking, obliged to indulge in any cosmological speculation about those epochs, because, on my theory, any proposition about them is of the nature of what A. F. Bentley, in well-chosen terms, calls *"extrapolation,"* under certain conditions, be it understood, perfectly legitimate, but nevertheless an extrapolation.[23]

As far as cosmological speculation on the indeterminate situations in astronomical and geological epochs is relevant to my theory (or my theory to it), *any* view which holds that man is a part of nature, not outside it, will hold that this fact of being part of nature qualifies his "experience" throughout. Hence the view will certainly hold that indeterminacy in human experience, once experience is taken in the objective sense of interacting behavior and not as a private conceit added on to something totally alien to it, is evidence of some corresponding indeterminateness in the processes of nature within which man exists (acts) and out of which he arose. Of course, one who holds, as Mr. Russell seems to do, to the doctrine of the existence of an independent subject as the cause of the "doubtfulness" or "problematic quality" of situations will take the view he has expressed, thus confirming my opinion that the difference between us has its basic source in different views of the nature of experience, which in turn is correlated with our different conceptions of the connection existing between man and the rest of the world. Mr. Russell has not envisaged the possibility of there being another generic theory of experience, as an alternative to the pre-Darwinian conceptions of Hegel, on the one hand, and of Mill, on the other.

---

[23] *Behavior, Knowledge and Fact* (1935), Section XIX, "Experience and Fact," especially, pp. 172–179. The passage should be read in connection with section XXVII, "Behavioral Space-Time." I am glad to refer anyone interested in that part of my view that has to do with prehuman and pre-organic events to Mr. Bentley's statement, without, however, intending to make him responsible for what I have said on any other point.

The qualification in my theory relating to the necessity of consequences being "operationally instituted" is, of course, an intimate constituent of my whole theory of inquiry. I do not wonder that Mr. Russell finds the particular passage he cites "somewhat obscure," if he takes it in isolation from its central position in my whole theory of experience, inquiry, and knowledge. I cite one passage that indicates the intrinsic connection existing between this part of my theory and the point just mentioned—that concerning the place of indeterminate situations in inquiry. "Situations that are disturbed and troubled, confused or obscure, cannot be straightened out, cleared up and put in order, by manipulations of our personal states of mind." [24] This is the negative aspect of the position that operations of an existential sort, operations which are actions, doing something and accomplishing something (a changed state of interactivity in short), are the only means of producing consequences that have any bearing upon warranted assertibility.

In concluding this part of my discussion, I indulge in the statement of some things that puzzle me, things connected, moreover, not just with Mr. Russell's view, but with views that are widely held. (i) I am puzzled by the fact that persons who are systematically engaged with inquiry into questions, into problems (as philosophers certainly are), are so incurious about the existence and nature of problems. (ii) If a "subject" is one end-term in a relation of which objects (events) are the other end-terms, and if doubt is simply a state of a subject, why isn't knowledge also simply and only a state of mind of a subject? And (iii) the puzzling thing already mentioned: How can anybody look at *both* an object (event) and a proposition about it so as to determine whether the two "correspond"? And if one can look directly at the event *in propria persona*, why have a duplicate proposition (idea or percept, according to some theories) about it unless, perhaps, as a convenience in communication with others?

I do not wish to conclude without saying that I have tried to

[24] *Logic*, p. 106.

conduct my discussion in the spirit indicated by Mr. Russell, avoiding all misunderstanding as far as I can, and viewing the issues involved as uncontroversially as is consistent with trying to make my own views clear. In this process I am aware of the acute bearing of his remark that "it is because the difference goes deep that it is difficult to find words which both sides can accept as a fair statement of the issue." In view of the depth of the difference, I can hardly hope to have succeeded completely in overcoming this difficulty. But at least I have been more concerned to make my own position intelligible than to refute Mr. Russell's view, so that the controversial remarks I have made have their source in the belief that definite contrasts are an important, perhaps indispensable, means of making any view sharp in outline and definite in content.

PART IV

About Thinkers

I

JAMES MARSH AND AMERICAN PHILOSOPHY

IN THE YEARS 1829, 1831, AND 1832, AN EVENT OF CONSIDERABLE intellectual importance took place in Burlington, Vt. For in these years Chauncey Goodrich published there editions of three of the more important writings of Samuel Taylor Coleridge, namely, *Aids to Reflection, The Friend* and *The Statesman's Manual.* The first of these contains the well-known Introduction by James Marsh.

In associating the name of romantic philosophy with the work of James Marsh, it is important that we should appreciate the sense in which the word "romantic" is employed. Words change their meaning, and today such a title may seem to imply a certain disparagement, since realism in some form is the now prevailing mode. In the sense in which the word was earlier used, a somewhat technical one, the opposite of romantic was not realistic, but rather classic. The word was used to denote what was taken to be the modern spirit in distinction from that of antiquity, and more particularly the spirit of the Teutonic and Protestant North in distinction from the Latin and Catholic South.

Fortunately an essay written during Dr. Marsh's last year in Andover Seminary and published in the *North American Review* for July, 1822, enables us to seize, independently of labels, what Marsh himself thought the difference in question to consist of. "The modern mind," he says, "removes the centre of its thought and feelings from the 'world without' to the 'world within'." More in detail he says, in speaking of the Greeks, that "they had no conception of a boundless and invis-

357

ible world in the bosom of which all that is visible sinks into the littleness of a microcosm." [1] In contrast with this attitude he says: "In the mind of a modern all this is changed. His more serious thoughts are withdrawn from the world around him and turned in upon himself. All the phenomena of external nature, with all the materials which history and science have treasured up for the use of the past, are but the mere instruments to shadow forth the fervors of a restless spirit at last conscious of its own powers and expanding with conceptions of the boundless and the infinite." The change is definitely connected with the influence of Christianity in general and of the Protestant and earlier Barbarian North in particular.

I am concerned with the ideas and principles of the philosophical work of Marsh rather than with its historical origin, development, and influence.[2] But it would be unfitting to pass the occasion by without noting the broad and deep scholarship of March as it is made evident even in this the earliest of his published writings. He had mastered Italian, Spanish, and German, as well as Latin, Greek, and Hebrew, at that early date. This was no attainment since he had never been abroad, and since there were few facilities for study at the time. His writings show that he not only knew the languages, but had an extensive and familiar acquaintance with their literatures. I may not go into detail, but it is not too much to say that he was probably the first American scholar to have an intimate first-hand acquaintance with the writings of Immanuel Kant, including not only the *Critiques of Pure* and *Practical Reason,* but his *Anthropology,* and especially his writings on the philosophic basis of natural science. In the latter connection it is worthy of note that Marsh's readings in the scientific literature of his day were wide and influenced his speculations; Oersted with his principle of polarity influenced him chiefly along with Kant.

[1] *North American Review.* Vol. XV, p. 107.
[2] A careful and thoroughly trustworthy account of the latter has already been given by Professor Marjorie Nicolson. See the article entitled "James Marsh and the Vermont Transcendentalists," in the *Philosophical Review* for Jan. 1925.

His interpretation of Kant was affected, of course, by his admiration of Coleridge, but also by his reading of Fries.

While his indebtedness to Coleridge was great, it was some-what less than his distrust of his own powers would intimate. He came to Coleridge with a preparation both in reading and in his thinking, which fitted him to appreciate the latter, but which also absolves him from any charge of being a mere disciple. The interest that Marsh had in Coleridge sprang primarily from a common interest in religion and a common desire to arouse among believers in Christianity a vital realization of its spiritual truth. There is much in Coleridge's *Aids to Reflection* that is far outside the main currents of present-day thought even in religious circles. Aside from penetrating flashes of insight, a reader today is likely to be left indifferent to its substance and repelled by its form. He may easily find it of only antiquarian interest. To employ a juster statement, it is mainly of historical interest. To say this is to say that to grasp its meaning and its influence in its own time we must place it in its own context in the intellectual and moral atmosphere of the early nineteenth century. We must recall that it was a period before Darwin and the evolutionists; before, indeed, modern science had itself left any great impress on the popular mind; a period when the peculiar problems forced upon modern society by the industrial revolution were only beginning faintly to show themselves. It was a time when, outside of a few radicals, there was nominal acceptance of established institutions and doctrines but little concern for their own meaning. It was, on the whole, a period of intellectual apathy and indifference.

The two essays of John Stuart Mill upon Bentham and Coleridge respectively give a clear picture of the general temper of the day. Among other things Mill says, "The existing institutions in Church and State were to be preserved inviolate, in outward semblance at least, but were required to be, practically, as much of a nullity as possible." More specifically in speaking of the Church he says, "On condition of not making too much noise about religion, or taking it too much in earnest, the church was supported, even by philosophers, as a 'bulwark against fanaticism,' a sedative to the religious spirit, to prevent it from disturbing the harmony of society or the tranquility of states." He sums it up by saying that "on the whole, England had neither the benefits, such as they were, of the new ideas, nor of the old. We had a government which we respected too much to attempt to change it, but not enough to trust it with any power, or look to it for any services that were not compelled. We had a Church which had ceased to fulfill the honest purposes of a Church but which we made a great point of keeping up as the pretence or simulacrum of one. We had a highly spiritual religion (which we were instructed to obey from selfish motives) and the most mechanical and worldly notions on every other subject." As he says, "An age like this, an age without earnestness, was the natural era of compromises and half-convictions."

In this situation, Bentham was the innovator, the critic, and destroyer of the old. Coleridge was the unusual type of conservative, the thinker who demanded that the *meaning* of the old be comprehended and acted upon. As Mill says, "Bentham asked of every custom and institution 'Is it true?' while Coleridge asked, 'What is its meaning?' " The latter question, in the existing state of things, was as disturbing as the other; its import was as radical, for it was a challenge to the existing state of belief and action. The more obvious phase of the radicalism of Coleridge in religion is found in his attack on what he called its bibliolatry. He condemned the doctrine of literal inspiration as a superstition; he urged the acceptance of the teachings of Scripture on the ground that they "find" one in the deepest and most spiritual part of one's nature. Faith was a state of the will and the affections, not a merely intellectual assent to doctrinal and historical propositions. As Mill says, he was more truly liberal than many liberals.

But while he disconnected faith from the Understanding, he connected it with a higher faculty, the Reason, which is one with the true Will of man. Coleridge said: "He who begins by loving Christianity better than truth will proceed by loving his own sect or church better than Christianity and end in loving himself better than all." But he held with equal firmness that Christianity is itself a system of truth which, when rightly appropriated in the rational will and affection of men, is identical with the truth of philosophy itself. This assertion of the inherent rationality of Christian truth was the animating purpose of his *Aids to Reflection,* and it was this which appealed to James Marsh; and it is in this sense that he may be described as a disciple of Coleridge. It was in a combination of the teaching of the great English divines of the seventeenth century, themselves under the spell of Plato, and the German transcendental philosophy of the late eighteenth and early nineteenth century, that Coleridge found the especial philosophical framework by which to support his contention of the intrinsic philosophical truth of the Christian faith. Since Marsh himself was already a student of the same sources, all the circumstances conspired to attach his exposition to Coleridge.

If I dwell upon the inherent liberalism of Coleridge's teaching under the circumstances of his own day, as described by Mill, a member of the opposite school, it is because without allusion to that fact we are without the historic key to the work of Marsh also. In our own idea, and under present conditions, the philosophy of Marsh seems conservative. There is comparatively little interest, even in theological circles, in the doctrines to whose clarification, in the light of reason, he devoted himself. One sees his thought in its proper perspective only as one places it against the background of the prevailing interests of his own day. By temperament, Marsh shrank from controversy; he deprecated becoming involved in it. But the most casual reader of the Introduction prefaced to the republication of Coleridge's *Aids to Reflection* will see that its undercurrent is the feeling that what Coleridge says and what he himself says goes contrary to the doctrines that possess the mind of contemporary religious circles, while conjoined with this is the sense that he is under a religious as well as a philosophical obligation to combat the tendency of these beliefs. It was not just the fate or the spread of a particular philosophical system that he was concerned with, but the reawakening of a truly spiritual religion which had been obscured and depressed under the influence of the prevalent philosophies of John Locke and the Scottish school. It was as an ally of spiritual and personal religion that he turned to the German philosophy, actuated by the conviction that the same evils which Coleridge found in England were found also in his own country.

It is worth while to quote from the Introduction at some length what he has to say upon this subject. "It is our peculiar misfortune in this country that, while the philosophy of Locke and the Scottish writers has been received in full faith as the only rational system and its leading principles especially passed off as unquestionable, the strong attachment to religion and the fondness for speculation, by both of which we are strongly characterized, have led us to combine and associate these principles, such as they are, with our religious interests and opinions, so variously and so intimately, that by most persons they are considered as necessary parts of the same system." He himself held that the philosophical principles thus popularly read into the Christian faith were, in fact, profoundly discordant with the latter. As he says, "A system of philosophy which excludes the very idea of all spiritual power and agency cannot possibly co-exist with a religion essentially spiritual." Like Coleridge, he anticipates being regarded as a heretic in religion because he is desirous of searching out a philosophy that is consistent instead of inconsistent with the spiritual truths of Christianity which are to him its essence.

In the attempt, to which I now turn, to expound the positive philosophy of Marsh, one may appropriately return to the essay of 1822, to which allusion has already been made. Christianity presented itself to him not only as the great cause of the intellectual and emotional change from the world of classic to that of modern mind, as expressed in literature, politics, and social life, as well as in religion, but as inherently a revelation of philosophic truth. Revelation from without was required because of the fallen state of man. But the revelation was not external, much less arbitrary in *content*. It was rather a recovery of the essential ultimate truths about nature, man, and ultimate reality. It is for that reason that I said that Christianity was to him a truly philosophic revelation. Were I to attempt to select a single passage that might serve as an illuminating text of what he thought and taught, it would be, I think, the following: A thinking man "has and can have but one system in which his philosophy becomes religious and his religion philosophical."

As I have already indicated, the full meaning of this position can hardly be recovered at the present time. It must be considered in relation to the time in which Dr. Marsh lived. It had nothing in common with the views upon philosophy which prevailed in the academic audiences and popular thought of the time. These, as we have also noted, were based upon Locke as modified by the ruling Scotch school, and upon Paley. The orthodox conceived of Christianity as a merely external revelation; the dissenters from orthodoxy relied upon proof from design in nature of the existence of God and upon what Marsh, following Kant and Coleridge, called "Understanding" in distinction from "Reason." There is much evidence that Dr. Marsh felt himself between two dangers. One was that he should be thought to reduce Christianity to a mere body of doctrines, a speculative intellectual scheme. The other was that he should be thought faithless to the living power of Christianity in re-making life and thus be classed with unbelieving critics. The situation in which he thus found himself accounts, I think, for the air of apologetic timidity which surrounds the expression of his deepest thoughts. In part it was due, undoubtedly, to his modest distrust of himself, but in larger part, to the situation with which his period confronted him. He was quite right, no one who reads him can doubt that fact, in thinking of himself as a deeply devoted man in his own personality. Indeed, for inner and humble piety and spirituality he had few peers among his contemporaries. But he had, in addition, the distinctively philosophic instinct. He wanted to see the universe and all phases of life as a whole. When he gave rein to his instinct in this direction, he found himself at once conscious that he was coming into conflict with the ideas which dominated not only American society but the churches themselves. He neither mitigated his own Christian sense nor ceased to philosophize. But his activity in the latter field was, it seems to me, restricted. He never developed the independence in thought which matched his philosophic powers. It is probable, as Dr. Nicolson has made clear, that he, as the means of directing Emerson to Coleridge, and indirectly at least, made a profound impress upon the American "transcendental" movement. But he never had the detached position which marked Emerson, for example, and accordingly did not reach an unimpeded development of his own powers.

It is, however, time to turn more directly to his basic thought in which for him the religious truth of Christianity was found to be one with the truth of philosophy as a theory of God, the universe, and man. Formulas are somewhat dangerous. But for the sake of brevity, if for no other reason, a formula or label seems necessary. I shall, accordingly, venture to say that his philosophy is an Aristotelian version of Kant made under the influence of a profound conviction of the inherent *moral* truths of the teachings of Christianity. The formula involves, unfortunately, considerable technical reference to historic systems. The external evidence shows that he was more of a student of Plato and of the great divines of the seventeenth century who are more influenced by Plato than of Aristotle. But we know also by external testimony that the *Metaphysics* and the *De Anima* of Aristotle were always by him. And it seems fairly evident that his objective interpretation of Kant, his disregard for the phenomenalism and subjective view of nature found in Kant, came to him ultimately, whether directly or through Coleridge, from Aristotle.

To explain what meaning this statement has in connection with Marsh's own metaphysical system, it is necessary to digress into a technical field which I would otherwise gladly avoid. In Kant, as all students know of him, there is a definite separation made between sense, Understanding, and Reason. In consequence, the affections of the mind called sensations are regarded by him as "mental" in character, and as organized by forms of space and time which are themselves ultimately mental in character. The categories of the Understanding, while they provide universality and constancy for these sense impressions, do not, therefore, get beyond knowledge of phenomena. While Reason furnished ideals of unity and complete totality, which go beyond the scope of the Understanding, they are for us unrealizable ideals. When we suppose that Reason gives us knowledge of the real nature of things, we are led into illusions. Knowledge must remain within the bounds of phenomena, that is, of the logical organization of the materials of sense.

Now it is a striking fact that, while Dr. Marsh freely employs the Kantian terminology, and while he uses constantly not only the general distinctions of sense, Understanding, and Reason, but also special conclusions reached by Kant in treating them, he never even refers to the Kantian limitation of knowledge to phenomena—what is usually termed the "subjectivism" of Kant.

For example, while he treats, like Kant, mathematics as a science of space and time as necessary and hence *a priori* forms of perceptual experience, he also has in mind the absolute space and time of Newtonian physics and not just mental forms. They are forms of actual and external things of nature, not merely forms of mind. Thus our geometry and other mathematics is a rational science of the conditions under which all physical things exist, not merely a science of our conditions of experiencing them. In and of themselves as conditions of the possibility of physical things and their changes, they "constitute," in his own words, "the sphere of possibility and of those possible determinations of quantity and form which are the objects of pure mathematical science." The free development of these possibilities, independent of the restrictions imposed by actual existence, is the work of the productive imagination. But they are also necessary principles of the existence of all physical things and events, since the latter are and occur in space and time. Thus mathematics forms the basis of physical science.

He was probably influenced by Fries in this objective interpretation. But there is the deeper influence which I have called Aristotelian. This influence appears in his treatment of the relations of sense to Understanding and of both to Reason, and also in his entire philosophy of nature, in its relation to mind. Instead of making a separation between sense, Understanding, and Reason, they present themselves in Marsh's account as three successive stages in a progressive realization of the nature of ultimate reality. Each of the two earlier, namely, sense and Understanding, forms the conditions under which the third manifests itself and leads up to it. For each contains in itself principles which point beyond itself and which create the necessity of a fuller and deeper apprehension of the nature of the real.

What I have called the Aristotelianism of his position is seen in the fact that he did not isolate this ascending series of sense, Understanding, and rational will from the natural universe, as did Kant, but rather saw in it a progressive realization of the conditions and potentialities found in nature itself. I have not run across in him any allusion to Hegel, although he seems to have known Fichte. But like Hegel, instead of putting the subject in opposition to the object or the world, he regarded the subject, who comes most completely to himself in the rational will, as the culmination, the consummation, of the energies constituting the sensible and physical world. While not a scientist, in any technical sense, Marsh was widely read in the science of his day, and thought he found in it the evidence for the truth of the conception that nature presents to us an ascending scale of energies in which the lower are both the condition and the premonitions of the higher until we arrive at self-conscious mind itself.

His conception of sense is, in the epistemological language of today, realistic. He holds that in sense we can distinguish the received material, the seen, heard, and touched qualities from the acts of mind that form seeing, hearing, touching, and that we refer the material of sensed qualities to a ground of reality outside ourselves, just as we refer the acts of sensing to the self as the abiding ground of their reality. We perceive qualities of sense as qualities of an object existing outwardly and independently. Sense, however, does not give knowledge, even of the physical world, but only material for knowledge. The Understanding is necessary to judge the sensory material and to know *what* is presented in them. We have to interpret the material of sense. The Understanding operates by acts of distinguishing, comparing, and thus brings out the relations implicit in sensuous material. Without these connective and organizing relations, we do not know an object but merely have a number of qualities before us. We have the power to become self-conscious of the relating activities of the mind. We note that they proceed by certain necessary laws in as far as they result in knowledge. The Understanding is not free to judge in any arbitrary sense of freedom. To attain knowledge we must judge or understand in necessary ways, or else we do not attain knowledge of objects but only personal fancies. This law of understanding or knowing objects proceeds from the mind itself, and it, when we recognize it and take note of it, forms what is termed Reason. In the Understanding (that is, in scientific knowledge of nature) this agency operates spontaneously; but when it notes its own operation and becomes self-conscious, we recognize it as rational will, which is the animating principle, one and the same in character, or universal in all knowing minds; and hence identical with the divine intellect which is the light that lighteth every man that cometh into the world. It is reason because it operates by necessary principles; it is will when it is viewed as an agency complete and self-sufficient in itself.

This technical excursion into what Marsh calls rational psychology may help express the sense of what has been called the Aristotelian element in him. He insists that the powers of the mind or self are called forth only by objects correlative to them. The sensibility remains a mere potentiality until it is called into action by nature. We cannot hear or see or touch except as the mind is affected by things having color, sound, and solidity. There is no difference between this and the action and reaction of iron and a magnet upon each other. In the same way, the powers of the Understanding remain mere possibilities until they are called into action by the actual relations which subsist among objects. The orderly, logical structure is both the condition that calls the powers into action and realizes their potentialities, and the object upon which they expend themselves, just as much as the qualities of things are both the actualizing conditions and the objects upon which the capacities of the mind terminate in exercise or sensibility. Similarly, the objective of self-conscious, rational will is both the condition and the object of the exercise of our Reason.

The essentially Aristotelian nature of this conception of each lower stage forming the conditions of the actualizing of some potentiality of mind and then supplying the material upon which a higher expression of the same mind exercises itself will be obvious, I think, to every philosophic student. It is through the use of this conception that Marsh escapes from the charmed circle of limitation within the self that holds the Kantian philosophy spell-bound. The world in its status as a manifold of qualities, as a logically interconnected whole, and as summed up in universal self-conscious will, has to be there independently of our minds in order that the capacities of our minds may be stimulated into real existence and have material upon which to work.

It was said, however, that this Aristotelian interpretation of Kant is made under the influence of ideas derived from Christian faith. Marsh separates himself from Greek thought, whether that of Plato or Aristotle, in two ways. First, he conceives of mind as identical with the self, the "I" or personality, an identification that is like nothing found in ancient thought, and one which he associates with the influence of Christianity. It is another way of saying the same thing to point out that he introduces into the classic conception of reason an element foreign to it in its original statement—namely, the conception of reason as *will*—that is, of a power to institute and seek to realize ends that are universal and necessary, that are supplied by nature but which flow from its own nature as a personal rational self. It is the very nature of these ends that they cannot be realized by themselves or by any merely intellectual process. Their nature demands that they be embodied in the material of sense and of the natural world as an object of knowledge, or that all the material of appetite connected with the senses or of desire directed upon natural objects be subdued and transformed into agencies of expressing the true ultimate nature of the rational will. To put it a little more concretely, Aristotle held that reason could be actualized in contemplative knowledge apart from any effort to change the world of nature and social institutions into its own likeness and embodiment. Following the spirit of Christian teaching, Marsh denied any such possibility. He held that Reason can realize itself and be truly aware or conscious of its own intrinsic nature only as it operates to make over the world, whether physical or social, into an embodiment of its own principles. Marsh constantly condemns what he calls speculation and the speculative tendency, by which he means a separation of knowledge and the intellect from action and the will. By its own nature, reason terminates in action and that action is the transformation of the spiritual potentialities found in the natural world, physical and institutional, into spiritual realities.

The other point of connection of Marsh's philosophy with the Christian faith is more specific, less general. Accepting the idea that man is a fallen creature, he accepted also the idea of Coleridge that original sin is not a mere historic fact, going back to a historic progenitor, but is the act of the will itself by which it takes as the principle and moving spring of its own action something derived not from its own inherent nature but from some source outside itself—the appetites of sense, or the desires that are used by the thought of ends derived from the world about us. I shall not extend my excursion into technicalities to trouble you with his philosophic rendering of the theological doctrines of sin, conscience, and freedom of the will. But no exposition of his basic idea of the equation of philosophy with religion would be complete without reference to the particular way in which he applies his conception of the necessity of a correlative object in order to awaken the potentialities of the self into reality. The correlative object of the conscience and will, through which they, as they exist in man, can be aroused into actuality of operation and being, is no abstract law. As will and conscience are personal, belonging to a self, so their correlative object must also be personal. At this point, the religious character of his philosophy most clearly reveals and expresses itself. This correlative personal object is the manifestation of the divine in Christ. In his own words: "The true end of our being presented by the spiritual law is the realization, practically, in our own being, of that perfect idea which the law itself presupposes, and of which Christ is the glorious manifestation." And again, "the spiritual principle may be said to have only a potential reality, or, as it enters into the life of nature, a false and delusive show of reality, until, awakened from above by its own spiritual correlatives, it receives the engrafted word, and is empowered to rise above the thralldom of nature."

The discussion will now turn to a consideration of somewhat more concrete matters (although not, according to the view of Marsh, more genuinely human interests and concerns) —to what Marsh has to say upon society in general and education in particular. Unfortunately, what is left to us in the published record is all too scanty. But there are suggestions adequate to a reconstruction of his fundamental philosophy. Here, too, we may fittingly begin by recourse to Coleridge, in spite of the fact that there is less direct evidence of his connection with Coleridge in this matter than in that of the identification of the Christian religion with true philosophy. Coleridge, in common with the German school which he represented, conceived social institutions as essentially educative in nature and function. They were the outward manifestation of law and reason by means of which the intelligence and conscience of individuals are awakened and by which they are nourished till they become capable of independent activity, and then express themselves in loyalty to social institutions and devotion to improving them until these institutions are still better fitted to perform their educative task for humanity.

Coleridge with considerable courage applied this conception to the Church as an institution in distinction from the inward and spiritual communion of the faithful—an application that took its point, of course, from the fact that there was an established Church allied with the political order in England. With rather surprising daring, he proclaimed that the Church, in this institutional sense, is not inherently a religious corporation. In his own words, "Religion may be an indispensable ally but is not the essential constitutive end of that national institute which is unfortunately, at least improperly, styled the church; a name, which in its best sense, is exclusively appropriate to the Church of Christ." Then with an obvious etymological reference to the original meaning of clergy as connected with clerks or writers, he goes on to say "the clerisy of the nation, or national church in its primary acceptation and original intention, comprehended the learned of all denominations, the sages and professors of law and jurisprudence, of medicine and physiology, of music and civil and military architecture, with the mathematical as their common organ; in short, all the arts and sciences, the possession and application of which constitute the civilization of a nation, as well as the theological." The latter, he goes on to say, rightfully claimed the precedence but only because "theology was the root and trunk of the knowledge of civilized man; because it gave unity and the circulating sap of life to all other sciences, by virtue of which alone they could be contemplated as forming the living tree of knowledge." It is primarily as educators that those especially called clergy of the established church are to be regarded, and it was even well, according to Coleridge, that they should serve an apprenticeship as village schoolmasters before becoming pastors.

It is evident that, owing to the non-existence of an established church in the United States, this portion of Coleridge's teaching could not directly influence the thought of Marsh. Indeed, he naturally thought that the condition in which the institutional church was but the outward expression or body of the inner and spiritual church represented a higher principle than could be expressed by any politically established church. But indirectly, Marsh's ideas move in a like direction, although with such differences as the difference between the political organization of Great Britain and of our country would naturally suggest.

It is interesting to note that Marsh makes, in a sermon at the dedication of the chapel of the University, a distinction between civilization and culture similar to that drawn by Kant and other German thinkers. Civilization, he says, in effect, is concerned with the adaptation of the acts and services of the individual to the needs and conditions of existing society. It is a discipline of the faculties with reference to the occupations of civil society. Culture is the development of the powers of individuals with reference to the ends that make them truly human; it transcends any existing social order and régime because it elevates them into the possession of the spiritual law of reason, of universal will, and the end of humanity as such. It aims at control by this inner law of rational will instead of by the ordinances and customs of a given society. From the obligations imposed by the interests of higher and common humanity, no state policy can absolve us. The peoples of the East, he says, are, perhaps, more civilized than those of the West, for their institutions and the discipline they provide fit the individual to some definite place and work in the social order. But we, he says, are not destined to be the working instruments for attaining the lower ends imposed by the state of civilization. And he adds these very significant words: "We can hardly, indeed, be said to be subjects of any state, considered in its ordinary sense, as body politic with a fixed constitution and a determinate organization of its several powers. But we are constituent members of a community in which the highest worth and perfection and happiness of the individual free persons composing it constitute the highest aim and the perfection of the community as a whole. With us there is nothing so fixed by the forms of political and civil organization as to obstruct our efforts for promoting the full and free development of all our powers, both individual and social. Indeed, where the principle of self-government is admitted to such an extent as it is in this state, there is, in fact, nothing fixed or permanent, but as it is made so by that which is permanent and abiding in the intelligence and fixed rational principles of action in the self-governed. The self-preserving principle of our government is to be found only in the continuing determination and unchanging aims of its subjects." From this Dr. Marsh draws the inevitable conclusion that the function of an educational institution is a cultivation of the community, which is identical with the full development of all the powers of its individual persons.

It is to be regretted that Dr. Marsh never achieved a complete exposition of his social and political philosophy. While changes in vocabulary might be needed to adapt the principles he here expresses to present conditions, he has stated, it seems to me, a principle which is fundamental to the distinctive American social system, if we have any such system, and one which stands in need of enforcement at the present time. When Dr. Marsh wrote, the idea of nationalism, in its modern sense, had hardly made its appearance in this country. There was little if any worship of the state as a political organization. Individuals were still conscious of their power organized as a free community to make and unmake states—that is, special forms of political organization. There was, indeed, great admiration for the American form of government and much patriotism in loyalty to it. But it was devotion to its underlying principle as an expression of a free and self-governing community, not to its form. It was regarded as a symbol and as a means, not as an end fixed in itself to which the will and conscience of individuals must be subordinated.

In my judgment, this subordination of the state to the community is the great contribution of American life to the world's history, and it is clearly expressed in the utterances of Dr. Marsh. But recent events have tended to obscure it. Forces have been at work to assimilate the original idea of the state and its organization to older European notions and traditions. The state is now held up as an end in itself; self-styled patriotic organizations make it their business to proclaim the identity of the loyalty and patriotism of individuals with devotion to the state as a fixed institution. The constitution of the state is treated not as a means and instrument to the well-being of the community of free self-governing individuals, but as something having value and sanctity in and of itself. We have, unconsciously in large measure but yet pervadingly, come to doubt the validity of our original American ideal. We tend to submit individuality to the state instead of acting upon the belief that the state in its constitution, laws, and administration, can be made the means of furthering the ends of a community of free individuals.

Dr. Marsh wrote in the full if insensible consciousness of the pioneer period of American life. The true individualism of that era has been eclipsed because it has been misunderstood. It is now often treated as if it were an exaltation of individuals free from social relations and responsibilities. Marsh expresses its genuine spirit when he refers, as he does constantly, to the *community* of individuals. The essence of our earlier pioneer individualism was not non-social, much less anti-social; it involved no indifference to the claims of society. Its working ideal was neighborliness and mutual service. It did not deny the claims of government and law, but it held them in subordination to the needs of a changing and developing society of individuals. Community relationships were to enable an individual to reach a fuller manifestation of his own powers, and this development was in turn to be a factor in modifying the organized and stated civil and political order so that more individuals would be capable of genuine participation in the self-government and self-movement of society—so that, in short, more individuals might come into the possession of that freedom which was their birth-right. Depreciation of the value of our earlier pioneer individualism is but the negative sense of our surrender of the native idea of the subordination of state and government to the social community and our approximation to the older European idea of the state as an end in itself. If I may be allowed a personal word, I would say that I shall never cease to be grateful that I was born at a time and a place where the earlier ideal of liberty and the self-governing community of citizens still sufficiently prevailed, so that I unconsciously imbibed a sense of its meaning. In Vermont, perhaps even more than elsewhere, there was embodied in the spirit of the people the conviction that governments were like the houses we live in, made to contribute to human welfare, and that those who lived in them were as free to change and extend the one as they were the other, when developing needs of the human family called for such alterations and modifications. So deeply bred in Vermonters was this conviction that I still think that one is more loyally patriotic to the ideal of America when one maintains this view than when one conceives of patriotism as rigid attachment to a form of the state alleged to be fixed forever, and recognizes the claims of a common human society as superior to those of any particular political form.

Dr. Marsh's views of education were a reflection of his general social philosophy. It goes without saying that he conceived of education in a deeply religious spirit and that to him religion was in words reminiscent of a passage already quoted from Coleridge, "the sap of life to the growing tree of knowledge." But we have also in interpreting his words to recall that to him religious truth was one with rational truth about the universe itself and about man's nature in relation to it. In his own words again, religious truth "is not so much a distinct and separate part of what should be taught in a system of instruction, to be learned and stored up in the mind for future use, as a pervading and life-giving principle and power that should act upon the mind in every stage and process of its development, and bring all the powers of the soul, as they are unfolded, under its holy and humanizing influence." The concepton of what religion and religious truth are may change; they have undergone change since Marsh taught and wrote. But some organizing, pervading, and life-giving principle to bind together all the specialisms and details which so abound is still as greatly needed in education today as it was when Marsh spoke.

The ideas of Dr. Marsh upon more specific matters of the organization and conduct of university education reflect his fundamental conceptions. In stating them I depend chiefly upon the record of his successor in the chair of philosophy, Professor Joseph Torrey in the Memoir he prefixed to the collection of Marsh's writings. It was the latter's opinion "that the rules for the admission of students are too limited and inflexible." There is no reason why those unfortunately prevented from taking advantage of the whole of the course should not have the privilege of taking the part that lies within their means. "He was also for allowing more latitude to the native inclinations and tendencies of different minds. It was absurd to expect every young mind to develop in just the same way; and equally absurd to confine each one to the same kind and quantity of study." Again, "he thought the methods of instruction in use too formal and inefficient. There was not enough of actual teaching, and too much importance was attached to text-books. He wanted to see more constant and familiar intercourse between the mind of teacher and learner." It was more important to invigorate and sharpen the student's powers of independent thought and judgment than to bend them to apprehending the ideas of others. As to college discipline and morals, he also distrusted the system of minute external regulation and conformity. He was also opposed to the then prevailing methods of classification and promotion of students. Merely formal examinations he thought of little value.

These points sound strangely like the criticisms and proposals of educational reformers from his day to this. They were not, however, with him concessions to practical expediency. They were reflections of his fundamental faith in individuality and in the spirit as opposed to the letter and mechanical form. But this emphasis upon the value of individuality was accompanied, in his views on education as elsewhere, with an equal sense that the ultimate end was a community of cultivated individuals. The ultimate purpose of education is "to elevate the condition and character of the great body of the people." Nowhere as much as in the United States were schools "made, as they are here, an important and leading object in the policy of government," and nowhere else was the experiment given a fair trial of "placing all classes and all individuals upon the same level providing for all the same system of free, public instruction." [3]

I have chosen to try to get some idea of the relation of Dr. Marsh's thought to that of his own time rather than to engage in general eulogy of him. But the record discloses a mind at once deeply sensitive and deeply rational. The period was not favorable to far-reaching thought, which always demands a certain audacity lacking both to the period and to Dr. Marsh's temperament. He did not carry his questionings beyond the received order of beliefs in religion. He depended upon others, notably Coleridge and the German idealists, for the language in which to clothe his philosophic speculations. But, none the less, because of his sensitivity one feels that, even when he speaks of things that do not make the appeal now that they did in a time when men were more engrossed in theology, there is nothing second-hand in his thought. There were realities of

[3] These words were spoken, be it noted, before the great public school revival of the eighteen-forties occurred in this country.

which he had an intimate personal sense behind his most transcendental speculations. It is characteristic of him that he holds that knowledge of "spiritual" truth is always more than theoretical and intellectual. It was the product of activity as well as its cause. It had to be lived in order to be known. The low rating which he gave sense as compared with Understanding was not, for example, a merely cognitive matter. The "thralldom of sense" was a moral and personal affair. And so his depreciation of Understanding in comparison with Reason was not technical. In what he called Understanding he saw the root of the skills and the conventions which enable men to make a shrewd adjustment of means to ends, in dealing with nature and with fellowmen. It was the key to what is termed success. But the ends which it prescribed were just those of worldly success, and so Reason was to him the symbol of the ability of man to live on a higher and more inclusive plane which he called that of spirit, and in which he found the distinctive dignity of man. Religion was to him the supreme worth, and yet his conception of what constitutes religion was a virtual condemnation of a large part of that which passed in his time and still passes for religion, as being merely an attempt to include God and the next world in a scheme of personal advancement and success. Underneath the somewhat outmoded form of his philosophy one feels a rare personality, gifted in scholarship, ever eager for more knowledge, who wished to use scholarship and philosophy to awaken his fellowmen to a sense of the possibilities that were theirs by right as men, and to quicken them to realize these possibilities in themselves. His transcendentalism is the outer form congenial in his day to that purpose. The underlying substance is a wistful aspiration for full and ordered living.

2

THE PHILOSOPHY OF WILLIAM JAMES

THE IMPRESSION THAT I CARRY AWAY FROM READING THE RECORD
of the activities and connections of William James is that in
respect to many-sidedness he is the most significant intellectual
figure the United States has produced. There are those who
surpass him in special points: Jefferson, for example, in depth
and range of political thought, and Emerson in consistency and
concentration of pure intellectual flame. But James seems all
but unique in his variety of conjunctions with vital matters.
As I reflect upon the full and ordered record which we owe
to the thorough and intelligent art of Professor Perry,* I can
think of but one aspect of human interest that is not expressed.
There are no signs of concern with the spectacle of history.
Yet this fact seems to be positive in import—an indication not
of an insufficient but of an abundant sense of life, of life irrespective of chronology. One may say that he is intensely contemporary; *is* rather than *was*. For his contemporaneousness
concerns not the incidents that make up the passing show but
springs from the problems and predicaments in which mankind
finds itself implicated under all skies at all times.

The story of William James is of enormous interest when
it is viewed simply as an account of an extraordinarily gifted
family. Dr. Perry has done well to devote one-fifth of the first
volume to the father, Henry James, Sr. A commentator could

* *The Thought and Character of William James*, by Ralph Barton Perry.
Vol. I, *Inheritance and Vocation*; Vol. II, *Philosophy and Psychology*. Boston:
Little, Brown and Company, 1935. (The subtitle—"As revealed in unpublished
correspondence and notes, together with his published writings"—is worth quoting in full.)

379

profitably devote an entire review to this remarkable man and his equally remarkable ideas and associations. Putting heredity to one side, one can hardly form an adequate picture of the gift of William James for lucid and picturesque diction and of the unconstrained originality of his thinking, without some knowledge of the father and the way in which he ignored the intellectual conventionalities and respectabilities of his day. I should like to pause to dwell on the family environment in which the budding capacities of James were formed. The spontaneity of affection that held it permanently together is not only a complete refutation of the notion that genius is hard to live with but is a heartening picture of what domestic life is capable of being. The respect which each member of the family shows for the personality of every other member can hardly have failed to be an important factor in shaping the idea of the individual which, as we shall see, is fundamental in the philosophy of William James.

Throughout the volumes runs the current of the affection and admiration in which William James and his brother, the novelist, Henry James, Jr., held each other. And there are occasional glimpses of the other children, each of whom rose far above the commonplace and mediocre. The pages of William himself could be searched in vain to find criticism more penetrating, expressed in any more vivid way, than that of the sister Alice, directed toward William. "William expressed himself and his environment to perfection when he replied to my question about his house in Chocorua. 'Oh, it's the most delightful house you ever saw; it has fourteen doors, all opening outwards.' His brain isn't limited to fourteen, perhaps unfortunately." And when she said that he "could lend life and charm to a treadmill," she stated precisely the feeling of everyone who enjoyed contact with the unconquerable vivacity of his interests; a persistent animation that was sustained throughout recurrent physical and mental ill-health. The novelist brother was constant in his affectionate admiration for his older brother, and while he had no interest in philosophy and professed incapacity for understanding it, he nevertheless put his finger upon the spirit of William's philosophizing when he wrote enthusiastically after the receipt of *Pragmatism* that its author had made philosophy more interesting and living than anyone had made it before, through creation of a philosophy that was "relevant and assimilable and referable."

The second part of Perry's work is entitled "Education and Career" and is a welcome substitute for what often passes as biography. For Perry permits the story to develop largely in terms of letters written by and to James, while he himself supplies just the quality and quantity of interpretive comment that is needed to make the story consecutive. Here too, as well as in family relations, there is a certain uniqueness of significance. William James had no schooling in the ordinary sense of that word. But he was exposed to an unusual variety of contacts, and most of them, unlike the themes of ordinary schooling, "took." His father had reacted strongly against the Calvinistic zeal of *his* father, expressed in desire to form his children in his own moral image. He wrote in an almost Rousseauan vein, "The great worth of one's childhood to his future manhood consists in its being a storehouse of innocent natural emotions and affections, based upon ignorance . . . I am sure that the early development of my moral sense was in every way fatal to my natural innocence, the innocence essential to a free evolution of one's spiritual character." In consequence, he withheld himself, to a degree extraordinary for his day and age, from the attempt to mould his children's beliefs and characters. At first sight this abstinence appears to conflict with the unusual depths of his personal convictions. In reality it is a tribute to the fidelity with which he lived up to his deepest conviction: the necessity of *free* evolution of spiritual character. The apparently haphazard nature of the education of the children and its actual issue in fruitful achievement cannot be understood apart from the loyalty of the father to his faith in human nature, when the latter is free from the distortions of convention and the paralysis of rigid institutionalism.

In an optimistic moment, he once wrote, "My sole hope for

humanity is that men will go on more and more to such a complete obedience of their natural instincts that all our futile old rulers, civil and religious, will grow so bewildered as to abandon their thrones and leave the coast free to scientific men"—not that obedience to natural instinct was the desired goal but that it was a necessary condition of its attainment. The actual or practical result was finely summed up in the comment of the daughter Alice. "How grateful we ought to be that our excellent parents had threshed out all the ignoble superstitions, and did not feel it their duty to fill our minds with the dry husks— leaving them *tabulae rasae* to receive whatever stamp our individual experience was to give them, so that we had not the bore of wasting our energy in raking over and sweeping out the rubbish."

Not the least important factor in the education of William was his temporary and experimental adoption of the career of a painter. Apropos of the fact that he abandoned the career of artist in behalf of that of scientist and philosopher, while Henry fell by sheer force of temperament into that of literary artist, Mr. Perry makes one of the most discriminating of his many discriminating comments. Of Henry he says:

> Experience afforded patterns or *scenes,* having for him some mysterious affinity of order or rhythm by which they were apprehended feelingly as units, and by which they became possessions to be stored against the day of their literary use. William shared this passion, but though an insistent it was always a subordinate motive. His own proper and deeper passion was to look behind the scene for causes or to look beyond in behalf of governing purposes . . . William had a painter's eye. He had a capacity, perhaps never equaled, of seizing and exposing the evanescent moments and fugitive sequences of conscious life . . . But he never indulged this interest without a revulsion against it, a revulsion that took one or the other of two forms—either *action* or *explanation.*

Henry speaks of the "inveteracy of his [William's] interest in the 'queer' or the incalculable effect of things. There was apparently for him no possible effect whatever that might not be more or less rejoiced in as such—all exclusive of its relation to other things than merely knowing." This aggressive catholicity of interest, with a bias, on the whole, in favor of the odd, involved an experimental attitude that was not congenial to the profession of painting, at least as that was pursued in the early sixties.

There seems to be no clear explanation of why he left painting save that it failed to hold him. His feeling that he could never be more than a mediocre painter appears to me to be but a translation of the fact that the art did not absorb him. Nor does there seem to have been, at the outset, a definite indication of a "call," as the religious people used to term it, to science. He had been interested from boyhood in experiments, chemical and electrical, and when the scales went down for art, the other pan went up for science. His upbringing as well as his temperament predisposed him to tentative search for a vocation rather than predestined him to a particular career. His movement from art to chemistry, from chemistry to medicine, on to physiology and to physiological psychology, and from that to psychology and to philosophy, and to philosophy of a progressively "metaphysical" cast, is the record of a mind and personality that was continuously striving to find itself. While external physical conditions, such as the weakness of his back that made prolonged laboratory work impossible, played a part in determining his choice, I can but think there is an intimate connection between his enduring search, through many turns and windings, for himself and his own potentialities, and that sense of an unfinished and still developing world that colors all his philosophizing.

However this may be, the path that took him through a variety of interests and pursuits assuredly enriched his store of knowledge, added cumulatively to his resources, and prevented that premature hardening which is perhaps the bane of most

persons who follow philosophy professionally. Above all it
extended his range of personal contacts and associations. It
would take, I fancy, a page of print simply to list the names of
persons with whom he had intellectual companionship and
with whom he carried on a stimulating exchange. This wide
acquaintance expressed his genius for friendship. A reader who
should dip casually here and there into these large volumes
might wonder whether at times letters of no great moment were
not too extensively reproduced. But one who reads consecu-
tively will, I am sure, come to the conclusion that nothing could
well be spared. As with the painting of a portrait, the multipli-
cation of strokes, many minute in themselves, build up a solid
figure. A great debt of gratitude is due Mr. Perry for the skill
and patience with which he has accomplished his task. The
obligation extends far beyond the circle of professional psychologists and philosophers. The range of intellectual connections of William James was so wide and the fervor with which
he went out to meet them so intense, that the volumes give an
irreplaceable portrayal of a most significant aspect of the development of American culture in the last two-thirds of a
century.

An account of William James as a philosopher cannot, then,
be separated from the development of William James the man,
as this development was influenced by his family relations, his
informal but vital education, and his varied contacts with vocations and men. This fact is, indeed, the point which reading of
these volumes has most impressed upon me. To my mind,
William James constitutes a memorable turning point in the
story of American philosophic thought precisely because the
human man always took precedence of the professional philosopher. He says of himself, "I originally studied medicine in order
to be a physiologist, but I drifted into psychology and philosophy from a sort of fatality. I never had any philosophical instruction. The first lecture on psychology I ever heard being
the first I ever gave." It would be easy to exaggerate the element of "drift." A drift that occurs because of fatality is an

impulsion from within, not a floating on an external current of chance. But the struggles of James within himself, the tardiness of his recognition as a genuine philosophic thinker, his final crucial influence in redirecting much of American philosophical thought, all of these things, in my opinion, have an intimate connection with the fact that he never underwent academic and professional philosophic instruction.

I do not mean, of course, that mere absence of such instruction is a warrant of philosophic independence and originality, or even a contributing factor. The contrary is the case. Self-taught philosophic "geniuses" usually exhibit lack of proportion and perspective, and exhibit swollen conceit of originality when they awkwardly reproduce some one or other of the most familiar of philosophic conceptions. James doubtless suffered at times from lack of the technique which is about all that formal philosophical instruction can confer. But his native gifts, his family environment, his range of contacts, combined with the instruction he obtained through his own studies, render in his case a defect of technique of slight import. His escape from the cramping influence of intellectual traditions, which in the hands of the average teacher are hardened into lifeless conventions, had something to do, in my opinion a great deal to do, with the intensity with which he laid hold of philosophical problems. As I have already intimated, they were for him first of all problems of urgent personal force and vitality; since they were not covered over by things learned at second hand, they retained the freshness and immediacy that are such striking factors of the thought of James, so striking as to make him all but unique among philosophers. To say these things does not imply lack of respect for technique. Original vision in order to endure and make its way must take on the resources afforded by competent technique. But there is always the danger that mastery of the tools of the intellectual trade will become a substitute for vision, while the inherent sincerity of an experience such as that of William James may be trusted in the end to generate its own relevant technique.

It is for this reason that I feel justified in including such remarks as I have made about the environment and career of William James under the general caption of his *philosophy*. The philosophical writings of James have, to an unusual degree, their own luminosity. But the record of his correspondence and his otherwise unpublished notes take us behind the printed word; they bring us face to face with the generative experiences from which the written word is derived. I do not know of any other case in the whole available record of intellectual origins and development in which we are so fully taken behind the scenes and initiated into the vital personal experiences out of which formulated doctrines finally sprang. Interest in the initiation and the gratitude due Mr. Perry for making the record accessible are not confined to those especially occupied with philosophy. They are shared by all those interested in the history of American intellectual life and by all those who are concerned with the mysterious conditions that lie back of original creative productivity.

Before coming to what seems to be *the* problem that entered so deeply into the experience of James as to determine the structure of his philosophy (even accounting for certain features that taken by themselves seem eccentric), I want to quote some things that were said by James at various times about philosophy and the teaching of philosophy. James remarked, in a letter to Hodgson, that every philosopher is motivated by some bogey in the background that he wants to destroy. The remark seems to me profoundly true; failure to realize what it is that a philosopher feels the pressure of and wants to get rid of is one of the main sources of the infertility of philosophical controversy. James goes on to add that *his* bogey is *dessication*. It is in this context that I would place remarks like the following, made about Wundt in the course of a letter to Stumpf.

> Surely, you must admit that since there must be professors in the world, Wundt is the most praise-worthy and

never-too-much-to-be-respected type of the species . . .
a professor, a being whose duty is to know everything and
to have his opinion about everything connected with his
Fach. He says of each possible subject, "Here I must have
an opinion. How many possible opinions are there? three?
four? Yes, just four." Thus he acquires a complete assortment of opinions of his own and as his memory is good,
he seldom forgets what they are.

I cannot but think that this passage throws, by contrast, a
good deal of light upon the aims and procedure of James himself, including the things for which he has been most criticized
—such as the inconsistencies of expression that are found because in dealing with one subject James forgets just what he
has said upon some other occasion. His correspondent, the
English thinker Shadworth Hodgson, expressed the characteristic quality of James with great moderation when he wrote
that James "makes us see the reality of things, the real common
sense of the questions and problems at issue." When James
Ward complained, in a review, complimentary on the whole,
of James' lack of systematic treatment of psychological topics,
James replied admitting that he was too unsystematic, but
added: "In this case I permitted myself to remain so *deliberately,* on account of the strong aversion with which I am filled
for the humbugging pretense of exactitude in the way of definition of terms and descriptions of states that has prevailed in
psychological literature." The conviction expressed in this
remark is the reason why James at times seems to lean over
backward in fear of system-making that is artificial, and it certainly helps explain his later overresponsive attitude to Berg-
son's attack on logic and conceptual constructions generally.
The fact is, however, that much in James that was attacked by
his early contemporaries as lack of sufficient respect for logical
form is in reality an expression of his superior intellectual con-
scientiousness. He was keenly sensitive to the danger of forcing unity and system beyond what facts themselves indicated.

There is a reflection of his basic intellectual conscientious-
ness in the reasons that he gave, in accepting an instructorship
in anatomy, for not taking up philosophy as a career—for he was
quite aware even then that his chief interest was in philosophical or general problems. He draws back, he says, from adopting
the career of a philosophic teacher, in spite of the fact that his
deepest interest is in philosophic issues, because he is so constituted that he needs some stable reality upon which to lean,
while "a professional philosopher pledges himself publicly
never to have done with *doubt* on these [the fundamental]
questions, but every day to be ready to criticize and call in
question the grounds of his faith of the day before." There are,
I suppose, many occupants of philosophic chairs who go
through the form, as a matter of pedagogic technique, of such
persistently renewed questioning. But it would be difficult, I
think, to find cases where the sense of the obligation of the
philosopher to be ready to carry out the doubts and questionings in good faith was so strong as to lead him so to doubt his
own enduring strength to assume the responsibility that he
was deterred from the career of the philosopher. It would be
impossible, it seems to me, to find better evidence of the profound seriousness of James' sense of intellectual responsibility
—a sense which his early critics, perhaps because of his occasional irrepressible levity of verbal expression, were loath to
credit him with.

A few years later, while still teaching physiology, he uttered golden words as to what philosophy and its teaching
should be. "Philosophic study means the habit of always seeing
an alternative, of not taking the usual for granted, of making
conventionalities fluid again, of imagining foreign states of
mind . . . What doctrines students take from their teachers
are of little consequence provided they catch from them the
living philosophic attitude of mind, the independent, personal
look at the data of life and the eagerness to harmonize them."
Although James is conventionally supposed to be opposed to
unity and system on principle, he expressed one of the leading

motifs of his life when he said that one can never be a great philosopher who lacks "that personal, unitary, all-fusing point of view which the great ones have." What he objected to was the unitary point of view that is *merely* dialectical, not personal, and in which parts are externally held together by mechanical logic rather than fused in and by emotional and volitional conviction. Later when he had arrived at relative philosophic maturity he said of Royce's *World and Individual,* "The subject is not really vital to him, it is just fancy-work." When one recalls his genuine admiration for Royce's gifts in comparison with those of most other teachers of philosophy, one gets a glimpse of the gulf that separated his idea of what constitutes genuine philosophy from the academic practice frequently followed.

The justification for quoting at length these incidental comments is that they convey by contrast the vitally personal source of James' own philosophizing. I do not know any other modern thinker whose philosophy owes so little to dialectics and to tradition, to the second hand generally, and so much to predicaments that were vitally experienced; that in the large and proper sense of the word were moral in quality. In him the need for working out a viable philosophy was one with the need for finding a solution of matters that weighed heavily upon him as a living being. Mr. Perry justly emphasizes the importance attached by James to the motives from which philosophizing proceeds. I hope I do not do him injustice in saying that he would recommend James' *Essay on the Sentiment of Rationality* in the form in which it included the *Essay on Rationality, Activity, and Faith* (together with James' own notes now made available) as the natural introduction to James' own philosophy. The needs to be satisfied are, on the theoretical side, clearness and unity. Their demands are so different as to tax thought to the uttermost. For clearness moves in the direction of diversity, the Many, while the simplicity that results from one-sided emphasis upon the One, is often specious. The incapacity of monistic systems to resist analysis

from the standpoint of either fact or logic is one of James'
favorite themes. But even when the conjoint need for unity
and clarity is satisfied, we are only at the threshold of an adequate philosophical system. The practical needs of man, emotional and volitional, must also be satisfied. It is the depth with
which James felt the urgency of the latter need that marked
him off from most of his contemporaries, and that, as I have
already suggested, explains both the early uncomprehending
and often scornful rejection he experienced and the power of
inspiration exhibited later by his thought.

There exists a letter written by James as early as 1869, the
year in which he received his M.D., the time at which, probably, the influence of natural science was at its height with him,
in which one finds the clue to the problem that was central in
the formation of his own philosophy. After saying that there
was once a period in which the ideas of nature and of human
fate were conglomerated in one, he says that in their later
development "the nature-lore and the individual-fate-lore or
religion have become so differentiated as to be antagonistic."

The remark might be interpreted in the sense of the conventionally recognized conflict of science and religion, since nature-
lore is so evidently a name for science. But such an interpretation misses the point. The identification of religion with "individual-fate-lore" and the feeling that the effect of science is to
submerge, to deny, the importance of individuality and of what
happens in and to the individual as such is the significant matter. It is significant both negatively and positively. The early
environment and rearing of James had made it impossible for
him to conceive of religion in the terms of any historic religion,
even that of Christianity in its purest and most sublimated
form. There is hardly a word in all of his numerous writings
about religion, about either any special doctrine of Christianity
or the figure of its reputed founder. Such allusions as he makes
to churchly creeds and practices are, for him, unusually un-
sympathetic in tone. They are in the vein of the following:

My training in natural science has completely disqualified me for sympathetic treatment of the ecclesiastic universe. It is impossible to believe that the same God who established nature should also feel a special pride at being more immediately represented by clergymen than by laymen, or find a sweet sound in church-phraseology and intonation, or a sweet savour in the distinction between deacons, archdeacons and bishops. He is not of that prim temper.

It is sometimes said that the essence of Protestant Christianity is the assertion of the immediate relation of God and the individual soul. With this conception as a basis, it may be said that James carried the spirit of Protestantism to a point where any connection with Christianity became meaningless. The "individual-fate-lore" in which he was interested was universal. All individuals looked alike to him as far as individuality is concerned in its relation to the universe. Hence the special treatment of religion that appears, say, in his *Varieties of Religious Experience* is but a part of his general philosophy and cannot be justly appreciated apart from the latter. On the face of the pages of that book, he selected cases so extreme that he himself called them pathological. But his selection was based on the belief that certain generic features in the relation of the individual as such to the universe were thrown into high relief in these cases, and could accordingly best be studied through them. The root idea is that in the religious experience, the essential individual—call it his soul—stands in communication with the universe at a level more primitive and at the same time more fundamental, in a certain way more veridical, than is attainable at the level of conscious and rational observation and thought. The result is "a kind of experience in which intellect, will and feeling, all our consciousness and all our subconsciousness together, melt in a kind of chemical union." Hence every genuinely religious experience is that which for lack of a better name we call mystical. In this experience, the "less articulate but more profound parts of our nature hold out against the attempt of a more superficial and loquacious part to suppress it." James was quite aware that this notion of the essentially irrational and instinctive origin of religious experiences was capable of being used as an argument against the validity and utility of religion. He himself deliberately chose to give the idea another and favorable interpretation. This choice roots partly in a temperamental feeling of the importance of vital instincts, on the ground that they represent the *process of life* more effectively than can rational thought, and partly springs from his philosophical doctrine that in any case immediate experience is more fundamental than are the ideational constructions built upon it. The underlying conception, I should say, is that the individual after all must have some vital connection with the universe in which he lives and that this connection can ultimately be but of two kinds. It is either such as to depress the individual or such as to support and invigorate him. Morally, we are entitled to adopt the latter attitude for the purpose of action even though rational proof of its validity be lacking. Short of the existence of overwhelming evidence of the invalidity of the belief, we may choose to live, to act, heroically, upon the assumption that something in the universe feeds our ideal aspirations and is actively on the side of their realization.

I have, then, dwelt at length upon the concern of James with religion and his understanding of its nature just because the latter is so different from what is usually called religion. The nub of the whole matter is the problem of the genuine relation of the individual and the universe, and this is the question which is final for philosophy itself. The growing opposition of James to monism in every form, idealistic as well as materialistic; his struggle against absolutisms of every sort, metaphysical, ethical, political; his pluralism; his indeterminism —all the determining *motifs* of his philosophy spring from his extraordinarily intense and personal feeling for the worth of the individual, combined, however, with an equally intense realiza-

tion of the extent to which the findings of natural science (to
which he was loyally devoted) seemed hostile to rational justification of the idea that individuality as such has any especial
value of justification in the universal scheme of things. His long
preoccupation with the philosophy of his colleague, Royce,
vividly portrayed in the volumes before us, is a record of his
dissatisfaction with the effort to give value to the individual on
the basis of monistic idealism. As he once wrote, "Make the
world a unit, and worship and abhorrence are equally one-
sided and equally legitimate reactions." Treat the world as a
plurality, and the difference between good and bad has a
meaning, and because of this difference, choice, loyalty, adora-
tion, have also a meaning. But James was equally unconvinced
by the attempts of his chief fellow pluralists, Davidson and
Howison, to find a strictly *rational* support for the doctrine of
the primacy and ultimacy of individuals as such. Their views
seemed to him to be, on one side, abstractly dialectical, and,
on the other side, to be based on lack either of adequate
empirical and scientific knowledge or else of adequate respect
for such knowledge (probably on both). A certain act of faith
in the sense in which faith means the resolve to live as if a
certain doctrine were true until evidence appears to the contrary, was to him the way out. Meantime, the act of faith has a
certain amount of rational support in our instinctive emotional
life and in the deliverances of immediate experience as a mode
of acquaintance-knowledge.

The biographic roots of this basic philosophic attitude of
James seem to be found, rather especially, in the crisis of his
own life, that was undergone in connection with extreme
depression due to ill-health, in 1870. He found the only promise of a way out in the assumption of a certain attitude of
resolute action. The philosophical implications involved in this
attitude are strangely prophetic of the most fundamental ideas
of his later philosophy. He asked, in his diary, "Can one with
full knowledge and sincerely ever bring himself so to sympa-
thize with the *total process of the universe* as heartily to assent

to the evils that seem inherent in its details? . . . If so optimism is possible." But the distinctive interests and sympathies of the individual may seem so important to him that they refuse to be swallowed up in the "feeling for the total process." In this case, the resulting attitude must be such hostility to the structure of the universe that pessimism is the only outcome. However, between the two extremes there is an alternative. "If a *divided* universe be a conception possible for his intellect to rest in, and at the same time he have vigor of will enough to look the universal death in the face, without blinking, he can lead the life of moralism." The conception of the intrinsic connection between a "divided" (pluralistic) universe and the attitude of resolute choice and action that is implicit in this passage, was reinforced as James came to see that certain volitional and emotional attitudes are the vital, although unexpressed, premises underlying both the optimistic monisms and the pessimistic dualisms that set the self and its interests in stark opposition to the cosmos as a whole.

The intensity of feeling that marks what James wrote in his diary and to his intimate friends in the time of crisis subsided as the years passed. But unless I have completely misunderstood the course of his development, as that is so skillfully and fully portrayed in the volumes before us, the sense of the problem involved remained basically the fountainhead of all his philosophy. It is at the root of his feeling of the conflict between science as nature-lore and religion as individual-fate-lore. It is the source not only of his pluralism and his indeterminism, but of his more special doctrines of the right to adopt in action a sincere belief in the absence of objective evidence and of that part of his pragmatism that emphasized that consequences, rather than origins, are the ultimate test and criterion of meaning and validity.

The sixth and final part of the present volumes is entitled "The Ultimate Philosophical System." Students of the metaphysical doctrine of James, especially as regards the meaning of *Pure Experience*, will find much to assist them in these pages.

If I forego further reference to them, it is not only because of limitations of space, but because I believe that the earlier exposition of the vital temperament and vital experiences of James is fundamental for the understanding of his more technical doctrines. The connection between the two becomes increasingly tenuous and indirect. But it is never lost. The sincerity and depth of the personal experiences which gave to James the key to the genuine meaning of philosophical issues remained the groundwork of his teaching. They are to my mind the enduring source of what we still have to learn from even the more technical aspects of his thought. In his attempts at developed formulation he was subject to the limitations from which every independent thinker suffers. The more original the thought, the more it is betrayed by the fact that the only language in which original insight can be expressed is that formed by the very doctrines against which one is reacting. Hence it is doubly important that the students of the philosophy of James never lose hold upon its vital springs and source.

3

THE VANISHING SUBJECT IN THE PSYCHOLOGY OF JAMES

THERE IS A DOUBLE STRAIN IN THE "PRINCIPLES OF PSYCHOLOGY" by William James. One strain is official acceptance of epistemological dualism. According to this view, the science of psychology centers about a *subject* which is "mental" just as physics centers about an *object* which is material. But James's analysis of special topics tends, on the contrary, to reduction of the subject to a vanishing point, save as "subject" is identified with the organism, the latter, moreover, having no existence save in interaction with environing conditions. According to the latter strain, subject and object do not stand for separate orders or kinds of existence but at most for certain distinctions made for a definite purpose *within* experience.

The first view is explicitly set forth by James in the following words:

> *The psychologist's attitude toward cognition* will be so important in the sequel that we must not leave it till it is made perfectly clear. *It is a thorough-going dualism.* It supposes two elements, mind knowing and thing known, and treats them as irreducible. . . . They just stand face to face in a common world, and one simply knows, or is known unto, its counterpart. This singular relation is not to be expressed in any lower terms, or translated into any more intelligible name. . . . Even in mere sense-impression the duplication of the object of an inner construction must take place. . . . The dualism of Object and Subject and their pre-established

harmony are what the psychologist as such must assume, whatever ulterior monistic philosophy he may, as an individual who has the right also to be a metaphysician, have in reserve.[1]

The *Psychology* was published in 1890. Much of the book was written some years before. The material of the important chapter on the "Stream of Consciousness," which verbally is probably the most subjectivistic part of the whole book, was published in *Mind* in 1884.[2] In 1904 in his article "Does 'Consciousness' Exist?" he says of the "consciousness," which the passage quoted takes as the basis and source of the material of his *Psychology*, that it is "mere echo, the faint rumor left behind by the disappearing 'soul' upon the air of philosophy." And what is especially significant for the present theme, the tendency of the separate subject as knower to disappear even in the *Psychology*, he adds "for twenty years past I have mistrusted 'consciousness' as an entity; for seven or eight years past I have suggested its non-existence to my students." [3] "Twenty years" takes his distrust well back of the date at which his *Psychology* appeared. A moderate amount of psycho-analysis might lead one to infer that the explicitness with which he states that the assumption of dualism is necessary for the psychologist means that he entertained doubt about the *ultimate* soundness of the dualistic position.

That he did not go further than he did go in his *Psychology* is not surprising in view of the state of the subject at the time he wrote. In view especially of the fact that he attacked both of the only two trends which then existed in psychology, namely, associationalist and "rational" psychology, one can understand why he hesitated to carry his scepticism to an even more radical extreme. For the only alternative to these two

[1] *The Principles of Psychology*, Vol. I, pp. 218–220, *passim*. Italics in original text. Referred to hereafter as *Psychology*.

[2] I say "verbally" because it is quite possible to translate "stream of consciousness" into "course of experience" and retain the substance of the chapter.

[3] Essay reprinted in *Essays in Radical Empiricism*, pp. 2 and 3.

views that existed at that time was a dogmatic materialism with its "automaton" theory of psychological phenomena. In spite of the tenderness of James on the topic of the *soul* he wrote that there was no scientific need whatever for a substantial soul or permanent mind; he went so far as to give a strictly empirical account of personal identity.[4]

His reduction of the "subject" to a "passing Thought" is itself sufficient proof of the way he whittled down the knowing subject. And it is worth special note that in one passage, written in direct connection with his discussion of the Self, he goes so far as to express a doubt about the existence of even a separate "thought" or mental state of any kind as the knower, saying that it might be held that "the existence of this thinker would be given to us rather as logical postulate than as that direct inner perception of spiritual activity which we naturally believe ourselves to have."[5] However, he dismisses this conclusion, although it is a direct result of his actual analysis, as "speculative" and says that speculation "contradicts the fundamental assumption of *every* philosophic school. Spiritualists, transcendentalists, and empiricists alike admit in us a continual direct perception of the thinking activity in the concrete. However they may otherwise disagree, they vie with each other in the cordiality of their recognition of our *thoughts* as the one sort of existence which scepticism cannot touch" (p. 305). But he adds in a footnote a remark that is especially significant in view of the article of 1904 to which reference has been made. For he says that there is one exception to the statement about all philosophical

[4] For his tenderness see the *Principles of Psychology*, Vol. I, p. 181, where he says, "The fact is that one cannot afford to despise any of these great traditional objects of belief." As to the substantial soul and permanent mind, see Vol. I, p. 346, where he says, "As *psychologists*, we need not be metaphysical at all. The phenomena are enough, the passing Thought itself is the only *verifiable thinker*, and its empirical connection with the brain-process is the ultimate known law." As to personal identity, as evidence for a permanent substantial subject or self, he was influenced by the recently discovered facts of split personality and wrote (Vol. I, p. 350), "The definitively closed nature of our personal consciousness is probably an average statistical resultant of many conditions, but not an elementary force or fact."

[5] *Principles of Psychology*, Vol. I, p. 304.

schools, namely, the important article of M. Souriau, the conclusion of which is "que la conscience n'existe pas." That James's own denial of the existence of consciousness involves a complete repudiation of the dualism earlier officially professed is obvious from the following words of his later essay in which he says what is denied is an "aboriginal stuff or quality of being, contrasted with that out of which material objects are made, out of which our thoughts of them are made."

Before taking up in detail the whittling down of the mental or psychical subject as it occurs in the *Psychology*, I shall say something about the position which, if it had been developed positively and in detail, would have rendered unnecessary from the start any reference even to the "passing thought" as that which remains from the old substantial subject. This position is suggested in the passage already quoted in which James refers to the brain process as "the ultimate known law." James came to the study of psychology from a grounding in physiology in connection with a preparatory medical education. His naturalistic strain, as far as constructively stated, and its conflict with the professed epistemological dualism, was derived from this source. If it had been consistently developed it would have resulted in a biological behavioristic account of psychological phenomena. In his first expression of opposition to both the "rational" and the "associational" psychologies, he says that certain deficiencies in both of them proceed from their inability to take into account obvious physiological facts which demand recognition of the organism and the nervous system. He goes on to say that the Spencerian formula according to which biological and psychological phenomena are one in essence, both being adjustments of "inner" to "outer" relations, while very vague, is immensely more fertile than the old-fashioned rational psychology "because it takes into account the fact that minds inhabit environments which act on them and on which they in turn react." [6] On this side, James's fundamental doctrine is that psychological phenomena (called by him the *mental life*) are

[6] *Principles of Psychology*, Vol. I, p. 6.

intermediate between impressions received from the environment and the responsive adjustments the organism makes to the environment. If what is involved in this view had been consistently maintained, the dualism that existed in Spencer's two sets of "inner" and "outer" relations would have been overcome, and organisms or personal beings, not "minds," would have been said to "inhabit the environment." The behavioral position is maintained when James says that "pursuance of future ends and choice of means for their attainment are the mark and criterion of presence of mentality in a phenomenon," since the passage suggests that the whole meaning of *mentality* consists in objectively observable facts of the kind mentioned. But as the matter is finally left, it may be doubted whether James intended to go further than to say that this pursuance and choice is the external sign of something called "mental" operating behind. For he limits the scope of the statement by saying that the view just stated would be adopted as the mark and criterion by which to circumscribe the subject-matter of this work *as far as action enters in.*[7] The clause I have italicized indicates that he held to the existence of phenomena so "mental" in nature that action (behavior) does not enter into them. At the same time, the position of James is free from that defect of the latter "behaviorism" which locates behavior, and hence psychological phenomena, *inside* the organism. For he says that the function of the nervous system "is to bring each part into harmonious co-operation with every other" part so as to make possible acts which are of service in connection with the sensory impressions proceeding from the environment.[8]

Since the biological approach does not control subsequent analyses to the extent that the introductory chapters would by themselves have led one to expect, it is worth while to note instances in which it is definitely influential. The chief cases are the treatment of habit and the effect of practice. The former,

[7] *Principles of Psychology*, Vol. I, pp. 8 and 11.
[8] *Ibid.*, p. 12.

treated as a biological factor having its basis in the constitution of matter, is said to be the "cause" of "association of ideas," and hence of retention and recollection, and also of imagination.[9] Even more significant in its implications (which, however, are not developed) is his statement that "attention and effort . . . seem in some degree subject to the law of habit, which is a material law." [10] The operation of practice, understood in terms of motor activities, is made central in discrimination. "Where . . . a distinction has no practical interest, where we gain nothing by analyzing a feature from out of the compound total of which it forms a part, we contract a habit of leaving it unnoticed." [11] He makes a great deal of Helmholtz's view that we notice "sensations" not *per se* but as "far as they enable us to judge rightly of the world about us; and our practice in discriminating between them usually goes only just far enough to meet this end" (p. 517). The ambiguity, noted later, between "sensation" as a strictly physiological process in the afferent structures and as a perceived quality of an object, influences James's treatment, since he seems to assume that the "sensation" is there all the time but is sometimes noted and sometimes not— a position all the more surprising because of his elaborate criticism of the doctrine of "unconscious mental states." He uses such expressions as the following: "Helmholtz's law is that we leave all impressions unnoticed which are valueless to us as signs by which to *discriminate things*. At most such impressions fuse with their consorts into an aggregate effect." Only the influence of an inveterate dualism could lead James to call sensory processes "impressions."

The later pragmatism of James is implicit in what he says about reflective thinking or reasoning. "My thinking is first and last and always for the sake of doing, and I can only do one thing at a time." There are no "truer ways of conceiving [understanding or interpreting]" things than any others; there are

[9] *Ibid.*, pp. 566 and 653, and Vol. II, p. 44.
[10] Vol. I, p. 126.   [11] *Ibid.*, pp. 515–516.

"only more important ways; more frequently serviceable ways." [12] Finally, in contrast with the current theory of perception, James gives an account which is definately biological and behavioral.

> We certainly ought not to say what usually is said by psychologists, and treat the perception as a sum of distinct psychic entities, the present sensation namely, *plus* a lot of images from the past, all "integrated" together in a way impossible to describe.

The simple and natural description is

> that the process aroused in the sense-organ has shot into various paths which habit has already organized in the hemispheres, and that instead of our having the sort of consciousness [perception] which would be correlated with the simple sensorial process, we have that which is correlated with this more complex process. [13]

When we ask why James did not develop his treatment in the direction indicated by these considerations, we come back to the influence exercised by the surviving metaphysical dualism. For as long as this dualism is postulated, the connection the nervous system, including the brain, indubitably has with psychological phenomena is a "mystery," and the more detailed and complete the evidence for the connection the more the mystery deepens. The influence of the dualism is so strong that James does not follow out the implication of his hypothesis that the brain—and nervous system generally—functions as an organ in the behavior constituted by interaction of organism and en-

---

[12] Vol. II, pp. 333–334. On page 335 we read the following: "The essence of a thing is that one of its properties which is so *important for my interests* that in comparison with it I may neglect the rest." The important rôle of "interest" in the entire scheme of James's account of psychological phenomena is a well-known fact. Officially he assumes interest to be mentalistic. What he actually says about it is most readily understood in terms of the selections effected by motor factors in behavior.

[13] *Ibid.*, Vol. II, pp. 80 and 79; cf. pp. 103–104.

vironment. Consequently, instead of applying the idea to the description of each one of the diversity of observed psychological occurrences, showing how it links up in detail with the general doctrine of the function of the nervous system as an instrumentality of effective interaction of organism and environment, he goes so far as to express adherence to the most miraculous of all the theories about the "mystery," namely, the parallelism or pre-established harmony of physical and psychical.

There is indeed a problem. But it can be broken down into a large number of things to be investigated. It is not a wholesale metaphysical problem, but a special problem like that of any scientific inquiry: namely, the problem of discovering the conditions of the occurrence of an observed phenomenon. Certain experienced situations occur, some of them mainly emotive or affectional in quality; others that of knowledge of this or that thing. The question of how these experienced situations come into existence is important because knowledge of conditions is always a prerequisite of control. Knowledge of organic conditions is part of the knowledge required if having of desired experiences and not having of unwanted experiences is to come under our control, knowledge of environing conditions being, of course, the other part. Knowledge of processes in the nervous system and brain is an important, although far from exclusive, part of the required knowledge of organic conditions. But in principles there is no difference between discovering the cerebral conditions involved in a hallucinatory or a veridical perception and the chemical conditions involved in occurrence of water. The difference is one of greater complexity. But our comparative ignorance of concrete conditions in the case of situations, as matters of experience, does not make a "mystery" out of them.

I now come to discussion of some psychological matters where James admits that the duplication in an "inner construction" of what is experienced is no part of the fact which is observed, but is a later theoretical interpretation. In the passage about dualism, quoted at the outset, James says that this dupli-

cation is demanded even in the case of "mere sense impression."
In his chapter on sensation James says:

> A *pure sensation is an abstraction;* and when we adults talk
> of our "sensations" we mean one of two things: either cer-
> tain *objects,* namely, simple *qualities* or *attributes,* like *hard,*
> *hot, pain;* or else those of our thoughts in which acquaint-
> ance with these objects is least combined with knowledge
> about the relations of them to other things.[14]

The latter part of this sentence retains the reference to the inner
"thought" as that which knows its outer counterpart. But
James's sense for empirical fact caused him to recognize that
in the actual experience of qualities as objects no reduplication
in inner sensations is to be found. For immediately afterward he
says:

> *The first sensation which an infant gets is for him the*
> *Universe.* . . . The infant encounters an object in which
> (though it be given in a pure sensation) all the "categories
> of the understanding" are contained. . . . Here the young
> knower [the infant, not a mental state] meets and greets his
> world. [P. 8.]

This position about sensory qualities is the one in line with the
objective stand he takes whenever guided by evidence into the
particular issue with which he is dealing.[15] The following pas-

> Take the example of an altogether unprecedented expe-
> rience, such as a new taste in the throat. Is it a subjective
> quality of feeling, or an objective quality felt? You do not
> even ask the question at this point. It is simply *that taste.*

[14] *Principles of Psychology,* Vol. II, p. 3.
[15] There is nothing intrinsically *sensory* about *red, hot, pain.* They are so
named because experience has shown the importance of the organic apparatus
by which they are mediated. That color is visual and sound auditory is an item
of knowledge gained through study of the conditions of the *occurrence* of the
quality; it is no part of the quality.

sages are representative:

But if a doctor hears you describe it, and says: "Ha! now you know what *heartburn* is," then it becomes a quality already existent *extra mentem tuam* which you in turn have come upon and learned. The first spaces, times, things, qualities, experienced by the child probably appear, like the first heartburn, in this absolute way, as simple *beings*, neither in nor out of thought.[16]

This view is probably the germ of his later theory of "neutral entities." The direct empirical meaning of *neutral* in this connection would seem to be that of indifference to the distinction between subjective and objective, this distinction arising when the proper guidance of behavior requires that we be able to tell whether a given sound or color is a sign of an environing object or of some process within the organism. Unfortunately his later writings seem at times to give the impression that these entities are a kind of stuff out of which both the subjective and objective are made—instead of the distinction being a question of the kind of object to which a quality is *referred*. If the latter position is taken then one of the problems of the psychologist is to determine the conditions under which a given *reference* occurs, the question of proper reference being the same *kind* of question that comes up when we inquire whether a given sound is produced by gunshot or by back-firing of an automobile.

Again, James says that "experience, from the very first, presents us with concreted objects, vaguely continuous with the rest of the world which envelops them in space and time, and potentially divisible into inward elements and parts."[17] This passage is meant to apply to primitive as well as to highly elaborated experience of objects. For in the same context he speaks of "sensible totals . . . subdivided by discriminative attention."[17] In another place he writes "No one ever had a simple sensation by itself. Consciousness [experience], from our natal day, is a teeming multiplicity of objects and relations and what we call simple sensations [qualities] are results of discriminative

[16] Vol. I, p. 272.   [17] Vol. I, p. 487.

attention, pushed often to a very high degree." [18] Surely such passages as these indicate what is intended when it is said that the child's first sensation (experience) is for him the Universe, and that the "Universe which he later comes to know is nothing but an amplification and an implication of that first simple germ." [19] To hold that there is at the same time inner reduplication in thought or feeling is a case of what James elsewhere calls the psychologist's fallacy, reading into the original experience an inferential conclusion which the psychologist arrives at in his special investigations—in this case a wrong inferential result.

I now come to the central case in which the issue is clinched —the account given by James of the nature of the self and our consciousness of it, in which the "subject" of dualistic epistemology disappears and its place is taken by an empirical and behavioral self. In speaking of the nature of "self-love" or egoism, he wrote:

> The words ME, then, and SELF, so far as they arouse feeling and connote emotional worth, are OBJECTIVE designations, meaning ALL THE THINGS which have the power to produce in a stream of consciousness excitement of a certain peculiar sort.[20]

This position is developed in detail in connection with the bodily or material and the social selves which he has mentioned earlier. The general or theoretical position is that

> To have a self that I can *care for*, nature must first present me with some *object* interesting enough to make me instinctively wish to appropriate it for its *own* sake.
> What happens to them [our bodies] excites in us emotions and tendencies to action more energetic and habitual than any which are excited by other portions of the "field."

[18] *Ibid.*, p. 224.   [19] Vol. II, p. 8.
[20] *Ibid.*, Vol. I, p. 319. The dualism is verbally retained in the mention of the "stream of consciousness." But aside from the fact that no difference is made in the argument when we substitute the words "the ongoing course of experienced things," the self or person is here expressly defined in objective terms, the small capitals being in the original text.

ABOUT THINKERS

407

My *social* self-love, my interest in the images other men have have framed of me, is also an interest in a set of objects external to my thought.[21]

James, however, had postulated what he calls a "spiritual" self in addition to material and social selves. It might then well seem as if this psychical self, consisting of acts of choosing, consenting, refusing, and emotions like fearing, hoping, etc., remained *the* inner self, as an inexpugnable object of direct observation. But in fact it is in dealing with this aspect of the self that James puts forth his most explicit and detailed biological interpretation. For he says all that he can directly and empirically observe shows that this " 'Self of selves,' when carefully examined, is found to consist mainly of the collection of these peculiar motions in the head or between the head and the throat." [22] In the context "these peculiar motions" are said to be "a fluctuating play of pressures, convergences, divergencies, and accommodations in my eyeballs," and "the opening and closing of the glottis," with "contractions in the jaw-muscles" and the chest. These bodily movements, which are all that is directly experienced as the innermost centre, the "sanctuary within the citadel" of the self, are expressions of "a constant play of furtherances and hindrances, of checks and releases, of tendencies that run with desire and that run the other way." The theoretical interpretation is expressly stated in the following words:

The nuclear part of the Self . . . would be a collection of activities physiologically in no essential way different from the overt acts themselves. If we divide all possible physiological acts into *adjustments* and *executions*, the nuclear self would be the adjustments collectively considered; and the

[21] Vol. I, pp. 319–321. Cf. the following: "The fact remains . . . that certain special sorts of thing tend primordially to possess this interest, and form the *natural* me. But all these things are *objects*" (p. 325). The discussion of the special topic of egoism is an amplification of the earlier statement that a man's self is *"the sum total of all that he* CAN *call his,"* all the objects he appropriates through the medium of a positive interest (Vol. I, p. 291).

[22] Vol. I, p. 301.

less intimate, more shifting self, so far as it was active, would
be the executions. [*Ibid.*, p. 302.]

He then says, since the adjustment activities are "entirely unimportant and uninteresting except through their uses in furthering or inhibiting the presence of various things, and actions,"
it is not surprising they are commonly overlooked. But the fact
that adjustment activities are involved in all interactions with
environing conditions, save in the acts that are most routine
and "automatic," confers upon them a certain special position,
for "they are the permanent core of turnings-towards and turn-
ings-from, of yieldings and arrests, which naturally seem central
and interior." [23]

What is further said about personal identity is consistent
with this behavioral interpretation. The appropriations of the
passing thought are "less to *itself* than to the most intimately
felt *part of its present Object, the body, and the central adjustments*, which accompany the act of thinking, in the head." [24]
Furthermore, the belief in the sameness of the self arises on
empirical grounds in the same way as belief in the sameness of
any object whatever, "*the sense of our own personal identity*"
being "*exactly like any one of our other perceptions of sameness
among phenomena.*" [25] Nevertheless the dualism reappears, for
he still assumes that a "passing thought" must be there as the
knowing subject. Hence, after recurring to his doctrine that
"'perishing' pulses of thought" are what know, he makes what
on the face of it looks like an extraordinary compromise between
the "pulse of thought" as *I* and the "empirical person" as *Me*. [26]

Were it important to do so, more evidence could be cited for
the proposition that there are two incompatible strains in the
Jamesian psychology, and that the conflict between them is
most marked in the vase of the self. But there is also evidence
that on the side of the empirical strain there are the elements
needed for a behavioral theory of the self. What he finally said
in 1904, after he had thrown over his knowing Thought for

[23] Vol. I, p. 302.
[24] Vol. I, p. 341.

[25] Vol. I, p. 334.
[26] Vol. I, p. 371.

Consciousness as a mere echo of a departed soul, was, after all, but an expression of ideas put forth in his *Psychology*, freed from hesitation and ambiguity. There is "the elementary activity involved in the mere *that* of experience, . . . and the farther specification of this *something* into two *whats*, an activity felt as 'ours' and an activity ascribed to 'objects.'" The former, he goes on to say, is

> part . . . of the world experienced. The world experienced . . . comes at all times with our body as its centre, centre of vision, centre of action, centre of interest. . . . The body is the storm centre, the origin of co-ordinates, the constant place of stress in all that experience-train. . . . The word "I," then, is primarily a noun of position, just like "this" and "here." [27]

But, as I have already intimated, he never reworked his *Psychology* so that all phases and aspects of psychological phenomena were observed and reported from this point of view. In consequence psychological theory is still the bulwark for all doctrines that assume independent and separate "mind" and "world" set over against each other. The idea originally came into psychology from philosophy. But now it is advanced by philosophers as having the warrant of psychology and hence possessed of the authority of one of the positive sciences. Philosophy will not be emancipated to perform its own task and function until psychology is purged, as a whole and in all its special topics, of the last remnant of the traditional dualism. And the purge requires more than a statement nominally made in terms of the living organism but in fact simply carrying over to the body distinctions that originated when there was a current belief in mind (or in consciousness) as a distinctive entity. This importation occurs whenever the phenomena are described in terms of the organism exclusively instead of as aspects and functions of the interactivity of organism and environment.

[27] *Essays in Radical Empiricism*, pp. 169–170 n.

4

WHITEHEAD'S PHILOSOPHY

Mr. WHITEHEAD'S PHILOSOPHY IS SO COMPREHENSIVE THAT IT invites discussion from a number of points of view. One may consider one of the many special topics he has treated with so much illumination or one may choose for discussion his basic method. Since the latter point *is* basic and since it seems to me to present his enduring contribution to philosophy, I shall confine myself to it.

Mr. Whitehead says that the task of philosophy is to frame "descriptive generalizations of experience." In this, an empiricist should agree without reservation. Descriptive generalization of experience is the goal of any intelligent empiricism. Agreement upon this special point is the more emphatic because Mr. Whitehead is not afraid to use the term "immediate experience." Although he calls the method of philosophy that of Rationalism, this term need not give the empiricist pause. For the historic school that goes by the name of Rationalism (with which empiricism is at odds) is concerned not with *descriptive* generalization, but ultimately with *a priori* generalities from which the matter of experience can itself be derived. The contrast between this position and Mr. Whitehead's stands out conspicuously in his emphasis upon immediately existent actual entities. "These actual entities," he says, "are the final real things of which the world is made up. There is no going behind actual entities. They are the only *reasons* for anything." The divergence is further emphasized in the fact that Whitehead holds that there is in every real occasion a demonstrative or denotative element that can only be pointed to: namely, the element referred to

in such words as 'this, here, now, that, there, then'; elements that
cannot be derived from anything more general and that form,
indeed, the subject-matter of one of the main generalizations,
that of real occasions itself.[1]

Mr. Whitehead's definition of philosophy was, however,
just given in an abbreviated form. The descriptive generalizations, he goes on to say, must be such as to form "a coherent,
logical, necessary system of general ideas in terms of which
every element of our experience may be interpreted. Here 'interpretation' means that each element shall have the character
of a particular instance of a general scheme." [2] The wording of
this passage suggests a point of view nearer to that of traditional Rationalism than the conception just set forth. If it means
that philosophers should proceed as logically as possible, striving to present findings that are coherent, that are even 'necessary', if the necessity in question be that of close-knit relation
to one another without omissions and superfluities in the
generalized descriptions of experience that are obtained, the
empiricist need not dissent. The statement is, however, open
to another interpretation, and to that I shall later return.

I first wish to dwell upon the complete extension of Mr.
Whitehead's conception of 'experience'. It is customary to find
the application of the term confined to human and even to
conscious experience. Denial of this restriction is fundamental
in Mr. Whitehead's thought. Everything that characterizes
human experience is found in the natural world. Conversely,
what is found in the natural world is found in human experience.
Hence the more we find out about the natural world, the more
intellectual agencies we have for analysing, describing, and understanding human experience. We cannot determine the constituents of the latter by staring at it directly, but only by interpreting it in terms of the natural world that is experienced.

The completeness of the correspondence between the elements of human experience and of nature is exemplified in each

[1] *Process and Reality*, pp. 27 and 37.
[2] *Ibid.*, p. 4; *Adventures of Ideas*, p. 285.

one of Whitehead's ultimate generalizations. I mention five of these correspondences by way of illustration. (1) Change is such a marked trait of conscious experience that the latter has been called, rather intemperately, a mere flux. Every actual entity in the universe is in process; in some sense *is* process. (2) No two conscious experiences exactly duplicate one another. Creativity and novelty are characteristic of nature. (3) Conscious experience is marked by retention—memory in its broadest sense—and anticipation. Nature also carries on. Every actual occasion is prehensive of other occasions and has objective immortality in its successors. (4) Every conscious experience involves a focus which is the centre of a determinate perspective. This principle is exemplified in nature. (5) Every conscious experience is a completely unitary pulse in a continuous stream. The continuity of nature includes atomicity and individualizations of the ongoing stream.

I do not mean to imply that Whitehead arrived at the generalizations, of which those just cited are examples, by instituting *directly* such a set of one-to-one similarities. But unless I have completely misread him, the correspondences are there and are fundamental in his method and his system. As he himself says: "Any doctrine that refuses to place human experience outside nature must find in the description of experience factors which enter also into the description of less specialized natural occurrences. . . . We should either admit dualism, at least as a provisional doctrine, or we should point out the identical elements connecting human experience with physical science."[3]

I now turn to the other aspect of the correspondence: the utilization of the results of natural science as means of interpreting human experience. A noteworthy example is found in his treatment of the subject-object relation. In this treatment, it stands out most clearly that his denial of bifurcation is not a special epistemological doctrine but runs through his whole cosmology. The subject-object relation is found in human ex-

[3] *Adventures of Ideas*, p. 237.

perience and in knowledge because it is fundamentally characteristic of nature. Philosophy has taken this relation to be
fundamental. With this, Whitehead agrees. But it has also
taken this relation to be one of a knower and that which is
known. With this, he fundamentally disagrees. In every actual
occasion the relation is found; each occasion is subject for itself
and is reciprocally object for that which 'provokes' it to be
what it is in its process. The interplay of these two things "is
the stuff constituting those individual things that make up the
sole reality of the Universe." There are revolutionary consequences for the theory of experience and of knowledge involved in this view of the subject-object relation.

I select, as illustration of these consequences, the relation
of his philosophy to the idealism-realism problem. Simplifying
the matter, idealism results when the subject-object relation is
confined to knowledge and the subject is given primacy. Realism
results when the object is given primacy. But if every actual
occasion is 'bipolar' (to use Mr. Whitehead's own expression)
the case stands otherwise. The terms 'real' and 'ideal' can be
used only in abstraction from the actual totalities that exist.
When we talk about the physical and the psychical as if there
were objects which are exclusively one or the other, we are, if
we only know what we are about, following, and in an over-
specialized way, the historic routes by which a succession of
actual occasions become enduring objects of specified kinds.
Nor are these routes confined to institution of just two kinds
of objects. Some are in the direction of those objects that are
called electrons; some in that of astronomic systems; some in
that of plants or animals; some in that of conscious human beings. The differences in these objects are differences in historic
routes of derivation and hereditary transmission; they do not
present fixed and untraversable gulfs. (I am obliged to omit
reference to the complementary principle of societies or communities of these objects.)

I give one further illustration, without comment, in Mr.
Whitehead's own words. "The brain is continuous with the

body, and the body is continuous with the rest of the natural world. Human experience is an act of self-origination including the whole of nature, limited to the perspective of a focal region within the body, but not necessarily persisting in any fixed co-ordination with a definite part of the brain." [4] Just one more illustration will be given of the use of the findings of physical science in analysis of human experience. I do not see how any-one not familiar with modern field-theories in physics and who did not have the courage of imagination to apply these theories to the descriptive generalization of human experience could have arrived at many of the conclusions about the latter which Whitehead has reached: I mention, as a special example, the fallacy of simple location.

I have selected, I repeat, a few points in order to illustrate the method which to me is his original and enduring contribution to philosophy, present and future. I should be glad to con-tinue in this strain, and to suggest how the results of this method, were it widely adopted, would assuredly take philos-ophy away from by-paths that have led to dead-ends and would release it from many constraints that now embarrass it. But I must return to that aspect of his thought which seems to imply that, after all, his method is to be understood and applied in a direction which assimilates it, with enormous development in matters of detail, to traditional Rationalism. I say 'seems'; for it is a question I am raising. The issue in brief is this: Is it to be developed and applied with fundamental emphasis upon ex-perimental observation (the method of the natural sciences)? Or does it point to the primacy of mathematical method, in accord with historic rationalism? I hope the word 'primacy' will be noted. This occasion is a highly inappropriate one in which to introduce bifurcation. The two directions are not opposed to each other. Mathematics has its own established position in physical science. But I do not see how the two can be co-ordi-nate, meaning by 'co-ordinate' being upon exactly the same level. One, I think, must lead and the other follow.

[4] *Ibid.*, p. 290.

A mathematical logician proceeds, if I understand the matter aright, in some such way as the following. He finds in existence a definite body of mathematical disciplines. The existence in question is historical. In so far, the disciplines are subject to the contingencies that affect everything historical. Compared therefore, with the requirements of logical structure, there is something *ad hoc* about them as they stand. The logician has then a double task to perform. He has to reduce each discipline to the smallest number of independent definitions and postulates that are sufficient and necessary to effect logical organization of the subject-matter of that discipline. He has also to bring the various definitions and postulates of the different branches of mathematics into coherent and necessary relation to one another. There is something in the extended definition of philosophy, which was quoted earlier, that suggests that Whitehead would have us adopt such a mathematical model and pattern in philosophizing. On this basis a philosopher would set himself the aim of discovering in immediate experience the elements that can be stated in a succinct system of independent definitions and postulates, they being such that when they are deductively woven together there will result a coherent and necessary system in which "each element shall have the character of a particular instance of the general scheme." In this case, it is not simply the philosopher who must proceed logically. The scheme of nature and immediate experience is itself a logical system—when we have the wit to make it out in its own terms.

Nevertheless, that which I have called Whitehead's basic method is capable of another construction. As far as experience-nature and descriptive generalizations are concerned, there is an alternative method open: that which I called that of the natural rather than the mathematical sciences. For in the former, while mathematical science is indispensable, it is subordinate to the consequences of experimental observational inquiry. For brevity I shall call this contrasting method 'genetic-functional,' though I am aware that 'genetic' in particular is exposed to serious misapprehension.[5] Upon the mathematical model, the resulting generalizations, it seems to me, are necessarily morphological and static; they express an aboriginal structure, the components of which are then deductively woven together. Upon the basis of the other model, the subject-matter of the generalizations is distinctions that arise in and because of inquiry into the subject matter of experience-nature, and they then function or operate as division of labor in the further control and ordering of its materials and processes.

As far as method is concerned, the only opposite I can find for 'genetic' is 'intuitional'. Generalized distinctions are there ready-made, so to speak, and after analysis has taken place, we just see and acknowledge them by a kind of rational perception which is final. The opposite of 'functional' is, of course, 'structural.' Somehow, when put together rightly, the various generalizations represent different parts of a fixed structure; they are like morphological organs when these are viewed in abstraction from differentiations of functioning activity. Thus we are led back to the question: Which aspect is primary and leading and which is auxiliary?

Adequate discussion of this issue would demand consideration of each one of Whitehead's ultimate generalities or categories, there being at least seven of them.[6] Time forbids such consideration. I confine myself to the position of 'eternal objects'. The fact that the word "ingression' is constantly used to designate their relation to actual entities suggests quite strongly the mathematical model. For ingression suggests an independent and ready-made subsistence of eternal objects, the latter being guaranteed by direct intuition. The conception of God in the total system seems to indicate that this is the proper interpretation, since some principle is certainly necessary, upon this premise, to act selectively in determining what eternal objects ingress in any given immediate occasion. The alternative

[5] Such misapprehension will occur if the idea of genesis is taken to be of a psychological order. It is meant in an objective sense, the sense in which the origin and development of astronomical systems and of animals is genetics.

[6] In *Adventures of Ideas*, these are connected, with appropriate modifications, with the Platonic scheme. See pp. 188, 203, 240, and 354.

view is that of the egression of natures, characters, or universals, as a consequence of the necessity of generalization from immediate occasions that exists in order to direct their further movement and its consequences. This capacity of intelligence performs the office for which Deity has to be invoked upon the other premise.

Upon the genetic-functional view, such objects (which are 'eternal' in the sense of not being spatio-temporal existences) emerge because of the existence of problematic situations. They emerge originally as suggestions. They are then operatively applied to actual existences. When they suceed in resolving problematic situations (in organizing otherwise conflicting elements) they part with some or most of their hypothetical quality and become routine methods of behavior.

Upon the basis of the generalized idea of experience of Whitehead, there is something corresponding to this in nature. There exist in nature indeterminate situations. Because of their indeterminate nature, the subsequent process is hesitant and tentative. The activity that is 'provoked' is incipient. If it becomes habitual, it is finally determinately egressive as a routine of nature, and it harmonizes the aggressively conflicting elements to which is due the indeterminacy of the original natural situation. When this routine-established mode of processive activity is observed it becomes the subject-matter of a natural law.

I am not affirming positively that this way of interpreting the basic conception of experience and the relations of its generalized descriptions to one another is necessary. It does decidedly appear to me to be a genuine alternative way. While my own preference is markedly in *its* favor, I am presenting it, as I have already said, for the purpose of presenting and making clear, as far as limits of time permit, a question.[7] Upon the negative side, the absence of any attempt in Mr. Whitehead's writings to

[7] The point of the choice between alternatives would be clearer still if there were time to discuss immediate qualities (usually called *sensory* because of one of their causal conditions) which Whitehead regards as eternal objects; for upon the other theory they are just what gives actual occasions their unique singularity, so that there is no actual entity without them.

place the ultimate generalities in any scheme of analytic-genetic derivation points to his adoption of what I have called the mathematical pattern. Upon the positive side there is the rather complex intermediary apparatus of God, harmony, mathematical relations, natural laws, that is required to effect the interweaving of eternal objects and immediate occasions. I do not think that the difficulties found in reading Mr. White-head are due to his fundamental conception of experience. On the contrary, given a reasonable degree of emancipation of philosophic imagination from philosophic tradition and its language, that idea seems to me extraordinarily luminous as well as productive. The difficulties seem to me to arise from the inter-mediary apparatus required in the interweaving of elements; the interweaving being required only because of the assumption of original independence and not being required if they emerge to serve functionally ends which experience itself institutes.

Because Whitehead's philosophy is fraught with such poten-tialities for the future of the philosophizing of all of us, I have raised the question of basic method, instead of limiting myself to the more congenial task of selecting some one of its many suggestive developments for special comment. As currents of philosophy are running at present, it is altogether likely that its immediate influence will be mainly upon the side of what I called the mathematical model. Its enduring influence in behalf of the integrated Naturalism to which Whitehead is devoted seems to me to demand the other interpretation. There is, without doubt, a certain irony in giving to Mr. Whitehead's thought a mathematical interpretation, for that implies, after all, the primacy of the static over process, the latter, upon this in-terpretation, being limited to immediate occasions and their secondary reactions back into what is fixed by nature; as in the case of the change in Primordial God. The plea, then, for the alternative direction of development of his thought is in essence a plea for recognizing the infinite fertility of actual occasions in their full actuality.

ACKNOWLEDGMENTS

Grateful acknowledgment is due to the editors of the following journals, who have given permission to reprint the articles mentioned below:

The Journal of Philosophy, for "The Future of Liberalism" (vol. XXXII, No. 9); "The Ambiguity of 'Intrinsic Good' " (vol. XXXIX, No. 12); "Valuation Judgments and Immediate Quality" (vol. XL, No. 12); "Further as to Valuation as Judgment" (vol. XL, No. 20); "Some Questions about Value" (vol. XLI, No. 17); "By Nature and by Art" (vol. XLI, No. 11); "How Is Mind to Be Known?" (vol. XXXIX, No. 2); "The Objectivism-Subjectivism of Modern Philosophy" (vol. XXXVIII, No. 20); "Inquiry and Indeterminateness of Situations" (vol. XXXIX, No. 11); "Propositions, Warranted Assertibility, and Truth" (vol. XXXVIII, No. 7); "The Vanishing Subject in the Psychology of James" (vol. XXXVII, No. 22);

The Social Frontier, for "Toward Administrative Statesmanship" (vol. I, No. 6); "The Teacher and His World" (vol. I, No. 4); "United, We Shall Stand" (vol. I, No. 7); "The Social Significance of Academic Freedom" (vol. I, No. 6); "The Crucial Role of Intelligence" (vol. I, No. 5); "Youth in a Confused World" (vol. I, No. 8); "Liberty and Social Control" (November, 1935); "The Meaning of Liberalism" (December, 1935); "Liberalism and Equality" (January, 1936); "Liberalism and Civil Liberties" (February, 1936);

School and Society, for "Authority and Resistance to Social Change" (No. 1137); "Democracy and Educational Administration" (No 1162); "The Future of Liberalism" (No. 1047); "The Relation of Science and Philosophy as the Basis of Education" (No. 1215);

The Southern Review, for "Religion, Science and Philosophy" and "The Philosophy of William James":

The Philosophical Review, for "Nature in Experience" (March, 1940) and "Whitehead's Philosophy" (vol. XLVI, No. 2);

Progressive Education, for "The Challenge of Democracy to Education" (vol. XIV, No. 2) and "What Is Social Study?" (vol. XV, No. 5);

The Antioch Review, for "The Democratic Faith and Education" (vol. IV, No. 2);

The American Scholar, for "The Problem of the Liberal Arts College" (vol. XIII, No. 4);

The Journal of the History of Ideas, for "James Marsh and American Philosophy" (vol. II, No. 2);

Forum and Century, for "The Need for Orientation" (vol. XCIII);

Fortune, for "Challenge to Liberal Thought" (August, 1944);

The Rotarian, for "Does Human Nature Change" (vol. LII, No. 2);

The Humanist, for "The Revolt against Science" (vol. V, No. 3); and the *Society for Ethical Culture,* for "Democracy and Education in the World of Today" (Felix Adler Lecture, 1938).

INDEX

absolutism, 136 ff.
acquaintance, 306
act, 215 f., 242, 247
Adler, F., 35
Agricultural Adjustment Act, 119
American Philosophical Association, 3
anarchy, 175
anti-semitism, 42
Aristotle, 98, 151, 152, 162, 185, 189, 282 f., 286, 296, 313, 364 ff.
Arnold, M., 5, 20
art, 84, 286 ff.
assertibility, 331 ff.
astronomy, 151
atom, 196 ff.
authority, 93 ff., 106, 169, 296
Ayres, C., 281, 291

Bacon, F., 106, 296, 312
Barnard, H., 38
Beethoven, L., 191
behavior, 314, 400
behaviorism, social, 253 ff.
being, 286 ff., 313
Benedict, R., 314
Bentham, J., 129, 359 f.
Bentley, A. F., 260, 351
Berkeley, G., 297
Bill of Rights, 61, 118 f.
biology, 151
Bradley, F. H., 223, 224
Brandeis, L., 120
Brotherston, B. W., 259 f.
Bryce, J., 49
business, 131, 305

categories, 233 ff., 239, 416
cause, 287, 316
Cave of Adullam, 152
certainty, 302
character, 231, 237, 239
China, 49
Christianity, 359 ff., 390 f.
church, 6, 99, 298, 359, 371

citizenship, 51, 79, 119, 147
civilization, 190, 372
Cohen, M. R., 195 ff., 202 f.
Coleridge, S. T., 357, 359 ff., 370, 375, 377
college, 83 ff.
commerce, 6, 131
communism, 52
community, 374 f.
conclusion, 211 f.
conditions, 315 ff.
consciousness, 237 f., 299, 302 f., 397, 406
conservatism, 186
Constitution, 51, 77, 119 f.
continuum, 228 f., 244 f., 325
cooperation, 167 f.
cosmology, 197
criteria, 143, 311
criticism, 88, 207, 311
curriculum, 85, 88, 144
custom, 151

Darwin, C., 359
Davidson, T., 393
Declaration of Independence, 119
deduction, 218
democracy, 32, 34 ff., 46 ff., 57 ff., 78, 114, 133, 157
Democritus, 313
Descartes, R., 297, 303
Dickens, C., 126
dictatorship, 175
dogmatism, 157 f.
doubt, 349 f.
dualism, 6, 15, 396, 406, 408

economic questions, 180 f.
education, 23 ff., 34 ff., 46 ff., 57 ff., 88, 90, 122, 143 ff., 164 ff., 183
empiricism, 194, 259, 312
enterprise, 102, 107 f., 131, 134
equality, 30, 60, 114
eternity, 12

421

logical conditions, 211 ff.
Lucretius, 313

Mackay, D. S., 322 ff.
Magna Carta, 118
majority, 36
Mann, H., 38 ff., 46 f.
Marsh, J., 357 ff.
Marx, K., 56, 137, 139
materialism, 117, 162, 244
mathematics, 5, 8, 219 f., 365, 415
meaning, 194, 212, 267
Middle Ages, 148 f., 299
Mill, J. S., 351, 359 f.,
mind, 299, 301 ff.
Moore, G. E., 283
morale, 187
morality, 152, 211 ff.
moral judgments, 213 f., 229 ff., 235 ff.,
    241 ff.
Mussolini, B., 34, 56, 139

Napoleon, 134
nationalism, 175
naturalism, 418
nature, 25, 193 ff., 286 ff., 315, 320,
    417
Nicolson, M., 358, 364

objectivity, 250 ff., 309 ff., 319
observation, 267, 301
Oersted, H. C., 358
orientation, 88ff.

pacifists, 188
Paley, 363
Parliament, 66
peace, 24, 30
Peirce, C. S., 156 f., 228, 260
Perry, R. B., 379, 381 f., 384 f., 389
perspective, 193
pessimism, 23, 25, 32
philosophy, 3 ff., 96, 100, 118, 134,
    155 f., 164 ff., 169 ff., 196, 201, 296,
    301 f., 309 ff., 335, 362, 384 ff., 409,
    410 ff.
planning, 26, 111
Plato, 313, 364, 368
pluralism, 393 f.
politics, 6
possibility, 317, 365
poverty, 25

power, 112 f., 123
practice, 400 f.
pragmatism, 11, 167, 223, 259, 380
press, 82, 92
prizing, 273 ff.
probability, 335
propaganda, 82
propositions, 278 f., 331 ff.
Protestantism, 296, 299, 391
psychological analysis, 235 ff.
psychology, 53, 64, 237 f., 396 ff.
pugnacity, 187

radicalism, 132, 138, 190
rationalism, 410 f., 414
realism, 413
reality, 5 f., 10 f., 205 f.
reason, 367 ff., 378
Reconstruction Finance Corporation,
    70, 131
relativism, 12 f.
religion, 106, 127, 169 ff., 371, 390 f.
Rice, P. B., 250 ff., 261 ff.
Rockefeller Foundation, 3
Rousseau, J. J., 126
Royce, J., 19, 389, 393
Russell, B., 169 ff., 331 ff.
Russia, 133

Santayana, G., 303, 313
Savery, B., 282 f.
school, 30, 36 f., 39, 43, 47 f., 50 ff.,
    62 ff., 69, 76, 89 f., 122
science, 7, 11, 15, 26 ff., 29, 31, 52,
    85, 98, 106 ff., 151, 155, 160 ff.,
    164 ff., 169 ff., 200, 218, 246 f., 252,
    288, 296, 298, 302, 316
scientific judgments, 215 ff.
scientific method, 157, 170
scientific technique, 172 ff., 211 ff.
scientific temper, 172
security, 25, 90
self, 398, 406 ff.
sensation, 404
sensum, 333 f.
situations, 322 ff.
slavery, 185
Smith, A., 127
social changes, 93 ff., 135, 186, 190
social control, 111 ff., 132
socialism, 159
social study, 180 ff.